Long-Term Memory Problems in Children and Adolescents

Long-Term Memory Problems in Children and Adolescents

Assessment, Intervention, and Effective Instruction

MILTON J. DEHN

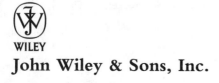

WILEY

John Wiley & Sons, Inc.

For general information on our other products and services please contact our Customer Care Department within the United States at (800) 762-2974, outside the United States at (317) 572-3993 or fax (317) 572-4002.

Wiley also publishes its books in a variety of electronic formats. Some content that appears in print may not be available in electronic books. For more information about Wiley products, visit our website at www.wiley.com.

Library of Congress Cataloging-in-Publication Data:

Dehn, Milton J.
   Long-term memory problems in children and adolescents : assessment, intervention, and effective instruction / Milton J. Dehn.
      p. cm.
   Includes bibliographical references and index.
   ISBN 978-0-470-43831-2 (pbk.); 978-0-470-77048-1 (ebk); 978-0-470-87206-2 (ebk); 978-0-470-87207-9 (ebk)
   1. Long-term memory in children. 2. Short-term memory in children. 3. Long-term memory in adolescence. 4. Short-term memory in adolescence. I. Title.
   BF723.M4D44 2010
   155.4'1312—dc22   2010005948

Printed in the United States of America
10 9 8 7 6 5 4 3 2 1

For my children, Sonya, Alisha, Ted, and Amber.
May the good memories we share last a lifetime.

Contents

Foreword

Long-term memory plays a crucial role in the formation and maintenance of our personal identity. Recalling the name of our first-grade teacher or a second cousin, remembering where we went on vacation the past summer, or remembering our first kiss are all memories of past personal experiences. Memories provide us a frame of reference based on experience and help shape our personalities. Long-term memory also includes over-learned and automatic daily activities such as remembering how to brush your teeth or drive to work. And finally, long-term memory includes our encyclopedic knowledge of information such as who the first president was or how many days there are in a calendar year.

We often take for granted the sophisticated neurological system within the brain that is required to make long-term memory a seamless process when our ability to form, store, and retrieve long-term memories is intact. However, when memory systems become impaired or disrupted there can be devastating effects on the acquisition of new learning or the retrieval of previously stored information. Dr. Dehn's book will provide clinicians and educators a useful and timely guide on how to identify and treat memory impairments.

In this book, Dr. Dehn provides the reader with a framework of how long-term memory relates to other types of memory (e.g., short-term memory, working memory, etc.). He has also discussed the subcomponents of long-term memory and how they relate to academic achievement. Dr. Dehn reviews what is known about the neuroanatomy of how memories are formed, the developmental trajectory of memory and learning, and the common types of memory dysfunction. An important part of this book is the chapter on recognizing the risk factors that can lead to long-term memory impairments. If a memory dysfunction is suspected, it is important to pick the proper assessment instrument to confirm the presence or absence of the memory difficulties. Dr. Dehn provides a concise review of the subcomponents of long-term memory that should be assessed and reviews the major standardized instruments that assess memory and learning.

Clinical practitioners and educators have a wide variety of assessment instruments designed to assess memory and learning, many of which are theoretically based and psychometrically sound. However, the identification of memory and learning deficits cannot be the end point. Once a memory deficit has been identified, educators need guidance on what evidence-based intervention strategies are readily available. Assessment must be linked to prescriptive intervention. Dr. Dehn provides a quality review of educational interventions designed to improve memory functions. Finally, Dr. Dehn presents several case study examples that illustrate how memory can be assessed and what interventions can be linked to the results of the assessment.

Long-Term Memory Problems in Children and Adolescents: Assessment, Intervention, and Effective Instruction by Milton Dehn will be a valuable resource for psychologists and educators who work with children or adolescents who are having difficulties with memory and learning. Translating theory and research into practice is a talent that Dr. Dehn possesses, and we will benefit from his professional skills. This book will be a useful addition to Dr. Dehn's other book, *Working Memory and Academic Learning: Assessment and Intervention* (2008), published by John Wiley and Sons, Inc.

Daniel C. Miller, Ph.D.,
ABPP, ABSNP, NCSP

Preface

One day when I was reading an article about recently discovered cases of developmental amnesia (a rare condition without identified cause in which children have extreme difficulty remembering), I was reminded of students with severe learning disabilities whom I had often encountered during my years of work as a school psychologist. It struck me that I had been missing something when I evaluated those students and made recommendations for their educational programs, and I began to wonder how many other children with academic learning and performance problems actually had underlying memory impairments. When I worked in the schools, I, like most school psychologists, seldom assessed students' long-term memory functions. In fact, I had never been trained to do so, probably because there were no long-term memory batteries for children in existence when I was in graduate school. As I switched to private practice, I began paying more attention to the possibility of memory problems when children were brought in for evaluations and tutoring. When I administered memory scales to these children, I was astounded to discover that about half of children with significant learning problems had deficits in working memory and that a sizable number also had impairments in long-term memory. I felt for these children. So often, their poor academic performance had been attributed to everything but neurologically based memory problems. Furthermore, those who were trying to help them were neglecting the memory problems.

With all of the resources our culture invests in the education of children and adolescents, I find it incredible that educators, parents, psychologists, and everyone else involved in the education and psychology of youth do not pay more attention to the most important variable in the learning equation—memory. Obviously, learning and memory go together; one cannot exist without the other. Yet, initial learning does not guarantee long-term retention and recall. Some students who learn easily also forget quickly, while others who struggle with learning retain the information well once it reaches long-term memory. Children and adolescents who forget too much or who struggle with learning because of memory problems are not difficult to understand or to help. Adults who want to understand and help can begin by learning more about memory. Books and research articles on memory from the fields of neuroscience, neuropsychology, cognitive psychology, and educational psychology are abundant and readily available. The applied science also exists. We know how to help children learn and remember more effectively. For example, one approach involves teaching strategies that improve encoding and retrieval. If what is known about memory functions was consistently applied in the classroom and everyday life, learning and memory would be enhanced, and wasted effort and frustration with learning would be reduced.

Perhaps scant attention has been paid to memory assessment, intervention, and memory-enhancing instruction because of the pervasive belief that memory impairments in youth are so rare. Everyone knows that children and adolescents who have experienced a traumatic brain injury are likely to have persistent memory problems that will make learning a challenge. But what everyone doesn't know is that there are many other children who fail to realize their academic potential because they have memory dysfunctions or because they have not learned how to effectively utilize their memory capabilities. How many? There's almost no hard data to answer that question. One study in the United Kingdom found that up to 5.9% of normal, elementary-age children had specific long-term memory difficulties (Temple & Richardson, 2006). Given that approximately one quarter of K–12 students struggle with academic learning and perhaps half of them have underlying memory problems, I estimate that as many as 10 to 12% of students have long-term memory impairments or don't know how to effectively use their memory abilities. Also, the large numbers of children with disorders and health conditions, such as diabetes, who are at–risk for long-term memory problems, is undeniable (see Chapter 4). Whatever the exact figure, it is evident to me that we are failing to identify and serve a population of children who are failing to achieve because of underlying memory problems. How could we be missing so many children with memory impairments? The answer is that we and the students themselves misattribute the behaviors and problems to factors such as motivation or low average intelligence. The situation is similar to Attention Deficit Hyperactivity Disorder (ADHD). We were unaware of the existence of ADHD in so many children until we learned what it was and how to diagnose it. Prior to "discovering" ADHD, we misattributed the behaviors and problems it causes.

This book is not solely about the children and adolescents with diagnosable memory disorders or severe memory dysfunctions. Rather, this book is primarily about the large numbers of children and adolescents of school age who have mild to moderate difficulties with one or more aspects of long-term memory. Although the memory difficulties of the majority of these students go unrecognized, their memory challenges often impede their academic learning and the long-term retention of knowledge that they will need throughout their lives. In addition to those students who have neurologically based memory impairments, there are many other students who are not realizing their scholastic potential because they have not discovered or learned how to use effective memory strategies and mnemonics. Often these students are naïve in regards to their memory functions and don't understand how to regulate them. A minimal amount of metamemory and strategy instruction may be all that is necessary to improve their retention and recall.

I have written this book so that those adults who educate and work with youth can learn more about identifying, helping, and educating the memory-impaired children and adolescents that we so often overlook. This book is written for school psychologists, clinical psychologists, neuropsychologists, special educators, classroom teachers, and related professionals who teach and work with children and adolescents. Although the school environment is emphasized in this text (as it is where children and adolescents spend most of their daytime hours), the information also can be applied in medical and private-practice settings. In this book I have mainly attempted to: (a) describe the various memory systems and processes; (b) explain how memory works at the neurological level; (c) interpret memory research; (d) identify the disorders and conditions that put children at-risk for memory problems; (e) emphasize the importance of metamemory development and the acquisition of effective memory strategies; (f) structure selective, cross-battery testing of memory so that memory assessment is comprehensive but efficient; (g) explain how to interpret results from various memory scales; (h) review contemporary memory scales that are designed for children and adolescents; (i) apply interventions to school settings; and (j) encourage educators to adopt more memory-enhancing instructional practices (see Chapter 1 for an overview of each chapter). For those who will pursue memory assessment, intervention, and instruction, this book is intended to be a resource and reference. Those who read and apply the information in this book will acquire enough expertise in long-term memory functions to effectively identify and help children and adolescents with memory problems.

Acknowledgments

I am indebted to my soul mate and intellectual partner, Paula A. Dehn, whose ideas, encouragement, and support made this book a reality. I wish to thank Benjamin R. Burns for gathering the literature, editing the manuscript, and providing feedback from a practitioner's viewpoint. I am also grateful to Joci Newton for providing feedback on chapters.

Long-Term Memory Problems in Children and Adolescents

Introduction and Overview

Memory is an unique psychological construct and cognitive function in that almost everyone is interested in or concerned about his or her memory at some point in life. Nearly every person, even a 4-year-old child, has a concept of memory and an awareness of how his or her memory functions. Almost everyone knows that short-term memory is limited in capacity and duration, that long-term memory has an immense capacity, and that memories can last for a lifetime. Even a young child knows that people quickly forget most information and that there are strategies that help memories endure. Nearly everyone also understands that memory is necessary for learning to occur and that personal memories define each individual. Yet, most children have misconceptions about memory and how it functions, misconceptions that can be detrimental to learning. For example, many children erroneously believe that the intention to remember something will increase the probability of later retrieval or that delayed recall will be just as strong as immediate recall. Similarly, there are disagreements about memory structure and functions among researchers and practitioners who are concerned with human memory. For example, there has been an ongoing dispute about how memories become solidified through the process of consolidation. Most of the discord arises from the fact that memory is extremely complex, consisting of several systems, with each system serving different purposes and incorporating somewhat different cognitive processes (Tulving, 1985). Indeed, memory is not a single homogenous entity but a composition of many distinct interacting brain systems (Emilien, Durlach, Antoniadis, Van Der Linden, & Maloteaux, 2004). It is only recently that neuroscientists and other researchers have begun to unravel the incredibly sophisticated mental function known as memory.

Driven by advances in neuroscience and brain imaging, the past 20 years has seen a resurgence of research on the memory functions of children and adolescents. Although many of the contemporary investigations have focused on working memory (see Dehn, 2008), a sizable portion concern long-term memory systems and processes and how they relate to academic learning. The subjects of these studies are no longer limited to children with severe acquired brain injuries. A variety of at-risk populations (see Chapter 4), as well as normal learners, have been studied. A few investigations have reported on low incidence disorders, such as developmental amnesia, while numerous studies have focused on children with more common medical conditions, such as childhood diabetes, that can damage the hippocampus (the brain's key long-term memory structure). Also, more studies are taking place in educational environments in an attempt to understand how memory impairments affect academic learning. Furthermore, there has been an explosion of neuro-psychological research on the memory dysfunctions of adults with debilitating medical conditions, such as Alzheimer's. Although the memory problems suffered by adults are somewhat different from those experienced by youth, most of the empirical findings are applicable to children because long-term memory systems and processes are essentially in place by 6 years of age. For example, depression affects memory functioning in youth in much the same way it affects the memory functioning of adults. As the number of references in this text will attest to, there is an abundance of scientific literature on populations with memory impairments, the characteristics of memory disorders, measurement of memory, interventions, and even on instructional practices that enhance memory for what has been learned. This scientific literature, along with books like this one, allows psychologists, educators, and related professionals to more fully understand how to identify and help youth with memory problems.

The growing interest in memory has made many psychologists and related practitioners realize that there are many school-age youth with unidentified memory impairments. This realization, coupled with advances in understanding memory functions, has led to a growing demand for memory assessment instruments and to the refinement of existing measures. For example, more cognitive scales have recently added working memory subtests, and memory batteries like the Wechsler Memory Scale®-Fourth Edition (Wechsler, 2009) have incorporated the latest empirical findings about long-term memory. Despite the availability of technically adequate tools, practitioners who evaluate children and adolescents seldom conduct comprehensive assessments of memory. Consequently, many students with long-term memory dysfunctions remain unidentified or are misidentified. For example, students receiving educational services for learning disabilities are likely to have underlying memory impairments. Yet, this significant learning impediment often goes unrecognized. In addition, there are significant numbers of children and adolescents with memory problems who are never referred because they appear to be "normal" students. In the United Kingdom, Temple and Richardson (2006) screened more than 300 normal children aged 8 to 12 years for episodic and semantic memory problems. Temple and Richardson discovered that 5.8 to 5.9% of the students with average IQ had specific memory difficulties. Given that this study excluded children with below-average IQ and identified learning problems, the number of students actually suffering from memory problems may be twice as high. One reason for the under-identification is that young children rarely complain of memory problems (Middleton, 2004). Even adolescents who have had memory deficits all their lives may be unaware of their deficits. Another reason students with memory problems are not referred or identified is that their academic learning and performance problems are attributed to other causes.

Furthermore, beliefs regarding the efficacy of memory interventions and instruction may limit the number of students referred for a memory assessment, based on the belief that there's no point in identifying problems that can't be remediated. Many educators and psychologists assume that there are no scientifically based interventions for memory impairments and dysfunctions, or that such interventions cannot be applied in an educational environment. Neither assumption is true; efficacious memory interventions that can be applied in education settings are well documented in the scientific literature (see Chapters 7 and 8). Adding to the lack of identification and intervention is the No Child Left Behind and Response-to-Intervention (Brown-Chidsey & Steege, 2005) educational movements, where the emphasis is strictly on academic skills interventions. Proponents of Response-to-Intervention argue that the cognitive cause of a student's learning problems is irrelevant and that generic academic interventions will work regardless of the underlying reasons for the learning problems. Sadly, this philosophy may deprive many students of the understanding, assistance, and interventions that might allow them to succeed (Kipp & Mohr, 2008). For instance, some reading disabilities are due to long-term memory problems rather than deficient phonological processing skills. Addressing the long-term memory problems of such children will be more beneficial than additional training in phonemic awareness, a skill they already possess.

In the school environment, the rapid acquisition and long-term retention of facts and concepts is fundamental to success. The ability to rapidly and continuously process new information and store it for later recall is essential in the relentlessly demanding educational environment where a new memory may need to be created as often as once every 10 seconds (Newall & Simon, 1972). Every aspect of acquiring and applying academic skills and knowledge depends on adequately functioning long-term memory structures and processes. Reading decoding, reading comprehension, mathematics, spelling, basic writing skills, written expression, and academic subjects, such as science and social studies, all require effective encoding, storage, and retrieval of vast amounts of information. For example, progress in mathematics depends on the retention and efficient recall of basic math facts, and advances in written communication depend on remembering grammatical rules. The acquisition of academic knowledge depends on both the episodic (memory for events) and semantic (memory for facts and concepts) systems, as well as the effective functioning of memory processes, such as encoding, consolidation, and retrieval (see Chapter 2). Because many semantic memories result from the accumulation of episodic memories acquired during multiple learning events, episodic memory ability (once thought to be autobiographical only) is just as important for classroom learning as semantic memory. For example, a student's recall of the personal experiences and contextual cues stored as episodic memories can facilitate retrieval of academic knowledge stored in semantic memory (Hood & Rankin, 2005). Thus, all long-term memory systems, including the subconscious implicit memory system (see Chapter 2) play a role in academic learning and performance. Moreover, the short-term and working memory systems are indispensible when students are committing information to memory (Dehn, 2008).

When students experience learning and memory problems in the classroom, there is often an underlying impairment, dysfunction, or inefficiency in encoding, consolidating, or retrieving information. That is, apparent long-term memory problems are seldom due to an inability to store a tremendous amount of information for long periods of time. The first potential impediment is impaired encoding, which can arise from ineffective encoding procedures or from a less than fully functional hippocampus. Encoding transfers information from short-term and working memory into long-term storage. Many times, the target information has been encoded but it is difficult to recall over time because it was not encoded in a manner that facilitates retrieval. At other times, encoding may be functioning properly but memories are not maintained because they are not integrated with related memories or are not transferred to permanent storage regions in the brain, a process known as consolidation (see Chapter 2). Difficulties retrieving information from long-term storage can also be the source of memory performance problems. In addition, poor self-awareness and self-regulation of memory functions (known as metamemory), along with the use of ineffective memory strategies, can reduce efficiencies and exacerbate minor memory problems. Also, subaverage related cognitive and executive processes, such as inhibitory control, can further complicate matters. Consequently, ferreting out the impaired processes underlying memory problems can be an assessment challenge.

MEMORY AND LEARNING

Differentiating Memory and Learning

There is no learning without memory, and there is no memory without learning. Memory, the indicator that learning has occurred, can be inferred from the ability to recall information, performance on a measure of retention, or a change in behavior. The bilateral relationship between learning and memory is not limited to directed efforts to acquire and retain facts and knowledge. Because people learn from their experiences, the interdependency of memory and learning exists any time humans are mentally processing information. Although learning and memory are tightly interwoven and often viewed as equivalent constructs, it is possible to distinguish between the two. As memory expert L. R. Squire (1987, p. 3) put it, "Learning is the process of acquiring new information, while memory refers to the persistence of learning in a state that can be revealed at a later time." In this book, a similar division of learning and memory is applied. "Learning" refers to the acquisition of knowledge; in other words, getting information into memory is considered the learning phase. Because learning depends primarily on the memory process of encoding, learning and encoding are viewed as essentially equivalent. Of course, learning opportunities are seldom limited to a single episode. Multiple opportunities to learn mean that consolidation and retrieval processes also become involved, as initially learned information is recalled, restructured, and reinforced. Nonetheless, in this text "learning" mainly refers to the initial learning event and is mainly associated with encoding. In contrast, "memory" includes and depends on the learning (encoding) phase, but the term is mainly applied to retention processes and the ability to recall information when needed. Thus, learning refers to the initial acquisition and immediate retention of new material, as measured within seconds and minutes; whereas, memory involves retrieval of that learning after an interval of several minutes, hours, or days. Consequently, learning is associated more with short-term than with long-term memory, and memory is mainly associated with retention of learning over extended intervals of time. Evidence for the separability of learning and memory is provided by the fact that individual differences in learning do not always translate into similar differences in memory. For example, an individual who learns new material very quickly may not retain the material as well as an individual who takes longer to learn it. Furthermore, many variables that have sizable effects on the rate of learning appear to have very little, if any, effect on how long information is retained in memory (Bloom & Shuell, 1981). Consequently, it is possible to obtain substantial improvements in memory without corresponding improvements in initial learning and vice versa.

Learning Rate and Forgetting

As learning proceeds, more and more information is retained and recalled. Each round of exposure, practice, or study of new material or a new skill produces higher recall. The degree of improvement over multiple learning episodes is known as the learning rate, and plotting learning across trials produces a learning curve. Learning curves demonstrate that acquisition of new knowledge or skills increases rapidly at first but then levels off, with each subsequent round of practice, review, or study producing smaller and smaller improvements in performance (Anderson, 2000). Despite diminishing improvements, the old adage that "practice makes perfect" definitely holds true for learning and memory: Recall of information improves the more it is practiced. Even after a learner has reached 100% recall of the material, further practice improves memory, as indicated by faster retrieval speed. Moreover, with each round of practice, the skill or knowledge is relearned more quickly, indicating that memory for the material is becoming stronger and stronger. Although most skills and knowledge eventually become ingrained in memory after numerous rounds of practice, rehearsal, review, or study, there are scientifically based learning and encoding methods that can improve the efficiency and effectiveness of learning (see Chapters 7 and 8). For example, strategies that involve in-depth processing of information produce better recall than rote learning. Given the fact that most students do not engage in enough study to fully master material, strategies that enhance learning and memorability are definitely advantageous. For students with memory problems, the application of effective strategies becomes even more important.

According to classical learning theory, a faster learning rate translates into slower forgetting, and slower learning is connected with faster forgetting. However, for many students, learning rate and forgetting rate may actually have a weak and inconsistent relationship (Brainerd & Reyna, 1995). In fact, Shuell and Keppel (1970) reported only minimal differences between fast and slow learners' rates of forgetting. Thus, assumptions about retention of information should not be based on rate of learning. Some individuals are fast, and apparently successful, learners but don't retain new learning very well. Others are slow learners but successfully retain what they have acquired. Instead of initial learning speed, the number of additional learning events required to fully retain material may be a better predictor of forgetting rate. A potential confound when examining these relationships is the fact that students who learn more slowly are usually provided with more learning opportunities. The fact that learning opportunities increase as learning rate decreases may compensate for the faster forgetting rates among slow learners (Brainerd & Reyna, 1995).

One of the goals of education is for students to retain important knowledge and skills for a lifetime. When learning is effective, students with normal memory functioning are capable of just that. In studies of very long-term retention of academic knowledge (reviewed in Cohen, 2008a), a prominent finding is that the level of original learning predicts the degree of retention. That is, students who initially learned more, mastered the material, or acquired more advanced knowledge, remembered more over extended periods of time. Other factors that influence long-term retention include the amount and spacing of the original training, the level of expertise originally attained (grades being one method of determining this), and the extent to which the information can be reconstructed from schemas. In one study of Spanish language retention, individuals who had not used Spanish during their lifetime were tested 50 years after initially studying it. Amazingly, 40% of the original knowledge could still be recalled and 60% of it was recognized (Bahrick, 1984). These longitudinal studies reveal that knowledge declines exponentially for about three to six years and then stabilizes before a final slight decline after 30 years.

MEMORY PROBLEMS

As used in this book, the term "memory problems" is used in a generic, inclusive sense. Memory problems exist whenever an individual has significantly subaverage ability in one or more aspects of memory, as indicated by subaverage performance on a formal measure of memory, difficulties performing tasks that require effective memory functioning, or difficulties retaining scholastic learning at a normal level. Memory problems are especially indicated when the subaverage performance or difficulty is also a significant intra-individual weakness relative to overall learning potential or intelligence. Thus, memory problems include memory weaknesses, impairments, deficits, disorders, dysfunctions, and deficiencies (see Chapter 3 for further clarification). It is presumed that there is either a neurological impairment underlying the memory problem or ineffectual use of normal memory capabilities. Memory problems in children and adolescents become worthy of concern, and assessment and intervention, when they either impede academic learning or impair daily functioning.

Because memory problems cover a continuum from mild to severe, they can be much more than minor inconveniences. In extreme cases, such as global amnesia, the individual may have difficulty coping with daily routines. In children and adolescents, even mild to moderate memory problems can impair many types of learning, leading to lifelong limitations. For example, a verbal memory impairment in a young child will affect the development of language and literacy. However, even significant memory problems can be difficult to detect and identify, leading to some assessment and diagnostic challenges. For example, not all memory problems are evident during early childhood. Most tend not to become apparent until learning challenges are encountered during the school years. Even then they are likely to be attributed to other factors. Also, many memory problems are subtle, which is why they are misunderstood. Subtlety, however, does not mean that the memory problems are not interfering with the effective learning and functioning of otherwise normal individuals. Nor does subtlety obviate the need for investigation, evaluation, and appropriate interventions and instruction. Educators and psychological practitioners need to remember that subtle or mild memory problems have an additive effect during the educational years, with the end result being fewer acquired skills, less knowledge, and failure to achieve important life goals.

Memory problems and their undesirable consequences may occur even when there is no underlying memory impairment. There are times when problems with encoding, storing, and retrieving information are not due specifically to abnormalities in the brain's memory structures. What is observed as a limitation in one or more memory structures or functions may actually stem from a broader cognitive disability or from a domain-specific impairment. For example, a child or adolescent with a general intellectual impairment is unlikely to demonstrate average memory performance. Also, individuals with a general verbal processing disability, such as those with a language impairment, are typically going to have weaknesses in any type of verbal memory function. Separating memory functions from the influences of related cognitive processes should be attempted during assessment, but whether or not poor memory performance is part of a broader cognitive disability is somewhat irrelevant. The fact is that students with cognitive disabilities benefit from memory interventions and memory-based instruction as much as students with intra-individual memory deficits. Therefore, those with cognitive disabilities also should be considered as having memory problems and provided with appropriate services. Finally, there is another group of children and adolescents whose subaverage memory performance is due to neither cognitive processing limitations nor specific memory impairments. These are youth with otherwise normal cognitive and memory abilities who have not yet figured out how to effectively utilize their memory capabilities due to delayed metamemory development or failure to apply effective strategies. In this book, they are also classified as having memory problems.

APPLYING MEMORY RESEARCH IN THE CLASSROOM

For decades, research by experimental, cognitive, and educational psychologists, as well as neuropsychologists and neuroscientists has documented the efficacy of numerous memory interventions, strategies, mnemonics, and instructional practices. Yet, many of these evidence-based practices have not been consistently applied in the classroom, an environment that continually places high demands on memory. The lack of application originates with teacher training programs that pay little attention to psychological research on memory and the educational applications of memory research. Consequently, relevant empirical findings and evidence-based practices have had very little influence on pedagogy and instructional practices in the classroom. Although effective teacher behaviors and evidence-based instructional practices generally support memory functioning (Rosenshine, 1995), approaches that specifically address memory functions can further enhance the academic learning and performance of all students (see Chapter 8). Teachers who address memory challenges, teach memory strategies and mnemonics, and adopt more instructional practices that specifically support memory, may ultimately reduce their burdens rather than adding to them, mainly because memory-based methods should increase the efficiency of student learning. Even students recognize the benefits of memory-based instruction. For instance, Scruggs and Mastropieri (1990) reported that the learning disabled students in their study greatly preferred memory-based instruction over traditional instruction. In reality, classroom-based memory interventions may be the only viable approach to serving the needs of students with memory impairments, as the funds, resources, and personnel available for pull-out services is very limited. Accordingly, one of the primary objectives of this book is to provide educational consultants, school psychologists, special education teachers, and class-room teachers with all of the information they need to successfully implement evidence-based memory practices in the classroom.

OVERVIEW OF THE CHAPTERS

Chapter 2, *Memory Systems and Processes*, describes and differentiates the functions of the major memory systems, the types of memory that comprise each system, and the memory processes involved. After discussing the structure, organization, and inter-relationships of short-term, working, and long-term memory, the focus shifts to the two major divisions of explicit memory—episodic and semantic—and the primary long-term memory processes: encoding, consolidation, and retrieval. Following an explanation of the interdependency of episodic and semantic memory, the pivotal role of consolidation in the formation of enduring semantic memories is proposed. Essentially, the chapter provides a comprehensive review of theories and research about human memory. The chapter concludes with implications for the assessment and intervention topics addressed in subsequent chapters.

Chapter 3, *Memory Neuroanatomy, Development, and Dysfunction*, examines memory from a neuropsychological perspective, as opposed to the cognitive perspective in Chapter 2. The neuroanatomy section describes how memories are formed through synaptic changes and strengthening, as well as alterations in neural pathways that connect related networks of neurons spread throughout the brain. The focus is on the medial temporal lobe and hippocampus, the two most critical brain structures in the encoding, consolidation, and retrieval of long-term memories. The section on development of long-term memory includes an in-depth discussion of metamemory and the vital role it plays in developing the child's ability to remember more and more information. The chapter concludes with a discussion of memory dysfunctions, such as amnesia, that can impair learning and daily functioning.

Chapter 4, *Risk Factors for Memory Impairments*, is potentially the most interesting and alarming chapter in this text because it reviews the memory research on approximately 30 disorders and medical conditions that place children at-risk for memory impairments. For example, the hippocampus of children with poorly controlled diabetes can suffer irreparable damage from repeated hypoglycemic episodes. The review attempts to identify specific memory components and processes that are most likely to be affected by each risk factor, leading to identification of specific memory components that should be addressed during assessment and intervention when a child or adolescent has experienced one of these risk factors.

Chapter 5, *Long-Term Memory Assessment Strategies*, promotes a hypothesis-driven approach to comprehensive memory assessment that incorporates selective, cross-battery procedures. The chapter begins with the identification of and rationale for specific memory components that should be considered for testing. In addition to standardized testing, the chapter details informal assessment procedures, including sample items for interviews and observation. The recommended assessment strategies are unique in that the assessment of metamemory development, strategy use, and classroom examination performance is included. The chapter concludes with a case study that illustrates clinical analysis procedures for identifying intra-individual weaknesses and deficits.

Chapter 6, *Assessing Long-Term Memory with Standardized Tests*, critically examines memory batteries and memory subtests from cognitive scales that are suitable for testing the memory functions of children and adolescents. For each memory scale reviewed, there is information on the structure, technical properties, and general interpretative procedures, followed by a brief critique of the scale. For each long-term memory subtest included, there is a description of the task, identification of the specific memory components it measures, and interpretative suggestions, along with implications of low performance. To facilitate selective, cross-battery testing, the chapter includes tables that identify the specific memory components tapped by subtests from several memory and cognitive scales.

Chapter 7, *Interventions for Memory Problems*, guides the reader through a step-by-step approach to selecting interventions, setting goals, measuring progress, and general training procedures for strategies. After confronting the challenges and concerns regarding memory interventions, there is an emphasis on metamemory training and demonstrating the efficacy of strategies and mnemonics. Then the details needed for implementation are provided for several evidence-based memory strategies and mnemonics, followed by an overview of non-strategic interventions, such as memory aids. Following a discussion of special methods recommended for children with traumatic brain injury, the chapter concludes with the typical sequence and activities recommended for a one-on-one intervention with a child or adolescent who has mild to moderate memory problems.

Chapter 8, *Classroom Instruction That Supports Memory*, focuses on instructional practices that enhance the memory functioning of students, especially those with memory problems. Underlying the recommendations in this chapter is the presumption that these instructional practices and the teaching of memory strategies will be most successful in a classroom that is oriented towards supporting the memory of learners, an environment and approach referred to as the "mnemonic classroom." The chapter, written with teachers and educational consultants in mind, includes details for evidence-based instructional practices that can easily be incorporated in the classroom. For each of the recommended practices and memory strategies, there is a discussion regarding what it is, how it works, why it works, who it benefits, the research supporting it, and how to apply it in the classroom. The chapter concludes with tips for reducing working memory load in the classroom and a summary of key memory principles that apply to classroom instruction.

Chapter 9, *Case Studies and Recommendations*, integrates many of the ideas discussed throughout the book by illustrating how memory impairments might be manifested in children's behavior and learning. In addition to providing all the assessment details about two cases introduced earlier in the book, the chapter relates everything that occurred during the actual intervention sessions with a 13-year-old student. In addition, student comments, reflections, and plans are reported from another intervention case. The chapter concludes with recommendations for future research and memory test development.

LEARNING OBJECTIVES

After reading, studying, and applying the information and practices discussed in this book, the reader will be able to:

1. Describe the unique characteristics of and key differences among short-term, working, and long-term memory systems.

2. Delineate the functions of episodic and semantic memory and the inter-dependency between them.
3. Explain the roles of encoding, consolidation, and retrieval on the formation, retention, and recollection of memories.
4. Envision the creation, strengthening, and interconnectivity of memories at the cellular and neural network levels.
5. Unequivocally understand the crucial role of the hippocampus in the encoding and consolidation of episodic and semantic memories.
6. Describe various aspects of metamemory and how a well-developed meta-memory can enhance memory functions.
7. Explain how comparing performance on uncued recall tasks with performance on recognition tasks helps to determine whether a retention or a retrieval problem underlies difficulty recalling information.
8. Recognize more than two dozen medical conditions and disorders that place children and adolescents at-risk for memory impairments.
9. Plan a comprehensive, but efficient assessment of memory and related processes that addresses the referral concerns.
10. Complete informal memory assessment procedures that include interviews, observations, and an evaluation of metamemory development.
11. Properly analyze and interpret test scores derived from a cross–battery assessment.
12. Given a variety of memory and cognitive scales, select appropriate subtests for the measurement of specific memory components.
13. Given a child or adolescent with mild to moderate memory problems, select appropriate evidence-based strategies, mnemonics, and other methods.
14. Convincingly illustrate the efficacy of memory strategies and mnemonics while conducting an intervention.
15. Provide training that promotes the development of metamemory self-awareness and self-regulation.
16. Recognize the procedures and rationale for memory interventions reserved for students with severe memory impairments, such as those who have suffered a severe traumatic brain injury.
17. Effectively consult with classroom teachers about evidence-based instructional practices that enhance students' encoding, consolidation, and retention of learning.
18. Provide the rationale for teaching evidence-based memory strategies and mnemonics in the classroom.
19. Understand many of the intricacies that will need to be incorporated if a one-on-one intervention with a student is to succeed.
20. Structure and write an evaluation report about an examinee's memory functions that is understandable to all readers.

2

Memory Systems and Processes

A middle school student named "Abby" was brought in by her mother for an evaluation and tutoring. Abby had been adopted at birth. Not much was known about the birth mother's health or behavior during pregnancy, but the use of crack cocaine was suspected. Academics had always been challenging for Abby, but with tutoring and her parents' support, she had acquired average skills in oral language, reading decoding, mathematics calculation, and spelling. Abby was well organized, well behaved, very attentive, and studied much longer than the average student. Despite her skills and efforts, Abby, who wanted to do well in school, was struggling in most of her academic subjects, especially science, social studies, and mathematics. Her borderline failing grades were mainly due to poor performance on classroom exams, even though her mother helped her study for each exam. Abby's mother reported that Abby seemed to know and understand the material when they studied but often performed poorly when tested. Most of Abby's teachers attributed her poor performance to lack of effort and motivation, an attribution her mother thought was untrue. When her mother suggested that Abby might have a memory problem, Abby's teachers were skeptical. The teachers argued that Abby seemed to learn new material just fine, and when quizzed immediately following a lesson, she could recall the information as well as other students. Abby's early development was normal and there was nothing noteworthy in her health history. Abby's adoptive mother reported that the first indication that Abby might be having learning problems came to light when Abby was having difficulty remembering nursery rhymes that were read to her day after day.

After a comprehensive psychoeducational evaluation was completed, the explanation for Abby's poor test performance became evident. Abby had mid-average verbal and auditory abilities, with low–average visual processing, fluid reasoning, and processing speed. Her academic skills were commensurate with her intellectual abilities. There was no evidence of a specific learning disability. The telling scores were her memory scores. Her learning, short-term memory, and working memory scores were average. As observed by her teachers, Abby could learn new material and recall it well immediately and shortly after it was learned. However, Abby's long-term retention of that same information was clearly deficient. Within 30 minutes, she was forgetting more content than would be expected. Even with prompts and cues her recall did not improve much, and on the standardized memory test her recognition standard scores were not significantly higher than her uncued recall scores, an indication that the information had actually been forgotten. Only her long-term memory for narrative information was normal. Abby's long-term memory deficit was corroborated by her mother and by the tutors who would later work with her. Without frequent review, Abby had an unusually rapid rate of forgetting. The explanation for Abby's poor test performance and rapid forgetting was obvious. Abby had significant difficulty consolidating and retaining new learning. Abby's teachers had been correct. Abby's "memory" was fine; however, the memory that was normal was only short-term memory, not long-term memory. (See Chapters 5 and 9 for more details on Abby's assessment and intervention results.)

Abby's case illustrates what most people know: There's more than one type of memory. Humans have multiple, distinct, but interrelated memory systems, and each of these systems is comprised of storage components and a set of correlated processes (Tulving, 1985). Memory systems can be defined in terms of content, structure, and function (Squire, 2004). Wilson (2009, p. 1–2) neatly summarized the different types of human memory systems and functions:

> We can consider memory in terms of the length of time for which memories are stored, the type of information to be remembered, the modality the information is in, the stages in the process of remembering, explicit or implicit memory, whether recall or recognition is required, (and) whether the memory is retrospective or prospective.

Human memory systems have different functions and handle distinct types of information. Not only do separate memory systems deal with distinct kinds of information, but they operate according to different principles and rely on different neural structures and processes (Tulving, 1993). Nonetheless, each cognitive event or learning experience draws on a unique combination of components from one or more memory systems. That is, there is seldom a one-to-one correspondence between the information being encoded and a particular memory system. However, memory systems can operate independently of one another. For instance, an individual who appears to have total amnesia for explicit forms of memory can still learn and remember through the implicit (unconscious) memory system. Despite the diversity of storage systems, a common set of cognitive processes enables much of the encoding, storage, and retrieval of information.

The purpose of this chapter is to help readers begin to unravel the complexities and mysteries of human memory and to gain an understanding of how all the pieces and processes work in unison. The chapter will begin by discriminating among short-term, working, and long-term memory, and by examining the components of each. The discussion will then focus on the divisions of long-term memory, with emphasis on the types of memory most closely related to academic learning. Details on all of the memory processing from input to output will then be provided, along with a discussion of forgetting and some cognitive theories of memory organization.

By the end of the chapter the reader should have a grasp of memory fundamentals and begin to foresee assessment possibilities and educational implications. This chapter focuses on cognitive models of memory, whereas Chapter 3 describes memory functions from a neurological perspective.

THE FLOW OF INFORMATION

Memory has been investigated since the early days of psychology (Ebbinghaus, 1913), but only in recent decades have psychologists reached a consensus about its structures and functions. There was even uncertainty over the division of memory into short-term and long-term components until early neuropsychological studies in the 1940s confirmed the distinction. Building on this finding, cognitive models of memory and information processing originated in the 1950s and evolved into the elaborate multi-component models that are now supported by neuroscientists' brain imaging research. It is difficult to represent complex human memory structures and functions in a figure, and consequently the general information processing model has been criticized as being overly simplified. Nonetheless, the classic model (see Figure 2.1) illustrates the usual flow of information and the fact that memory components and processes form the core of information processing.

Information flows through several components as it travels from the environment to long-term memory and then from long-term memory into a behavior or expression. Incoming information passes through sensory memory, short-term memory, and working memory before taking up residence in long-term memory stores. Outgoing information is activated in long-term memory before passing through working memory and being expressed behaviorally. Along its course, the information is selected, winnowed, manipulated, transformed, stored, retrieved, evaluated, and expressed. In memory terminology, the information is encoded, consolidated, stored, and retrieved. As information from the external world proceeds through the sequence of processes, progressively higher level representations of the perceived information are formed (Simons & Spiers, 2003). In the process, different

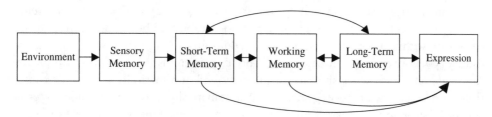

Figure 2.1 The flow of information through memory components

features of the event or related information are associated and integrated into a bound memory representation. Current goals and task demands may guide the construction of these representations, and these structures will be modified as they are accessed in the future.

SENSORY MEMORY

The first memory system to process and store incoming information is usually referred to as sensory memory (Atkinson & Shiffrin, 1968) but is also known as the *sensory register*. Visual sensory memory is known as *iconic memory*, and auditory sensory memory is known as *echoic memory*. Sensory memory is not a specific brain or memory structure, but rather a stage of processing. Environmental stimuli that impinge on the human senses and are perceived by the brain are momentarily held in perceptual form. This perceptual information is available for a fraction of a second before it is overwritten by new incoming information. The duration is barely long enough for attentional processes to select input for further processing in short-term memory. Individuals with a dysfunction in the sensory memory systems are usually considered as having visual or auditory perceptual disorders, not a memory impairment. Given that sensory memory relates more to perception than memory, it will not be discussed further in this book.

SHORT-TERM MEMORY

Very little of the sensory information that is perceived and briefly stored actually reaches short-term memory. When humans are actively processing information, they can consciously influence which incoming information is selected for further processing and storage by selectively attending to it. Thus, attentional processes are crucial learning and memory functions. If an individual wants to learn and remember information, she or he must first pay attention to it. When a person is not interested in or not paying attention to available input, some sort of automated filtering device is presumed to allow only a limited amount of the vast information in the passive sensory store to transfer to short-term memory. In short-term memory, active processing of the input is possible or short-term memory can just passively hold information. Active processing consists mainly of rehearsal that serves to extend the retention interval. Without rehearsal, information will be lost from short-term memory within a matter of seconds. In addition to temporal limits, short-term memory has a typical adult capacity of about seven items or chunks. Much of the information that reaches short-term memory will automatically be encoded into long-term memory processing areas or will automatically activate relevant long-term memory structures. Information that is the focus of attention will be processed further in working memory before being encoded or used to achieve an immediate goal. In common usage, people think of short-term memory as extending for several minutes if not hours. Actually, any information recalled after several seconds is most likely being retrieved from long-term memory. Thus, *immediate memory* may be a more accurate descriptor of short-term memory.

In contemporary memory models, short-term memory is thought to be embedded within the working memory system (Dehn, 2008). In an unconscious mode, short-term memory can operate independently of working memory, but whenever short-term memory content is being managed, working memory is performing that executive function. Both short-term memory and working memory can be divided into auditory-verbal and visuospatial components. Although short-term and working memory are not the focus of this book, they are inextricably linked with long-term memory and thus need elaboration.

Phonological Short-Term Memory

Although frequently referred to as auditory or verbal short-term memory, *phonological short-term memory* is a more appropriate term because auditory input is processed and encoded phonologically. Phonological short-term memory, also referred to as the *phonological loop* or the *articulatory loop*, is a limited capacity, speech-based store of verbal information (Baddeley, 1986, 2003). Oral input gains immediate, direct, and automatic access to short-term memory, where it is briefly stored in phonological form (Hitch, 1990; Logie, 1996). Baddeley (1986), who developed the predominant working memory model, subdivides phonological short-term memory into passive phonological storage and subvocal, articulatory rehearsal. Short-term phonological capacity is analogous to an audio tape recorder loop of a specific length. Words or other auditory units are recorded in the order they are perceived, and they will quickly decay or be recorded over by new auditory units unless rehearsal rerecords them onto the tape. Amazingly, this *phonological loop* is only two seconds in duration, regardless of the individual's age.

The number of verbal items that can fit into the phonological loop depends on the time taken to articulate them. Longer words take longer to articulate and therefore take up more of the phonological loop. This phenomenon explains why recall of one-syllable words is better than that of multiple-syllable words. Adult sequential recall of five monosyllabic words is about 90%; whereas, it drops to about 50% when the equivalent number of words consists of five syllables each (Baddeley, 2003). The capacity of the phonological loop can be expressed as this: number of retained words equals the length of the loop times speech rate (Hulme & Mackenzie, 1992). That is, the typical adult can recall only a sequential span that he or she can articulate within 2 seconds (Baddeley, 1986; Hulme & Mackenzie, 1992). For instance, if an individual's speech rate is two words per second, his or her memory span will be about four words. The number of words recalled is not a function of how many items are presented within 2 seconds but rather the number of words the individual can articulate within 2 seconds. The implication is that the amount of information that can be rehearsed and consequently retained is constrained by the 2-second loop and speech rate. Furthermore, subvocal rehearsal rate is thought to be equivalent to overt speech rate. This relationship accounts for the findings that verbal short-term memory span varies according to the length of the items and the individual's speech rate; individuals with faster articulation rates can maintain more items than individuals who are slow articulators (Hulme & Mackenzie, 1992).

For adults, normal phonological memory span has long been assumed to be approximately seven units (Miller, 1956). The span is typically measured with tasks such as digit or word span and is often referred to as verbal span. The finding that span is highly related to the time it takes to articulate the stimulus words implies that short-term memory is not necessarily limited to seven, plus or minus two, units of information as is usually believed. The immediate serial recall of word sequences decreases as the constituent words become longer (Baddeley, 1990). This phenomenon, known as the *word length effect*, has been attributed to the greater time it takes to subvocally rehearse items of longer articulatory duration. The crucial feature is the spoken duration of the word and not the number of syllables. When subvocal articulation of the sequence exceeds the brief retention interval, errors begin to occur. Therefore, verbal memory span can be equated with the number of words that can be articulated in approximately 2 seconds, rather than thinking of it as a specific number of spoken words. Even the classic digit span task is subject to this rule. For instance, the digit span of Welsh children is substantially lower than that of English speaking children because Welsh digits consist of more than one syllable (Ellis & Hennelley, 1980).

Despite the strong evidence that word length and articulatory rehearsal speed determine auditory short-term memory span, other influences also affect memory span. One influence is prior knowledge. Meaningful phonological information may activate relevant long-term memory structures, which may then facilitate recall in the absence of short-term retention. For instance, the average adult has a longer span for meaningful words than for pseudo-words. The degree of chunking, the grouping of items into larger units, also affects span. For example, the separate digits "5" and "8" can be chunked as "58." Nevertheless, subvocal rehearsal seems to largely determine verbal span because whenever individuals are prevented from rehearsing, performance is markedly impaired. The typical interference task prevents rehearsal by requiring the participant to engage in an unrelated attention-demanding task. Prevention of rehearsal allows researchers and examiners to assess pure phonological short-term memory capacity. The impact of disrupting phonological short-term rehearsal provides evidence of the importance of rehearsal to the short-term retention of information, and it provides evidence for the subdivision of the phonological loop into a passive store and a rehearsal function. In summary, phonological short-term memory span is primarily a joint function of rate of decay and rate of rehearsal. Articulation rate determines how much information can be repeated before it decays. Repeated subvocal rehearsal also extends the interval over which information can be retained. When individuals are prevented from rehearsing information, their short-term memory performance decreases dramatically, as well as the amount of information they can encode into long-term memory (Henry, 2001).

Visuospatial Short-Term Memory

Visuospatial short-term memory is responsible for the immediate storage of visual and spatial information, such as objects and their location. Like the phonological component, it consists of passive temporary storage and active rehearsal. Decay in the temporary visuospatial store seems to be as rapid as phonological decay, taking place within a matter of seconds. The rate of forgetting seems to be a function of stimulus complexity and of how long the stimulus is viewed. Refreshment of the visual trace appears to result from eye movement, manipulation of the image, or some type of visual mnemonic (Baddeley, 1986). Visuospatial short-term memory seems primarily designed to maintain spatial or patterned stimuli rather than temporal sequences of visual items, which explains why it has been linked to the control and production of physical movement (Logie, 1996). It may also serve an important function during reading, as it visually encodes printed letters and words while maintaining a visuospatial frame of reference that allows the reader to backtrack and keep his or her place in the text (Baddeley).

Visuospatial short-term storage divides into two subcomponents: visual and spatial (Pickering, Gathercole, Hall, & Lloyd, 2001). The visual subcomponent is responsible for the storage of static visual information (i.e., information about objects' shape and color), and the spatial subcomponent is responsible for the storage of dynamic spatial information (i.e., information about location, motion, and direction). The visual subcomponent is a passive system that stores visual information in the form of static visual representations. In contrast, the spatial subcomponent is an active spatial rehearsal system that maintains sequential locations and movements. According to Olive (2004), the spatial subcomponent requires rehearsal to continually update dynamic information, as well as to refresh decaying information. Visual short-term storage is limited in capacity, typically to about three or four objects for a matter of seconds. Because of the limitations, individuals may not notice when objects in a series move, change color, or disappear. Of course, in the real world, objects and their characteristics often persist over time, making detailed visual retention and rehearsal unnecessary (Baddeley, 1996).

Complex patterns are more difficult to retain than simple patterns. Complexity refers to the amount of variety in a stimulus. For example, blocks displayed in a matrix are easier to recall than a random display, and asymmetrical figures are more difficult to recall than symmetrical ones. These findings indicate that structured visuospatial information consumes less short-term storage capacity than unstructured. The fact that visuospatial span is better for familiar material suggests that long-term memory representations are facilitating short-term visuospatial memory, much like recognizable words extending phonological memory span.

Better recall for familiar images may also be accomplished by the conversion of visual information into verbal information, which is more likely to occur when images are recognizable.

Although the visuospatial component can operate independently from the phonological component, visuospatial storage and rehearsal appear to depend a great deal on phonological rehearsal. The phonological rehearsal of visuospatial information is initiated by the deliberate recoding of visuospatial information into verbal information, which occurs when the individual verbalizes the names of objects and locations to be remembered (Richardson, 1996). By 10 years of age, most individuals verbally recode much of their visuospatial input by naming objects and rehearsing them verbally. Not all visuospatial input is easily transformed; the individual has to be able to identify and name the object or location in order for the transfer to occur. Visually presented patterns that are difficult to name must be encoded visually. Failure to create a verbal representation of visual material may prevent rehearsal and affect retention. The visual–verbal conversion process seems to be one of the functions of the phonological rehearsal component.

Relationships With Learning and Long-Term Memory

Numerous studies have investigated phonological short-term memory span and found it to be an incredibly robust phenomenon that is highly predictive of verbal learning (for more discussion, see Dehn, 2008). For example, it plays a crucial role in the acquisition of vocabulary and arithmetic facts (Baddeley, 2003). It is also highly interrelated with phonological processing. Clearly, adequate short-term memory capacity, an adequate retention interval, and effective rehearsal are essential for initial learning and for encoding into long-term memory. The presumption is that the longer information can be held in short-term memory the more likely it will be encoded into long-term memory. Although this relationship may be true, there is more to effective learning and encoding than just passive retention and encoding.

For its part, long-term memory supports short-term memory functioning. Long-term memory representations directly enhance short-term span. When information enters short-term memory, related information in long-term storage is immediately and automatically activated. Long-term memory then sends cues to short-term memory that can be used to reconstruct partially decayed information, thereby extending short-term memory span and retention intervals (Nairne, 2002). This interaction explains why people can recall some recently experienced material for longer than a few seconds. In conclusion, normal short-term memory functioning may be a necessary prerequisite for learning and long-term encoding, but it is insufficient for optimal long-term retention of information. In contrast, short-term memory can function well when there is a dysfunctional long-term memory, as demonstrated by cases of total amnesia. Thus, long-term memory and short-term memory are intertwined but still dissociable systems. Table 2.1 highlights some of their similarities and differences.

Table 2.1 Similarities and differences between short-term memory and long-term memory

Similarities

Both have verbal and visual components	Both necessary for learning
Both interact with working memory	Both transform information
Both affected by strategies	Both affected by interference
Both can function automatically	Both can be monitored
Both related with other cognitive processes	Both involve forgetting

Differences

Short-Term Memory	Long-Term Memory
Very limited capacity	Extensive capacity
Retention for seconds	Retention for minutes to years
Conscious access to all content	Not all content has conscious access
Only two types	Multiple types
Depends on attention	Less dependent on attention
Immediate retrieval only	Retrieval can be extended
Forgetting is immediate	Forgetting is gradual
Amenable to simple strategies	Amenable to elaborate strategies
Easy to assess	Difficult to assess
Less susceptible to brain injury	Very susceptible to brain injury

WORKING MEMORY

The working memory system utilizes temporarily stored or retrieved information in the performance of complex cognitive tasks (Hulme & Mackenzie, 1992). The information may be drawn from short-term or long-term memory. Essentially, working memory is conceptualized as the processing of information while trying to retain the same or different information. The main distinction between working memory and the other two global systems is that working memory involves conscious processing; whereas, short-term and long-term memory functions are considered more passive, automatic, and unconscious. Overall, working memory can be viewed as a comprehensive system that unites various short- and long-term memory subsystems and functions. Working memory's primary functions include encoding, effortful retrieval from long-term memory, enactment of strategic processes, control of attentional processes, and executive management of memory systems. The combination of moment-to-moment awareness, efforts to maintain information in short-term memory, and the effortful retrieval of archived information constitutes working memory. In general, working memory involves the management, manipulation, and transformation of information drawn from either short-term or long-term memory.

It is difficult to delimit working memory and disentangle it from related cognitive processes, such as reasoning. From a broad perspective, working memory is a central cognitive process that is involved with the active processing of information. It appears to be a fundamental capacity that underlies complex, as well as elementary cognitive processes (Lepine, Barrouillet, & Camos, 2005). Working memory supports human cognitive processing by providing an interface between perception, short-term memory, long-term memory, and goal-directed actions. Working memory is particularly necessary for conscious cognitive processing because it permits internal representation of information to guide decision making and overt behavior. Working memory is one of the main cognitive processes underlying thinking and learning. By utilizing the contents of various memory storage systems, working memory enables individuals to learn and to string together thoughts and ideas. For more details on working memory, see Dehn (2008).

Verbal Working Memory

Verbal working memory consists of complex working memory operations in which analysis, manipulation, and transformation of verbal material takes place. One of the primary functions of verbal working memory is to extract a meaningful representation that corresponds to the phonological information taken in by phonological short-term memory. In essence, verbal working memory involves processing of verbal information that either is in current short-term storage or has been retrieved recently from long-term storage. In contrast to phonological short-term memory, verbal working memory is viewed as higher-level, meaning-based processing, whereas phonological short-term memory is simple, passive processing.

Visuospatial Working Memory

The main distinction between visuospatial short-term and visuospatial working memory is that the short-term component involves only passive retention of information, whereas visuospatial working memory adds a processing component, such as reversing the sequence of objects or manipulating an image. Visuospatial working memory is also involved in the generation, manipulation, and maintenance of visual imagery (Gathercole & Baddeley, 1993). Maintenance and manipulation of visual images are demanding processes, beyond the capacity of visuospatial short-term memory. Therefore, working memory is required whenever internally generated visual images are being consciously manipulated. Because imagery mnemonics are often used to create enduring long-term memory representations, the possession of adequate visuospatial working memory capacity is important. Verbal working memory may also lend some assistance during imagery processing by attaching labels to the images involved. Consequently, reconstruction of the images during recall may depend heavily on verbal representations. Image manipulation and the coordination of the verbal and visual subsystems are functions of executive working memory. Hence, manipulation of visuospatial information, such as images, appears to involve all aspects of the working memory system and to consume many of its resources as well.

Executive Working Memory

According to Baddeley (2003), there is no verbal or visuospatial division of working memory. Rather, working memory is not modality specific, and it is primarily executive in nature. Baddeley refers to the working memory core as the *central executive* and views it as responsible for controlling short-term memory components and regulating and coordinating all of the cognitive processes involved in working memory performance, such as allocating limited attentional capacity. The central executive is involved any time information is transformed or manipulated, such as during mental arithmetic. The central executive is analogous to an executive board that controls attention, selects strategies, and integrates information from several different sources. It is modality or domain free, acting as a link between subsystems that are dependent on auditory or visual processing. As described by Baddeley (1986, 1996), the central executive, which does not itself have storage capacity, draws on the overall limited capacity of short-term and working memory. Despite its important role, the functioning of the central executive is the least understood component of working memory. The lack of a clear construct is due to measurement challenges and to its multiple functions (Richardson, 1996). Nevertheless, there is a consensus among theorists that general executive processing plays a central role in working memory. Most experts agree that individual differences in working memory are primarily determined by executive aspects of working memory.

Working memory's central executive is involved whenever an individual must simultaneously store and process information. Tasks that introduce interference or a secondary processing task while requiring the retention of information will necessarily involve the central executive. For instance, the central executive is responsible for managing dual-task situations, which typically involve processing information while trying to retain the same or different information. Multi-tasking is actually the norm in modern daily life, especially in an academic learning environment. The added demands of coordinating multiple tasks may slow down processing and reduce short-term span. Because working memory has limited resources for storage and processing, there is a need to maintain short-term, modality-specific stores and to incorporate long-term memory structures that can assist with storage and retrieval.

In general, the main functions of executive working memory seem to be: (a) coordinating performance on two separate tasks (i.e., simultaneous storage and processing of information); (b) switching between tasks such as retrieval and encoding; (c) attending selectively to specific information (Engle, 2002); (d) selecting and executing plans and strategies; (e) allocating resources to short-term memory components; and (f) retrieving, holding, and manipulating temporarily activated information from long-term memory. In addition to these operations, cognitive inhibition and updating are other crucial functions. Inhibition is the ability to attend to one stimulus while screening out and suppressing the disruptive effects of automatically generated or retrieved information that is not pertinent to the task at hand. Inhibition also discards previously activated but no longer relevant information and suppresses incorrect responses. In effect, inhibition reduces interference. Updating is the ability to control and update information. It is a process of constant revision whereby newer, more relevant information replaces older, no longer relevant information (Swanson, Howard, & Saez, 2006).

The Episodic Buffer

To explain the interface between long-term memory and working memory, Baddeley (2000, 2006) recently added a fourth component—the episodic buffer— to his model. The episodic buffer is considered a limited capacity component, consciously accessible, that interfaces with long-term episodic and semantic memory to construct integrated representations based on new information. The episodic buffer also allows direct encoding into long-term episodic memory (Pickering & Gathercole, 2004), and controls directed searches of long-term memory. In particular, the episodic component can account for temporary storage of large amounts of information that seem to exceed the capacities of the phonological and visuospatial storage systems, without relying on storage in the executive component or direct retrieval from long-term memory (Baddeley, 2003). It was added to Baddeley's model (2006) after research (Hulme & Mackenzie, 1992; Logie, 1996) found that short-term memory span depends substantially on information from long-term memory. The episodic buffer is also a response to competing models of working memory that claim working memory is little more than activated long-term memory representations. From Baddeley's perspective, the episodic buffer compliments long-term memory storage. The episodic buffer also addresses the reality that working memory processes conceptual knowledge, which is composed of more than the basic phonological and visuospatial codes found in the model's two short-term memory buffers (Cowan, Saults, & Morey, 2006).

The functioning of the episodic buffer is important for learning because it uses multimodal codes to integrate representations from components of working memory and long-term memory into unitary representations. The episodic component combines visual and verbal codes and links them to multidimensional representations in long-term memory. The episodic buffer may also be responsible for binding separate episodes or units of information into chunks, and it may even integrate elements into new coherent structures. Undirected changes in long-term representations occur slowly, after many repeated exposures to the same information. In contrast, conscious episodic working memory processes can quickly represent and integrate information for immediate learning and processing.

Relationship With Short-Term Memory

Many cognitive psychologists and memory experts view short-term and working memory as interchangeable or consider one to be a subtype of the other. However, for assessment and intervention purposes, the two components are best viewed as distinguishable memory systems (see Figure 2.2). Although short-term and working memory can function somewhat independently, they are, to a large extent, dependent on one another. Adequate short-term capacity allows working memory to manipulate and transform information without losing it; for example, short-term capacity is needed to retain the facts and partial solutions during mental arithmetic. For its part, working memory enhances short-term memory functioning through implementation and management of strategies. The main distinction between the two systems is that short-term memory passively holds information; whereas, working memory consciously processes information. See Table 2.2 for a summary of their similarities and differences.

Relationship With Long-Term Memory

The relationship between working memory and long-term memory is bidirectional (Ericsson & Kintsch, 1995). Working memory is involved during effortful long-term encoding and retrieval (Cantor & Engle, 1993; Rosen & Engle, 1997). Working memory also operates on memory representations, for example, modifying semantic memory structures as new information is added. For its part, long-term memory contributes to performance on working memory tasks, and may even extend working memory capacity by maintaining a pool of recently activated schemas (Unsworth & Engle, 2007). Furthermore, working memory capacity and functioning are affected by the acquired skills and knowledge retained in long-term

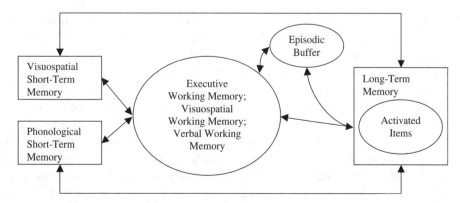

Figure 2.2 Integrated memory systems

Table 2.2   Similarities and differences between short-term memory and working memory

Similarities		
Both have very limited capacity		Both connected with long-term memory
Both involved in encoding		Both necessary for learning
Both susceptible to interference		Both can be monitored
Differences		
Short-Term Memory		Working Memory
Storage is main function		Processing is main function
Average span of seven items		Average capacity of four items
Passively holds information		Actively manipulates information
Domain specific storage		Multimodal storage
Non-executive functions		Executive functions
Automated processing		Effortful processing
Involved in encoding		Involved in encoding and retrieval
Enhanced by simple strategies		Enhanced by elaborate strategies

memory. As knowledge and skills become consolidated in long-term memory, less processing is required of working memory, as automated responses and procedures occur. When automated retrieval and processing are insufficient for the task, working memory initiates and conducts effortful searches that deliberately retrieve information for active restructuring and encoding. Nonetheless, long-term and working memory are not as interdependent as short-term and working memory. That is, most activation of long-term memory representations is automatic and is initiated by short-term memory content (Logie, 1996). The subsequent automatic responses also bypass working memory.

Relationship With Academic Learning

Working memory's relations with various aspects of academic learning mainly arise from its limited capacity (Gathercole & Pickering, 2000, 2001). Although there are individual differences, the capacity of working memory is quite restricted, even in individuals with normal working memory resources. For example, the typical individual can only manipulate about four pieces of information at a time (Cowan, 2001). Because of the central role working memory plays in cognitive functioning and learning, successful learning is largely a function of the individual's working memory capacity (for more details, see Dehn, 2008). For instance, a child with an impairment in verbal working memory is likely to have difficulties with reading comprehension. Moreover, given the inherent limitations of working memory, efficient utilization of its resources is important for all learners, not just those with working memory deficits.

LONG-TERM MEMORY SYSTEMS

There are several ways the organization of long-term memory can be modeled and understood. For example, there is certainly a memory store associated with each of the five senses: visual, auditory, tactile, olfactory, and taste. Although most assessment instruments have simply divided long-term memory into visual and auditory components, research and applied psychologists have developed a more elaborate organization of long-term memory structures that is now widely accepted and seems consistent with actual brain structures and functions. The primary division of long-term memory is into explicit and implicit memory. There are two recognized aspects of explicit memory: episodic and semantic. There are three major categories of implicit memory: priming, classical conditioning, and procedural learning (see Figure 2.3).

Explicit (Declarative) Memory

Explicit, or declarative, memory is the kind of memory people are usually referring to when they discuss memory. In contrast to unconscious implicit memory, explicit memory stores contain consciously accessible information. Explicit memory is divided into two formats: episodic and semantic. Essentially, episodic is memory for events and semantic is memory for facts. However, each memory system includes autobiographical knowledge and knowledge of the world. The inclusion of factual knowledge in episodic memory blurs the traditional lines between episodic and semantic memory, as information that lacks personal information is generally considered semantic. Consequently, these two memory systems can be viewed as parallel but partially overlapping processing and storage systems (Tulving, 1993).

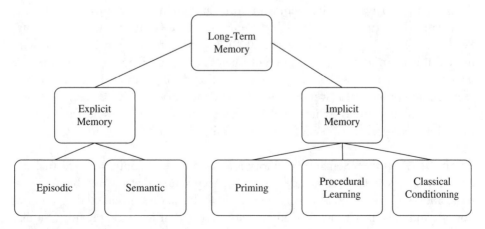

Figure 2.3 Long-term memory systems

Episodic Memory   Episodic memory is the storage and recollection of experiences and events. Specifically, episodic memory consists of personal experiences and the specific objects, people, and events that have been encountered at a particular time and place (Williams, Conway, & Cohen, 2008). Although episodic memory seems primarily visuospatial and contextual, it also includes verbal content. The construct of episodic memory has evolved since it was first proposed by Tulving in 1972 (Tulving, 1985). At first, the emphasis was on autobiographical content and the recollection of personally experienced events. More recently, there is less emphasis on the autobiographical component and more on the recall of specific episodes. These episodes include formal learning events, as well as personal experiences.

Academic learning does not go directly to semantic storage; the acquired information is initially stored as episodes. When recently learned factual material is recalled, it is actually retrieved from episodic storage, along with the source, details, and context of the learning event. For instance, Conway, Cohen, and Stanhope (1992) reported that when college students were tested within a few days of learning psychology course material, they recalled the information as episodes. When retested a few months later they could not remember the learning episodes but could retrieve the facts and concepts from their semantic memory. Thus, initial exposure to new material in the classroom should be considered episodic learning. The new knowledge will be stored primarily in the episodic system, for at least a few days or weeks. Accordingly, when memory is tested in the laboratory, clinic, or school, most of the tasks involved are classified as episodic memory paradigms, even when the stimuli have no personal or autobiographical connection for the examinee (Gathercole, 1998). For example, learning a list of words or trying to recall a story is categorized as episodic memory.

An already existing cohesive memory representation, usually associated with a schema or script stored in semantic memory, is crucial for the functioning of episodic memory. In the creation of a new episodic memory, associative processes bind details from a specific event with established structures that function like templates. Perhaps the lack of enduring episodic memories from early childhood results from the lack of schemas or scripts with which new episodic traces can be integrated (Shing, Werkle-Bergner, Li, & Lindenberger, 2008). In addition to being connected with pre-existing memory structures, different aspects of an experience or episode must be linked in a fashion that will allow their reintegration during recall. These binding and reintegration processes, as well as other episodic memory functions, seem to rely on the brain's hippocampus, which explains why episodic amnesia results from hippocampal atrophy (see Chapter 3 for more details).

Semantic Memory   Semantic memory is a storehouse of context-free factual and conceptual knowledge that includes general concepts, specific facts, autobiographical facts, and language. Factual knowledge, such as the names of cities, the colors of flowers, and the characteristics of animals are all stored in semantic memory. Similar to episodic memory, the storage capacity of semantic memory appears limitless and

Table 2.3 Differences between episodic and semantic memory

Episodic	Semantic
Memory for events	Memory for facts
Remembering	Knowing
Context dependent	Context free
Subjective focus	Objective focus
Vulnerable to pathology	Resistant to pathology
Develops later	Develops first
Known source	Unknown source
Mostly visuospatial	Mostly verbal
Unintentional encoding	More intentional encoding
Chronological	Categorical
Organized spatiotemporally	Organized by meaning
Subject to rapid forgetting	More resistant to forgetting

the information that resides there can remain accessible for a lifetime. In contrast with episodic memory, which depends on contextual associations, the organization of semantic memory is based on meaning and conceptual relationships. Although episodic acquisition seems to be immediate, semantic acquisition appears to be a more involved process (see the section on Consolidation in this chapter). Nonetheless, the semantic knowledge base can grow rapidly. For example, during the ages of 7 to 16, the average child acquires new vocabulary at the rate of 3,000 words per year. See Table 2.3 for key differences between episodic and semantic memory.

Cognitive psychologists believe that semantic memories are organized into conceptual or relational categories that are arranged hierarchically. This model explains semantic memory's efficient storage because common properties, such as characteristics of an animal species, need only be represented once (Cohen, 2008a). There is considerable behavioral evidence in support of this model, with reaction times for retrieving related content being quicker than when the content is not related. Neuropsychological support for categorical storage comes from the fact that specific knowledge is forgotten before general knowledge. The tendency to preserve general knowledge instead of details explains why much of human knowledge is approximate and probabilistic instead of exact.

The organizational structure of semantic memory lends itself well to academic learning that places a heavy emphasis on conceptual and factual learning. For most people, semantic structures are more verbally than visually based, which also is consistent with traditional academic instruction and knowledge. Therefore, it is appropriate to think of academic learning as primarily dependent on semantic memory, even though episodic memory plays a critical role. If academic learning is to be retained for more than a few days or weeks, the information that is initially stored episodically must ultimately be transferred to semantic memory.

Relationship between Episodic and Semantic Memory   The general perspective on the relationship between episodic and semantic memory is that information encountered in repeated episodes gradually becomes general knowledge (semantic memory). When knowledge is first acquired, it is represented episodically, and its memory includes recall of the learning episode(s). As learning proceeds, the memory representation shifts from episodic to semantic, with the outcome that the individual simply "knows" the information without having to recall or being able to recall any specific learning events (Conway, Gardiner, Perfect, Anderson, & Cohen 1997). Exactly how this transition occurs is unknown, but the assumption is that rule-based and conceptual knowledge is somehow abstracted from learning episodes. That is, a series of similar episodes leads to extraction of meaning and the formulation of knowledge. What begins as personally experienced, separate events ends up as semantic knowledge. Once information has been stored as semantic knowledge, people typically forget the learning or experiential episodes that led to the acquisition of that knowledge. In other words, they simply know the facts to be true although they can't recall when, where, how, or with whom they learned them.

The implication is that semantic memory development is, at least partially, dependent on episodic memory. The functioning of individuals with acquired brain injury is often cited as evidence. When these individuals have impaired episodic memory they have difficulty expanding semantic memory (Sohlberg & Mateer, 2001). Yet, there are recent indications that semantic memory is capable of acquiring new information when episodic memory is dysfunctional, as long as there are repeated opportunities to learn (Temple & Richardson, 2006). On the other hand, developmental psychologists have generally proposed that episodic memory is dependent on semantic memory because semantic memory appears to develop first (Tulving & Markowitsch, 1998). Although it is unclear as to which memory system develops first, episodic and semantic memories can be viewed as interactive and interdependent aspects of explicit memory, not as two separate, compartmentalized structures. After all, semantic knowledge is derived from the accumulation of personal experiences, and episodic memory is interpreted from the perspective of semantic knowledge structures.

Autobiographical Memory   Autobiographical memory refers to memories individuals hold about themselves and their relations with the world around them (Baddeley, Eysenck, & Anderson, 2009). Autobiographical memories, composed of recollections of experiences from one's life, as well as self-facts, give individuals a sense of self. Autobiographical memory is not really a distinct kind of memory system. Rather, these types of memories are stored in both episodic and semantic memory. Remembered experiences that include contextual details, such as when, where, and with whom the experience occurred, are stored in episodic memory, whereas autobiographical facts, such as a birth date, are retained in semantic memory. Autobiographical memories can be forgotten just like other kinds of explicit memories. When they are forgotten, specific experiences stored episodically tend to be lost before autobiographical facts stored semantically.

Implicit (Nondeclarative) Memory

Types of human learning and memory that do not require conscious awareness of stored information are classified as implicit memories. These memories are acquired through experience and learning just like explicit memories. However, unlike explicit memory's conscious recollection of learning events and awareness of what is known, implicit, or non-declarative memory, is inaccessible to conscious awareness. For example, bicycle riders remember how to balance a bicycle even though they cannot explicitly retrieve that information. Less is known about implicit memory, and implicit memory may not be a unitary memory system, but it's clear that implicit memories are not stored in the explicit memory system. Nonetheless, implicit memories may be organized in a fashion similar to semantic memories; for example, implicit memories are bound together by associations. Because implicit memory operates subconsciously, its functions do not demand attentional resources and working memory capacity. Although implicit memory cannot be tested by asking examinees to recall information, the existence of implicit memories can be documented by observing performance or a change in behavior. At least three types of memory are typically ascribed to implicit memory: priming, classical conditioning, and procedural learning.

Priming In humans, priming is the most studied type of implicit memory. Priming refers to an unconscious process whereby identification or performance is enhanced by recent, prior exposure to related information. The term *priming* relates to the fact that seeing a word or image seems to prime the individual's ability to come up with the correct response. During priming, cues prompt accurate recall or performance without the individual's recollection of the acquired information or that it was previously learned. Priming occurs even when people say that they do not remember any exposure to the stimulus. In the experimental research, stimuli typically consist of word lists or pictures of objects. After being exposed to the stimuli, subjects are tested with both old and new items and asked to name words or objects as quickly as possible. Verbal priming is demonstrated in such tasks as word identification or word-stem completion. For example, a few letters of a word, e.g., MOT_ _ for MOTEL, are presented. The subjects invariably select a recently exposed word to complete the fragment instead of other possible words. Prior exposure to stimuli also speeds retrieval of the items, especially when partial cues are provided. Priming is associated with the perceptual processing of information that occurs prior to conscious recall and recognition. Thus, individuals may retrieve the correct response before it ever enters conscious awareness. In cases of amnesia, priming is intact even though individuals report that the stimuli are unfamiliar and they cannot remember being recently exposed to the stimuli.

Priming seems to be rooted in a perceptual representation system that functions independently of explicit memory. That is, part of the stored information about a stimulus is perceptual, and this aspect seems to be what is stored in implicit memory and later observed as priming. Tulving and Schacter (Schacter, 1996) even proposed a memory structure known as the *perceptual representation system* that allows people to identify common objects and recognize familiar printed words. Perceptual priming is quite material specific compared with declarative memory. Priming effects are strongly determined by structural features of the words or objects that are presented (Squire, 1992). For instance, when words are presented in the auditory modality during study and in the visual modality during testing, priming effects are reduced significantly, an effect not observed with explicit recall (Schacter, 1992).

In addition to perceptual priming, some researchers consider conceptual priming to be a type of priming. According to this position, perceptual priming is an unconscious form of human memory that deals with perceptual identification of words and objects. In contrast, conceptual priming occurs when one concept evokes retrieval of related items, such as when a person is asked to name members of the animal category. Conceptual priming is displayed during free association tasks, such as when pre-exposure to *cry* elicits *baby*, or the production of category exemplars, such as when pre-exposure to *strawberry* elicits the names of other fruits. Conceptual priming's influence on the specific information recalled has led to the proposal that priming may assist declarative memory recall, particularly recognition. However, it seems that priming and recognition are independent of one another and that priming makes no contribution to the accuracy of recognition memory (Levy, Stark, & Squire, 2004). Nonetheless, it is difficult to separate conceptual priming from semantic memory functioning.

According to Mandler (2007), priming should probably be classified as a memory process instead of a type of memory structure. Indeed, the effects of priming are observed for semantic material, not just perceptual material. But because the process occurs without awareness, it is typically classified as a type of implicit memory. One of the distinguishing characteristics of priming is that it occurs whether or not there is explicit memory recognition for what has been presented. In fact, priming can occur when exposures are so brief that people cannot even be aware that something was presented. Neurological evidence also supports the classification of priming as implicit learning (see Chapter 3). Apparently, there is a lack of hippocampal activity (necessary for explicit memory) during priming's exposure and recall phases. Finally, priming even seems to operate by different rules than explicit memory. For example, the priming effect is unrelated to whether information is encoded deeply or shallowly (Schacter, 1996).

Clearly, implicit memory and priming play a role in learning and recall. For example, priming can facilitate retrieval and performance even when people have forgotten the learning event. Knowledge of priming functions can be useful in cases of anterograde amnesia where the individual has little or no ability for new explicit learning. For instance, neuropsychological case studies have reported the successful learning of computer skills in individuals who could not recall being taught the skills and denied any knowledge of the skills. Another educational application of priming is that learning can be improved through pre-exposure to stimuli. For example, using an advance organizer before a lesson can be considered an example of conceptual priming.

Procedural Memory   Procedural memory is knowing how to do something; it includes skills and habits. Although conscious processes are involved in the early stages of most procedural learning, and the training can generally be recalled, procedural learning can happen without the ability to recall the training. Even when individuals can consciously access the steps involved in a learned procedure or skill, conscious retrieval is not necessary for performance of the skill. Hence, it is considered a type of implicit memory. Other indications that procedural learning is part of the implicit memory system are that procedural learning is not dependent on explicit memory and that procedural memory is still retained when explicit memory becomes inaccessible, such as in cases of amnesia or dementia. Procedural learning includes cognitive, perceptual, motor, and other types of learning. For example, it involves learning to blend phonemes into smoothly pronounced words or learning to dribble and shoot a basketball. Procedural memory accrues through experience and is evidenced by changes in behavior. Conscious awareness of procedural memory is not necessary for accurate performance of a skill. For instance, the automated and reflexive actions involved in driving an automobile depend on procedural memory. Procedural memory accumulates slowly through practice and repetition. Once a procedural memory is established, it usually lasts a lifetime. For example, people never forget how to ride a bicycle, and even individuals with advanced Alzheimer's retain their procedural knowledge.

Classical Conditioning   In classical conditioning, the individual learns the predictive relationship of one environmental stimulus with another. The conditioning begins when an initially neutral stimulus is paired with an unconditioned stimulus that elicits a reflex response. The conditioning is complete when the neutral stimulus elicits the response in the absence of the unconditioned stimulus. The classic example is Pavlov's dog learning that a sound reliably predicted the delivery of food. Retrieval and the resulting behavior are elicited by cues similar to those encoded during learning. The retrieval of the associative relationship is quick and usually unconscious, with the expected behavior indicating that there is memory of the connection.

Relationship Between Implicit and Explicit Memory

At first glance, the implicit and explicit memory systems seem completely unrelated. In addition to the behavioral evidence, neuroscientific research has identified two separate functional systems located in different areas of the brain.

Table 2.4   Differences between explicit and implicit memory

Explicit	Implicit
Conscious	Unconscious
Knowledge	Skills
Flexible expression	Rigid expression
Hippocampus-dependent	Hippocampus-independent
Expressed through recollection	Expressed through performance
Cognitive only	Non-cognitive components
Effortful recall may be required	Automatic, unconscious recall only
Symbolic encoding	Nonsymbolic encoding
Develops until adulthood	Developed by age three
Vulnerable to brain injury	Resistant to brain injury

Neuropsychological studies report that implicit memory continues to function after complete loss of explicit memory. There are also differences in the developmental trajectories of explicit and implicit memory. Implicit memory reaches an adult asymptote at a relatively early age and remains stable over the life span (Yeates & Enrile, 2005), whereas explicit memory starts out slower but continues to develop until adulthood. The many differences between explicit and implicit memory clearly demonstrate their disassociability (see Table 2.4). Their independent functioning is supported by the Parkin and Russo (1990) finding of very low correlations between implicit and explicit performance. Also, IQ is highly predictive of explicit but not implicit memory, and explicit memory is more highly correlated with academic achievement. Neurologically, explicit memory is more susceptible to injuries and insults from disorders, illnesses, and injuries. Yet despite the evidence of two separable memory systems, implicit and explicit memory are interactive. Both are important for the learning of academic skills, such as learning to decode words. Reading decoding could not develop from explicit learning and memory alone. Priming and procedural learning are essential for automated word recognition and learning the skills of segmenting phonemes and then blending them into a whole word.

Prospective Memory

In addition to remembering what has happened in the past, humans also encode, store, and retrieve intentions and plans for future actions. Remembering to perform an intended action in the future is known as *prospective memory*, as opposed to recalling previously acquired information, which is termed *retrospective memory*. In contrast with retrospective memory, prospective memory is usually self-generated, consists of a small amount of information, and involves an action, not just information. There appears to be a disassociation between these two types of memory, as there is typically little or no correlation between them (Ellis & Cohen, 2008). Nevertheless, prospective memory is generally considered a subtype of episodic memory because it involves personal memories and actions. Prospective memory, which involves planning and monitoring, has a declarative component (the information to be recalled) and a temporal-contextual component (when and where the action is to be executed). Time-based prospective memories are generally more difficult to remember than event-based. According to some experts (e.g., Sohlberg & Mateer, 2001), prospective memory is not so much a type of memory as a set of processes. Also, because prospective memory requires planning, it may be more of a function of the frontal lobes and working memory than long-term memory.

Cues that are highly distinctive, unfamiliar, or unique are effective at cueing a prospective memory. Opportunities to review one's intentions and mentally rehearse them also increase the likelihood of enactment. Of course, external aides, such as lists, timers, and appointment calendars are used by the majority of adults. Prospective memory is an important element of functional, everyday memory (Cohen, 2008b). In the elderly, health and safety depend on it; for example, remembering to consume vital medications depends on prospective memory. With children and adolescents, parental supervision and school routines reduce their need to depend on their own prospective memory. Accordingly, prospective memory concerns and interventions will not be emphasized in this book.

LONG-TERM MEMORY PROCESSES

The long-term memory systems discussed earlier in this chapter are distinguished mainly by content or types of learning. In order for information to become a memory and remain accessible it must go through a series of cognitive processes. The big three processes are encoding, consolidation, and retrieval but several other processes and factors are also involved in the creation, duration, and recall of a memory.

Encoding

Encoding refers to the process of transforming sensory and perceptual information into a representational code that can be stored in long-term memory. Because encoding is a process of transformation, memories are coded records of experience, not exact replicas of the events or materials themselves. The records created by encoding are referred to as *memory traces*. Memory traces are not immutable because they are frequently updated and restructured during ongoing learning. Modifications also may occur during storage and retrieval processes. Encoding differs according to the type of sensory or processing system involved, as well as by the content. The form and extent of encoding is in part determined by the stimulus and in part determined by the individual's interpretation of the event or material. Consequently, any given experience or piece of information can be encoded in multiple formats and multiple brain locations (Brown & Craik, 2000). For example, verbal information may be encoded in terms of its phonological features, or it could be coded in terms of its semantic characteristics. Also, multiple modality encoding may occur, such as when information is encoded in both an auditory and visual mode. Furthermore, information may be encoded with multiple memory representations. As implied by this complexity, different aspects of an event or specific information end up being stored in different regions of the brain (see Chapter 3).

Most encoding is relatively automatic and unconscious as information passes directly from perceptual structures, sensory memory, and short-term memory into long-term memory stores. Automatic encoding operates at a constant level under a variety of circumstances. It occurs without intention and does not involve practice or repetition. The automatic processes encode certain attributes, such as spatial or temporal, of whatever event is occurring. Because it is automated, this type of encoding makes no demands on executive or attentional resources, such as working memory (Hasher & Zacks, 1979). Because these automated processes are innate, they are only minimally influenced by age, culture, motivation, education, or intelligence. In contrast, conscious, effortful encoding is intentional and its efficiency increases with practice. Effortful encoding typically involves thoughtful processing or mnemonic strategies, and it consumes some attentional capacity, thereby limiting the ability to simultaneously engage in other cognitively demanding tasks. Poor performance on memory tasks is often attributed to ineffective use of effortful encoding processes. Used effectively, memory strategies can enhance encoding so that information will be more memorable.

In addition to enactment of strategies, several other variables can influence the effectiveness of encoding. Foremost among them is attention. Focused attention is essential for successful encoding of explicit memories; however, implicit memory encoding does not require selective attention. Encoding of explicit information often fails because insufficient attention is devoted to the stimulus at the time of encoding (Schacter, 1999). In particular, divided attention during encoding substantially reduces later recall (Emilien, Durlach, Antoniadis, Van Der Linden, & Maloteaux, 2004). Another variable is preexisting knowledge. Prior knowledge not only influences how an event or information is perceived but provides memory structures and representations with which the incoming information can be integrated (Howe & Brainerd, 1989). (See the section on the "Organization of Memory" later in this chapter.) Certainly, without encoding there would be no memories, and effective encoding is a prerequisite for subsequent memory processing. How information is encoded partially determines how long it will remain in storage and how easily it can be retrieved. For example, a considerable amount of empirical evidence indicates that retrieval is more effective when encoding variables match retrieval variables. However, even with effective encoding there's no guarantee of long-term retention.

Levels-of-Processing Theory   In addition to the fundamental, unconscious forms of encoding, there are effortful, conscious forms of encoding, at least theoretically. Conscious attempts to influence encoding range from rote repetition to effortful, elaborate strategies. An individual need not employ mnemonics to enhance the quality of conscious encoding. How information is processed during learning will influence how well it is encoded. According to Craik's and Lockhart's (1972) levels-of-processing theory, information that is processed more "deeply" will have a higher likelihood of being recalled than information that is processed "shallowly." Deep processing includes meaningful and semantic processing, whereas shallow processing includes perceptual or rote processing. Accordingly, semantic clustering of words produces better recall than simply making phonetic associations. Elaboration, a conscious process of connecting incoming information with related information, is a prime example of deep processing and encoding. Elaborative encoding produces better recall because the process makes the information available to a broad range of retrieval cues, whereas shallowly encoded information can only be accessed by a few perfectly matched cues. The benefits of deep processing over shallow processing have been supported in many empirical investigations (e.g., Metcalfe, Kornell, & Son, 2007), and the theory is consistent with findings that elaborate encoding strategies are more effective than simple, rote strategies.

Encoding Specificity Theory and Transfer-Appropriate Processing   According to the encoding specificity principle, retrieval is facilitated when the cues available at retrieval match those present at the time of encoding (Haist et al., 1992; Hannon & Craik, 2001). That is, what is remembered depends partly on the compatibility between how information is encoded and the circumstances or cues present at the time of retrieval. Thus, encoding is effective to the extent that it overlaps with the operations required at the time of retrieval. For example, retrieving and producing responses during testing is more successful when the processing during encoding is very similar to the testing structure. In particular, encoding specificity theory stresses the importance of the cues that are attached to incoming information. Because retrieval depends heavily on cues, a cue that is available during retrieval will aide recall to the extent that it was encoded along with the learned material (Koriat, 2000). Thus, a retrieval cue will be effective if the cue was incorporated during the original encoding. For example, if "piano" is encoded as a musical instrument, a later retrieval cue of "something heavy" will not lead to recall as well as the cue of "musical instrument." Essentially, the encoding specificity principle means that successful recall is a function of the similarity between encoded information and the information provided at retrieval (Hannon & Craik, 2001).

The retrieval cues can be derived from the context or situation, as well as the meaning and structure of the interrogatives. When cues incorporated into the memory trace at the time of encoding match a retrieval cue, recall is successful. With academic learning, the semantic congruency of cues is paramount. For example, if a set of objects is grouped according to function during encoding, it will be easier to recall the objects when asked questions about their functions, as opposed to being asked about their colors. Another example of incongruence is learning new vocabulary by associating the terms with synonyms, such as *female-woman*, but then being tested with an antonyms format, such as *female-male*. Of course, once the new item or concept acquires multiple semantic connections, a shift in semantic context at retrieval makes less difference (Hannon & Craik, 2001). An underlying assumption is that performance on scholastic tests depends primarily on meaningful, semantic information. Therefore, encoding that includes semantic processing enhances later test performance. Deeper processing of the new information at the time of encoding also serves to reduce its dependence on compatible retrieval cues.

A related theory known as the transfer-appropriate processing theory also postulates that good memory performance is a function of the degree of overlap between encoding and retrieval processes (Blaxton, 1989; Brown & Craik, 2000). The theory contrasts with encoding specificity in that it focuses on processes rather than cues. Specifically, the theory predicts that memory test performance with benefit to the extent that the operations required during testing recapture the operations used during encoding.

Storage

Storage of memories, also referred to as *retention*, is not just a passive holding function; storage includes processing. After encoding, storage processes manipulate memories until they reach a form and location that allows permanent retention. Although storage processes are nonconscious, they are affected by conscious activities. For example, reviewing information increases the probability that it will be retained and accessible. Memories are stored in the same brain regions where the perception and processing of the information took place. Given the multisensory characteristics of most events, it is assumed that memories of a single event are stored in several different regions of the cortex (see Chapter 3). Even semantic memories are not localized, as phonetic, linguistic, and visual characteristics of a fact all need to be stored separately. Despite the distributed storage, most memories are unified by the synaptic connections among them and are reconstructed into a whole during retrieval.

Consolidation

During the early stages of storage a process known as *consolidation* operates on the memory traces that have been encoded. Consolidation refers to an extended, multistage process whereby a memory becomes more stable and resistant to interference and forgetting. It is a post-encoding process that involves maintenance, elaboration, and storage of new information. Consolidation begins immediately but can extend for days, weeks, and months. It probably occurs in stages, with initial consolidation, also referred to as *synaptic consolidation*, taking place with seconds or minutes after encoding and long-term consolidation (system consolidation) taking hours to months (Dudai, 2004). These two phases of consolidation are essentially different (Squire & Alvarez, 1995). One distinction between the two is that initial consolidation involves the deposit of an item trace in long-term memory whereas long-term consolidation involves acquiring a retrieval operation for accessing the memory trace (Miller & Matzel, 2006). Without consolidation, long-term retention of events and knowledge would be at–risk.

Controversies over the memory consolidation construct have been existent for more than a century (this is the reason why it is often omitted from texts on memory), mainly because it has not yet been determined how the process actually takes place (Meeter & Murre, 2004). Despite the controversies, there seems to be consensus about the following: (a) if information is not being effectively consolidated from the beginning, it will rapidly be forgotten; (b) consolidation seems to be primarily an unconscious, automated process that mainly occurs during sleep (see the subsection on sleep later in this chapter); (c) consolidation not only stabilizes memories but modifies, condenses, and enhances them (Siegel, 1999); (d) consolidation includes processes that incorporate newly encoded memories with preexisting memories; (e) consolidation not only includes cellular and molecular processes occurring at the synaptic level but systems-level reorganization as well (Stickgold, 2005); (f) consolidation involves hippocampal structures, but once consolidation is complete, retrieval of stored information no longer requires hippocampal functioning; and (g) over time, memory storage is gradually reorganized so that memories eventually reside in various regions of the neocortex instead of the hippocampus and adjacent medial temporal lobe structures (McClelland, McNaughton, & O'Reilly, 1995).

Although the details of the process are speculative, there's no disputing that consolidation is mediated by the hippocampus (see Chapter 3), especially consolidation of explicit memories (Squire, Cohen, & Nadel, 1984). Neuropsychological evidence for hippocampal involvement and for the consolidation process itself comes from cases of acquired retrograde amnesia that have been caused by hippocampal atrophy. In such individuals, more recent memories are lost while more distant memories are spared. This phenomenon is attributed to incomplete consolidation. After encoding and initial learning, explicit memories exist in a fragile state. During this stage newly formed memories seem to reside in the hippocampal region until they are reprocessed and transferred to the cerebral cortex. When the hippocampus is damaged, recent memories that are still undergoing the process of consolidation have not yet been transferred to cortical regions and therefore are permanently lost. The existence of a consolidation process is also supported by the effects of interference. The shorter the interval between initial learning and related learning, the greater the retroactive interference. Apparently, interference has more impact when there has not been adequate time for consolidation to stabilize the memory trace. Thus, the susceptibility of a memory to disruption decreases over time. Although the brain's long-term storage capacity appears to be unlimited, its ability to consolidate new memories before they are forgotten or become irretrievable is certainly limited (Wixted, 2004).

Some contentious issues about the consolidation process remain. First, memories may not be simply transferred from the medial temporal lobe to cortical regions, but rather the hippocampus may build connections between separate but related cortical representations (Paller & Voss, 2004). During consolidation the medial temporal lobe binds together memories of the same event that are stored in separate cortical regions so that during recall the separate aspects are perceived as one event (Milner, Squire, & Kandel, 1998). These new connections also enrich the memory and provide additional routes for subsequent retrieval. Second, it seems that movement of information from the hippocampal region to cortical regions may apply more to the semantic than the episodic system. According to some theorists, autobiographical memories, no matter how old, permanently reside in the medial temporal lobe and hippocampus (Moscovitch, Nadel, Winocur, Gilboa, & Rosenbaum, 2006). Although many episodic memories are retained for a lifetime, they are not consolidated and interconnected in cortical regions in the same manner as semantic memories. Thus, the recall of some episodic memories may always be dependent on the hippocampus (Nadel & Moscovitch, 1997). Furthermore, some of these episodic memories may remain intact, especially those that are novel, highly significant, or emotionally laden. Third, it has been postulated that the amygdala also plays an important role in consolidation (McGaugh, 2000). Finally, the textbook account of consolidation is that it applies to hippocampal-dependent memories only, implying that consolidation does not apply to implicit memory. Yet, sleep studies have revealed that consolidation of procedural learning definitely occurs during sleep.

Memory consolidation is very relevant for education because consolidation plays a crucial role in semantic learning and knowledge acquisition. Consolidation appears to be involved in the transition from episodic to semantic storage. Essentially, consolidation is the process of abstracting information from episodic memory and transforming it into conceptual knowledge arranged schematically. That is, the consolidation process can be thought of as extracting factual information from an episode or series of episodes and integrating that information with semantic representations. In effect, the facts are separated from the episode and its context. The separation accounts for why people remember the facts even though the learning episodes have been forgotten. Thus, consolidation is crucial for the accrual of semantic knowledge. Classic concepts of memory consolidation typically emphasize passive, unconscious, biological operations that occur over time. However, conscious cognitive processes may also enhance consolidation, especially where semantic memory is concerned (Weingartner & Parker, 1984). For example, consciously linking recently processed information to related memory structures in semantic memory is known to create more persistent memory traces. Also, consciously reactivating memory traces may facilitate consolidation. If conscious cognitive processes play a role in consolidation, then the implications for learning and education are many. For example, elaborative rehearsal techniques may enhance consolidation (see Chapter 7).

From an assessment perspective, consolidation failure is implicated whenever free recall and recognition are equally deficient. In such instances, it is unlikely that the sought after information remains in long-term storage. The reason it has been forgotten is that it was not consolidated. If it had been consolidated, it would have been fairly impervious to forgetting.

Reconsolidation   Consolidation is an iterative process; previously encoded and stored information is processed and reprocessed. The presumption is that ongoing processing is unconscious and biological and that it occurs during storage. Yet, information is also reprocessed and consolidated during retrieval (Spear & Mueller, 1984). In effect, the act of retrieval may initiate another round of encoding and consolidation, thereby increasing the odds that a persistent set of memory traces will be created. Regardless of the exact mechanisms, it is undeniable that some information receives repeated opportunities for consolidation. These additional opportunities are referred to as *reconsolidation*.

One thing consolidation does not do is create permanent memories that are immutable. Activation of a consolidated memory returns it to a labile state and it must then be reconsolidated, according to the thinking of many memory theorists (e.g., Nader, 2003). Although activation mainly results from overt retrieval, even subtle reminders can activate memory traces and initiate reconsolidation. After activation, the memory once again becomes dependent on the hippocampus. Although reactivated memories may remain in this state before being reconsolidated, the process is thought to be far quicker than the initial consolidation period. Nader, Schafe, and LeDoux (2000) reported that reconsolidation appears complete within six hours after reexposure, and Dudai (2004) reported that system reconsolidation lasts for only two days. Often, new information will be added to the original trace, creating the necessity for reconsolidation and a memory trace that is different from its original version; essentially, the modified trace now holds the memory of a memory. Despite modifications, the core of the original memory trace is thought to remain, being somewhat immune to changes because of its maturity and integration with other memories.

Basically, the reconsolidation process is the same as consolidation. Similar to the original consolidation phase, memory traces are somewhat fragile during reconsolidation and may be destabilized and lose accuracy (Hupbach, Gomez, Hardt, & Nadel, 2007). For instance, eyewitness accounts of criminal activity may change because they are frequently activated and reconsolidated. However, reconsolidation is mostly viewed as a beneficial process as it serves to update memories and thereby strengthen them. Another explanation for how the reconsolidation process strengthens memories is that each time an episode is retrieved, it is subsequently re-encoded, leading to the formation of more memory traces of the same event (Moscovitch et al.,

2006). The evidence for consolidation and reconsolidation demonstrates that memory storage is a dynamic process, not a static one.

The Influence of Sleep   Some of the most fascinating memory research conducted over the past two decades concerns the role of sleep in memory consolidation. Nearly everyone knows that sleep deprivation can severely impair encoding and retrieval of declarative memories. What has not been known until recently is that consolidation and enhancement of memories actually occur during sleep (Gais, Lucas, & Born, 2006). Memory consolidation seems to occur during both rapid eye movement (REM) and non-REM sleep, with each stage making unique contributions. REM sleep seems to have more influence on implicit memories; whereas, non-REM sleep, also referred to as slow wave sleep, enhances explicit memories (Born, Rasch, & Gais, 2006; Drosopoulos, Wagner, & Born, 2005; Stickgold, 2005). Although the mechanisms remain unclear, it is thought that explicit memories are consolidated by hippocampal reactivation and replay of previously encoded events. This repeated reactivation facilitates the storage and consolidation of explicit information in the neocortex (Plihal & Born, 1997), perhaps by forming and strengthening associations within memory networks. Clearly, sleep provides an efficient method of strengthening memory traces without additional study and training. Undoubtedly, it is a critical component of the memory consolidation process. Although not all memories may need sleep to consolidate, consolidation is clearly amplified by sleep.

Another reason why sleep may enhance memories is that it reduces interference, especially when one goes to sleep shortly after exposure to new information. This proposal makes sense if newly encoded memory traces are considered fragile and thus more susceptible to interference. In particular, sleep seems to be especially beneficial for weaker declarative associations that would be easily disturbed by retroactive interference (Drosopoulos, Schulze, Fischer, & Born, 2007). The interference reduction position is also consistent with the finding that going to sleep immediately after studying material is most effective. For instance, students forget more declarative information they learn in the morning than they learn in the evening (Born et al., 2006). Wixted (2004) reviewed a study in which subjects who went to sleep immediately after learning recalled 81% of the material whereas those who learned the material at the beginning of the day recalled 66%. Nonetheless, while sleep does seem to counteract retroactive interference, this perspective ascribes only a passive role to sleep, contrary to a plethora of evidence that favors an active sleep role.

In addition to consolidating declarative memories, sleep seems to enhance procedural memories (Walker & Stickgold, 2006). Not only does sleep strengthen memories, it even enhances skill performance. The performance of subjects who sleep after learning new motor skills actually improves after a good night's sleep. For instance, Walker and Stickgold (2005) reported a 24% motor performance improvement overnight. Across six studies reviewed by Stickgold (2005), sleep accounted for an average of 69% of the variance in next-day improvement in procedural tasks. It seems that the brain replays the same pattern that was learned during daytime practice, in effect practicing the procedure during non-REM sleep. The sub-conscious practice may improve performance by strengthening synaptic connections or by integrating the procedural units into single memory elements, thereby optimizing motor speed and accuracy. Brain imaging research has confirmed the relationship: The amount of next-day improvement is directly proportional to the amount of reactivation in the hippocampus during sleep (Walker & Stickgold, 2006). Even daytime naps have been demonstrated to enhance procedural memory and skill performance. Apparently, a 90-minute daytime nap can have as much effect on learning as a full night's sleep, and a nap followed by a night of sleep provides as much benefit as two nights of sleep (Mednick, Nakayama, & Stickgold, 2003).

Retrieval

Retrieval refers to the processes involved when one accesses information that has been stored in long-term memory. Retrieval actually involves two types of processes: a spontaneous, automatic process that brings information into consciousness and a controlled, strategic process that guides a search for information. The automatic process is initiated by external cues. The controlled process may be activated by external or internal cues. According to Koriat (2000), the consciously controlled process might best be framed as goal-oriented problem solving that begins with a goal and proceeds strategically until the solution is found. Strategic retrieval involves the deliberate use of cues to probe one's memory for more cues that will bring one closer to the target information. Of the two types of retrieval, automatic retrieval is the more essential. When the automatic retrieval system is dysfunctional, conscious efforts to search memory will also fail. However, when conscious retrieval processes are impaired, an intact automatic retrieval system can still retrieve information, provided there are appropriate cues (Schacter, 1996). The success of conscious retrieval processes depends on the frontal lobes and working memory to control, monitor, coordinate, evaluate, and revise search processes while holding partially retrieved information in temporary storage and inhibiting irrelevant information.

Of all the memory problems attributed to processing, retrieval failures seem the most pervasive, probably because everyone experiences them frequently. When retrieval failure occurs, the individual usually "knows" the information is in storage, but can't access it at that moment. Retrieval failure, sometimes referred to as *blocking*, can have many causes. First, successful retrieval is critically dependent on cues that are created or associated during encoding and consolidation. In everyday life the conditions that initiate retrieval normally provide many useful cues. However, in the classroom typically fewer cues are provided or available. For example, when a teacher queries a student, the query itself may provide the only cue. Often such a cue is insufficient for direct retrieval of the desired knowledge. Retrieval in such an instance depends on how well the individual can regenerate the cues to which the memory is associated. Second, blocking is often created by interference caused by prior retrieval of related but incorrect information. When individuals are aware of a blockage, it is referred to as the tip-of-the-tongue state. This type of blocking often involves word or name retrieval failure. When blocking of a word occurs, individuals can usually describe the semantic, syntactic, and phonological properties of the word but not identify the word itself. However, repeated retrieval attempts will often produce the blocked information (Klimesch, 1994). Third, successful retrieval is dependent on organized memory structures where related events and concepts are interlinked. Although the amount of storage capacity in long-term memory may be unlimited, humans' ability to retrieve any and all memories is constricted. Clearly, the amount of information stored in long-term memory is much greater than the amount than can be retrieved at any given moment. The discrepancy between stored information and accessible information highlights the need for effective encoding and retrieval processes (Koriat, 2000).

Unfortunately, retrieval of information does not mean the information is accurate or correct. Everyone evaluates activated information to determine if it's the desired information, but sometimes people are unable to determine the accuracy or veracity of what they have retrieved. Sometimes, individuals really don't know whether the information is correct or incorrect, especially when the cue that prompted the retrieval is not very familiar (Metcalfe, 2000). One type of retrieval error is called *source error*. Source error occurs when information or an event is misattributed to an incorrect, time, place, or person (Schacter, 1999). In these instances, people correctly remember an item or fact but connect it to the wrong source. Source confusion can have serious outcomes, such as when a child asserts that he or she saw a particular face involved in a criminal act, but the face was actually encountered in a different situation.

Another aspect of retrieval that can cause memory performance problems is retrieval speed or fluency. Retrieval speed is as important as accuracy in determining the overall efficiency of the operation. Slow retrieval speed may have a neurological basis and may be just one aspect of slower cognitive processing speed. However, the speed and efficiency of retrieval also depend on the degree of interconnectivity among memory representations of related concepts and events, according to Klimesch (1994). It is assumed that experts have more highly integrated memory structures and that this increased interconnectedness results in quicker retrieval. The fact that working memory has temporal limitations may compound the problem in that items that need to be compared for accuracy are not simultaneously active in working memory due to slow retrieval. On the other hand, deficits in working memory capacity may interfere with otherwise efficient retrieval. Naturally slow retrieval speed can also confound the individual's evaluation of the activated information because an individual's confidence in the accuracy of retrieved information is mainly determined by the speed with which the information is retrieved.

Because stored memories are not replicas of the world, retrieval is actually a process of reconstruction. Of necessity, it is reconstructive because neural codes must be transformed back into images and language. Moreover, retrieval is necessarily reconstructive because different aspects of a memory are stored in different neural structures and must therefore be reintegrated. Conscious retrieval processes are also reconstructive because not all the details of an event or concept can be remembered (sometimes because they were never encoded). Organizational structures known as schemas and scripts (see "The Organization of Memory" section later in this chapter) often serve as templates in this reconstructive process. For instance, an individual may not remember all the details from a dining-out experience the evening before but is able to logically fill in the missing gaps by utilizing a well-known script of what is involved in dining-out behavior. Inferential reasoning is also relied on to fill in unrecoverable information. Obviously, retrieval is not an all-or-none process. Many times only some of the desired information is retrieved and individuals must make inferences based on what they could access. When people fail to retrieve enough desired information, they are usually able to access partial cues that can then be used to guide further searching. This process often amounts to a narrowing process that begins with retrieval of a general attribute followed by retrieval of specifics (Koriat, 2000). A metaphor for reconstructive retrieval is an archaeological dig in which pieces of what was once a whole item are recovered and then logically reconstructed until the archaeologist determines the identity of the object. Accurate reconstruction also depends on the ability to evaluate the information that has been retrieved. Reconstructive processes, along with other retrieval processes, utilize working memory functions and capacity.

Retrieval is facilitated by practice, specifically practice that involves the actual retrieval of the desired information. Practicing retrieval not only makes retrieval more automatic and accurate but also improves long-term storage. For example, research on the *testing effect* (see Chapter 7) has established that testing (which requires retrieval) is an extremely effective method of ensuring long-term retention. However, too much retrieval of specific information may actually be detrimental for the retention of related but unretrieved information. This phenomenon is known as *retrieval-induced forgetting*. The act of remembering separates relevant from irrelevant knowledge and experience to satisfy the requirements of the task (Emilien et al., 2004). The unwanted information is then inhibited. The act of inhibition can lead to subsequent inhibition, which can result in at least temporary forgetting of that information. Moreover, retrieval of erroneous information increases the probability of retrieving the incorrect information in the future.

There are two main types of conscious retrieval: recall and recognition. When contrasted with recognition, *recall* refers to retrieval without any deliberate or direct external prompts and cues, whereas *recognition* refers to selecting the response from a set of provided items. That is, recognition involves a process of discriminating the correct response from incorrect or irrelevant responses. During a recognition task, the individual examines the response options and either immediately recognizes one of the responses or feels that one of the responses is familiar. In a normally functioning memory, more correct information is retrieved through recognition than through recall because recognizing an item is easier than freely recalling it.

Hence, recalling an item requires more readily available information in storage than recognizing an item (Haist, Shimamura, & Squire, 1992).

The distinction between recall and recognition is important because comparison of the two can provide insight into whether a memory performance problem is primarily a storage or a retrieval problem. Most individuals can correctly recognize more information than they can accurately recall without cues. However, when recognition surpasses free recall by a highly unusual amount, it indicates that the information is in storage but the individual is having difficulty retrieving the information. In such instances, storage problems can be ruled out while a retrieval impairment is implicated. When recognition of information is not substantially better than free recall of the same information, the implication is that the information has been forgotten and is no longer stored in long-term memory. Therefore, it's important to include recognition tasks during memory assessment and compare performance to free recall performance. When assessing academic learning, testing recognition is important for another reason: During the learning process, recognition precedes recall (Stone, 1993). For example, a child still learning the alphabet will recognize more letters than she or he can produce through free recall.

Unfortunately for assessment purposes, free recall and recognition are not so much distinct processes, but rather two ends of a retrieval continuum. The implication of free recall is that no cues are provided in the stimulus that initiates retrieval processes. However, this is nearly impossible; even an open-ended question can contain one or more cues about the answer. Furthermore, unless the recall of desired information is automatic, recognition is actually part of recall. That is, recall is a two-stage process where the search for and retrieval of candidate items is followed by a selection of the most recognizable item. As for recognition, it is defined as heavily cue-laden and requires that the individual simply select a response, such as when provided a multiple-choice item. Although recall involves a recognition process, recognition need not involve a recall process.

Although recall and recognition are difficult to separate, some differences between them can be identified. First, free recall involves actually remembering an event or fact; in contrast, recognition involves a sense of familiarity or knowing (Knowlton & Squire, 1995). Recognition is accompanied by either conscious recollection or by feelings of familiarity when the information cannot actually be recalled. When there are feelings of familiarity, the knowledge is probably stored in semantic memory but cannot be accessed at the moment (Gardiner, Gawlik, & Richardson-Klavehn, 1994). Whereas recall depends solely on declarative memory, recognition is partially influenced by unconscious retrieval from implicit memory (Knowlton & Squire). Priming, in particular, plays a role by improving detection and identification of target information (Haist et al., 1992). For example, an individual may recognize a stimulus because of previous exposure but yet have no conscious recollection of ever having learned the stimulus or having any awareness of knowing the stimulus.

Frequent retrieval failures are considered normal in the elderly population. To a certain extent, retrieval failures in children and adolescents are normal. However, with children and adolescents, memory performance problems due to abnormal retrieval can hinder academic progress. Consequently, there are many educational implications of retrieval functions. First, successful retrieval depends on effective encoding, which requires undivided attention, organized instruction, elaborative rehearsal, and cuing methods (see Chapter 8). Second, instructional methods must support consolidation and retention because information must be stored effectively before it can be retrieved. Third, because retrieval is cue dependent, classroom instruction should facilitate the incorporation of cues with new information. Fourth, retrieval is more successful when the features present at encoding are reinstated during retrieval. Finally, the best determinant of acquired knowledge may be recognition, not uncued recall.

FORGETTING

Most of what humans experience and learn is forgotten. Everyone knows what forgetting is, and everyone experiences this normal process of decay on a daily basis. Forgetting refers to prospective memory failures (e.g., forgetting an appointment), the irretrievable loss of information from memory storage, or the inability to access information despite conscious attempts to retrieve it. Traditionally, forgetting was viewed primarily as a retrieval phenomenon. The presumption was that storage is permanent but at times information is inaccessible. Reminiscence (remembering something at time 2 that could not be recalled at time 1) was cited as evidence that forgetting is simply a retrieval problem. However, researchers (e.g., Howe & Brainerd, 1989) who have analyzed the relative contributions of encoding, storage, and retrieval failures to forgetting have reported that storage failures contribute more to forgetting than retrieval failures. Thus, forgetting is the observable behavior that results from the brain's inability to permanently retain all information in long-term memory storage. However, in this discussion the term "forgetting" can refer to either the actual loss of information from storage or the inability to retrieve it on demand. As discussed previously, comparing free recall with recognition can help to differentiate between the two causes of memory failure. When information or an event is not recognized, or remains completely unfamiliar despite cues, it is most likely no longer in storage.

The old adage "Here today, gone tomorrow" sums up the ephemeral nature of information that is encoded into long-term memory. It's a well-known fact that memory for information and events becomes less accessible over time. Psychological study of forgetting began with Ebbinghaus (1913) in the latter part of the 19th century. Ebbinghaus, an early experimental psychologist, documented the typical rates of human learning and forgetting. He discovered that after material has been learned, there is rapid forgetting over the first few hours and next two days, with a more gradual but steady decline over subsequent days, weeks, and months.

Ebbinghaus also discovered that forgetting of nonsense words decreases with multiple relearnings and that widely distributed study was more effective than a massed series of reviews. A more recent investigation of student's forgetting of textbook material (Sprenger, 2005) reported these retention percentages: 54% after 1 day, 35% after 7 days, 21% after 14 days, and 8% after 21 days. Approximately half of what is known after a study period or lesson is forgotten within 24 hours. After the first month, the rate of forgetting is negligible but gradual forgetting continues for several years (Squire, 1989). For example, in Bahrick's (1984) longitudinal study, most foreign language vocabulary was forgotten within four years. After that, there was remarkably little forgetting of the vocabulary over the next 30 to 50 years.

There are three basic accounts of what causes normal forgetting: the decay hypothesis claims that memories simply decay, weaken, or erode over time (Schacter, 1999); the interference hypothesis asserts that other memories block retrieval of the desired information; and the retrieval-cue hypothesis posits that memories can't be accessed because the cues have been lost (Anderson, 2000). Decay is presumed to be a natural process whereby the memory representation increasingly degrades over time, ultimately leading to the complete loss of the once-stored information. Decay is more likely to occur when a memory is not used. The impact of interference depends on how much related information is learned within a relatively short interval; the greater the similarity of the material, the greater the interference. Consistent with the interference hypothesis, some forgetting results from an alteration in what was stored. As time passes, surviving memories become more resistant to interference. Cues may be lost because of contextual changes in daily life or because they have become irrelevant. Also, cues may never have been established due to incomplete or superficial encoding. All three of these factors probably contribute to the forgetting process, although many researchers believe that interference is the primary cause.

There are several factors to consider when evaluating whether or not a child's level of forgetting is abnormal. First, normal forgetting is not an all-or-nothing process. Some bits of information about an event or fact are retained while others are lost. The details of episodes and information are often lost while the main features and gist are retained. Second, in educational settings, lesson content that is difficult to learn is usually forgotten more quickly than content that is easily acquired. Third, excessive forgetting is not just due to an inability to retain information over time. It also can result from dysfunctions and inefficiencies in any of the constructive and reconstructive memory processes. Amnesia, usually caused by brain damage, is an extreme level of forgetting where some prior knowledge and/or most new learning is completely lost (see Chapter 3). Partial memory loss, or dysmnesia, also can result from brain damage. Finally, dysfunctions in related cognitive processes can also exacerbate forgetting; for instance, attention deficits can interfere with effective encoding. Children and adolescents with excessive levels of forgetting should be referred for a neuropsychological evaluation.

Of course, forgetting need not be permanent; sometimes the information becomes accessible at a later time. If the material has not been retained, it can be re-encoded and relearned. Fortunately, relearning of forgotten material can be accomplished more quickly than learning completely new content, a phenomenon also discovered by Ebbinghaus (1913). Furthermore, despite the constant lamenting about human forgetting, it actually serves an adaptive purpose (Storm, Bjork, & Bjork, 2007). Without some means of reducing outdated and irrelevant information, encoding and retrieval of new learning would be subject to more and more interference. Therefore, it is adaptive to forget trivial experiences and details lest the mind becomes overwhelmed. Also, retaining the gist or the meaning is more important than remembering all the details. Luckily, this is something most humans are adept at doing.

INTERFERENCE

Memories are often lost or become inaccessible due to interference. There are two types of interference: proactive and retroactive. *Proactive interference* occurs when prior knowledge or recently learned material impedes the learning of additional material. It also occurs when storage and retrieval of new learning is disrupted by previously acquired information. *Retroactive interference* occurs when retrieval of information learned earlier is impeded by subsequent exposure to additional material. The classic retroactive interference paradigm consists of learning a list of word pairs through repeated trials, followed by the learning of another list, which is followed by recall of the first list. Subjects who learn both lists recall significantly fewer items from the first list when compared to subjects who learn only the first list. On the other hand, poor recall of the second list is an example of proactive interference. Given that there are almost continual encounters involving previously encoded information, the opportunities for interference are many, especially in the classroom. A prime educational example of how interference retards learning is the difficulty children have learning arithmetic facts. Because the same numbers appear in many different addition and multiplication facts, the facts create interference with each other, thereby causing confusion and slower learning.

The influence of interference also can be observed during the learning of a single list of words by noting primacy and recency effects. The *primacy effect* occurs when more words are recalled from the beginning of the list, and the *recency effect* occurs when more words are recalled from the end of the list. The most recent words are the easiest to recall because they are still in short-term memory. Long-term memory is required to recall the words at the beginning of the list. The words in the middle are the most difficult to recall because of proactive interference from the beginning words and retroactive interference from the final words. Learners who recall words from the beginning and middle of the list are thought to possess efficient long-term memory encoding, whereas those who recall only the most recent words are more likely to have encoding weaknesses or be very susceptible to interference. Those who are highly susceptible to interference will experience learning and memory problems.

Although interference is thought to occur mainly during storage and retrieval (Howe, 1995), it can occur at any stage of information processing. During storage the introduction of subsequent related information alters the initial memory representations, thereby weakening the initial memory trace and leading to forgetting even before there is an opportunity for retrieval. During learning, previously learned information can hamper encoding of new input. Interference also disrupts consolidation and retrieval processes (Wixted, 2004). Even when retrieval is successful, interference can slow retrieval speed. Despite its pervasive meddling, interference is most observable at the time of retrieval. Although interference can be somewhat restricted through conscious and unconscious inhibition of unwanted information, everyone experiences interference during retrieval.

The degree of interference depends on several factors. The predominant factor is the similarity between the target information and the interfering information (Hockley, 1992). The greater the similarity between the interfering and the target information, the greater the level of interference (Howe, 1985). This phenomenon can be observed in memory tasks where items that are phonetically similar are more difficult to recall than phonetically dissimilar items. Second, interference is modality specific; visual material following verbal information will be less disruptive than verbal input following verbal information. For example, studying the same type of material all day will be less productive than studying different subjects. Finally, details are more susceptible to interference than the gist or main idea (Brainerd & Reyna, 1995). Nevertheless, ordinary mental activity unrelated to the target material also causes interference (Wixted, 2004). Thus, interference is unavoidable; humans must simply learn to cope with it.

Humans can minimize interference mainly by inhibiting irrelevant and incorrect information that becomes activated during learning and retrieval. Inhibition is the ability to attend to one piece of information while screening out and suppressing the disruptive effects of automatically generated or retrieved information that is not pertinent to the task at hand. Inhibition also discards previously activated but no longer relevant information and suppresses incorrect responses. Inhibition is mostly an unconscious executive function that seems to be associated with working memory capacity. Thus, executive dysfunctions or working memory impairments can indirectly degrade long-term memory performance, particularly during retrieval. Consequently, an individual's inhibition ability will influence performance on memory tasks. For instance, a child or adolescent with Attention Deficit Hyperactivity Disorder (ADHD) may have difficulty retrieving correct information because of a general inhibitory deficit.

There are several factors, cognitive processes, and strategies that can reduce interference. First, interference can be reduced through overlearning of material; the stronger the learning of material the better it will withstand interference from related information. Second, extending the interval between learning sessions curtails interference, especially when the sets of material are related. Third, when additional material is consistent with existing knowledge, it causes minimal interference. When it is inconsistent, there is greater interference. Fourth, unique context cues can serve to counteract interference by allowing a distinction between materials that would otherwise suffer from interference. For instance, students with a changing learning environment remember more than those who learn different material in the same environment (Anderson, 2000). Fifth, expertise, or in-depth knowledge of a subject, can serve to limit interference. Finally, forgetting of irrelevant information also curtails interference (Altmann & Gray, 2002).

THE ORGANIZATION OF MEMORY

Undoubtedly, one of the main functions of memory structures and processes is to organize information. It would be disastrous if input were simply encoded into the brain without some type of organization. A well-organized memory allows individuals to fill in missing gaps when only some of the information can be recalled. For example, when recalling a specific event, people rely on general knowledge structures to supply missing elements and infer what must have happened. The exact organizational structures of memory, as well as the underlying neurological structures (see Chapter 3), are difficult to examine and identify. Thus, psychologists and neuroscientists have developed several explanatory models.

Schemas

Schema theory is an attempt to explain how explicit memory, especially semantic memory, is organized. The theory accounts for the generality of memory and the interrelationships among memory representations. Schemas represent abstract knowledge about concepts and facts. They can vary in size, be arranged hierarchically, linked together, and be embedded within one another. Essentially, schemas are prior knowledge structures that represent all types of knowledge, including objects, situations, events, actions, and categories. Examples of schemas include objects (e.g., dogs, houses, tools) and common routines (e.g., making a phone call). Schemas are acquired from experiences and continue to evolve as more information related to the schema is obtained. A schema is often viewed as a categorical clustering of information that goes together. For example, items that serve the same function, such as tools, will be grouped into a tool schema, or mammals will be integrated into a mammal schema. From a brain-based perspective a schema is mostly likely stored in neural networks that are linked together.

There are several other important characteristics of schemas. Once a schema is established, it influences how people perceive, encode, store, consolidate, and retrieve information. In particular, a schema provides a framework with which new, but related, information can be integrated. Thus, schemas serve to organize incoming information, facilitating encoding and storage in the process. The influence of schemas is so strong that they can distort perception of an experience or information so that it is consistent with the existing schema, such as when people see what they expect to see. Associating new information with an appropriate schema will enhance retrieval, as individuals can search through a schema to retrieve a particular memory. Additionally, schemas endure for a lifetime and are impervious to interference (Cohen, 2008a). Another interesting characteristic of schemas is that new knowledge is immediately assimilated into an appropriate schema and that an updated version that eliminates any inconsistencies is produced. When original schemas turn out to be untrue, people easily correct and modify them.

Scripts

Episodic memories of an autobiographical nature are organized and interconnected in much the same way semantic memories are organized. For episodic memories, these general knowledge structures are known as *scripts*. Scripts, a subtype of schemas, represent the knowledge abstracted from a class of similar events. People have scripts for common experiences, such as going to the library and visiting a doctor. A script, sometimes referred to as a template, includes roles, scenes, and props but does not include the details of particular events. A script can also consist of a sequence of actions, such as steps involved in dining at a restaurant. The main advantage of scripts is that they can be used to infer forgotten events and details. However, scripts can make individual events of the same type difficult to remember because familiar, frequent events often become fused into a common generic memory (Williams, Conway, & Cohen, 2008). Just like schemas, scripts are dynamic, constantly being reorganized as different experiences are encountered. Of course, many events are unique experiences for which there is no script. Human memory is quite capable of retaining the elements and details of these novel experiences.

Fuzzy Trace Theory

According to Reyna and Brainerd (1995), the stage of memory development also determines the structure and content of memory representations. Fuzzy trace theory posits that memory traces range from literal to fuzzy (gistlike). Young children are more likely to store and retrieve literal, verbatim traces, rather than fuzzy, gistlike traces. As development proceeds, children are more likely to extract the gist of the information and store the knowledge in that form. Fuzzy traces, which are stored separately from the verbatim traces, are more easily accessed and less susceptible to interference and forgetting. Fuzzy trace theory is consistent with the notion of schemas and scripts. It takes time for children to develop schema and script-like structures. Once children have attained these structures, gistlike traces are all that is necessary for successful functioning in the world because schemas and scripts can be used to fill in missing elements and infer reasonable details.

Constructivism

The theory of constructivism holds that people actively build their perception of the world and interpret objects and events that surround them in terms of what they already know. The roots of constructivism can be traced to Piaget (1968). Regarding memory, the theory of constructivism posits that memories are not recalled verbatim; rather, the gist of an episode or related facts is recalled and then the details are inferred and the memory is reconstructed. Memory is constructive in that experienced events and learning episodes are integrated with inferences and elaborations that go beyond what is actually retrieved (Reyna & Kiernan, 1994). Reasoning is centrally involved in the constructive process. For example, Piaget demonstrated that improvements in memory are correlated with improvements in reasoning. Sometimes reasoning actually distorts memories, especially when reasoning based on gist takes precedence over verbatim memory. In such instances, erroneous responses can result, usually responses that are consistent with correct reasoning. Sometimes the constructive process goes so far that completely false memories are produced.

IMPLICATIONS FOR MEMORY ASSESSMENT

1. By definition, standardized memory scales mostly measure episodic memory rather than semantic memory. This is because most scales test long-term recall after only 30 minutes (see Chapter 6), an interval too short for information to transfer from episodic to semantic memory.
2. Although implicit memories cannot be tested by asking examinees to recall information, the existence of implicit memories can be documented by observing an examinee's behavior.
3. It is easier to identify which memory system is impaired, as opposed to which memory process is impaired, because memory systems can be differentiated by content and retention interval. It's also difficult to determine which memory process is having the most influence on memory performance.
4. Despite the challenge, an effort should be made to differentiate among the influences of encoding, consolidation, storage, and retrieval upon memory performance.
5. Focused attention is a prerequisite for effective encoding. Because of their strong relationship, the two can be difficult to differentiate during assessment.
6. Recognition tasks are a crucial component of a comprehensive memory assessment. Comparing recognition performance with recall performance allows the evaluator to determine whether memory impairments are mainly due to retrieval failure or storage failure.

7. Long-term memory should not be tested in isolation. Short-term memory, working memory, and related cognitive processes should be included.
8. Memory challenges and limitations are normal. For example, an evaluator must know the difference between normal forgetting and excessive forgetting.

EDUCATIONAL AND TRAINING IMPLICATIONS

1. Educators and psychologists who work in education should be required to fully understand the complexities of human memory. Such knowledge will enhance their ability to help students learn and remember.
2. Instructional methods that support initial learning and encoding may not be the most effective for facilitating long-term retention and retrieval.
3. Instruction should be structured in a manner that supports the normal limitations of memory, and material should be organized in a manner that meshes with inherent organizational structures in memory.
4. Learning and memory goals should specifically address how to slow the forgetting rate, enhance consolidation, and facilitate retrieval.
5. Reduction of interference is important. Trying to teach too much material at one time is ineffective because of the buildup of interference. Recently formed memories need a chance to consolidate before more material is introduced.

MEMORY FUNDAMENTALS

1. Human memory is complex. There are many different types of memory, memory systems, and memory processes.
2. Although the memory systems and components are interrelated, there are varying degrees of independent functioning. Thus, individuals will demonstrate relative strengths and weaknesses across memory systems and components.
3. Some types of memory, classified as implicit memories, are inaccessible to conscious control. Yet, these memories support conscious, explicit memory performance.
4. Long-term memory is dynamic; it's not a passive repository of information. Even during sleep the brain is constantly processing and updating memory representations.
5. Memory has a natural ability and tendency to organize information in a logical and efficient manner.
6. Related memory representations, such as related schemas, are inter-connected.

7. Semantic memories are acquired by extracting meaning from a series of similar learning episodes that are initially stored in episodic memory.

8. Memories need time to consolidate and make the transition from the hippocampus to cortical regions. After initial encoding, memories are manipulated and gradually integrated into cortical storage structures.

9. Despite effective learning and memorization practices, memories are ephemeral. Rapid forgetting of new material is normal.

10. Some information is maintained in memory storage but cannot be retrieved on demand, often because of interference.

11. Memory processes are highly interdependent. For example, successful retrieval depends on effective encoding and consolidation.

12. Working memory and long-term memory are interdependent. Effective utilization of long-term memory representations depends on adequate working memory capacity, and working memory functioning is enhanced by firmly established long-term memory representations.

Memory Neuroanatomy, Development, and Dysfunction

At the end of a school year, a mother and father brought in their 8-year-old, third-grade daughter for a summer of academic skills tutoring and memory training. "Agnes" was having difficulties in reading comprehension, mathematics, remembering information, and oral expression. The parents had adopted Agnes at 13 months of age after briefly serving as her foster parents. Early in her infancy, Agnes had been removed from her birth parents because she had sustained a non-accidental broken arm and severe head trauma while in their care. The abusive incident caused a right parietal skull fracture for which a craniotomy was performed. The neurosurgeon informed the adoptive parents that there should be no long-term cognitive repercussions from the head trauma. This prediction initially appeared true as Agnes's development was within normal limits when she was tested at 18 months and 3 years. However, when she entered kindergarten, significant delays in expressive language were documented and she began receiving speech and language services. As formal schooling increased the demands on memory, it became evident to her parents that Agnes had some significant memory problems. By third grade, Agnes's academic struggles were extensive and she was placed in special education for part of the school day. When they signed her up for tutoring, Agnes's parents were concerned because they believed her learning progress was slowing down in spite of expanded school services. They would later withdraw her from school (to be homeschooled) because of the lack of individual attention she was receiving in her special education setting.

Prior to special education placement, Agnes was administered the Wechsler Intelligence Scale for Children®-Fourth Edition (WISC®-IV; Wechsler, 2003). The results indicated that her Full Scale IQ, her verbal comprehension abilities, and working memory were all in the borderline to low average range, whereas her perceptual reasoning and processing speed were average. Beyond the working memory factor embedded in the WISC®-IV, no memory testing had been conducted. Follow-up psychological testing administered at the time of her enrollment in tutoring services, revealed that Agnes had subaverage scores in visual-auditory learning (16th percentile), long-term retrieval (9th percentile), short-term memory (16th percentile), and fluid reasoning (13th percentile). The rest of the information about Agnes' abilities and skills had to be gathered informally, as Agnes's parents did not want more testing. Through interviews and observations it became apparent that Agnes had difficulties with encoding, storing, and retrieving information, and that her memory problems involved short-term, working, and long-term memory systems. For example, her parents reported that they often repeated information for Agnes's benefit and that she obviously knew some information that she could not retrieve on demand. In interviewing and working with Agnes, it also became evident that she was not using any memory strategies. For example, when practicing a basic rehearsal strategy, Agnes reported that she had never done that before. Her metacognitive development was also delayed. She knew she had significant memory problems, and she seemed to be fearful and worried about forgetting information. However, she had very little knowledge of memory functions and her own memory strengths and weaknesses. To her credit, Agnes was very interested in trying to improve her memory, and she diligently applied herself to learning memory strategies throughout the summer. Significant gains in her memory performance were documented at the end of the summer.

The case of Agnes brings up many questions that are relevant to the topics in this and the next chapter: (a) What role do the parietal lobes play in memory? (b) Did Agnes sustain unidentified injury to other brain regions that are crucial for memory functioning? (c) How did her age at the time of injury influence her subsequent memory development? (d) Why hadn't her memory impairments been identified earlier? (e) Were her language delays related to her memory impairments? (f) What is expected of an 8-year-old regarding metamemory development and memory strategy acquisition, and why was Agnes delayed in these skills? (g) Did her memory deficiencies warrant a diagnosis of a memory disorder? After finishing this chapter and Chapter 4, the reader should have several insights regarding the answers to these questions.

THE NEUROANATOMY OF MEMORY

Whereas the previous chapter examined memory structures and functioning from a cognitive perspective, this chapter will review memory from a neuropsychological perspective. Initial neurological evidence for separate memory systems came from 1950s case studies of individuals with brain lesions. With advancements in brain imaging technology, the fields of neuropsychology and neuroscience have been able to expand the study of memory functions and systems. Functional magnetic resonance imaging (fMRI) has been an especially productive tool because it allows viewing of neural activation as a person performs a cognitive task (for a review of other imaging techniques, see Berninger & Richards, 2002). In general, brain imaging research has identified the neural basis of memory and has provided support for the memory models and classification schemes that were discussed in Chapter 2. The particular set of neural structures that underlies each memory system has been well established. With recent advancements in neuroimaging, some specific learning and memory functions have been linked to specific neurological structures. Yet, because of the complexity of the brain's memory systems and functions, much remains to be elucidated.

The challenge of mapping memory function and storage sites in the brain is that no single memory center exists, either for declarative or non-declarative memories. Many parts of the brain participate in the processing and storage of any single event, with each aspect of the event being stored in a different location. For example, imagine a minor automobile accident. Memories for the sounds, spatial location, people involved, facial expressions, smells, words, and emotions will end up being stored in different brain structures. Yet, they are linked or bound together so that the different aspects of the event can all be recalled simultaneously. Despite the complexity of storage, it is known that permanent storage of memories involves changes in the same cortical regions responsible for perceiving and processing specific materials or types of sensory information (Milner, Squire, & Kandel, 1998). That is, visual memories are stored in visual processing regions, and linguistic memories are stored in language processing regions.

As discussed in Chapter 2, incoming information goes through a series of processes in the brain before it ends up as a stored memory. Upon experiencing an event, sensory inputs are registered in multiple regions throughout the cortex (i.e., visual and auditory cortices). Inputs from these primary sensory areas are then sent to sensory association areas for each sensory modality, and the information is then integrated into wholistic perceptions (i.e., what an object looks like). These perceptions then proceed to multisensory association areas where the different sensory inputs converge (Bauer, DeBoer, & Lukowski, 2007). The information is then encoded as memory traces in the medial temporal lobe structures, including the hippocampus. These memory traces are then integrated and consolidated by the hippocampus. Over time, the information is transferred to the sensory association areas in the cerebral cortex where the input was first registered. Neuroimaging research has confirmed that episodic memory storage for an experience resides in the same neural units that processed the experience when it happened (Roediger, Gallo, & Geraci, 2002). The same is true for semantic memory: Brain activation patterns during retrieval mimic the processing that occurred at the time of study. Essentially, these studies suggest that similar neural structures support perception, encoding, storage, and retrieval.

Different brain cells and structures specialize in the performance of different tasks. Nonetheless, there is usually not a one-to-one relationship between a brain structure and a specific function. Some functions, such as sensory and motor functions, are highly localized, but higher-level cognitive processes are more diffuse. Although higher-level processes such as memory are widely distributed throughout the brain, the brain tissues involved are linked together in neural networks. Fibrous connections referred to as *pathways* link cells within neural networks and related networks with each other. Learning and memory seem to depend on the creation of neural networks and the neural pathways between them. In essence, the interconnections at the cellular and network level underlie the organization and storage of memories. Retention, consolidation, and retrieval of memories depend on the creation, strengthening, and durability of these pathways. Also, memories are enhanced when the brain creates alternative or redundant pathways that link the same information (Berninger & Richards, 2002).

Microstructure

The human brain has an estimated 180 billion cells consisting of glial cells and nerve cells called neurons. Glial cells, also referred to as neuroglia, provide structural, nutritional, and other types of support to neurons; for example, some glial cells form the myelin sheath around axons. Neurons have three components: a cell body, an axon, and dendrites. The axon is a trunklike attachment to the cell body that transmits information from the cell. The dendrites are branchlike structures with receiving terminals that collect information from other neurons. Each neuron can have thousands of dendrites but only one axon. A synapse is the small space that separates the axon terminals from the dendrites. The synapse contains chemicals, referred to as neurotransmitters, that, when released, influence the activity of other neurons (Berninger & Richards, 2002). Thus, communication between neurons takes place as chemical signals travel from axons to dendrites across synapses. Learning and memory involve specific changes in neuronal connections. These changes involve how neurons communicate (or fire) with each other, as well as which neurons are communicating with each other. Neurons that fire in a pattern are called neural networks. Neural networks change as new information is combined with related information already stored. Thus, at the neurological level, each memory and each aspect of a memory requires a network of neurons. Humans store millions of these networks.

Memories are encoded into long-term storage through a chain of biochemical and cellular processes that occur over an extended period of time, as opposed to short-term storage that relies on patterns of electrical activity that are established in a matter of milliseconds. According to research on the molecular basis of memory, changes in the strength of existing synapses are crucial for the storage of memories in neural networks (Emilien et al., 2004). A persistent increase in synaptic strength is known as long-term potentiation (LTP). The physical changes that occur during LTP consist of the growth of additional spines on the dendrites onto which axons synapse (Milner et al., 1998). These changes enhance synaptic neurotransmissions and increase neural representations of cues in the brain (Miller & Blasik, 2010). Because LTP depends on joint activation of two neurons, it is thought to involve some type of associative learning. LTP, which can last for weeks, is one of the critical neural processes that underlie learning and memory formation. In addition to the growth of new dendrites and the strengthening of synapses, the long-term storage of memory also requires physical changes in neurons. As information is converted from immediate or short-term memory into long-term memory, protein synthesis takes place at the cellular level.

Another way of explaining how memories are formed and stored neurologically has been offered by Schacter (1996), who describes how episodic memories are consolidated and preserved through the formation of *memory traces*. According to Schacter, the brain records episodic information by creating, modifying, and strengthening the connections between groups of neurons that participate in the encoding process. The resulting pattern of connections, referred to as a *memory trace* or an *engram*, is the brain's record of the event. Essentially, the brain stores memory traces by increasing the strength of synaptic connections between different neurons. When an event or information is encoded, the connections between active neurons become stronger, and this specific pattern of brain activity constitutes the memory trace (Schacter). Memory traces vary in strength, and they are thought to fade or disintegrate over time. The greater the strength, the better the retention and retrieval. Traces are difficult to retrieve when they become weak and indistinguishable from similar traces. Eventually, they may be lost from storage altogether. Numerous traces are required to store any given episodic memory. Thus, during retrieval constituent memory traces must be reassembled. Retrieval also restores trace strength and alters the memory because every reactivation of a memory trace is thought to produce a different but related trace (Nadel & Moscovitch, 1997). The formation of multiple traces increases the probability of successful retention and retrieval.

In summary, the incorporation of new events and knowledge leads to changes in brain structure. At the cellular level, the neurons participating in memory storage undergo reorganization. A memory is not stored in a single neuron but rather clusters of neurons, and these clusters, or networks, are interconnected. There are also synaptic changes among cellular and network connections. Neuroscientists continue to investigate the synaptic, biochemical, and cellular changes involved in the brain's storage of memories.

Macrostructure

The human brain consists of numerous structures but the focus in this chapter is on the structures involved in memory. Memory functions take place in the cerebrum, the largest part of the brain, which lies in front of and above the cerebellum, which is involved in motor movement and coordination and is located at the base of the skull. The cerebrum is divided into left and right hemispheres joined by the corpus callosum. The left hemisphere specializes in language and sequential processing, and the right hemisphere specializes in visuospatial processing and simultaneous processing. Effective brain functioning requires that both hemispheres work together cooperatively. The cerebral hemispheres are surrounded by the cortex (or neocortex), a thin covering of cells up to six layers thick. Although the cortex is very thin, it accounts for 80% of the brain because of all of its folding. Each hemisphere has

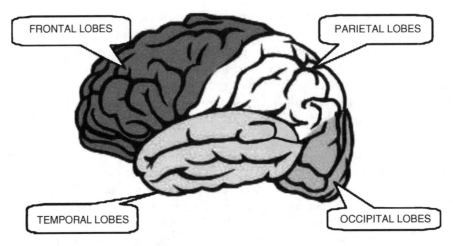

Figure 3.1   The brain's four lobes

Source: Neuropsychological Perspectives on Learning Disabilities in an Era of RTI: Recommendations for Diagnosis and Intervention, by E. Fletcher-Janzen and C. R. Reynolds (Eds.), 2008, Hoboken, NJ: Wiley.

four lobes: frontal, parietal, temporal, and occipital (see Figure 3.1). The parietal, temporal, and occipital lobes are involved in fundamental perception and information processing, whereas the frontal lobe specializes in higher-level cognitive processing. There are also subdivisions of each lobe; for example the temporal lobe is divided into the inferior, middle (medial), and superior temporal lobes.

The Frontal Lobes and Prefrontal Cortex   The frontal lobes, which are located behind the forehead, can be divided into the motor cortex, which is involved in movement, and the prefrontal cortex, where executive functioning takes place. (In this text references to the frontal lobes refer to the prefrontal cortex.) The prefrontal cortex, located in the most forward part of the frontal lobe of each hemisphere, is instrumental in attention allocation, impulse control, problem solving, and organization. It is also the seat of working memory. Along with the medial temporal lobes, the prefrontal cortex plays an important role in long-term memory processing. The encoding and retrieval of several types of long-term memory, especially explicit memories, depend, at least partially, on frontal lobe functioning. During encoding the degree of involvement seems to be a function of the complexity of the encoding process. For instance, there is more activation of the left dorsolateral prefrontal cortex during more demanding verbal encoding tasks (Pliszka, 2003). (The dorsolateral areas of the prefrontal cortex are toward the back and toward the sides.) The frontal lobes are also involved in retrieval, as indicated by the increased blood flow to the frontal lobes during conscious searching of memory. For instance, the right dorsolateral prefrontal cortex is activated during retrieval of verbal material. During retrieval, the frontal lobes are also involved in evaluating accessed memories and in applying inferential logic when partially recovered memories need to be reconstructed. Finally, the frontal lobes are essential for the development and functioning of metamemory and strategic memory. For example, frontal regions of the brain are involved during elaborative rehearsal, such as organizing and categorizing new information (Schacter, 1996).

The frontal lobes do not perform memory functions in isolation but rather in conjunction with the medial temporal lobe and the hippocampus (Emilien et al., 2004). For instance, if there is medial temporal lobe damage, the frontal lobes cannot instill new memories on their own. The close connection between the two brain regions is evidenced by the existence of a direct physical connection between them, known as the Papez circuit. Whether the hippocampus or the frontal lobes mediate retrieval of a memory seems related to whether or not the memory is dependent on environmental cues, in which case the hippocampus is more involved. The frontal lobes are also involved in recalling temporal information, as well as prospective memory and source memory (when and where an event occurred). However, much remains unknown about the interactions between the hippocampus and frontal lobes during memory processing. For example, it's not clear which brain region has primary responsibility for recalling temporal and spatial information (Sohlberg & Mateer, 2001). Although the prefrontal cortex plays a crucial role in memory processing, memories are not actually stored in the frontal lobes, in contrast with the medial temporal lobe and hippocampus, which actually store some memories.

Parietal Lobes   Somatosensory functioning, such as a sense of touch, is the primary function of the parietal lobes, which are located at the top rear of the skull, behind the frontal lobes. The parietal lobes also are involved in auditory activities, such as speech perception, and visual-spatial processing and recall, as indicated by increased parietal activity when people remember the location of objects. Along with the frontal lobes, the parietal lobes also play a role in some aspects of working memory. In fact, some neuroimaging studies (discussed in Klingberg, 2009) have linked the development of working memory to the myelinization of connections between the parietal and frontal lobes.

Occipital Lobes   The occipital lobes, also known as the primary visual cortex, are located in the middle rear of the skull. The occipital lobes process visual stimuli and are necessary for vision, visual perception, visual discrimination, visual integration, and identifying faces and objects.

Temporal Lobes   The temporal lobes, located at ear level, are responsible for auditory processing, language, short-term memory, and higher order visual processing, such as object identification. The temporal lobes are frequently involved in head injuries because they often make contact with the skull in accidents (Semrud-Clikeman, Kutz, & Strassner, 2005). The temporal lobes are also closely associated with the limbic system (see the section on other neural structures) that includes the hippocampus.

The Medial Temporal Lobe

The medial temporal lobe is the brain region most responsible for the formation, maintenance, retrieval, and reintegration of long-term memories (Broadbent, Clark, Zola, & Squire, 2002). It is a large region that contains the hippocampus, amygdala, fornix, and the entorhinal, perirhinal, and parahippocampal cortices. The complex processing and interrelationships among the different structures are not yet fully understood, but it is believed that each has specialized functions in memory storage and that each mediates different aspects of acquired information. Undoubtedly, the medial temporal lobe and its embedded structures are all involved in various aspects of memory processing, from encoding to retrieval. Encoding is initiated when the medial temporal lobe receives information from a range of sensory association areas (Simons & Spiers, 2003). Following encoding, the lengthy process of consolidation is orchestrated by the medial temporal lobe, especially the hippocampus. The classical memory consolidation position is that memories are initially stored in the medial temporal lobe until they are transferred to other cortical regions. Even after the transfer occurs, the medial temporal region is still involved in retrieval of information that is stored elsewhere in the brain. It seems that the medial temporal lobe stores the key for reassembling related memory traces into a coherent response to a cue. Apparently, the medial temporal lobe and the hippocampus are the sites of this reconstructive process. Despite all that is known about the neuroanatomy of memory, there has been a long-standing debate over the role of the medial temporal lobe in long-term memory storage. Although there is agreement that the medial temporal lobe is essential for the consolidation of memories, it's not clear how many memories actually remain stored in this region. Although there is recent evidence that at least some episodic memories are permanently stored in the medial temporal lobe (Moscovitch, Nadel, Winocur, Gilboa, & Rosenbaum, 2006), it appears that most memories are ultimately stored in cortical networks outside the medial temporal region, with different cortical networks retaining different kinds of information (Schacter, 1996).

The Hippocampus

The hippocampus is a small, horse-shoe-shaped structure that lies deep within the medial region of the temporal lobes (Giap et al., 2000). For more than 50 years it has been known that the hippocampus and adjacent structures play a fundamental role in the formation of new memories. Of all the medial temporal lobe formations, the hippocampus is the most directly responsible for the majority of explicit memory processes. For instance, the hippocampus is required for transferring information from short-term memory to long-term memory. But the hippocampus is involved in more than encoding of information; it is also essential for consolidation, storage, and retrieval. However, it's not yet clear which specific memory functions and processes are mediated solely by the hippocampus and which are primarily carried out by other medial temporal lobe structures. Consequently, when psychologists and neuroscientists refer to the memory functions of the medial temporal lobe, the hippocampus is implicitly included, and when they attribute a process to the hippocampus, the processing actually may be supported by adjacent medial temporal lobe structures. The hippocampus is also part of the limbic system, which is a loosely defined group of brain structures that are involved in emotion and learning. Anatomically, the hippocampus consists of two sheets of neurons. One sheet is the dentate gyrus, and the other is the cornu ammonis (Pliszka, 2003). The hippocampus also is comprised of a left and right hemisphere. The left hippocampus plays a more important role in verbal memory than the right; in contrast, visuospatial memory is clearly dependent on the right hippocampus.

The hippocampus has different relationships with various memory systems and types of memories. First, it is not involved with the implicit memory system, whereas all explicit memories require a functioning hippocampus. Second, as demonstrated in cases of childhood and adulthood amnesia, episodic memory formation fully depends on the hippocampus. Adequate hippocampal functioning is essential for the creation and recall of episodic memories, especially detailed episodic memories. In contrast, the hippocampus may not be necessary for all semantic memory formation, as proposed by Vargha-Khadem, Gadian, Watkins, and Connelly (1997). Third, spatial memory, an integral component of episodic memory, depends on adequate hippocampal functioning. Specifically, the hippocampus is needed for re-experiencing spatial memories, no matter how old they are (Moscovitch et al., 2006). The relationship between spatial memory and the hippocampus was documented in a study of London taxi drivers who depend heavily on spatial memory. Experienced drivers' posterior region of the hippocampus was larger than in novice drivers or London bus drivers (Maguire, Vargha-Khadem, & Mishkin, 2001). Fourth, the hippocampus may serve as the permanent repository of certain types of memory. For example, especially detailed autobiographical and spatial memories seem to be stored permanently within the hippocampus (Rosenbaum, Winocur, & Moscovitch, 2001).

Although the hippocampus may permanently store some memories, the majority of new memories are stored only temporarily until the process of consolidation transfers them to cortical regions. The consolidation of memories seems to rely primarily on the hippocampus. Although the actual process of consolidation is unknown and the construct is controversial (see Chapter 2), it seems to proceed something like this: (a) in the creation of memories, the hippocampus first binds neural elements together into a new memory trace; (b) these newly created traces are encoded and stored in the cortex; (c) a hippocampal-cortical connection is established; (d) the neural elements participating in storage of the memory trace undergo reorganization, and in the process, their synaptic efficiency and integration are increased (Shimamura, 2004); (e) the trace is gradually strengthened through retrieval or through the subconscious replaying of the trace by the hippocampus; (f) eventually, cortical-cortical interconnections are established, thus reducing the need for the hippocampus during retrieval and reintegration of memories. Until memory traces are permanently stored and interconnected in the neocortex, a process that typically takes weeks but may take years, the hippocampus and medial temporal lobe are essential for recovering memory traces. This is why retrograde amnesia resulting from brain injury affects recent memories more than remote memories, and episodic memories more than semantic memories. Cortical consolidation is an automatic and unconscious process that seems to take place during sleep (see Chapter 2 for more details).

Although the hippocampus is needed mostly for encoding and consolidation, it also plays a crucial role in retrieval, during which it binds together the multiple features of a memory that are retrieved from different cortical regions. The hippocampus seems to be involved primarily with the automatic retrieval that occurs when a cue immediately triggers an associated memory, whereas, conscious, effortful, and strategic retrieval seems to be more a function of the prefrontal cortex. There is controversy over whether the hippocampus is involved in retrieving only recent memories or memories across the entire life span. The traditional position is that once memories are consolidated in the cortex, the hippocampus is no longer necessary for their retrieval. This position also holds that the hippocampus is more involved in retrieval of recently acquired memories than of remote memories. In opposition, some researchers have claimed that the hippocampus continues to play a role in retrieval of even well-consolidated memories. Regardless of how this dispute is resolved, there is consensus that the hippocampus is more important for acquisition than for retrieval (Simons & Spiers, 2003).

Although most hippocampal processing of information is automated and unconscious (even occurring during sleep), it is by no means a passive or "thoughtless" neurological processing component. Amazingly, the hippocampus seems to be an associative device that contributes to the formation of new relationships between stimuli (Squire, 1992). In fact, the integration of contextual information is known to rely on the hippocampus. In effect, the medial temporal lobe and the hippocampus bind together cortical representations that are simultaneously active. That is, representations that are being processed at the same time are associated with each other, and this cognitive process is supported at the neurological level by the actual binding of the involved neural structures, thereby creating cortical-cortical interconnections (Shimamura, 2004). A critical point about the hippocampus is that it primarily stores associations between memories rather than the memories themselves. In effect, it establishes and maintains connections among neural networks, which explains why the hippocampus is necessary during effortful searches for information, especially for recently stored input. The hippocampus holds the key to the connections and consequently correctly activates all of the cortical connections that hold the diverse input associated with a single event or fact. These functions explain why the hippocampus is required for both semantic and episodic memory. For semantic memory, it creates neural connections between traces that are conceptually associated. In regards to episodic memory, it binds together elements of complex episodic memories, along with integrating contextual information. Simply put, without a functioning hippocampus, new explicit memories cannot be created and retained.

Other Neural Structures Involved in Memory

The Limbic System   The limbic system is a loosely defined brain network that is involved in emotion, memory, and learning. It involves the ability to control emotions and interpret emotional information. It includes the thalamus, cingulated gyrus, hippocampus, amygdala, septal area, and portions of the cerebral cortex (Willis, 2005). The system has extensive interconnections with many other brain structures, especially the frontal lobes.

Hippocampal Related Structures   The medial temporal lobe memory system also includes the entorhinal, perirhinal, and parahippocampal cortices. All of these structures have reciprocal connections with the hippocampus. Visual input and auditory input pass through the entorhinal cortex on their way to the hippocampus. The perirhinal cortex is thought to serve as the interface between visual perception and memory and to also play an important role in declarative memory (Broadbent, Clark, Zola, & Squire, 2004). The parahippocampal cortex (or gyrus) is thought to be involved in spatial and topographic memory. These integrated memory structures may support semantic memory formation when the hippocampus itself is severely damaged.

Amygdala   The amygdala, an almond-shaped limbic system structure that sits just behind the hippocampus, is known to be important for emotional learning in humans. In particular, emotional conditioning and fear conditioning, both types of classical conditioning, depend on the amygdala. For example, the amygdala is highly activated by the perception of faces with strong emotional content. The amygdala is also known as the brain area where the perception of stimuli is matched to information about its biological significance (Pliszka, 2003). Although the amygdala is part of the implicit memory system, it does influence explicit memories. That is, emotional arousal during explicit learning will enhance those explicit memories. It also has been reported that the amygdala is involved, along with the hippocampus, when cross-modal associations are required (Nelson, 1995). The amygdala does not seem to be a storage site for memories but rather a neural structure that modulates memory storage in other brain regions.

Thalamus   The thalamus, an egg-like structure that also lies near the hippocampus, functions as a relay station through which all sensory information, except smell, passes on its way from the back of the brain to the cortex in the front of the brain. The thalamus is an essential information processing structure, as damage to the thalamus can produce amnesia (Schacter, 1996).

Implicit Memory Structures   Less is known about the neurological structures and functions of implicit memory, other than the fact that they are not located in or primarily served by the medial temporal lobe. Recent evidence suggests that diverse posterior brain regions, particularly the parietal and occipital lobes, may play a greater role in implicit memory (Shum, Jamieson, Bahr, & Wallace, 1999). Additional implicit memory processing and storage areas include the cerebellum (for conditioning), the striatum (for procedural learning), the temporal cortices (for visual word priming), the amygdala, the basal ganglia, and the motor cortex (Nelson, 1995; Siegel, 1999). The diversity of brain regions reportedly involved with implicit memory is consistent with the several unique types of implicit learning and memory. The dispersion of implicit memory structures may serve as a protective function that makes implicit memory generally impervious to injury and degeneration.

SHORT-TERM AND WORKING MEMORY STRUCTURES

Short-term memory and working memory depend on a different set of neural structures than those associated with long-term memory. Depending on the short-term or working memory task, several brain regions may be activated simultaneously, including locations in the frontal, parietal, and temporal lobes (Cowan, 2005). Whereas the frontal lobes may allocate resources, the parietal lobes are involved in further processing and in the retention of modality-specific information. Cowan (1995) suggested that the frontal lobes keep active the appropriate neural systems in other parts of the brain so as to maintain representation of the stimuli. Studies have also demonstrated that the prefrontal cortex prolongs posterior activation, including activation of long-term memory storage areas. This evidence indicates that working memory processing is not confined to the frontal lobes, and it also lends further support to the belief that long-term memory and working memory are highly interactive. From a neurological perspective, working memory capacity might be an indication of how many brain areas the frontal lobes can simultaneously involve in working memory processing.

Despite wide-spread activation during working memory tasks, neuroimaging of short-term memory tasks (storage-only tasks) reveals that brain activation is restricted primarily to the areas related to the modality of the content (Prabhakaran, Narayanan, Zhao, & Gabrieli, 2000). Accordingly, phonological short-term storage is generally associated with left hemisphere functioning, whereas visuospatial storage is generally associated with the right hemisphere. Posterior activations are material related, with specific areas in parietal and temporal regions involved either in phonological or visuospatial short-term memory. For example, the right hemisphere pre-motor cortex is activated for visuospatial material (Smith & Jonides, 1997). Thus, the different activation sites reflect the neural separation of short-term storage for phonological versus visuospatial information, as well as the neural separation of working memory from the domain-specific short-term memory subsystem. To a lesser degree, the prefrontal regions are also involved with retention and processing of visuospatial and verbal material. The left prefrontal region (Broca's area) is activated when verbal material is being processed. In contrast, the right prefrontal region processes both verbal and visuospatial information (Prabhakaran et al., 2000). However, activation of the prefrontal cortex is more likely to occur when both verbal and visuospatial information are being processed. Hence, complex working memory activities (storage-plus-processing tasks) reveal content-specific activation but also more general activation of the dorsolateral prefrontal cortex and anterior cingulate (Jonides, Smith, Marshuetz, & Koeppe, 1998).

Phonological Short-Term Memory

Neuroimaging studies indicate that short-term phonological retention and rehearsal operate at a relatively deep, central level. According to Baddeley (2003), phonological activity is associated with left hemisphere activation, with Brodmann's area 40 associated with phonological storage and Broca's area associated with subvocal rehearsal. According to Gathercole, Pickering, Ambridge, and Wearing (2004), phonological storage is served by a neural circuit in the left hemisphere spanning inferior parietal areas, and rehearsal is associated with anterior temporal frontal areas. Baldo and Dronkers (2006) recently reported that the supramarginal gyrus subserves the phonological store while Broca's area subserves articulatory rehearsal. Despite the somewhat different explanations, there is clearly neurological evidence supporting the division of phonological short-term memory into a passive storage component and a rehearsal component.

Visuospatial Short-Term Memory

Neuroimaging research has revealed that visuospatial short-term memory is principally, but not entirely, localized in the right hemisphere of the brain (Baddeley, 2003), especially in the occipital and inferior frontal areas. Neuroimaging studies have also provided strong indications of separate neural systems serving the two visuospatial subcomponents of storage and rehearsal (Smith & Jonides, 1997). There is also evidence that visuospatial short-term memory can be divided into visual and spatial components, with the visual component located in the occipital lobes and the spatial component in the parietal lobes.

Working Memory's Central Executive

The functioning of core working memory processes, namely executive processes, is thought to reside in the prefrontal cortex. The executive aspects of working memory include allocation of resources, inhibition of interference, updating, shifting, monitoring, and strategy implementation. According to Kane and Engle (2002), the dorsolateral prefrontal cortex is responsible for inhibiting interference from a secondary processing task while trying to sustain the relevant information. Dorsolateral prefrontal activation is also observed whenever updating, shifting, and refreshing are needed, such as when a person is engaged in dual-task performance. Moreover, the prefrontal areas seem to have a special role in integrating different types of information in working memory, such as when both verbal and visual-spatial information about a stimulus is required. As the demands on working memory increase, there is greater activation in the prefrontal cortex (Prabhakaran et al., 2000). Despite these findings, more specific brain-mapping of executive working memory is a challenge because executive functions can't be implemented by just one brain structure. Moreover, some neuroimaging studies reveal considerable variability across individuals in the distribution of activated regions during executive working memory tasks, with no specific frontal region predominating (D'Esposito et al., 1995). Perhaps, this variability reflects the use of differing strategies to perform an executive processing task, or it could arise from differences in how demanding the task is for each individual.

After an extensive review of the literature on the role of the prefrontal cortex in working memory capacity, Kane and Engle (2002) came to the following conclusions: (a) the evidence consistently underscores the role of the dorsolateral prefrontal cortex (dPFC) in executive working memory; (b) normal individual differences in working memory capacity are mediated by individual differences in the dPFC; (c) the dPFC is a necessary but insufficient structure for working memory functions—other neurological structures are also necessary; (d) the primary role of the dPFC is to actively maintain information in the presence of interference by blocking distractions and irrelevant information; and (e) the neuroanatomic evidence supports a heirarchical view of working memory, with distinct working memory systems in the posterior regions networked to the dPFC. It has also been discovered that the same prefrontal regions are active during both working memory and long-term memory tasks (Ranganath, Johnson, & D'Esposito, 2003), lending support to the claim that the same executive processes located in the prefrontal regions support both working and long-term memory performance.

The Episodic Buffer

In addition to neurological evidence for the phonological, visuospatial, and executive components of short-term and working memory, there is also evidence for a buffer that interfaces between working and long-term memory. Prabhakaran et al. (2000) found evidence of a buffer that allows for the temporary retention of integrated information. Rudner, Fransson, Ingvar, Nyberg, and Ronnberg (2007) recently collected neuroimaging data supporting the existence of episodic buffer processing. The left hippocampus and the right medial temporal lobe are involved during episodic processing. This finding is consistent with the proposition that the hippocampus is responsible for transferring information from short-term to long-tem memory.

NEUROLOGICAL PRINCIPLES OF MEMORY

Despite the complexity of the brain's memory processes and the difficulty of mapping memory functions and storage sites, much has been discovered and reaffirmed in recent years. From the neuropsychological and neuroscientific research, some key principles have emerged that have implications for memory assessment and intervention. These principles include:

1. Memory structures and functions in the brain are both localized and distributed. Even those memory processes and types of storage that mainly occur within a specific brain structure are, at some level, distributed throughout related networks in the brain.
2. The creation and retention of memories depends mainly on the modification and strengthening of synaptic connections between individual neurons and among neural networks.
3. After consolidation, memories are stored in the same sensory association areas in the cerebral cortex where the input was first registered and processed. For example, phonological memories are stored in cortices that process phonological information.
4. The brain creates multiple pathways during encoding, thereby allowing parallel processing and increasing the probability that stored information can be accessed when needed.
5. Each time a memory trace is reactivated during retrieval another trace is formed, resulting in multiple traces for the same memory.
6. The prefrontal cortex and hippocampus are directly linked and share responsibility for several memory functions.
7. Although the hippocampus is not necessary for immediate (short-term) recall, it needs to be engaged at the time of learning if long-term memories are going to be created (Squire & Zola-Morgan, 1991).
8. The hippocampus is involved in all aspects of long-term memory processing. Encoding and consolidation rely on it exclusively, whereas other brain structures also provide storage and support retrieval.
9. The central executive activities of working memory are primarily associated with the dorsolateral prefrontal cortex. However, working memory processing is not confined to the frontal lobes.
10. Phonological short-term memory is located in the temporal lobes of the left hemisphere, and visuospatial short-term memory is situated in the temporal lobes of the right hemisphere.

THE DEVELOPMENT OF LONG-TERM MEMORY

As with other cognitive abilities, there is a developmental progression with long-term memory. It is well known that older children and adolescents retain more information than younger children (Moulin & Gathercole, 2008). In fact, there are consistent improvements in amount retained from early childhood through the adolescent years (Howe & Brainerd, 1989). The causes of this substantial improvement in memory storage are many: more effective encoding, quicker retrieval, and greater ability to store information for longer periods of time. Compared with older children (e.g., 12 years of age), younger children (e.g., 6 years of age) have retrieval deficiencies. The desired information seems to be stored but they have difficulty retrieving it without prompting (Pressley & Levin, 1980). Thus, between the ages of 6 and 12, improved memory performance mainly results from more efficient retrieval processes (Wright & Limond, 2004). Continued improvement after the age of 12 is attributed to greater ability to encode more and more features of the incoming information. More effective encoding underlies concurrent improvements in consolidation and storage. Overall, from early childhood to adolescence, the largest gains in long-term memory functioning are in consolidating information and retrieving information without prompting. Although more efficient and effective memory processing naturally unfolds with age, development of metamemory and strategic processing also plays a crucial role. Unlike short-term and working memory, the development of long-term memory is less about growth in basic capacities than about enhancement of memory processes through the use of effective strategies. Improved long-term memory performance is also related to growth in the amount of stored knowledge.

Infancy

Infants are born with a remarkable capacity to encode and retain information. Infants recognize the sound of their mother's voice within hours and their mother's face within three to four days. Long-term memory functions and retention of information go on to develop rapidly in early infancy. Recognition memory is the first to emerge, appearing within the first days of postnatal life (de Haan, Mishkin, Baldeweg, & Vargha-Khadem, 2006). Given two minutes of familiarization, 4- to 5-month-olds can recognize abstract patterns up to two days later and faces up to two weeks later. By 6 months, the infant is able to form mental representations and recall them after a delay. At 9 months of age, infants can remember individual actions for as long as five weeks. By 11 months, they can remember actions for as long as three months. At 14 months, infants can remember over delays of four to six months. In general, as infancy progresses, encoding is faster, retention is longer, retrieval is faster, a wider range of retrieval cues is utilized, and changes in context become less disruptive to retrieval (Hayne, 2007).

The biological factors that contribute to the early development of long-term memory include myelination, the growth of dendrites, and increases in synaptic density. At birth, the medial temporal lobe and the hippocampus are fairly well developed, although their functional maturity remains in question (Rose, Feldman, & Jankowski, 2007). After birth, the hippocampus matures rapidly and appears to be functional within the first month or so of life. Also, there are pronounced changes in the temporal lobe structure beginning late in the first year of life. Because these structures are involved in consolidation, the implication is that storage capabilities, not encoding or retrieval, are the major source of differences in long-term memory during infancy (Bauer et al., 2007). Although much remains to be learned about infants' memory development, the rudimentary functions of explicit memory seem to be in place by six months of age. Nonetheless, learning during infancy must depend more on implicit than explicit memory.

Early Childhood

Although infants and preschoolers under the age of 5 can learn and remember events and information over relatively long periods of time, as older children and adults they seldom remember much autobiographical information from the first few years of life. This phenomenon is known as *infantile amnesia*. One hypothesis to account for the loss of what was once known is that the contexts of children's lives change dramatically over the years. Another account of this phenomenon is that episodic memory does not become functional until somewhere between 2 and 4 years of age (Tulving, 2002). The current consensus seems to hold that rudimentary episodic memory begins around the age of 3. Regardless of the exact onset, memory theorists do agree that semantic memory development must precede episodic memory development because many episodic operations rely on semantic memory structures (Tulving, 1993). For example, episodic memories cannot be encoded in an organized way without some generalized semantic knowledge of the world, such as a schema or script, to which they can be connected. Consequently, young children can learn facts about the world and acquire semantic knowledge, such as vocabulary, before they can consolidate and permanently store specific experiences (Temple & Richardson, 2006). Another reason for the slower development of episodic memory is that the hippocampus does not mature fully until the fifth year of life. In addition to lacking a fully functioning hippocampus, young children are handicapped by incomplete development of the frontal lobes. During early childhood, there are several memory weaknesses that can be attributed to limited frontal lobe functioning. For example, young children have great difficulty with source memory (remembering when, where, and with whom an event occurred). They also easily confuse imagined episodes with real events. Furthermore, their recollections are easily influenced by suggestions and misleading information. These weaknesses make young children especially vulnerable to distorted memories and false recollections, as has been documented in sexual abuse cases where adults were wrongfully accused by preschool-age children (Schacter, 1996). Poor memory strategy development can also be attributed to immature frontal lobes.

Despite childhood amnesia and the other memory challenges faced by pre-schoolers, there is substantial growth in long-term memory abilities and performance during the early childhood years. The progression is so rapid that it can be stated confidently that normal children have fully mature memory systems by 5 or 6 years of age. In addition to maturation of the necessary neurological structures, young children are developing knowledge and control of their memory functions. They are also learning the utility of basic memory strategies. In fact, continued improvement in their memory performance hinges primarily on the development and utilization of increasing effective memory strategies. Parents can nurture their child's refinement of memory functions, knowledge, and strategy use through social interactions focused on memory. For example, it has been shown that when mothers regularly engage in highly elaborative conversations, such as posing many questions while helping their children reminisce about past events, their children grow up to have stronger recall abilities (Ornstein, Grammer, & Coffman, 2010).

Elementary School Years

Improvements in memory performance over the school years seem dependent on the growing use of strategies. Children become more proficient in the use of memory strategies as they grow older. In early elementary, spontaneous use of memory strategies is unlikely and the strategies are limited to basic ones such as rote rehearsal. However, young children can use memory strategies effectively when they are directed to do so or when the materials elicit strategy use (Best & Ornstein, 1986). By sixth grade, spontaneity and sophistication have increased. For example, sixth graders frequently self-test, create first-letter mnemonics, and organize information categorically (Cox, Ornstein, Naus, Maxfield, & Zimler, 1989). The greatest gains in long-term memory performance and functions occur during the late elementary school years. Increased knowledge, more organized memory representations, and effective strategy usage combine to produce a major developmental improvement in long-term memory performance. Greater processing efficiency and expanding working memory resources also enhance long-term memory functions. Thus, by late elementary years, improvements in long-term memory functioning reflect changes in knowledge and strategies, not expansion in long-term memory capacity per se.

Adolescence

The typical adolescent uses a broader range of strategies and selects strategies that match the task or the content. The improvement in strategic functioning is related to corresponding development in metamemory and other executive functions. Adolescents understand forgetting and other memory processes well and are more accurate at predicting delayed recall. With the maturation of executive processes, resistance to proactive and retroactive interference also improves. In addition, adolescents' rapidly expanding knowledge base facilitates memory performance. Long-term memory performance improves because prior knowledge provides cognitive structures that facilitate the encoding, retention, and retrieval of additional information. That is, it is easier to remember information that is not completely new and can be connected with a large store of related knowledge. For example, experts in a domain recall more domain-specific information than novices. Not surprisingly, there is a diminished need for strategy application when there is expertise or an elaborated knowledge base (Schneider & Bjorklund, 1992). Despite their expanded knowledge base and greater awareness and strategy use, most adolescents will never discover some of the most effective memorization and study techniques. They also continue to use relatively ineffective, basic rehearsal methods, especially as default strategies.

Implicit Memory

Less is known about the development of implicit memory, except that it probably precedes development of explicit memory. Infants as young as 8 months display learning on tasks that do not require explicit remembering. Some aspects of implicit memory, such as priming, have been observed during the early preschool years. Implicit memory abilities appear to remain intact throughout life, even surviving dementia. Whereas normal age-related decreases in explicit memory test performance can reach 50% or more, aging has little or no affect on implicit memory test performance (Graf, 1990).

DEVELOPMENT OF METAMEMORY AND EFFECTIVE STRATEGIES

As part of their theory of mind, most children and adolescents believe they understand memory and how it works. After all, human memory seems simple enough. Sometimes people remember events and information; sometimes they don't. Most individuals know other facts about memory functioning: Memories become stronger with repetition, they often are incomplete, and they fade over time. Normal school-age children also know that they can influence memory through the learning methods they employ and the mental searching they engage in when something is not automatically recalled. Despite their knowledge about memory functioning, children and adolescents frequently have misconceptions; for example, they might believe that the desire to remember something will significantly influence recall. How well children and adolescents understand memory functions, their own memory capabilities, and how to manage their memories has a significant impact on their memory performance and academic learning (Brown & Sproson, 1987; O'Conner, Moulin, & Cohen, 2008). This type of knowledge and regulation is known as metamemory.

Metamemory, a type of metacognition, refers to knowledge about and regulation of memory. Metamemory is comprised of beliefs, knowledge, awareness, and regulation components. For example, it includes the individual's knowledge of the contents of his or her memory and the beliefs regarding the probability of later recalling newly acquired information. What children and adolescents factually know about their own memory functioning is referred to as *declarative metamemory*. This type of knowledge is explicit and includes beliefs and knowledge concerning memory types, capacities, functions, limitations, and development (Pierce & Lange, 2000). The self-awareness aspect of declarative metamemory includes self-efficacy, which consists of judgments about one's abilities. Accurate self-efficacy judgments depend on understanding the difficulty level of various memory tasks and one's ability in relation to those tasks. Self-efficacy influences confidence and degree of effort applied to the learning task at hand. Another aspect of declarative metamemory is knowledge of memory strategies. Strategy knowledge includes knowing how to perform a strategy, as well as the range of tasks that a strategy applies to. Knowledge about specific strategies is an important component of metamemory (Flavell, 1979) because it is required for effective strategy deployment (Pressley, Borkowski, & O'Sullivan, 1984). In essence, declarative metamemory is the individual's personalized interpretation of how memory works.

In contrast, *procedural metamemory* refers to self-monitoring and self-regulation activities while solving memory problems (Wang & Richarde, 1987). In addition to monitoring learning, procedural metamemory includes self-assessments known as *judgments of learning*, which are appraisals of how well one has learned material. Self-regulatory functions include selecting and implementing a strategy, monitoring its effectiveness, and modifying the approach as needed. In addition to declarative and procedural components, metamemory includes *conditional metamemory*, such as knowing when, where, and why to use a strategy. For example, selecting an appropriate strategy for the task at hand is an element of conditional metamemory. When conditional knowledge is sufficient, the individual will realize the connection between strategy deployment and successful performance. That is, the individual will recognize the efficacy of the strategy for a particular task. Essentially, metamemory is needed to consciously initiate, monitor, and control memory processes and strategies.

The ability to self-monitor and predict future memory performance is one of the key components of metamemory. These personal assessments of learning and future recall are known as *judgments of learning*. As the term implies, judgments of learning refer to an individual's beliefs about how well information has been learned and how well he or she will later recall it. Typically, students based their judgments of learning on how easily items are mastered or how quickly items can be retrieved during self-testing (Koriat, 2008). In fact, both behaviors are positively correlated with recall. Nevertheless, judgments of learning and long-term recall tend to be very inaccurate, especially among children under age 10 and among adolescents with poorly developed metamemory (Son, 2005). Even average and mature students commonly overpredict their delayed recall after they have studied material. The correlations between their predications and performance are usually around .25 (Rawson &

Dunlosky, 2007). Inaccurate predictions of future performance are often derived from an overly simplified conceptualization of memory. That is, students are often fooled by the fluency or ease with which they can retrieve information in the short-term, not realizing that long-term retrieval will be more challenging (Benjamin, Bjork, & Schwartz, 1998). Consequently, the accuracy of judgments of learning is significantly improved when students make their judgments after delayed recall rather than after immediate recall (Nelson & Dunlosky, 1992). Accuracy is also improved when students base their self-assessments on how well they could actually retrieve the information versus how familiar the content feels when they simply review it (Rawson & Dunlosky). Accurate judgments of learning are critical because they are used to determine the allocation of study time. Youth with well-developed metamemory and more accurate judgments of learning differently allocate their study time between easy and difficult items, spending more time on difficult items (Mazzoni, Cornoldi, & Marchitelli, 1990). However, even when they allocate more time to studying difficult content, the additional study time is usually not enough to make a difference (Mazzoni et al., 1990). Judgments of learning are also poor when students are unsure of the correctness of their responses, a fact that illustrates the importance of corrective feedback.

Metamemory judgment also comes into play during retrieval, such as evaluating the accuracy of retrieved information or deciding whether to continue or terminate a search (Koriat & Goldsmith, 1996). Similar to their erroneous predictions, children generally overestimate the accuracy of the information they retrieve (Metcalfe, 2000). The ease with which a potential response comes to mind contributes to the confidence in its accuracy and gives rise to a subjective feeling of knowing. However, ease of retrieval can be misleading. For example, recent exposure to erroneous facts will increase the speed at which they are retrieved even though they are untrue (Kelley & Lindsay, 1993). Consequently, it is important to prevent and reduce errors during learning, and to provide immediate corrective feedback when a student responds incorrectly. Even the processing of corrective feedback is influenced by metamemory. The subjective certainty of whether or not a response is correct determines how much attention is paid to corrective feedback. When individuals are highly confident of the correctness of a response and it turns out to be erroneous, they pay much more attention to the feedback (Butterfield & Metcalfe, 2001). Regarding the persistence of searching, knowing what is known is an important metamemory variable because it influences the persistence and effectiveness of search strategies. When an individual believes that he or she knows the sought-after information, more effort will be invested in trying to retrieve that knowledge.

Metamemory is a crucial component of memory development and functioning. It is instrumental in the growth of explicit memory skills and performance. An adequate level of metamemory development is essential for successful memory performance, especially when learners encounter difficult or novel memorization tasks (Cavanaugh & Poon, 1989; Pressley et al., 1984). In fact, level of metamemory development may be the best predictor of memory performance. Among children and adolescents, those with better metamemory remember more information when they study. Metamemory level even predicts memory performance better than general intelligence (Kurtz et al., 1982). A meta-analysis containing 60 studies reported a moderately strong relationship (an overall correlation of .41) between children's metamemory and their effective memory behaviors (Schneider & Pressley, 1997). Metamemory also has a positive relationship with learning (Cull & Zechmeister, 1994). In a study by Emilien et al. (2004), the correlations between metamemory measures and actual performance on tests of learning ranged from .20 to .30. Of course, a well-developed metamemory that effectively manages memory processes does not ensure long-term retention of information. Although well-developed metamemory is a cornerstone of successful memory performance, it cannot fully compensate for impairments that may exist in various memory systems and processes. Motivation and attribution variables also may come into play. Well-developed metamemory and strategic knowledge is ineffectual if lack of motivation or erroneous attributions interfere with applications of strategies. In such instances, memory performance will suffer because the individual is not effectively utilizing strategies that have been acquired, a condition known as a production deficiency.

Metamemory Development

During the preschool years, a child's understanding of memory develops by leaps and bounds. Although few 3-year-olds are aware that memory endures over time, most 4- or 5-year-olds have a theory of long-term memory and understand the concept of forgetting over time. Also, 4-year-old children have some idea that memorization is an active process requiring deliberate effort (Sodian, Schneider, & Perlmutter, 1986). Yet, some of their early childhood naïve beliefs remain: They believe that memory reflects reality (O'Sullivan & Howe, 1998); that interest alone has a positive effect on memory (O'Sullivan, 1997); and that the desire to remember by itself will improve recall. Thus, it appears that preschoolers and young school-age children often have more misconceptions about memory than accurate beliefs. Unfortunately, naïve beliefs can have powerful influence on memory behavior and performance. By age 6, children are aware that retention of events can be inaccurate, but they continue to overestimate their delayed recall. Despite their overconfidence, first graders will allocate more study time to materials that are judged more difficult to learn. By age 8, children are more realistic about their memory capabilities; for example, they accurately predict that their forgetting will increase as the retention interval increases. Accordingly, 8-year-olds will spontaneously lengthen their study time if they know there will be a long retention interval prior to a test. By middle school, children have a more in-depth understanding of the intricacies of memory. For example, they are aware that memory performance varies across occasions, types of material, and individuals (Kreutzer, Leonard, & Flavell, 1975). Consequently, middle school children typically realize that more time should be spent studying items that are difficult to learn. During adolescence, learners acquire and hone more sophisticated strategies, such as creating meaningful connections among superficially related items. Adolescents also use strategies more flexibly, and their monitoring of memory performance continues to improve. Although 18-year-olds know more about memory and memory strategies than they did as children, they typically enter adulthood possessing only a fraction of the strategies and metamemory that they could possess. For instance, even adults with normal metamemory tend to over-estimate their delayed recall and will terminate study prematurely. In summary, metamemorial knowledge, effective regulation, and accuracy of metamemorial judgments improve with age. Furthermore, there is an increasing use of memory strategies and the variety of memory strategies employed (Beuhring & Kee, 1987).

Strategy Development

As metamemory develops, there is a corresponding growth in the acquisition and application of effective memory strategies. The level of metamemory development predicts the use of more advanced strategies; for example, children with substantial metamemories recognize that elaborative rehearsal is a more effective strategy than rote repetition (Kurtz, Reid, Borkowski, & Cavanaugh, 1982). Greater utilization of effective strategies not only enhances performance on specific tasks but accounts for much of general memory development, as growth in strategy knowledge and use is positively correlated with memory development (Harris, 1996). The relationship between strategic behavior and recall is very strong; for instance, Schneider (2010) reported a correlation of .81. The influence of strategy usage on memory develop-ment is so pervasive that it accounts for most of the improvement in memory performance after age 6. Unfortunately, some children and adolescents have poorly developed metamemory and consequently make little use of some important and powerful memory strategies (Schneider, 2000).

Strategy knowledge and application grow dramatically once children enter school. Not surprisingly, the adoption and proficient use of many memory strategies seems to be a byproduct of academic learning demands (Ornstein et al., 2010). Formal schooling (even without direct instruction in memory strategies) has a tremendous influence on strategy acquisition and utilization because academic learning places heavy demands on memorization and extended recall. Nonetheless, students' memory strategies mainly consist of those that are discovered or acquired naturally. Consequently, many children and adolescents have little or no knowledge of some important memory strategies despite the continual scholastic need to deploy effective memory strategies. Furthermore, untrained children and adolescents often reject time-tested strategies that could quickly produce results. Thus, formal instruction in memory strategies, something that seldom occurs in school, would benefit most students (see Chapter 8).

There seems to be a developmental progression in competent strategy use from early childhood through adolescence. Children begin to use memory strategies earlier than previously thought; even 2- to 3-year-olds appear to use rudimentary memory strategies (Miller & Seier, 1994). By the time they enter school most children know how to use one or more basic strategies, such as rote rehearsal. However, the deliberate use of strategies by young children only occurs under circumstances that encourage such use. For instance, young children will use a strategy when the materials fit the method well or when instructions prompt its use (Waters & Kunnmann, 2010). Younger children are also more likely to spontaneously employ a strategy when under lighter cognitive load conditions. For instance, young children seldom employ memory strategies during challenging learning conditions that place a heavy cognitive load on working memory. Between 6 and 12 years of age, children progress from simple to complex strategies, with some basic strategies being replaced by more intricate, sophisticated strategies that allow for more efficient encoding and retrieval. By the age of 10, children have progressed from rehearsing one item at a time to cumulative rehearsal. By fourth grade, they are typically using a semantic clustering strategy to organize many items that need to be memorized. Late elementary children may begin using an elaboration strategy but elaboration is not widely used until adolescence (Pressley & Schneider, 1997). There is also substantial development of retrieval strategies during the elementary years, with systematic use of retrieval cues occurring by 8 to 11 years of age. As strategy development continues into adolescence, less effective strategies compete with new, more effective ones until the ineffective strategies are dropped.

Another perspective on strategy development during the school years is to view it as a transition from passive to active strategy use. For instance, Pressley (1982) describes a study in which the percentage of children using only a passive repetition strategy declined from 53% at the fifth-grade level to 6% at the ninth-grade level, while those using an active elaboration strategy increased from 47% at the fifth-grade level to 94% at the ninth-grade level. The transition to more sophisticated strategies is important because at all age levels elaboration users outperform those who use repetition only. As children learn to proficiently use active, complex, and effective strategies their memory performance improves; for instance, Kron-Sperl, Schneider, and Hasselhorn (2008), reported a 30% improvement on memory performance tasks in children between the ages of 8 and 12. Interestingly, for many normal children the learning and adoption of a new strategy is not a gradual process but rather an abrupt transition. For instance, Ornstein et al. (2010) review a longitudinal study in which 80% of the children exhibited a pattern of an all-or-none transition from the nonuse of an organizational strategy to complete use. Of course, the speed of transition may depend on the complexity of the strategy and the cognitive resources available to the individual.

As children develop, they acquire more strategies and learn to use their repertoire in an integrated fashion. In a longitudinal study of children's development of memory strategies, Kron-Sperl et al. (2008) found that German children begin to effectively apply multiple strategies at age 8, even performing more than one memory strategy at a time. By the end of elementary school, children can integrate and simultaneously perform several strategies, such as sorting, rehearsal, and elaboration. The German longitudinal study also discovered that once encountered, children rapidly acquire individual strategies and add them to their repertoire, typically within a six-month interval. Over time, multiple-strategy users become more competent at integrating strategies and their performance exceeds that of single-strategy users. The development of multiple-strategy utilization parallels that of working memory capacity, as children with greater working memory capacity are more successful at integrating multiple strategies.

Discovering a strategy or learning to use a strategy does not guarantee successful application of the strategy or improved memory performance. Like other skills, there is a learning curve with strategies; proficient strategy use takes time. Until the strategy is mastered, its use may not benefit performance. Fortunately, children typically persevere during the ineffectual acquisition stage. Perhaps, they persevere because they are naïve. That is, children continue to use a strategy that is not making an immediate difference because they overestimate its effectiveness. Another possibility is that children persist at using an ineffectual strategy because they have been taught that effort makes a difference (O'Sullivan, 1997). Their naïve perseverance may be a developmental advantage because it allows time for them to master the strategy and increase its efficacy. After there have been ample opportunities to learn and apply a strategy, performance problems may continue because children have not learned how to use the strategy effectively or they use it infrequently.

Failure to use known strategies effectively or at all is referred to as a *production deficiency* or a *utilization deficiency*. A production or utilization deficiency occurs when a child or adolescent fails to apply a strategy that he or she knows how to use. The term also applies to children spontaneously engaging in a new strategy even though use of the strategy results in little or no improvement in their memory performance (Bjorklund, 1997). Both of these occurrences are natural phases in the course of strategy acquisition and development. When the deficiencies persist, they are most likely the result of poorly developed strategy knowledge from a metamemory perspective. That is, the child does not know when, where, or why to use the strategy even when he or she knows how. Also, the child may not understand how particular strategies match up with his or her memory strengths and weaknesses and the task at hand. Another reason for the occurrence of a utilization deficiency is that the application of a strategy may exhaust the child's working memory resources, leaving little processing capacity for actually memorizing the material or performing metamemory monitoring (Kron-Sperl et al., 2008). Furthermore, production deficiencies may result from difficulty integrating strategies or from the continued use of ineffective strategies. Thus, the knowledge and ability to perform a strategy does not mean that the strategy will be used proficiently.

FUNDAMENTALS OF MEMORY DEVELOPMENT

Much is known about the developmental progression of long-term memory functions. Understanding memory development allows psychologists and educators to set realistic expectations for student performance and design appropriate interventions and instruction. The following list summarizes some essential aspects of memory development.

1. Implicit memory develops before explicit memory, and implicit memory is generally impervious to injury and degeneration. Whereas implicit memory development is automatic, explicit memory development is influenced by conscious cognitive factors such as metamemory.
2. Long-term retention of episodic memories seems to require an established semantic memory system, as indicated by infantile amnesia.
3. Although children may process information qualitatively different than how adults process it, their memory structures and functions appear to be equivalent to those of adults by 6 years of age (Williams, Conway, & Cohen, 2008).
4. After the elementary school years, most improvement in long-term memory performance is due to an expanding knowledge base and more effective utilization of sophisticated memory strategies.
5. The growth of sophisticated memory strategies seems driven by environmental requirements rather than a natural developmental progression. Thus, the adoption and proficient use of many memory strategies seem to be a byproduct of academic learning demands.
6. As metamemory develops, judgments of learning and delayed recall become more accurate. Children with immature metamemory usually overestimate their future performance because they base their estimates on the ease of immediate recall.
7. Metamemory is more than self-awareness of one's memory functions and strengths and weaknesses. It also includes monitoring and regulation of strategic behaviors, as well as in-depth knowledge of memory strategies and their efficacy.
8. The level of metamemory is highly related with effective strategic behavior and memory performance. When metamemory is poorly developed, strategy production and utilization deficiencies are likely to exist.
9. There are several related cognitive processes that interact with and support memory processing. Consequently, memory performance improves along with the development of interrelated processes.

RELATED COGNITIVE PROCESSES

Improvement in long-term memory performance relies on more than the development of metamemory, strategies, and long-term memory processes, such as encoding and retrieval. Advances in long-term memory functioning also correspond with development in several related cognitive functions, such as the maturation of reasoning that occurs during early adolescence. Some cognitive processes are more closely linked with certain types of memory systems, especially those within the same domains. Individuals must first be able to adequately process information in a given modality or domain before they can encode and store memories in that domain. For example, visuospatial processing is required to encode and store visuospatial memories, and phonological, linguistic, and semantic processing is required to acquire and store verbal memories. In addition to modality-specific processes, broad cognitive functions such as attention and executive processes support explicit memory systems. Despite the strong relations memory has with other cognitive abilities, normal cognitive development and attainment of average processing capabilities do not ensure proficient memory functioning. It seems that normal development of related cognitive processes is a necessary but insufficient condition for effective memory functioning. Also, the relationship between memory systems and processes is frequently reciprocal; for example, the building of verbal abilities depends on semantic memory structures. An obvious implication for assessment is that related cognitive processes should be evaluated whenever there is a memory performance problem, as impairment in a related cognitive process may underlie the memory problem. (See Chapter 2 for a discussion of relationships among short-term, working, and long-term memory.)

General Intelligence

General intelligence, which is usually equated with a full scale or composite IQ score, is comprised of several cognitive and intellectual factors, with verbal and reasoning abilities traditionally contributing the most. General intelligence is highly predictive of long-term memory performance, and consequently IQ can justifiably be used to determine the presence of intra-individual memory weaknesses and strengths. Some data indicative of the strong relationships between Full Scale IQ and various types of memory are the correlations between the *Wechsler Adult Intelligence Scale-Fourth Edition* (WAIS®-IV; Wechsler, 2008) and the *Wechsler Memory Scale-Fourth Edition* (WMS®-IV; Wechsler, 2009). (Both scales are normed for individuals 16 years of age and older.) For instance, the correlation between the WAIS-IV Full Scale IQ and the WMS-IV Delayed Memory Index is .61 (see Table 3.1), which means that approximately 37% of the variance in delayed memory is accounted for by full scale IQ. Although this is a strong relationship, several cognitive and intellectual factors have correlations in the same range. The relationship between intelligence and long-term memory is higher in younger children than in older children (Cohen, 1997) because growth in strategy use mostly accounts for improved memory performance in late childhood and early adolescence. However, the acquisition and utilization of strategies is also related to intelligence, as children and adolescents with higher cognitive abilities tend to use strategies more than those with lower abilities. The influence of intelligence declines in adulthood because extensive prior knowledge or expertise has more influence on specific memory performance than general

Table 3.1   Correlations between WAIS®-IV and WMS®-IV factors

	WAIS®-IV Composites*				
	VCI	PRI	WMI	PSI	FSIQ
WMS®-IV Indexes					
Auditory Memory	.53	.44	.50	.40	.57
Visual Memory	.44	.62	.47	.45	.61
Delayed Memory	.51	.55	.51	.44	.61

Source: Wechsler, 2009, p. 75

*WAIS-IV abbreviations: VCI = Verbal Comprehension Index, PRI = Perceptual Reasoning Index, WMI = Working Memory Index, PSI = Processing Speed Index, FSIQ = Full Scale Intelligence Quotient

intellectual ability (Pressley & Schneider, 1997). Despite their strong relationship, the relative independence of intelligence and memory is demonstrated by individuals with acquired amnesia who retain their intellectual functions (O'Conner & Verfaellie, 2004).

Attention

Attentional control, along with inhibition, is a crucial component of information processing and effective memory functioning. Attention can be divided into several subtypes: selective, sustained, focused, and divided. Of the different memory processes, encoding is the most closely related with attention. All aspects of attentional control are necessary for successful explicit memory encoding, but divided attention ability may be the best marker. The inability to effectively divide attention results in poor encoding of important information because the individual is unable to inhibit less important information. Accordingly, the long-term memory difficulties of children with attention deficits, such as those with ADHD, usually originate with poor encoding due to poor attentional control. When there is poor attentional control, short-term and working memory performance also will be affected. If the examinee's performance on phonological short-term memory and verbal working memory tasks is normal, the possibility of attention problems influencing long-term memory is less likely. Interestingly, those with ADHD are more likely to have problems with visuospatial long-term memory than with verbal long-term memory. For instance, the Brown ADD Scales Total Score (Brown, 1996) has a correlation of .54 with the WMS-IV Visual Memory Index but a correlation of only .22 with the Auditory Memory Index (Wechsler, 2009). (See Chapter 2 for more discussion on the role of attention in memory.)

Verbal Abilities and Language Development

Verbal abilities and language development are essential for verbal memory encoding, storage, and recall. A child with poor receptive language ability will have difficulty comprehending and consequently may not link incoming information with related knowledge. A child with poor language expression may have encoded information adequately but perform poorly when asked to recall the material verbally (Hood & Rankin, 2005). As expected, general verbal abilities, as measured by IQ tests, have a moderately strong relationship with verbal long-term memory (see Table 3.1). This is expected because verbal abilities, such as vocabulary development, depend on semantic memory storage. At times, a verbal long-term recall score may be unrelated to an individual's verbal ability score. In such instances, the difference can be attributed to the fact that most conventional verbal memory scales are tapping episodic rather than semantic memory.

Visuospatial and Auditory Processing

Visuospatial processing is the ability to perceive, analyze, synthesize, manipulate, locate, and transform visual patterns and images, including those generated internally. The visual component relates to identification of objects, and the spatial aspect is related to the location and movement of objects. Auditory processing is the ability to perceive, analyze, synthesize, and discriminate auditory stimuli, such as the phonemes used to compose words. As discussed earlier, modality-specific information is thought to be stored in the same brain regions that sense, perceive, and process it. As predicted, verbal long-term memory has a strong relationship with auditory processing, and visuospatial memory has a strong relationship with visuospatial processing. For instance, the Perceptual Reasoning Index of the WAIS-IV, which relies on visuospatial processing, is highly correlated (.62) with the Visual Memory Index of the WMS-IV.

Fluid Reasoning

Fluid reasoning, a contemporary term for inductive and deductive reasoning, is the ability to reason and solve problems, especially when confronted with novel tasks. It is considered to be one of the primary intellectual factors (Carroll, 1993), if not the essence of what is considered general intelligence. Like executive processing, with which it is intertwined, fluid reasoning does not mature until early adolescence. Several studies have documented the strong relationship between fluid reasoning and working memory capacity. For instance, Kane and Engle (2002) report correlations of .6 to .8 between fluid reasoning and working memory span. Fluid reasoning is also highly related with long-term memory content and functions. Higher level fluid reasoning draws from the long-term memory storehouse of concepts and relations. In exchange, it facilitates memory performance by evaluating the accuracy of retrieved information and mediating the reconstruction of incomplete memories. Furthermore, it is integral to advanced memory strategies, such as elaborative rehearsal and categorical organization.

Executive Functions

Executive functions, performed by the prefrontal cortex, undoubtedly have a strong connection with long-term memory functioning. Executive processes mainly become engaged when there are challenges during encoding and retrieval. Although automated encoding of familiar material does not require executive resources, encoding of novel or challenging material does. For instance, encoding of unstructured material seems to be more difficult for individuals with executive dysfunctions (Tremont, Halpert, Javorsky, & Stern, 2000). During retrieval, executive processes monitor, evaluate, and verify activated representations. Executive processes also became involved with conducting a search for information that is not automatically recalled. Regarding memory systems, executive functioning seems to be more involved with visual memory than verbal (Busch et al., 2005). Also, executive dysfunctions have been associated with difficulties in remembering contextual details and discriminating the source of information (Simons & Spiers, 2003). Finally, the monitoring and regulation of memory strategies are executive functions. In particular, the application of sophisticated strategies requires adequate executive abilities. Because executive processes mature in later childhood and early adolescence, growth in acquisition and application of memory strategies may be restrained until there is adequate executive processing development.

Processing Speed

In general, processing speed refers to how quickly information moves through the information processing system and how efficiently simple cognitive tasks are executed over a sustained period of time. Processing speed is typically measured with tasks requiring an individual to perform overlearned procedures that require little reasoning or higher level processing. Because processing speed is integrally related with encoding and retrieval, it is sometimes difficult to separate from memory processing. For instance, slow retrieval speed or retrieval fluency may be the result of slow general processing speed rather than impaired search procedures.

MEMORY DYSFUNCTION

Like other cognitive dysfunctions, long-term memory problems lie along a continuum from mild to severe. So, when is a long-term memory "problem" serious enough to warrant assessment and intervention? The perspective taken in this book is that a memory problem should be addressed when it is serious enough to impede academic learning or create significant challenges in daily life. In a scholastic environment, this happens when a memory problem reduces learning

---

Table 3.2 *DSM-IV* **diagnostic criteria for amnesia due to a general medical condition**

A. The development of memory impairment as manifested by impairment in the ability to learn new information or the inability to recall previously learned information.

B. The memory disturbance causes significant impairment in social or occupational functioning and represents a significant decline from a previous level of functioning.

C. The memory disturbance does not occur exclusively during the course of a delirium or a dementia.

D. There is evidence from the history, physical examination, or laboratory findings that the disturbance is the direct physiological consequence of a general medical condition (including physical trauma).

Reprinted with permission from the *Diagnostic and Statistical Manual of Mental Disorders*, Text Revision, Fourth Edition, (Copyright 2000), American Psychiatric Association.

and retention of information, such that a student with otherwise normal intellectual abilities and learning potential is underachieving. A prime example would be a student who engages in seemingly effective learning and study behaviors but consistently can't remember information when tested in class. When memory is assessed, such a student may display an intra-individual weakness in memory, whereby overall cognitive or intellectual ability is significantly higher than some aspect of memory functioning. In such cases there may have been an underlying neurological impairment from early in life, an impairment may have been acquired through injury or illness, or crucial elements of effective memory functioning are developmentally delayed. When it comes to memory problems and dysfunctions there are more questions than answers because unlike other disorders and impairments there are no official childhood memory disorders. Although researchers and clinicians frequently refer to "memory disorders" in children, the term is usually applied in a loose, generic sense. Amnesia is the only memory disorder found in the *Diagnostic and Statistical Manual of Mental Disorders* (*DSM-IV*; American Psychiatric Association, 1994) and its criteria apply more to adults than children (see Table 3.2).

In this text several terms are used when referring to memory problems. Here are the definitions for each:

- Dysfunction—any impairment, disturbance, or deficiency in behavior or functioning.
- Impairment—any departure from the body's typical physiological structure or psychological functioning.
- Disorder—a group of symptoms involving abnormal behaviors or a disruption in physiological functioning.
- Deficiency—a lack or shortage of something, such as a lack of a skill, a lack of a biological process, or a lack of resources that enable specific functions and actions to be performed.
- Weakness—lacking the ability to function normally or fully. From an assessment perspective, a weakness can be either normative or ipsative. A

normative weakness is a skill or ability that is below average. An ipsative weakness is a relative, intra-individual weakness that is demonstrated by a memory test score that is significantly lower than the mean of the individual's other cognitive processes.

■ Deficit—a significant lack or shortage of something. From the assessment perspective in this text, a deficit occurs when the individual has both a normative weakness and an ipsative weakness.

Amnesia

Amnesia is the most severe type of memory loss and dysfunction that can occur. In extreme cases, the impairment is so global that it is readily observed. Amnesic syndrome is characterized (see Table 3.3) by a severe deficit in explicit long-term memory, normal short-term memory abilities, and retention of general intelligence, language functions, and implicit memory (Brizzolara, Casalini, Montanaro, & Posteraro, 2003). Individuals with amnesic syndrome are impaired in their ability to learn new information and/or to recall previously learned information or past events. There are two forms of amnesia: anterograde and retrograde. Anterograde amnesia is the inability to acquire new facts and events while being able to retrieve (at least partially) previously acquired information. Retrograde amnesia refers to the inability to retrieve some previously learned information while retaining the ability to acquire new information. In some cases, individuals suffer from both types. With retrograde amnesia, more recently formed memories are more likely to be lost than remote memories (Wixted, 2004), and semantic memories, especially overlearned ones, are more likely to be preserved than episodic memories. For example, the amnesiac may still recall that a dog is an animal but have no recollection of the dog he or she once owned. Anterograde amnesia usually involves some degree of retrograde loss. Also, anterograde amnesia is usually global, in that all types of explicit memory (i.e., verbal or visuospatial) are affected. There are permanent and transient forms of amnesia. In cases of head injury, amnesia may be permanent or temporary and partial recovery may occur (see Chapter 4).

Table 3.3   General characteristics of amnesia

■ Memory impairment can be enduring.
■ Episodic information is more affected than semantic.
■ Memory impairment is exacerbated by distraction.
■ Memory impairment is not limited to one sensory modality.
■ Forgetting occurs more quickly.
■ Procedural and other implicit memories are spared.
■ Short-term memory is spared.
■ Intelligence is unaffected.

Individuals with amnesia typically retain their semantic memories acquired before the onset of the amnesia but have great difficulty adding new information to their semantic memory knowledge base (Baddeley, Vargha-Khadem, & Mishkin, 2001). The complete loss of episodic memory functions may be at least partially to blame because retention of repeated episodes is necessary for the accrual of semantic memories and the recall of episodic content facilitates semantic retrieval. The inability to retain new information is not due to impairments in short-term memory or working memory. Individuals with amnesia usually have normal performance on short-term memory and working memory tasks (O'Conner & Verfaellie, 2004). Also, Full Scale IQ and Verbal IQ typically remain at their pre-amnesic levels, even when the memory impairment is global. Another characteristic of amnesia is preserved implicit memory in the presence of a marked decline in explicit memory functioning. Several case studies have demonstrated that individuals with anterograde amnesia can still acquire and express new implicit memories even though they have no conscious recollection of ever having learned the skill or information.

Amnesia results from damage to the hippocampus and medial temporal lobes. These lesions are usually acquired as the result of infectious diseases, substance abuse, head trauma, or other medical conditions. Examples of medical conditions include herpes simplex encephalitis, anoxia, stroke, and aneurysm (see Chapter 4 for more examples). Evidence from many neuropsychological case studies clearly documents that the memory dysfunctions associated with amnesia lie with the failure to encode, consolidate, and retain information, not with retrieval (e.g., Haist et al., 1992). The evidence comes from comparing amnesiacs' recall and recognition. Their recognition memory for recent learning is typically no better than uncued recall (Baddeley et al., 2001), indicating that enduring memories are not being formed. The only exceptions to this finding are cases where recall is impaired by frontal lobe lesions instead of hippocampal damage (Haist et al., 1992). Furthermore, in cases of permanent retrograde amnesia, consolidated episodic and semantic memories that were accessible in the past can no longer be retrieved by any means. That is, permanent retrograde amnesia is not a retrieval problem; the information is simply no longer available.

Table 3.4   Long-term memory components and processes that may be impaired

Explicit	Implicit
Verbal	Visuospatial
Episodic	Semantic
Encoding	Consolidation
Storage	Retrieval
Metamemory	Strategic

Specific Memory Dysfunctions

Many memory impairments are not severe enough to be classified as amnesia but nonetheless cause dysfunction in at least one dimension of memory. Although memory systems, subtypes, and processes are all interrelated, they can be affected differently. Memory impairments may occur in any of the memory subtypes and processes discussed in Chapter 2. Deficits in any one aspect of memory may underlie observed memory dysfunctions. Of course, impairment in one of the short-term or working memory components may also underlie memory dysfunctions. However, these are only minimally addressed in this book, as they are covered in depth in a companion volume (see Dehn, 2008). For a list of potential specific long-term memory dysfunctions, see Table 3.4. The perspective of this book is that an effort should be made to identify specific dysfunctional memory systems and processes in order to understand how the impairments are impacting learning and memory. Such identification will facilitate the selection and design of interventions that are likely to improve the memory functioning of affected individuals.

4 Risk Factors for Memory Impairments

"Sarah," who had just turned 16, was playing in a spring soccer match when she was accidently kicked in the forehead. Although she did not lose consciousness, she did "see stars" and feel dizzy. Sarah was allowed to remain in the game for a few minutes longer until it was obvious that she was disorganized and off balance. That same afternoon the school's sports trainer evaluated Sarah and concluded that she had a concussion. She was suffering from dizziness, a severe headache, fatigue, and nausea. Later that evening Sarah went to a hospital emergency room where a brain scan did not reveal any abnormalities, but a doctor advised her to stay home from school and avoid reading and bright overhead lights. At home the next day, she slept all day. Sarah returned to school after two days, but her headaches, fatigue, and bouts of dizziness continued for a few weeks. Sarah was suffering from the effects of mild traumatic brain injury, or what is more commonly referred to as post-concussion syndrome.

During the first week following the concussion, it was apparent to Sarah's parents that she was having memory problems. Sarah was having difficulty recalling episodic events; for example, she had very little recollection of the game in which she was injured. She also was having difficulty remembering information she studied for school, especially from day-to-day. Moreover, she could not remember some well-known semantic information and some procedures that she had known prior to the head injury, such as Spanish vocabulary, multiplication procedures, and the combination to her school locker. These performance problems indicated that Sarah was experiencing some mild posttraumatic amnesia. Sarah was frustrated and frightened, but, luckily, the vocabulary and multiplication skills came back after a few days, and Sarah relearned her locker combination. After a week, Sarah was performing normally in her school courses and denied any ongoing memory problems, even though her physical symptoms persisted. However, her parents observed some ongoing memory problems and became concerned enough to take Sarah to a psychologist for memory testing. By the time the memory testing was conducted, a month had elapsed since the injury and the psychologist did not expect to find any evidence of ongoing memory problems. However, the memory assessment revealed that, whereas Sarah's verbal memory was average, her visuospatial memory, both short- and long-term, was well below average, and her visuospatial working memory was at the 1st percentile. Fortunately, some cognitive testing had been conducted with Sarah only a few months before, providing some indications of pre-injury memory functioning. When current test results were compared with prior testing, it appeared that Sarah had experienced significant declines in verbal working memory and visuospatial memory (see Chapter 9 for more assessment details on this case). The case of Sarah illustrates how a concussion (mild head trauma) incurred during a school sporting event can cause temporary, if not persistent, problems with memory functions. Because of Sarah's concussion, knowledgeable educators and professionals would expect Sarah to have some temporary memory dysfunctions and other post-concussion symptoms. However, how many educators, psychologists, and related professionals would be concerned about the potential of persistent memory problems after the physical symptoms disappear?

When Sarah suffered a mild traumatic brain injury she joined the ranks of students who are at-risk for debilitating, chronic memory problems and impairments. There are numerous behaviors, injuries, medical conditions, developmental disabilities, and mental disorders that put children and adolescents at-risk for memory problems, if not actual memory impairments. Although some memory impairments are transitory, the majority are enduring. Thus, the purpose of this chapter is to make educators and psychologists aware of the numerous childhood diseases, disorders, and other conditions that can cause memory impairments or are associated with memory impairments. Unfortunately, it is unknown as to how many of these at-risk students have or will acquire memory deficits that will impede their learning and academic progress, but an awareness of the risk factors will increase the likelihood that more students with memory problems will be properly identified. So often memory dysfunctions are misattributed to laziness, stupidity, poor instruction, and other factors when the actual underlying problem is a memory impairment. The exact number of children and adolescents suffering from memory impairments is unknown, but the number is almost certainly higher than most educators and professionals would estimate. By some estimates (e.g., Alloway & Gathercole, 2006), approximately 10% of the school-aged population suffers from deficits in short-term or working memory alone. In a screening conducted in the United Kingdom, 3.4 to 4.3% of a sample of 309 children, 8 to 12 years of age, were found to have significant memory problems that were independent from intelligence level (Temple, 2004). Even 4% is a number that warrants serious consideration. Therefore, educators, psychologists, and related practitioners who encounter children and adolescents with a history including any of the conditions reviewed in this chapter should consider a referral for a memory evaluation when the child or adolescent is experiencing learning difficulties.

Memory impairments can be developmental or acquired (Temple, 2004). Developmental impairments are thought to be present from birth. In such cases, the child has never developed average memory skills and functioning but the impairment may not become manifest until learning and memory challenges arise. Acquired impairments occur in an infant, child, or adolescent who has had normally developing memory skills until an injury, disease, or some other medical condition affects memory development or functioning. Acquired memory problems are caused by damage to one or more of the brain regions associated with memory—the frontal lobes, medial temporal lobe, hippocampus, amygdala, or thalamus. Such damage may result from injury, inflammation, atrophy, hemorrhage, surgery, epilepsy, anoxia, and several other causes. There are also psychological causes, such as depression and anxiety.

When children and adolescents experience memory problems, there is almost always an anatomical basis. From a neurobiological perspective, the majority of the conditions discussed in this chapter have one thing in common—a damaged hippocampus or medial temporal lobe (see Chapter 3). Any injury or disease that impacts the brain makes it highly probable that memory structures in the brain, especially the vulnerable hippocampus, will suffer damage. Sometimes, the damage suffered is not in the hippocampus but in other brain regions that are involved with information processing. For example, damage to the frontal lobes can interfere with encoding and retrieval of information. When damage is restricted to the hippocampus, the medial temporal lobes and other brain regions that are unaffected may continue to support aspects of memory functioning that the hippocampus no longer provides. However, evidence of brain plasticity for memory functions is limited. The end result of insults to different brain structures and various degrees of hippocampal atrophy is that there are many different ways that memory impairments can be expressed (see Table 4.1 at the end of this chapter).

There are some limitations to the studies reviewed in this chapter. First, some of the studies fail to separate memory from related processes, making it difficult to determine if in fact memory is the primary deficit or if memory is just a related deficit. Second, many of the studies do not delineate the types of memory processes measured. When they do, there is always the challenge of comparing results across studies when each has used a different memory measure. Third, for some disorders, there has been little or no research with children, at least in regards to potential memory impairments. Although prudence is advised, the adult findings can be appropriately generalized to youth because memory structure and function are essentially the same in adults and in school-aged children (see Chapter 3). Despite these shortcomings, the studies reviewed here are mostly well-designed studies that controlled for confounding variables. For each condition reviewed, there were studies that eliminated subjects with related diagnoses and studies that included controls who were matched on critical variables such as IQ, age, and sex. Moreover, evidence of causality clearly emerges from the research—the connections between medical conditions and memory processes cannot be denied. Fortunately, only a fraction of the youth who experience any of these risk factors will develop memory impairments. However, a significant number will, and these are the individuals who need to be identified and served.

ACQUIRED BRAIN INJURY

Traumatic Brain Injury

Traumatic brain injury (TBI) is damage to brain tissue caused by external mechanical forces, as evidenced by skull fracture, loss of consciousness, or objective neurological findings. TBI is the leading cause of childhood death and disability in the United States, with an estimated .25% of children and adolescents sustaining a TBI each year. The frontal and temporal lobes are the most frequently damaged brain regions. Consequently, TBI can cause a broad spectrum of cognitive problems, with memory deficits and executive dysfunctions among the most frequently reported. With severe TBI, an estimated 54 to 84% of individuals (across all age groups) experience significant memory difficulties, known as posttraumatic amnesia, within the first few days or weeks following the injury (DeLuca, Schultheis, Madigan, Christodoulou, & Averill, 2000). Of these, up to 36% may suffer long-term impairments in learning and memory (Wilson, 2009; Zec et al., 2001). One study (cited in Emilien, Durlach, Antoniadis, Van Der Linden, & Maloteaux, 2004) reported that 53% of victims and 79% of their families report persistent memory deficits seven years post-injury. Even when intelligence and other cognitive functions recover, memory may not. Regardless of severity and persistence, when declines in memory functioning are observed, short-term, working, and long-term memory are all affected.

Although TBI can impact nearly every aspect of explicit memory, some memory systems, components, and processes generally fare better than others. For example, verbal memory functions tend to be more affected than visuospatial. A meta-analysis (Babikian & Asarnow, 2009) concluded that visuospatial short-term memory is the most resistant to head injury. Although retrieval from semantic memory is better than retrieval from episodic memory in cases of adult posttraumatic amnesia, severe head injury in children and adolescents does not seem to discriminate between episodic and semantic memory (Levin, Fletcher, Kusnerik, & Kufera, 1996). Regarding which processes are compromised, encoding, consolidation, storage, and retrieval have all been implicated. Also, impairments in metamemory often result from TBI (Hanten, Bartha, & Levin, 2001), even when memory performance appears relatively intact. For children and adolescents, the main concern following a TBI is how academic learning will be affected. More than 75% of those with severe TBI will be placed in special education.

The extent, severity, and chronicity of memory impairments depend mainly on the severity of the injury. When acquired brain injuries are mild, and 85% of them are, the likelihood of persistent memory impairments is minimal. For example, Roman et al. (1998) found that at one month post-injury, children with mild TBI did not have a higher incidence rate of memory impairment than control subjects. When memory impairments do result from a mild head injury, they can persist over a period of months or even years. However, there is gradual recovery in the vast majority of these cases. In a meta-analysis of 28 studies of pediatric TBI (Babikian & Asarnow,

2009), the memory problems of nearly all subjects were resolved within two years. With moderate injuries, verbal long-term memory impairments frequently persist beyond two years. In severe cases of TBI, the risk of acquiring chronic memory impairment is higher. Estimates vary, depending on the study. Roman et al. reported that 29% of their severely brain-injured subjects had a significant memory deficit (below the 5th percentile) one month after resolution of posttraumatic amnesia. With severe TBI, all of the memory structures seem to suffer damage, with moderate to large effects on working, short-term, and long-term memory. Both verbal and visuospatial memory are usually involved, with verbal long-term memory impairments being the most persistent, some actually increasing in severity over time. Age at time of injury is another variable related to outcomes. Although the empirical evidence is conflicting, the consensus seems to be that the earlier in development a traumatic brain injury occurs, the more likely there will be lifelong cognitive and memory deficits. In summary, the persistence of memory deficits is mainly related to the severity of the injury. When head injuries are mild, memory impairments are usually resolved within one to three months after injury. In contrast, those who experience severe injuries typically have enduring memory deficits (Levin & Hanten, 2004). Nonetheless, there is a wide variation in recovery of memory in survivors of severe head injury.

There are different stages of recovery from TBI. Immediately following an injury, the patient may experience temporary, posttraumatic, anterograde amnesia in which no information about ongoing events is retained (Levin & Hanten, 2004). Temporary retrograde amnesia can also occur. With retrograde amnesia, memory for events in the distant past is better than memory for more recent events that occurred just prior to the traumatic incident. Amnesia of some form may occur even in mild injuries but is most likely when the victim has lost consciousness or been in a coma. After awakening from a coma, 65% of adult patients display posttraumatic amnesia, as reported by Ellenberg, Levin, and Saydjari (1996). Despite the frustrations and fears caused by posttraumatic amnesia, for the majority of TBI victims, recovery of memory functions is rapid for the first three to six months and then levels off after 12 to 18 months. Improvement in memory functions can occur for up to 10 years. For most head injury victims, posttraumatic amnesia is only present in the early stages of recovery; however, a few will acquire a lifelong amnesic disorder. In studies of adults with severe head injuries, approximately 50% reported memory deficits seven years after the injury. In a study of adolescent victims with normal intellectual functioning (reported in Levin & Hanten, 2004), 15% of the moderate and 30% of the severe head-injured victims had significant memory deficits up to 42 months after the injury. There is much individual variation in the rate of memory recovery, but the best predictor is the severity of the injury.

Regarding the memory processes involved, encoding, consolidation, storage, retrieval, and metamemory have all been implicated (see Table 4.1). The relative involvement of each process depends on injury severity, affected brain regions, and the stage of recovery. Encoding new learning is clearly a problem immediately following a severe brain injury. Slower rates of learning, observed in many TBI students, are an indication of encoding problems. Regarding consolidation and storage, some researchers (e.g., Vanderploeg, Crowell, & Curtiss, 2001) have made a strong case for impaired consolidation as the primary deficit underlying memory impairment in TBI. Support for their case is demonstrated by rapid rates of forgetting, poorer performance on recognition tasks, and less proactive interference from prior learning that should have been stored. Other investigators (e.g., Roman et al., 1998) have found little evidence to support consolidation and storage problems after posttraumatic amnesia has been resolved. These investigators have reported that retention of new information over time seems to be normal. Retrieval also seems to be deficient in most cases of TBI memory impairment. In the initial stages of recovery, both recall and recognition are impaired. After several months of recovery, recognition tends to improve while a free recall deficit remains (Roman et al., 1998). Of all the memory processes, encoding, rather than consolidation and retrieval, seems to be the primary cause of memory dysfunction following TBI (DeLuca et al., 2000). Impaired encoding is consistent with hippocampal damage, as the hippocampus is the brain structure primarily responsible for encoding information into long-term memory. Despite evidence of specific encoding deficiencies and suspected damage to the hippocampus, the role of compromised executive functions should not be ignored, as TBI-affected learners are known to underutilize encoding strategies.

When there is damage to the frontal lobes, executive functions, attentional control, and working memory will certainly be affected. Children with frontal lobe damage will experience metacognitive and metamemory processing problems (Hanten, Bartha, & Levin, 2001). Metamemory deficiencies reported in TBI children include difficulty estimating how much material will be recalled and the reduced application of appropriate encoding strategies. Individuals with frontal lobe lesions are less likely to use organizational and other memory strategies, as these depend on executive functioning. Impaired development and utilization of memory strategies (Levin & Hanten, 2004) will have a detrimental impact on learning and encoding. For example, young children with TBI underutilize semantic clustering and even have difficulties performing and modifying basic rehearsal strategies (Harris, 1996). Fortunately, Gershberg and Shimamura (1995) found that patients with frontal lobe lesions benefit from strategy instruction. Retrieval impairments may also be associated with frontal lobe damage because some retrieval difficulties result from reduced ability to inhibit interference. In general, TBI victims are more susceptible to interference.

In addition to retrospective memory problems, severe head injuries in children can cause prospective memory deficits across a variety of tasks (Levin & Hanten, 2004). Prospective memory is an important element of everyday functional memory with which individuals with TBI often have significant difficulty. Several external memory aides, such as computerized reminders and memory notebooks, can be used to alleviate this concern but these may not be practical in every environment. Providing meaningful incentives, such as a monetary reward, is one alternative that was recently investigated with TBI children and adolescents (McCauley, McDaniel, Pedroza, Chapman, & Levin, 2009). The study's authors found that prospective memory can improve significantly under highly motivating conditions.

The only memory system that seems almost entirely resistant to TBI is implicit memory, probably because of its reduced dependence on the frontal and temporal lobes. Research with head trauma victims has discovered that implicit memory is less vulnerable to TBI than explicit memory (Yeates & Enrile, 2005). This makes sense because most brain injuries do not damage the posterior region of the brain where implicit memory is thought to reside. Even when there is full-fledged amnesia or limited explicit memory functioning, the child or adolescent's implicit memory usually remains intact (Shum, Jamieson, Bahr, & Wallace, 1999). For example, procedural memory is preserved in children with TBI (Ward, Shum, Wallace, & Boon, 2002).

When TBI victims return to school, they usually require accommodations and interventions, at least on a short-term basis. They should also be closely monitored to determine how well they are progressing through the stages of recovery. In cases where ongoing learning and memory problems are anticipated, comprehensive memory testing should be conducted so that instruction and interventions can be designed to match these students' needs. If neurocognitive testing was conducted immediately after the injury, there is no need for memory testing for a few weeks. It's perhaps best to wait until the short-term posttraumatic amnesia has naturally subsided. From that point on, recovery and response to intervention can be tracked through periodic memory testing every few months until full recovery or until functioning has stabilized. However, there are some challenges to memory assessment with TBI students. The first challenge is that there is seldom any pre-injury testing of memory performance. Thus, it's frequently difficult to determine whether there has been an actual decline in memory abilities. In fact, some studies have reported that students with learning, behavioral, and emotional problems are more likely to experience a head injury than those with average or above abilities. Another challenge confronting the evaluator is denial of memory problems and resistance to testing from the child or adolescent. The denial is probably related to reduced metamemory functioning resulting from frontal lobe damage but may also be motivated by the desire to appear normal and return to athletic activities. For instance, a child with TBI consistently overestimates how well he or she is recalling information, much like a more developmentally immature child (Hanten et al., 2001). There is also the concern that improved performance on a standardized test may be due to practice effects. Distinguishing practice effects from actual improvement can be a challenge.

Post-Concussion Syndrome

A concussion is a mild traumatic brain injury that disrupts brain function but is typically followed by spontaneous recovery. In the United States, the number of high school athletes who sustain a concussion each year is estimated at more than 62,000 (Lovell et al., 2003), and the number of concussed athletes of all ages may be as high as 300,000 per year. The likelihood of an athlete sustaining a concussion in any given year may be as high as 19%. Youth who sustain a concussion or mild traumatic brain injury often display short-term symptoms that include headache, dizziness, sleep difficulties, fatigue, irritability, sensitivity to light or noise, and attention and memory problems. This constellation of symptoms is referred to as post-concussion syndrome. Post-concussion symptoms usually clear up within a few days or within a month, but sometimes they persist for longer intervals. Chronicity is an indication of impairments in neurocognitive functioning. Some studies of patients with persistent symptoms have found deficits in attention and memory at 6 to 18 months post-injury (reviewed in Ryan & Warden, 2003). Multiple concussions or suffering a second concussion while recovering from an initial one increases the risk of long-term consequences. Of course, the degree of risk is also determined by the severity of the concussion. When there is a loss of consciousness, which happens in the minority of cases, the outcomes are likely to be more serious. Of those who remain conscious, amnesia or disorientation lasting longer than five minutes significantly increases the risk that memory problems will persist for more than seven days (Lovell et al., 2003).

School sports coaches and athletic trainers are quite familiar with post-concussion syndrome because mild traumatic brain injuries frequently occur during athletic competitions. Because recovery is usually rapid, with no observable long-term outcomes, concussions that occur at school are usually not considered to put students at risk for memory and learning problems. Yet, some school athletes will suffer repercussions that will affect learning and school performance, at least in the short-term. For instance, when 14 high school athletes who suffered concussions were closely followed after the incident, their memory impairments were unresolved until 10 days after the injury (Sim, Terryberry-Spohr, & Wilson, 2008). In some cases, persistent cognitive and memory problems may occur (Ryan & Warden, 2003). Educators and athletic coaches need to be aware of this possibility.

In youth sports management, the primary concern is whether it is safe for the athlete to return to sports play. Ordinarily, this decision is based on the athlete's self-report of symptoms. Because they want to return to sports play, many high school athletes will minimize their symptoms. For example, formal neurocognitive testing at four and seven days post-injury has revealed a significantly higher rate of memory problems than are self-reported (Lovell et al., 2003). To prevent this problem, some school districts and universities across the nation have implemented mandatory pre-season neurocognitive testing (which includes several memory tasks) for all athletes. These computerized assessments (see Chapter 6) provide a baseline to which post-injury performance can be compared. Establishing a baseline is important because traditional neurodiagnostic tests, such as brain scans, are too insensitive to measure neurologic changes after a concussion (Van Kampen, Lovell, Pardini, Collins, & Freddie, 2006). Pre-testing of athletes also eliminates the problem of determining the premorbid level of memory functioning. Pre-testing of athletes is especially beneficial in cases where persistent memory problems occur.

Frontal Lobe Lesions

Hippocampal damage is implicated for most of the conditions discussed in this chapter. However, sometimes frontal lobe lesions or atrophy are the cause of memory impairments. A lesion is defined as any disruption of or damage to the normal structure or function of a brain region due to injury, disease, or surgical procedure. Atrophy is a wasting away of a body part due to a degenerative disease. Although traumatic brain injury is the most frequent cause of frontal lobe lesions, they can result from several medical conditions. The nature of the memory impairments resulting from frontal lobe dysfunction can be discriminated from those resulting from hippocampal dysfunction. Generally, the pattern of memory deficits suggests difficulties with organization and monitoring during encoding and retrieval (Mangels, Gershberg, Shimamura, Arthur, & Knight, 1996). Individuals with frontal lobe lesions are less likely to engage in useful memory strategies. They also struggle during retrieval, and they benefit from cues and recognition formats. Their retrieval problems seem related to their poor ability to organize a productive search of memory. Their retrieval difficulties may also stem from greater susceptibility to interference. Whereas individuals suffering from amnesia due to hippocampal damage seem to have lost remote memories from storage, those with frontal lobe damage have retained the information but have difficulty retrieving it.

MEDICAL CONDITIONS

Prenatal to Neonatal Conditions

Prematurity Advancements in medical technology now allow very premature babies to survive. After extended stays in intensive care units, the majority of these infants go home with no apparent physical limitations and later reach developmental milestones normally. Nevertheless, they are still at-risk for learning and memory problems, as their increased incidence rate of learning difficulties attests to. Premature babies lack full development of their respiratory systems and are thus likely to experience hypoxia (a diminished availability of oxygen to the body). Hence, neonatal damage to the hippocampus may occur. In a study by Isaacs et al. (2000), 11 individuals born prior to 30 weeks gestation had significantly smaller hippocampi (despite equivalent head size) and scored lower on memory tests when they were examined during adolescence. Although there is little to support the claim that this population has impairments in semantic memory, they may have problems with episodic memory. In a study (Briscoe, Gathercole, & Marlow, 2001) with the Rivermead Behavioral Memory Test for Children

(Wilson, Ivani-Chalian, & Aldrich, 1991), the authors concluded that children born at 32 weeks gestation or less were at increased risk for everyday memory difficulties.

Perinatal Asphyxia   Asphyxia, sometimes referred to as anoxia, occurs when the level of oxygen in the blood falls below normal and the brain receives insufficient oxygen. Any time the brain is deprived of oxygen, permanent injury to the vulnerable hippocampus can result within minutes (Gadian et al., 2000). Birthing is the first life event that puts humans at risk for oxygen deprivation. Other life incidents that cause asphyxia include choking, drowning, electric shock, inhaled smoke or toxic fumes, and disease of or injury to the respiratory system. Asphyxia occurs during approximately 1 to 6 per 1,000 births. In severe cases of perinatal asphyxia the infant dies (15 to 20%). Of the survivors, 25% will show significant neurological impairments. Severe asphyxia can cause cerebral palsy and mental retardation. Several studies of full-term asphyxiated babies (reviewed in de Haan et al., 2006) have reported injury to the hippocampus, with bilateral volume reductions as high as 43 to 71%. Damage to the frontal lobes will also have an impact on memory functioning. The memory functions affected will vary depending on the extent of the asphyxia. Memory deficits have been reported in long-term visuospatial, verbal, and episodic memory. In some severe cases, developmental amnesia is diagnosed after these children enter school. A study of 28 Spanish individuals who suffered moderate perinatal asphyxia included only those with average IQ and good neurological outcomes (Maneru, Junque, Botet, Tallad, & Guardia, 2001). When tested during adolescence, these subjects exhibited deficits in long-term verbal and visuospatial memory.

Excess Bilirubin Levels   Another neonatal condition that has the potential to cause learning and memory problems is excess bilirubin (bile pigment). Approximately 60% of full-term infants and 80% of premature babies have excess bilirubin that is observable as jaundice, a yellowing of the skin and mucous membranes. Jaundice and hyperbilirubinemia are easily treated with exposure to light. Persistent, high levels of bilirubin can cause damage to select brain areas, including the hippocampus and basal ganglia. Severe or untreated hyperbilirubinemia causes kernicterus, a condition that is toxic to brain tissue and can even lead to death. In a study of 22 South African children who had excessively high levels of bilirubin shortly after birth, the researchers found that the majority of the subjects had impaired short-term and long-term memory (Pretorious, Naude, & Becker, 2002). These subjects appeared unimpaired during early childhood, but memory difficulties emerged once they began formal schooling.

Congenital Hypothyroidism   Congenital hypothyroidism is a neonatal disorder that affects 1 in 3,000 to 4,000 newborns. It is caused by the lack of the thyroid hormone, which is essential for normal brain development. Even though most cases are now detected at birth, thereby preventing mental retardation, even a brief period of postnatal thyroid hormone insufficiency can put these infants at risk for selective memory deficits. In addition to memory problems associated with abnormal hippocampal development, these children typically display deficits in language, attention, motor, and visuospatial abilities, with an increased risk for math disabilities (Rovet, 2002). Studies with early-treated subjects have reported deficits in short-term memory, delayed recall, recognition memory, and everyday memory. The types of memory most affected seem to be those that rely predominantly on the hippocampus (Hepworth, Pang, & Rovet, 2006).

Childhood Conditions

Childhood Diabetes   Type 1 Diabetes Mellitus (T1DM) is one of the most common chronic diseases of childhood, affecting as many as 1 in 60 children under the age of 18 (Wolters, Yu, Hagen, & Kail, 1996). The percentage of children developing childhood diabetes continues to escalate, raising widespread concerns not only for learning and memory problems but for the numerous health problems that ensue. Among children, learning problems and CNS dysfunctions frequently emerge early in the course of the disease, usually within one to three years. Students with T1DM typically score within the average range on measures of intelligence but may acquire memory problems. Memory dysfunctions (see Table 4.1) have been implicated in short-term memory and in both verbal and visuospatial long-term memory (Desrocher & Rovet, 2004) but not implicit memory (Hershey, Craft, Bhargava, & White, 1997).

As is the case with other risk factors, damage to the hippocampus underlies the memory dysfunctions experienced by this population. The brain, and in particular the hippocampus, is very sensitive to changes in insulin and glucose levels because the brain relies almost exclusively on glucose as its energy source, and brain cells are unable to store glucose (Desrocher & Rovet, 2004). Children with diabetes are constantly experiencing abnormal levels of insulin and glucose that affect brain function. Both hyperglycemia (high blood glucose from too little insulin) and hypoglycemia (low blood glucose from too much insulin) can cause brain damage, especially in children. One or the other of these conditions results when insulin level is poorly controlled, something that happens more frequently in younger children. Younger children have poorer control because they may be less aware of the onset of hypoglycemia and less able to verbalize their symptoms. Hypoglycemia is a greater concern than hyperglycemia, especially when it is severe and leads to seizures. As many as 31% of T1DM children experience one or more episodes of severe hypoglycemia (Desrocher & Rovet, 2004). Brain imaging research has revealed that adults with a history of hypoglycemic seizures have large decreases in hippocampal volume, on both the right and left side (Desrocher & Rovet, 2004). Accordingly, some studies have found correlations between the number of reported hypoglycemic episodes and memory performance in children (Hershey, Lillie, Sadler, & White, 2003).

There are also indications that children with T1DM suffer brain damage to areas other than the hippocampus. Verbal short-term memory deficits have been reported (Wolters et al., 1996), and frontal lobe damage has been implicated by the finding that diabetic children are deficient in the use of strategies to organize and recall information (Hagan et al, 1990). For example, the diabetic subjects in the Hagan et al. (1990) study did not utilize rehearsal strategies as frequently as controls. Wolters et al. (1996) discovered that children with better metabolic control of their disease were more likely to use a productive rehearsal strategy than children whose control was poor. However, even when those with poor control employed strategies, their recall was lower.

The two T1DM variables that are most predictive of memory impairments are age at onset and number of episodes of severe hypoglycemia (Ryan, Vega, & Drash, 1985). Those who develop the disease prior to age 5 are much more likely to acquire brain abnormalities than individuals who develop the disease later in life. For instance, children diagnosed before age 4 are more likely to have weaknesses in both visuospatial and verbal memory. Of the two variables, the incidence of hypoglycemia is more influential (Hershey et al., 2003). Regardless of age of onset, the number of severe hypoglycemic episodes, especially those that culminate in hypoglycemic seizures, are closely related to the extent of memory impairment. For example, Hershey et al. (1997) found that children with a history of severe hypoglycemic episodes recalled 33% less story information than normal controls and 22% less than diabetic children with no history of hypoglycemia. Hershey et al. (2003) reported that children with as few as three severe episodes performed worse on long-term spatial memory. There is also evidence that memory functioning of diabetic children declines over time. Northam et al. (2001) found poorer memory performance at six years after disease onset than at two years after onset. In addition to decrements in memory, verbal ability and visuospatial processing also decline over a period of years (Rovet, Ehrlich, Czuchta, & Akler, 1993).

Children born to diabetic mothers may also be at risk for neurodevelopmental problems, especially when the mothers have poor control of their insulin-dependent diabetes (Sells, Robinson, Brown, & Knopp, 1994). When mothers experience hypoglycemia, damage to the fetus's hippocampus can occur (Nelson et al., 2000). Furthermore, these infants encounter prenatal exposure to iron deficiency and hypoxemia (insufficient blood oxygen), additional risk factors for hippocampal damage. In research reviewed by Bauer, DeBoer, and Lukowski (2007), 12-month-old infants of diabetic mothers displayed impaired performance on ordered recall.

Even students without a diagnosis of diabetes may experience less than optimal memory functioning due to poor glucose tolerance or abnormal glucose regulation (Awad, Gagnon, Desrochers, Tsiakas, & Messier, 2002). These are often children and adolescents in a pre-diabetic state who may later be diagnosed with Type 2 diabetes. They display mild glucose intolerance and mild insulin insensitivity, resulting in poor assimilation of glucose and high blood glucose levels. Individuals with good glucose tolerance will have rapidly increasing blood glucose levels shortly after consuming glucose-containing drink or food, followed by falling glucose levels. Those with poor glucose tolerance do not assimilate the glucose as rapidly. In a study with undergraduate students, subjects classified as poor glucose regulators recalled 5 to 8% less verbal information on delayed recall measures than those with normal glucoregulation (Messier, Desrochers, & Gagnon, 1999). Attesting to the hippocampus's need for sufficient glucose, some studies (reviewed in Awad et al., 2002) have found ingestion of glucose (resulting in a mild hyperglycemic state) to improve verbal memory performance in subjects with poor glucose regulation. For example, Messier et al. (1999) found that ingestion of glucose by poor glucoregulators produced improvements in long-term verbal recall. Glucose ingestion improved performance regardless of whether it was taken at the time of learning or at recall, indicating that glucose facilitates both encoding and retrieval. However, individuals with normal glucose regulation did not benefit from higher glucose levels unless they were performing a very demanding cognitive task (Donohoe & Benton, 2000). Normal individuals with high glucose levels at the beginning of a cognitively demanding task outperformed those with lower levels of glucose (Benton, 2001). Those with better glucose tolerance also performed better overall.

Approximately 20% of children with diabetes are placed in some form of special education. When evaluating diabetic children for learning and memory problems, practitioners should inquire about the course of disease, keeping in mind that it takes about three years before diabetes' adverse effects on memory and school performance become evident. Age of onset, number and severity of hypoglycemic episodes, amount of school absenteeism, and degree of disease control are important variables. In general, practitioners and educators should be investigating how well the diabetes is being controlled, as children with poorer glycemic control are more likely to develop learning and memory problems.

Sleep Disorders Sleep disordered breathing is a condition characterized by collapse or narrowing of the pharynx that causes episodes of upper airway obstructions referred to as apneas. The prevalence of childhood sleep disorders has been estimated to be between 1 and 4% (Rhodes, Shimoda, Waid, O'Neil, Oexmann, Collop, et al., 1995). In children, upper airway obstructions are often due to enlarged adenoids and tonsils. Snoring is one observable sign that apnea is occurring. Apneas reduce oxygen supply and disrupt sleep. Children who experience fragmented sleep are often hyperactive, irritable, or excessively sleepy during the day. Although empirical findings are equivocal, there are studies (reviewed in Kaemingk et al., 2003) that have linked poor memory performance with sleep disorders. Memory performance on standardized tests is significantly reduced among children who have respiratory disturbances during sleep, with children who have higher respiratory disturbances displaying greater memory deficits (Kheirandish & Gozal, 2006). When memory difficulties co-occur with sleep disorders, the underlying cause seems to be sleep deprivation, as opposed to any permanent brain dysfunction. Consequently, memory performance typically improves when obstructive tonsils and adenoids are removed and normal sleep returns (Kaemingk et al., 2003).

Epilepsy Epilepsy is a group of chronic brain disorders associated with disturbances in the electrical discharges of brain cells and characterized by recurrent seizures. The types of seizure vary, depending on the nature of the abnormal electrical discharge and the area of the brain affected. There has been a considerable amount of research on memory function in children and adolescents with epilepsy (see Table 4.1). All youth with epilepsy are at-risk for memory dysfunction and poor academic achievement, with approximately 10% of them experiencing significant memory impairment (Wilson, 2009). The reason for the high risk is that the brain areas most involved with memory functions (the frontal lobes, temporal lobes, and hippocampus) are the areas most likely to sustain an epileptic seizure. The memory performance of children with epilepsy is deficient relative to their overall cognitive ability. For instance, Borden, Burns, and O'Leary (2006) reported on an epileptic group with a mean WISC®-III Full Scale IQ of 92.19 that had respective means of 83.81, 85.43, and 87.16 on the Verbal Immediate Index, Learning Index, and Verbal Delayed Index of the Children's Memory Scale. In addition to long-term storage problems, several studies have found children with epilepsy to display deficiencies in verbal short-term memory and verbal learning tasks. For instance, one investigation discovered that they require 50% more learning trials to reach 90% mastery (Davidson, Dorris, O'Regan, & Zuberi, 2007).

The severity and type of memory problem depends on several variables. First, reduced memory functioning is associated with earlier age of onset and longer duration of active epilepsy (Nolan et al., 2004). Second, the level of seizure control is related to degree of memory impairment, with greater seizure activity correlated with reduced memory performance (Jocic-Jakubi & Jovic, 2006). In fact, children with well-controlled epilepsy may not have any difficulties with new learning or verbal memory retention (Williams et al., 2001). Third, the type and location of the seizures are other important variables. Individuals with temporal lobe epilepsy are the most at-risk for severe long-term memory impairments, especially in the verbal domain. Those with childhood absence epilepsy are more likely to experience difficulties with visuospatial memory (Nolan et al., 2004) There is also evidence that children with frontal lobe epilepsy have significant memory deficits, but the type of memory dysfunction is not delineated in the research. However, it is unclear whether the location of the seizures makes much difference in terms of memory performance. Some studies have reported no direct relationship between the type of seizure disorder and the type of memory problem (Williams et al., 2001). Research that attempts to link seizure types and brain locations to specific memory impairments must deal with several potential confounds, including the length of each seizure. For example, the hippocampus is very sensitive to the effects of prolonged seizures (Williams, Sharp, Lange, & Bates, 1996).

Children and adolescents with epilepsy are particularly known for "accelerated forgetting," exhibiting normal delayed recall for short intervals while performing very poorly as the retention intervals are extended (Davidson et al., 2007). This phenomenon seems to result from ongoing seizures disrupting the memory consolidation process (Kapur et al., 1997). Consequently, students with epilepsy may have poorer retention over extended time periods, such as a day or more, than they do after a 30-minute interval (Blake, Wroe, Breen, & McCarthy, 2000; Davidson et al., 2007). Incomplete consolidation may also result from brain damage caused by epileptic activity that occurs during the retention interval. The finding of incomplete consolidation of new verbal learning is consistent with damage to the left temporal lobe, a brain region thought to be involved in verbal memory consolidation (Nolan et al., 2004). In contrast, right temporal lobe damage is correlated with visuospatial memory deficits. When inadequate consolidation is the source of memory impairments, deficits in encoding and retrieval can effectively be ruled out. However, the consolidation deficit hypothesis is not without controversy. Some researchers (e.g., Davidson et al., 2007) contend that the underlying problem is not disrupted consolidation but rather encoding and retrieval problems, as some subjects retrieve better during recognition tasks than during uncued recall tasks (Williams et al., 2001). Regardless of the actual cause, long-term recall of information decreases in conjunction with increased number of seizures (O'Conner, Sieggreen, Ahern, Schomer, & Mesulam, 1997).

When conducting cognitive and memory evaluations with this population, it is critical to establish the age of onset, duration of the epilepsy, treatment history, and frequency and severity of the seizures. Inquiry about medications is also important, as anti-convulsive medications, such as Phenobarbital, sometimes exacerbate memory problems (Temple, 2004). Moreover, children taking two antiepileptic medications may perform significantly worse on both verbal and visuospatial memory scales than those taking just one medication, according to Williams et al. (1996). For children and adolescents with temporal lobe epilepsy, in-depth verbal memory testing is essential. The possibility of disrupted consolidation should also be investigated. Children and adolescents with epilepsy may perform normally on 30-minute delayed recall subtests, yet experience significant difficulties retaining information over longer intervals. Consequently, examiners should conduct extended delayed recall measures (e.g., a day or a week) to determine the extent of accelerated forgetting over time, even if non-standardized testing is necessary. Furthermore, because of the possibility of consolidation dysfunctions, measures of semantic memory (see Chapter 6) should be included. Finally, practitioners should assess (at least informally) aspects of everyday memory functioning. In doing so, it's important not to rely on uncorroborated reports, as individuals with epilepsy tend to underestimate their everyday memory failures (Blake et al., 2000).

Regarding classroom interventions and instruction, students with epilepsy would certainly benefit from repetition and spaced study opportunities, as well as periodic testing. If memory consolidation is lacking, these methods will afford more opportunities to solidify the material. Most important, students and parents should be encouraged to report seizure activity so that students are not tested on material until they've had an opportunity to relearn it after a seizure. When tested, these students should be provided a recognition format, such as multiple-choice, to facilitate recall of the information that they have been able to consolidate (Williams et al., 2001).

Herpes Simplex Encephalitis   Encephalitis is inflammation of the brain, typically caused by a viral brain infection, the most common of which is herpes simplex. Herpes simplex encephalitis is a rare but very dangerous disease that can devastate the brain and cause amnesia. In the early stages, patients usually experience flu-like symptoms with fever, headaches, lethargy, and sometimes seizures. The virus tends to affect the temporal and frontal lobes. Approximately 70% of encephalitis survivors will incur a memory impairment (Wilson, 2009). There are variations in the degree of memory loss that reflect the extent of damage to the medial temporal lobe and hippocampus (O'Conner & Verfaellie, 2004). Although some individuals fully recover from encephalitis, others will experience lifelong cognitive and memory deficits.

Childhood Stroke   After a stroke, children are known to experience memory problems with short-term and long-term verbal memory. Pediatric stroke victims have been reported to have memory difficulties with encoding, use of memory strategies, and free and cued recall (Lansing et al., 2004). For example, children who have suffered a stroke have difficulty organizing words into semantic clusters. The earlier in development the stroke occurs, the greater the impairments. Unlike adult stroke victims whose deficits correspond with the damaged brain hemisphere, pediatric victims acquire verbal memory problems when the lesion occurs in the left or the right hemisphere (Block, Nanson, & Lowry, 1999). Functional everyday memory impairments may also result from lesions to either hemisphere.

Reye's Syndrome   Reye's Syndrome is most common in children ages 5 to 15 years, with earlier onset associated with a poorer prognosis. It begins with viral-like symptoms that lead to brain swelling and diffuse damage to cognitive and memory functions. When intellectual abilities are unaffected or recover, memory impairments may persist. These memory impairments include working memory, use of memory strategies, and verbal and visuospatial episodic memory (Temple, 2004). Of the processes involved, encoding is typically the most deficient.

Medulloblastoma   Medulloblastoma is a type of pediatric brain tumor that is treated through surgery, radiation, or chemotherapy. Although radiation therapy increases survival rates, it is associated with adverse effects on neuropsychological functioning. Children treated for medulloblastoma demonstrate a mixed profile of memory impairment. Post-treatment memory declines have been reported in long-term verbal and visuospatial memory, with retrieval deficits in both free recall and recognition. In a study of 40 treated children, the authors concluded that the subjects had deficiencies in both encoding and retrieval (Nagel et al., 2006). As expected, abnormal hippocampal development has been discovered in treated children. Although radiation dosage is not associated with degree of memory impairment, age of treatment is, with younger children having more difficulty with delayed recall.

Effects of Asthma Medication   Asthma is one of the most common chronic illnesses among children. With asthma, it's not the illness that can cause memory problems but rather the medication used to treat it. Each year in the United States approximately 10 million new prescriptions (for children and adults) are written for oral corticosteroids, the medication routinely used to treat asthma. This medication includes cortisone, which is known to adversely affect memory structures and functioning. Several researchers have reported psychological and cognitive side effects associated with corticosteroid therapy (reviewed in Naude & Pretorius, 2003). The cognitive deficits most frequently involve verbal declarative memory, but sometimes only short-term memory is impacted. For example, in a case study of a 9-year-old South African male who had been taking corticosteroids since the age of 1 year, the subject was found to have impairments in short-term memory, sustained attention, and reading fluency (Naude & Pretorius, 2003).

DEVELOPMENTAL DISORDERS

The relations between developmental disorders and memory functioning are different from the relations memory has with the other risk factors discussed in this chapter. Whereas risk factors such as medical conditions may cause memory impairments, developmental disorders do not cause memory impairments. In fact, memory impairments are more likely to be one of the "causes" of some developmental disorders, such as a learning disorder. With most disorders all that can be said with certainty is that memory impairments are likely to be associated with the disorder. What binds the developmental disorder and memory impairment together may actually be another factor they both share a relationship with. For example, both dyslexia and poor memory performance may stem from broader verbal processing deficiencies. Therefore, it is important to investigate the possibility of a memory impairment whenever an associated disorder is diagnosed, mainly because a memory impairment exacerbates the developmental disorder.

Specific Language Impairment (SLI)

At least 3% of youth are diagnosed with SLI, a developmental disorder characterized by deficits in expressive and/or receptive language skills that are disproportionally greater than other cognitive problems. The expressive type, which is characterized by limited ability to learn vocabulary, is more common in childhood. Several aspects of memory, especially verbal components, are inextricably intertwined with language development and functioning (Gilliam, 1998; Riccio, Cash, & Cohen, 2007). The strong connection between memory and language is illustrated by aphasia, which is an acquired loss of the ability to understand language or express oneself through language. Aphasia is caused by brain injury or disease, such as head injury or encephalitis. In the typical case of aphasia there are impairments in phonological short-term memory and verbal long-term memory (Emilien, 2004). Numerous studies (reviewed in Shear, Tallal, & Delis, 1992) have found evidence of diminished phonological short-term memory and verbal long-term memory among children with SLI (see Table 4.1). In addition, research has revealed that SLI children have difficulties with encoding and retrieval. Among the long-term memory systems, verbal semantic memory seems to be the most affected (Ceci, Ringstorm, & Lea, 1981). For example, children with SLI often perform better with recently encountered isolated words (episodic memory) than they do with semantically related information in stories (Riccio, Cash, & Cohen, 2007). Verbal semantic memory is essential for the ability to comprehend and produce language. Semantic memory not only stores word meanings but also grammatical rules. Furthermore, some researchers believe that children with SLI have less ability to use rehearsal, especially elaborative rehearsal, to maintain information (reviewed in Kirchner & Klatsky, 1985). For instance, Kirchner and Klatsky discovered that children with SLI are capable of semantic organization and elaborative rehearsal during encoding but are unlikely to use these strategies because of their working memory deficits. Some investigations have even found that SLI children do not benefit from semantic cues provided to them during retrieval.

Among children with SLI, the most common specific memory deficits are in phonological short-term memory and verbal long-term memory. Difficulty with the short-term retention of new words in their phonological forms slows vocabulary development. Normal children can acquire new words with as few as six exposures and learn as many as 10 new words per day (Rice, Oetting, Marquis, Bode, & Pae, 1994), a feat that SLI children cannot accomplish because their deficient short-term memory capacity limits encoding into long-term memory. Phonological short-term memory deficits can also interfere with language comprehension. Whereas nearly all investigations have found phonological short-term memory deficits (Records, Tomblin, & Buckwalter, 1995), fewer have found deficits in both short- and long-term memory. For instance, in a study (Riccio et al., 2007) where children with SLI were tested with the Children's Memory Scale (Cohen, 1997) the subjects performed significantly worse than controls on both immediate and delayed subtests of auditory and verbal memory. Results from other studies (e.g., Nichols et al., 2004) suggest that SLI children have difficulty with efficient and elaborative encoding, thereby slowing down their learning. However, once children with SLI have learned the material, they appear to retain it well and are able to retrieve it without depending on recognition. While it's unclear how frequently children with SLI have long-term verbal memory impairments, they almost always have auditory or phonological short-term memory deficits. As a result, they will need more exposures to new words than normally developing young children.

Learning Disabilities

In the United States, approximately 6% of children and adolescents are identified as having a learning disability. (In this text, learning disability is synonymous with learning disorder.) Students with a learning disability frequently have one or more specific memory deficits within the short-term, working, and long-term memory systems. The nature of their memory deficits varies somewhat by the type of disability they experience, although nearly every student with a learning disability has difficulty acquiring and retaining semantic information, relative to ability-matched, non-disabled peers. For most individuals with a learning disability, visuospatial memory ability is usually average and an area of strength, except for those who have a nonverbal learning disability. In such cases, visuospatial memory is impaired while verbal is normal (Liddell & Rasmussen, 2005). Acquisition and retention of knowledge seems to be a challenge that cuts across different specific learning disabilities (Gettinger, 1991). For example, youth with any kind of learning disability typically have difficulty incorporating new information into semantic memory. Those with a reading disability are especially poor at encoding and recalling semantic information (Nelson & Warrington, 1980). Other studies have attributed the learning and memory problems to underutilization of strategies, including categorical organization and rote and elaborative rehearsal (Ceci, 1985). Students with learning disabilities also have poorly developed metamemory and are more susceptible to retroactive interference.

Reading is the most investigated type of disability (herein equated with dyslexia). A considerable amount of empirical evidence supports the claim that students with reading disabilities have deficits in the verbal aspects of short-term, working, (see Dehn, 2008, for a review), and long-term memory (Kipp & Mohr, 2008; Kramer, Knee, & Delis, 2000). In particular, children with a reading disability perform poorly on short-term memory tasks compared with normally achieving peers. There have even been some experiments (Vicari, Finzi, Menghini, Marotta, & Petrosini, 2005) that implicate difficulties with procedural learning and memory, which involves implicit memory processes. In reading disability research, the debate over whether the primary problem lies with encoding, storage, or retrieval has been ongoing. Encoding has often been cited as the core deficit in reading-disabled children. Their encoding problems are usually associated with truncated phonological short-term memory spans. However, their encoding weaknesses may also arise from poor utilization of encoding strategies, especially higher-level strategies such as elaborative rehearsal. Regarding storage and retrieval, some experiments have found that children with reading disabilities have deficits in long-term verbal memory storage but not retrieval. For example, Kramer et al. (2000) reported that dyslexics do not perform better on recognition than they do on free recall, indicating that the information has been forgotten and that storage is the problem, not retrieval. Nonetheless, Swanson (1986) and others have long argued that the primary problem lies with retrieval. There is also an avenue of reading research that emphasizes the slow retrieval rates of reading-disabled children. In particular, these children are slow at what is known as rapid automatic naming, a function that is highly correlated with reading ability (Torgesen, 1985). Overall, the consensus seems to be that children with impaired reading are deficient in the ability to learn and remember verbal material and that the primary memory dysfunction is encoding. However, the broad range of empirical findings can only lead one to conclude that a variety of memory impairments can contribute to or be associated with reading problems. For instance, Kipp and Mohr (2008) describe the case of an 8-year-old male with developmental dyslexia that seemed to stem from the boy's inability to store and access letter-sound associations. Interestingly, the boy did not have a general memory deficit.

Regarding children with a mathematics disability, the constellation of memory problems is somewhat distinct from those experienced by children with reading and written language disorders. They often have deficits in visuospatial aspects of memory, in addition to verbal memory weaknesses. Children with math learning problems seem to have the most difficulty in learning and retrieving basic arithmetic facts from long-term memory (Geary, 1993). The exact cause of this problem is unknown, but working memory seems to play a role. After a meta-analysis of studies on math disabilities, Swanson and Jerman (2006) concluded that limited working memory capacity is the primary roadblock to learning arithmetic facts and perform- ing math operations. Given working memory's role in the retrieval of information stored in long-term memory, it's difficult to determine how much of the difficulty with recall and math performance can be attributed to long-term memory rather than working memory.

Attention Deficit Hyperactivity Disorder (ADHD)

ADHD is one of the most prevalent disorders diagnosed among school-aged American youth. Students with ADHD typically experience learning problems in academic settings. Of course, their learning difficulties are often attributed to problems with various aspects of attention. However, some individuals with ADHD also have memory impairments. In particular, working memory deficits frequently occur among youth with ADHD (Barkley, 1997). These and other potential short- term and long-term memory dysfunctions should not be overlooked. Parents and teachers often report that children with ADHD have excellent memory for personal information (autobiographical memory) while they are lacking in semantic memory (Barkley). Skowronek, Leichtman, and Pillemer (2008) found support for this belief; their ADHD subjects performed as well as non-ADHD subjects on episodic memory measures. At the encoding stage, those with ADHD may lose information because of difficulties with selective and sustained attention. Further- more, during retrieval, their recall is especially vulnerable to interference, a finding that is consistent with their poor ability to inhibit interference from irrelevant verbal information. For example, Cornoldi, Barbieri, Gaiani, and Zocchi (1999) reported that children with ADHD have many intrusion errors during recall. Accordingly, youth with ADHD tend to perform better on cued recall and recognition tasks than they do on free recall (Voelker, Carter, Sprague, Gdowski, & Lachar, 1989). ADHD students with a comorbid learning disability are even more at-risk for long-term memory problems. These students are more likely to demonstrate difficulties with both short-term and long-term memory than students with a diagnosis of ADHD alone (Webster, Hall, Brown, & Bolen, 1996).

With ADHD children and adolescents, memory dysfunctions may not originate with a compromised hippocampus but rather with inadequate frontal lobe functioning. Their poor memory performance may be an outcome of executive processing weaknesses that result in poor management of strategic memory. ADHD students have demonstrated difficulties memorizing material, especially when it needs to be associated or organized, indicating their lack of appropriate strategy knowledge and usage (Cornoldi et al., 1999). It seems that students with ADHD generally have adequate metamemory development and strategy knowledge. The problem seems to be their failure to use strategies that would be beneficial, consistent with a production deficiency or a developmental lag in implementation of known strategies (Voelker et al., 1989). Because they seldom employ strategies, youth with ADHD are often naïve as to which strategies would be the most effective (O'Neill & Douglas, 1991). Also, their minimal use of effortful strategies means the strategies are less practiced and automatized, thereby placing more demands on the youth's already inefficient cognitive processing when they actually attempt to use a strategy. In conclusion, youth with ADHD are most likely to exhibit poor memory performance when a challenging learning task requires the application of an effective organizational or elaborative strategy (August, 1987). On simple tasks, their memory performance is usually normal.

When administering a memory test to a student with ADHD it is essential that the examiner has the student's attention before each and every item is presented so that the lack of attention does not invalidate the memory test results. Close observation of the examinee's behavior is critical; for example, the examiner might wait until the examinee makes eye contact. At times, it may be necessary to modify the standard protocol and cue the student that presentation of another item is imminent.

In the classroom, students with ADHD may particularly benefit from context-related cues that allow them to utilize their strong episodic memory to support recall of recently learned semantic material. During lessons, teachers might help these students connect contextual and factual information through an elaborative technique (Skowronek et al., 2008). Regarding individualized memory interventions, this population would also benefit from the teaching of metamemory and effective monitoring and utilization of memory strategies, such as being taught to group verbal items on the basis of semantic categories (see Chapter 7 for details).

Autism

The growing number of children with autism spectrum disorders has spawned more research on their cognitive abilities. Early investigations reported apparent deficits in long-term verbal semantic memory when individuals with autism were compared with ability-matched controls (see Toichi & Kamio, 2003, for a review). The poor semantic memory performance of youth with autism seems to result primarily from a failure to use advantageous encoding strategies, such as categorical clustering and elaborative rehearsal, as children with autism perform normally with lists of unrelated words. Similarly, those with autism fail to use semantic cues to aid recall. Interestingly, a unique encoding strategy, known as subject-performed tasks, appears to benefit children with autism while having no effect on normal children. In this strategy, subjects are instructed to act out a word to be remembered; for example, for the word "comb" they are told to "comb your hair." In a study with eight autistic children, subject-performed tasks improved word recall by 92% (Summers & Craik, 1994). Although visuospatial memory tends to be an area of strength, children with autism spectrum disorder typically demonstrate deficits in memory for faces, a subtype of visual memory. This unique deficit is consistent with the social and communication deficits that accompany autism. Overall, deficits in long-term memory seem to be more prevalent among autistic individuals with lower cognitive abilities. Among those who are higher functioning, some recent studies have failed to find evidence for long-term memory impairments.

Down Syndrome

Down Syndrome is a genetic disorder caused by abnormalities of chromosome 21. Although most individuals with Down Syndrome have mental retardation, their long-term memory functioning tends to be even more deficient, with impairments in both verbal and visuospatial domains (Nichols et al., 2004). When mental age is controlled for, individuals with Down Syndrome still exhibit long-term verbal memory deficits. In short-term memory, they tend to display weaknesses in phonological short-term memory relative to strengths in the visuospatial component. Also, they seem to be particularly susceptible to interference (Nichols et al., 2004).

Williams Syndrome

Williams Syndrome is a rare genetic disorder, with an incidence rate of 1 in 7,500, that is characterized by significant cognitive impairments, especially in visuospatial processing. Some studies have reported auditory short-term memory to be preserved, in contrast with significant memory impairments in the visuospatial domain. However, one recent study found global memory impairments in a group of 14 subjects with Williams Syndrome (Sampaio, Sousa, Fernandez, Henriques, & Goncalves, 2008). The subjects had significant deficits in short-term and working memory, as well as deficits in long-term verbal and visuospatial memory. Prior research by Nichols et al. (2004) also reported that this population has poor long-term memory abilities and poor use of organizational strategies during learning.

Developmental Amnesia

Recently, there has been some neuropsychological literature on rare cases of developmental amnesia. Individuals with amnesia are significantly impaired in their ability to learn new information and/or their ability to recall past events (see Chapter 3). Amnesia is unique in that short-term memory and working memory are usually preserved. Also, Full Scale and Verbal IQ are typically normal, even when memory impairment is global. Another characteristic of amnesia is intact implicit and procedural memory in the presence of marked impairment in explicit memory. Amnesia is usually acquired as the result of a medical condition, substance abuse, or head trauma. The medical conditions include herpes simplex encephalitis, anoxia, stroke, and aneurysm (O'Conner & Verfaellie, 2004). The term "developmental amnesia" applies when there is no known cause for this severe memory impairment or when there is a very early acquired injury, such as one resulting from perinatal anoxia. In most of these cases, significant bilateral hippocampal atrophy has been documented (Vargha-Khadem, 2001). Similar to acquired adult amnesia, the majority of children with developmental amnesia have more difficulty with episodic than semantic memory. For instance, the children described by Vargha-Khadem, Gadian, Watkins, and Connelly (1997) had significant impairments in episodic memory. These children had difficulty in finding their way around in familiar surroundings, remembering where objects and possessions were usually located, and being oriented in time. None of them could provide a reliable account of the day's activities. There are also reports of some children with developmental amnesia having impairments in both episodic and semantic memory (Ostergaard, 1987).

Those with spared semantic and procedural memory may perform adequately in a scholastic environment because academic learning depends primarily on semantic and procedural memory functions. In fact, cases of developmental amnesia reported in the literature have emphasized how these children lack episodic memory for personal autobiographical events and the presentation of novel information in the classroom but somehow manage to adequately acquire and recall semantic knowledge. Most of these children have normal language development, average IQ, and are making average progress in academic skills and knowledge. These cases are significant in that they demonstrate that the development of semantic memory is not entirely dependent on episodic memory or an intact hippocampus (Temple & Richardson, 2006). The proposed explanation for this phenomenon is that a fully functional hippocampus may be necessary for episodic memory but not semantic memory. However, some memory theorists (e.g., Squire & Zola, 1998) continue to claim that semantic memories cannot accrue without a functioning hippocampus and episodic memory system. One counter explanation is that semantic knowledge can be acquired without a functioning hippocampus because the medial temporal lobe structures subjacent to the hippocampus, specifically the perirhinal and entorhinal cortices (Martins, Guillery-Girard, Jambaque, Dulac, & Eustache, 2006), perform some encoding and consolidation functions. Another argument is that there is enough residual hippocampal functioning to support semantic learning but not enough to maintain episodic memories. Nonetheless, semantic acquisition apparently has some dependence on episodic learning, as semantic learning in these reported cases is slower and memory performance is poorer. Interestingly, a successful intervention with a case of developmental amnesia indicated that semantic memory can be used to boost episodic recall (Brandt, Gardiner, Vargha-Khadem, Baddeley, & Mishkin, 2006).

Despite the similarities, children with developmental amnesia, which often is just an early form of acquired amnesia, will experience different consequences than adults who acquire amnesia later in life. For example, the language development of young children will be affected if amnesia is acquired before language is established. Thus, developmental amnesia may underlie developmental delays in language. Developmental amnesia also differs from acquired amnesia in that recognition memory is relatively preserved compared to recall (de Haan, Mishkin, Baldeweg, & Vargha-Khadem, 2006). The main concern regarding developmental amnesia is that there are probably many cases that go undetected. The expanding literature on developmental amnesia indicates that this disorder may be more common than has been recognized in the past (Temple, 2004). For example, children with normal intelligence who are diagnosed with severe learning disorders may be suffering from unidentified developmental amnesia.

MENTAL DISORDERS

Posttraumatic Stress Disorder (PTSD), Childhood Abuse, and Chronic Stress

PTSD results when an individual lives through or witnesses an event in which he or she believes there is a threat to life and safety. During the event the individual experiences fear, terror, or helplessness. PTSD is characterized by painful recollections of the trauma, as well as emotional numbing and chronic physiological arousal. The symptoms include disturbed sleep, exaggerated startle response, difficulty concentrating and remembering, guilt, and avoidance of activities that bring the traumatic event to mind. There are several hundred thousand American youth suffering from PTSD (Bremner & Narayan, 1998). Among youth, PTSD commonly results from being the victim of abuse or witnessing violence. Students attending inner city schools are especially at-risk for developing PTSD because as many as 70% witness a violent crime or homicide (Bell & Jenkins, 1991).

Although, it is well established that adults with PTSD suffer from memory impairments, less information is available regarding PTSD in children and adolescents. Recently, however, investigations have begun to document memory and learning problems in the PTSD youth population. For instance, Yasik, Saigh, Oberfield, and Halamandaris (2007) found the general memory functioning of PTSD youth to be one standard deviation below the mean. The childhood memory deficits most commonly reported are in short-term memory and verbal long-term memory, whereas visuospatial memory typically remains intact.

The stress resulting from childhood physical and sexual abuse may have a detrimental impact on memory functions even when the child or adolescent never develops PTSD. Although some researchers have argued that exposure to trauma is only associated with memory impairment when the individual subsequently develops PTSD (Yasik et al., 2007), it is well known that chronic stress can harm the hippocampus. A study of undiagnosed adult survivors of childhood abuse (Bremner, Randall, Scott, Capelli, et al., 1995) discovered that these victims had significantly lower short-term and long-term verbal memory test performance than comparable normal subjects. Furthermore, the degree of the memory impairment was correlated with the severity of the abuse, which often had occurred before the age of 5. These results are similar to those in a follow-up study with sexual abuse victims who were diagnosed with PTSD (Bremner, Vermetten, Afzal, & Vythilingam, 2004). In adulthood, diagnosed victims exhibit significant deficits in verbal declarative memory that are correlated with increased PTSD symptoms, as well as with greater severity of childhood sexual abuse. In a study not as removed from the maltreatment, 14 children with a mean age of 11.38 years performed poorly on a test of verbal delayed free recall (Beers & De Bellis, 2002).

As expected, these decrements in memory functioning can be associated with damage to the hippocampus that can be observed in reduced hippocampal volume (Bremner, Randall, Scott, Bronen et al., 1995). For example, in a study with Vietnam combat-related PTSD subjects, Curvits, Shenton, Hokama et al. (1996) discovered an astounding 26% decrease in bilateral hippocampal volume. With PTSD and chronic stress, the responsible neurochemical agents and mechanisms are well understood. Humans under stress release glucocorticoid hydrocortisone (also referred to as cortisol). Both the hippocampus and prefrontal cortex have a high number of receptors for cortisol and thus are very sensitive to cortisol released by the adrenal cortex (Schwabe, Bohringer, & Wolf, 2009). During an extremely stressful event, humans release high levels of glucocorticoids that cause damage to neurons in the hippocampus. The neuronal damage, which persists for many years after the original trauma (Sapolsky, Packan, & Vale, 1988), causes atrophy and significantly reduced hippocampal volume, especially on the left side. For example, Bremner and Narayan (1998) found a 12% left side reduction in adult patients with childhood, abuse-related PTSD.

Individuals need not experience abuse or trauma or be diagnosed with PTSD in order to sustain hippocampal atrophy or experience temporary memory problems. Recent research has discovered the impact of chronic and everyday stress on specific aspects of memory. Chronic stress and even everyday stressful events also cause the release of cortisol, and chronic exposure to cortisol destroys hippocampal neurons (Siegel, 1999). Accordingly, adults and youth who live with chronic stress are known to have persistent memory impairments (Elzinga, Bakker, & Bremner, 2005). However, even temporary, above normal secretions of cortisol, induced by everyday stressful events, may impact recall of information learned during or shortly after the interval of elevated cortisol. Acquisition of verbal, and even spatial information, is negatively correlated with cortisol levels during learning (Elzinga et al., 2005). When cortisol levels are elevated, encoding of information is affected. Moreover, stress-induced elevated cortisol levels may interfere with consolidation of declarative memories (Elzinga et al.) because high cortisol levels persist for at least 30 minutes after cessation of the stress-producing stimuli. Stress also may interfere with the consolidation of memories by reducing non-REM sleep, a critical sleep stage for consolidation of explicit memories (Maquet, 2001). Finally, a high level of stress, such as that induced by test anxiety, can impede or interfere with retrieval processes that are dependent on the hippocampus. Stress especially seems to impair retrieval of context-dependent memories (Schwabe et al., 2009). One limitation of research on stress-induced cortisol's impact on memory functioning is that most of this research has been conducted with adults. Cortisol is known to have a stronger negative impact on memory functioning in adults than among youth.

Reported learning problems in any child or adolescent with PTSD or a history of abuse, trauma, or chronic stress should lead to a referral for a memory evaluation. When conducting evaluations with this population, evaluators need to investigate the individual's age at the time of traumatic experience, the number and severity of the incidents, the youth's reaction, and the treatment received. If there is no diagnosis of PTSD, symptoms of stress should be reviewed to determine their severity and chronicity.

Obsessive-Compulsive Disorder (OCD)

OCD is characterized by recurrent intrusive thoughts and repetitive, ritualistic behaviors that cause severe distress and interfere with daily functioning. Obsessions are persistent ideas, thoughts, impulses, or images that are intrusive and inappropriate and cause marked anxiety or distress. In contrast, compulsions are repetitive behaviors that have the goal of reducing anxiety or distress. The main difference between childhood OCD and adult OCD is that children usually lack the awareness that their obsessions or compulsions are excessive or unreasonable. There are no known investigations into the links between OCD and memory functioning that have been conducted with children. In the adult literature, connections have been drawn between OCD and specific memory dysfunctions. Generally, studies have documented memory deficits in short-term memory and both verbal and visuospatial long-term memory, although findings of visuospatial memory difficulties predominate. Also, there seems to be problems with both encoding and free recall, whereas retention and recognition seem to be normal (Savage, Keuthen, Jenike, & Brown, 1996). The memory deficiencies of individuals with OCD appear to originate with poor encoding. These encoding difficulties have been attributed to problems with organization in both verbal and visuospatial domains (Deckersbach, Otto, Savage,

Baer, & Jenike, 2000; Emilien et al., 2004). For example, OCD subjects tend not to use semantic clustering and verbal elaboration strategies. Poor strategic processing is consistent with the evidence that prefrontal lobe dysfunction underlies OCD behaviors. OCD patients present with strategic processing difficulties whether or not they are on medication at the time of testing (Savage et al., 2000). Interestingly, there is speculation that OCD behaviors might be caused by memory problems. That is, compulsive checking might occur because the individual can't remember whether he or she has performed an action or because he or she can't distinguish performing an action from imagining an action. In contrast, several studies suggest that OCD behaviors arise from an intolerance of uncertainty, not from a problem with encoding or retrieval per se (Emilien et al., 2004).

Depression

It is well known that adults with depression exhibit impaired memory functioning of several types. Although very little research on depression and memory has been conducted with school-age populations (see Lauer et al., 1994), it is relatively safe to assume that depression affects memory functioning in children and adolescents much the same as it does in adults. Memory deficits in adults and youth with a history of depression have been reported in metamemory, short-term memory, working memory, and long-term memory (see Table 4.1). Within long-term memory, both the verbal and visuospatial domains are affected. Also, findings of poor performance on recognition tasks (Watts, Morris, & MacLeod, 1987) indicate that individuals suffering from depression have difficulties encoding and storing information. Memory dysfunctions associated with depression are especially evident when effortful encoding is required, probably because depression limits the attentional resources that can be devoted to encoding. The relationship between depression and memory dysfunction is mediated by the stress-induced secretion of glucocorticoids, which are known to have adverse effects on hippo-campal neurons, especially when a high level of secretion is sustained (Sapolsky, 1996). Accordingly, adults with depression have been found to have significant reductions in hippocampal volume, 12 to 15% in studies reviewed by Sapolsky. Adult studies also have found a significant correlation between the cumulative duration of recurrent depressive episodes and the extent of atrophy (Sheline, Wang, Gado, Csernansky, & Vannier, 1996). Likewise, studies of depressed children have found that memory impairment varies as a function of depression severity (Lauer et al.). Furthermore, the effects are enduring: Reduced hippocampal volume and memory dysfunctions are observed in subjects who are not currently suffering from depression. The main difference between the adult and youth populations is that adults with a history of depression are more likely to have received electro-convulsive therapy (ECT), which produces seizures. ECT has been implicated in structural damage and memory dysfunctions (Sheline et al., 1996).

Pediatric Bipolar Disorder

Bipolar disorder is a mood disorder in which both manic and depressive episodes occur. Bipolar disorder is an increasingly prevalent disorder in children and adolescents. From the research conducted with affected youth, it appears they are at-risk for the same memory impairments as adults with bipolar disorder. Adult populations frequently exhibit deficits in attention and verbal episodic memory. In a meta-analysis of the existing literature, the largest difference (.62 of a standard deviation) found between healthy controls and youth with bipolar disorder was in verbal memory (Joseph, Frazier, Youngstrom, & Soares, 2008). Effect sizes were also significant in visual memory (.51) and working memory (.60). A study with 21 affected children and adolescents by Dickstein et al. (2004) reported that the sample was impaired on measures of visuospatial memory (the study did not include any verbal measures). In another investigation with 41 subjects that included verbal memory testing, Glahn et al. (2005) found significant verbal memory impairments, but only in those subjects with a diagnosis of Bipolar I Disorder, not those with Bipolar II Disorder (manic episodes predominate in Bipolar I and depressive episodes predominate in Bipolar II). Their deficient verbal memory was attributed to poor encoding of the information, rather than rapid forgetting. Regarding the brains of adults with Bipolar Disorder, researchers have not found reduced hippocampal volume but rather reduced volume in the prefrontal cortex (reviewed in Deckersbach et al., 2004). Consistent with prefrontal lobe involvement, the poor memory performance of this population may be associated with difficulties organizing verbal information during encoding (Deckersbach et al., 2004). As expected, individuals with more lifetime manic and depressive episodes display more memory impairment. Also, people with bipolar disorder need not be in a manic or depressive state to experience learning and memory problems. Even when they are in a euthymic (neutral) state, memory problems persist. In the Kurtz and Gerraty (2009) meta-analysis of adult patients with bipolar disorder, there were large effect sizes for long-term verbal (.80) and visuospatial (.92) memory when subjects were tested during the absence of clinical symptoms. However, when these subjects were in a manic phase, their verbal learning impairments were more significant.

SUBSTANCE ABUSE

Children and adolescents may consume chemicals that can damage the brain's memory systems. Little is known about the cognitive effects of substance abuse during childhood or adolescence because there is very little research on how memory might be impacted by youthful abuse of illegal drugs, such as cannabis. One exception is research on Ecstasy, which has been widely abused by teens in recent years. Ecstasy is known to severely damage serotonin axons in the hippocampus, resulting in permanent impairments in both verbal and visual memory (Emilien et al., 2004). Also, inferences about chemical abuse can be drawn from the adult literature. For example, prolonged and excessive alcohol intake in adults causes Korsakoff's syndrome, which is characterized by retrograde amnesia (Emilien et al., 2004).

Prenatal Alcohol Exposure

The risks of maternal alcohol consumption during pregnancy have been well known since alcohol was officially identified as a fetal teratogen in the 1970s (Richardson, Ryan, Willford, Day, & Goldschmidt, 2002). The neurocognitive effects of alcohol exposure lie along a continuum that seems to be dose-related. Heavy consumption puts the fetus at-risk for fetal alcohol syndrome (FAS) or fetal alcohol effect (FAE). But even those fetuses with mild exposure to alcohol are at risk for lifelong neurocognitive damage (Streissguth, Barr, Bookstein, Sampson, & Olson, 1999) because the fetal brain is very vulnerable to alcohol exposure. Even one drink per occasion can be detrimental (Streissguth et al., 1999). The adverse neurocognitive consequences include impairments in learning, language, attention, executive functions, short-term memory, and various types of long-term memory. (See Table 4.1 towards the end of this chapter.) Based on the data collected in the Seattle Longitudinal Study, Streissguth et al. estimate the prevalence of alcohol-related neurodevelopmental disabilities to be as high as 1 in 100 births. Unfortunately, central nervous system (CNS) impairments resulting from prenatal alcohol exposure frequently go undetected and undiagnosed or are not attributed to maternal consumption of alcohol when they are identified. Furthermore, many children who do not meet criteria for the disorders may have memory weaknesses and impairments that affect academic learning (Willford, Richardson, Leech, & Day, 2004).

Heavy alcohol consumption causes FAS, the most severe manifestation of alcohol consumption during pregnancy. FAS, affecting from 1 to 7 per 1,000 live-born infants, remains the most common cause of mental retardation (Niccols, 2007). For example, Native American populations report incidences up to 3 per 1,000 births (Mattson & Riley, 1998). FAS is characterized by the coexistence of three features: prenatal-onset growth deficiency, facial dysmorphology, and evidence of CNS dysfunction. When the physical characteristics are present, FAS is identifiable at birth or during infancy. For example, FAS babies are usually small for their gestational age and continue to show evidence of growth deficiency. When postnatal physical appearances are normal, a diagnosis is sometimes made when health problems or developmental delays emerge later on. Brain imaging studies have discovered abnormalities in several brain regions, including the hippocampus, medial temporal lobes, and prefrontal cortex (Niccols). For instance, neuroanatomical studies (reviewed in Niccols) have found that children with FAS have a smaller left hippocampus than right. Damage to the hippocampus and prefrontal cortex is most likely the result of alcohol exposure during the third trimester of pregnancy. Not surprisingly, deficits in various aspects of memory have been reported by several researchers (see Table 4.1). Some investigators have concluded that the core deficit in FAS is working memory (Rasmussen, 2005). Attention Deficit Hyperactivity Disorder (ADHD) is the most frequently diagnosed disorder among FAS children (Niccols).

FAE is the label associated with children who only partially meet the criteria for FAS but nonetheless display some of the developmental and cognitive characteristics (Kaemingk, Mulvaney, & Halverson, 2003). Children with FAE are generally considered the result of light to moderate drinking. In a longitudinal study involving several hundred such children retested at age 14 (Willford et al., 2004), none of the subjects had an official diagnosis of FAS. Nonetheless, the cohort had deficits in learning, short-term memory, and auditory/verbal memory, as well as impairments in encoding, storage, and retrieval processes. The learning and memory deficits of these children typically do not emerge until their school-age years, and even then may remain undetected.

Even a child without a diagnosis of FAS or FAE may have neurocognitive damage from prenatal alcohol exposure. Patterns of neuropsychological dysfunction have been found to be consistent between alcohol-exposed children with and without a diagnosis (Mattson & Roebuck, 2002). That is, a diagnosis of FAS or FAE is irrelevant when it comes to potential learning and memory problems. Through repeated assessments of approximately 500 offspring, the Seattle Longitudinal Study has clearly documented the adverse learning and memory effects associated with minor and casual alcohol consumption during pregnancy (Streissguth et al., 1999). More than 80% of the mothers were white, married, and middle class. They had a mean educational level of 13.8 years, and 100% of them had received proper prenatal care. The children were evaluated within the first 2 days of life, at 8 months, 18 months, 4 years, 7 years, and 14 years. The most notable findings through the years are that the effects of alcohol are enduring and dose-dependent. Greater levels of alcohol consumption lead to more impairment. At 7 years, prenatal exposure was associated with poor performance on tests of attention, spatial memory, verbal memory, and short-term memory. The results of standardized rating scales completed by teachers revealed additional problems with organization, grammar, and word recall. At 11 years, poor achievement in all academic areas, especially arithmetic, was evident. Memory testing was conducted again at 14 years, and the cohort particularly struggled with tests of spatial memory. These outcomes are solely attributable to minor alcohol exposure, as the researchers controlled for such potential confounds as drug abuse, smoking, and demographic factors. Although researchers (e.g., Streissguth et al.) have concluded that no level of alcohol exposure is safe for every pregnancy, many children exposed to alcohol in utero never develop FAS or FAE. In fact, only a small percentage of the offspring of heavy drinkers actually display the physical symptoms (Streissguth et al.).

Neuroimaging and postmortem studies have documented diverse CNS abnormalities in fetal alcohol spectrum disorders (see Malisza, 2007, for a review). Abnormalities have been found in many brain locations including the basal ganglia, thalamus, corpus callosum, cerebellum, brainstem, hippocampus, medial temporal lobes, parietal lobes, and the frontal lobes (Malisza). Because there is a large amount of inter-subject variability, a neurocognitive profile of FAS-related insults cannot be determined. Several studies have found reduced volume in the hippocampus and frontal lobes, the brain systems most associated with explicit memory. In addition to structural abnormalities, functional magnetic resonance imaging (*f*MRI) studies have uncovered abnormal patterns of brain activation. For instance, Sowell et al. (2007) reported that children with heavy prenatal alcohol exposure exhibit an unusual increase in frontal lobe activation and a decrease in medial temporal lobe activity during verbal learning and memory tasks usually handled by the medial temporal memory systems. Sowell et al. hypothesized that the subjects might be relying more on the frontal lobe systems to encode and retrieve verbal information because the medial temporal lobes are deficient. Despite the brain's plasticity, these subjects remained impaired on verbal learning tasks.

When a child with a possible fetal alcohol spectrum disorder is evaluated, practitioners should review the syndrome's characteristics and carefully interview the mother about her prenatal care, behavior, and alcohol consumption. A detailed developmental history should be collected with a focus on infant growth rate and the developing child's motor skills, attention, activity levels, and language development. When parents deny prenatal alcohol consumption, medical records may contain clues, such as low birth weight at full term or reports of growth deficiency. With severe effects of alcohol exposure, IQ will be impacted; however, IQ alone does not fully account for memory deficits in this population (Kaemingk et al., 2003). Therefore, once testing is complete, evaluators should consider how the examinee's memory functions compare to overall intellectual ability.

Although implicit and procedural memory are intact, children with prenatal alcohol exposure are likely to experience difficulties in nearly all aspects of memory functioning (see Table 4.1). Learning and memory functions of particular concern in the classroom are short-term memory and verbal memory. Initial learning seems to be slower due to encoding problems. For example, FAS children in the Mattson and Roebuck (2002) study learned .75 new words per trial on the California Verbal Learning Test—Children's Version (Delis, Kramer, Kaplan, & Ober, 1994), whereas control children learned 1.21 new words. Thus, given the same opportunities, students on the fetal alcohol spectrum learn significantly less (Kaemingk et al., 2003). Nonetheless, once they have learned the information, they retain it as well as learning-ability matched, non-exposed children (Kaemingk et al., 2003). Regarding visuospatial memory, short-term memory is often normal but long-term retrieval of object and spatial information is more likely to be lacking (Olson, Feldman, Streissguth, Sampson, & Bookstein, 1998). The consensus seems to be that long-term visuospatial and verbal memory are equally vulnerable (Kaemingk et al., 2003). Although free recall problems have been reported, retention and recognition of verbal content does not seem to be a problem (Mattson & Riley, 1999). Nonetheless, spared retention of information may be insufficient for adequate academic performance because the memory of fetal alcohol–impacted learners is very susceptible to interference problems, such as perseveration (Kaemingk, Mulvaney, & Halverson). Consistent with the syndrome's attention deficits, FAS students typically demonstrate poor inhibition of interference. Because retention of learned verbal material is fairly normal (Mattson & Riley, 1998; Mattson & Roebuck, 2002), interventions and instruction should focus on enhancement of encoding and retrieval (see Chapters 8 and 9), such as using mnemonics to attach retrieval cues. Because their learning is slower, repeated exposure to material should be a basic instructional modification. Children on the fetal alcohol spectrum should also be tested with recognition items (matching, true-false, or multiple-choice items) so that they can demonstrate their knowledge. See Chapter 7 for more details on interventions and Chapter 8 for more information on classroom instruction.

Prenatal Cocaine Exposure

Compared to the extensive investigations of alcohol exposure, research on the cognitive effects of prenatal cocaine exposure has been limited and has produced inconsistent results. Neurological risks have been implicated by research with rats that found cocaine exposure to be associated with increased oxidative stress on the hippocampus. Some human studies (reviewed in Bennett, Bendersky, & Lewis, 2008) have reported deficits in verbal memory, whereas others have found no cocaine-related effects. In a study of 90 predominantly urban, African American children exposed in utero to cocaine, Bennett, Bendersky, and Lewis discovered that the boys exhibited more cognitive processing deficits than the girls. Only short-term memory was tested, and it was found to be deficient, along with visual abstract reasoning. Another study with 130 school-aged children (Mayes, Snyder, Langlois, & Hunter, 2007) reported that intrauterine cocaine exposure was related to impairments in visuospatial working memory and long-term visuospatial memory. The study's authors also concluded that prenatal exposure reduces consolidation of initial learning. Although some researchers have argued that children prenatally exposed to crack cocaine will have significant memory problems by school age (Allen et al., 1991), it is difficult to draw any firm conclusions about the relationships between prenatal cocaine exposure and memory functions. It's not just the controversial findings but the multiple confounds such as alcohol, marijuana, and tobacco exposure that have not been controlled for (Frank, Augustyn, Knight, Pell, & Zuckerman, 2001). Nonetheless, practitioners should consider a memory assessment whenever a student is known to have been exposed to cocaine prenatally.

Table 4.1 Types of memory reported to be significantly affected by risk factors*

Risk Factor	Episodic	Semantic	Implicit	Verbal	Visuospatial	Short-Term	Working	Encoding	Consolidation	Storage	Retrieval	Recognition	Metamemory**
Traumatic Brain Injury	X	X		X	X		X	X	X		X	X	X
Post-Concussion Syndrome	X												
Frontal Lobe Lesions								X			X		X
Prematurity	X												
Perinatal Asphyxia	X			X	X								
Excess Bilirubin Levels						X							
Congenital Hypothyroidism						X					X	X	
Childhood Diabetes				X	X	X							X
Sleep Disorders													
Epilepsy				X	X	X		X	X		X		
Herpes Simplex Encephalitis													
Childhood Stroke				X		X		X			X		X
Reye's Syndrome	X			X	X		X	X					X
Medulloblastoma				X	X			X			X	X	
Effects of Asthma Medication				X		X							
Specific Language Impairment		X		X		X	X	X			X		X
Learning Disabilities		X	X	X		X	X	X		X	X		X
ADHD		X					X						X
Autism		X		X	X								X
Down Syndrome				X	X	X							
Williams Syndrome				X	X	X	X						X

(continued)

Table 4.1 (continued)

Risk Factor	Episodic	Semantic	Implicit	Verbal	Visuospatial	Short-Term	Working	Encoding	Consolidation	Storage	Retrieval	Recognition	Metamemory**
Developmental Amnesia	X									X	X		
PTSD, Abuse, Chronic Stress				X		X		X	X		X		
Obsessive-Compulsive Disorder				X	X	X		X			X		X
Depression				X	X	X	X	X		X		X	X
Pediatric Bipolar Disorder	X			X	X		X						X
Prenatal Alcohol Exposure				X	X	X	X	X			X		
Prenatal Cocaine Exposure				X	X	X	X		X				

*Based on a review of empirical evidence. The absence of an "x" does not mean that type of memory may be unaffected. It may simply mean that there is insufficient research on the specific memory dysfunctions associated with a particular risk factor.

**Includes strategy development and use.

FINDINGS THAT APPLY TO ALL AT-RISK GROUPS

1. Damage (lesions or atrophy) to the hippocampus and/or surrounding medial temporal lobe structures is the underlying neurological cause of most memory impairments. Frontal lobe damage is the second most common cause.

2. The earlier in development the brain is affected, the more likely there will be diverse, significant, and enduring memory impairments. Unfortunately, many memory impairments originate during the prenatal, neonatal, and early childhood stages of life.

3. Long-term consolidation and storage of information is seldom affected. Most children and adolescents with medically related memory problems evidence normal consolidation and retention of information that they have learned.

4. Memory impairments may not immediately ensue after the commencement of a medical condition or mental disorder. With some conditions, such as chronic stress, epilepsy, or diabetes, it takes time for significant hippocampal damage to accrue.

5. The existence of a memory impairment may not become apparent until high demands are placed on the child or adolescent, such as demanding learning requirements when the child enters school.

6. Memory impairments do not occur in isolation. Other cognitive functions are usually involved. For example, there are often concurrent deficits in attention and executive functions.

7. Some form of episodic memory functioning is almost always affected when there is a memory impairment. Although episodic memory dysfunctions are not specifically addressed in much of the research (see Table 4.1), they are implicated when researchers refer to "verbal" or "visuospatial" deficits.

8. Implicit memory is more resistant to disease, injury, and other conditions than is explicit memory. In fact, implicit learning and memory is almost never affected. Even individuals with amnesia can learn new procedures and even some semantic knowledge through implicit memory without any episodic recall of the learning event. Also, they almost always retain their pre-amnesic implicit skills and "knowledge."

9. When it comes to memory functions, brain plasticity is limited.

10. A dysfunction in one memory process will influence the effectiveness of other processes. For example, encoding dysfunctions and inefficiencies will diminish the effectiveness of retrieval.

11. Children, adolescents, their parents, and sometimes their teachers are often unaware of existent memory problems. Even in cases of severe developmental amnesia, the adults involved usually don't realize that a

memory impairment underlies the child's learning and daily functioning problems.

12. Many memory problems and impairments go undetected, undiagnosed, and untreated because of the lack of awareness of the risk factors reviewed in this chapter.

ASSESSMENT IMPLICATIONS

The author of this book has evaluated (in schools and in a private practice setting) many children and adolescents with long-term memory problems. Nearly all of these students had experienced one of the events, illnesses, or disorders discussed in this chapter. The risk factors in these cases included autism, learning disability, language disability, fetal alcohol effects, childhood diabetes, traumatic brain injury, childhood stroke, prematurity, cocaine exposure, perinatal asphyxia, and ADHD. In cases of previously identified disabilities, very seldom had the prior testing expressly included long-term memory. At best, there were references to short-term or working memory problems. As for the parents who brought their children in for testing and tutoring, many had no idea that there was a significant memory problem, even though they often reported that their child would study hard and know the material only to fail a school exam the next day. Although Chapters 6 and 7 will detail memory assessment strategies and review memory scales, some assessment recommendations are made here while the characteristics of the at-risk populations are still fresh in mind.

1. Early screening should be conducted with children who have experienced events and illnesses that put them at-risk for memory impairments.
2. When children attend a preschool or kindergarten screening, educational staff should question parents about memory. Questions might include asking how well a child remembers where household items are placed or how well the child remembers stories that have been read to her or him.
3. A developmental and health history is absolutely essential (see Table 4.2 and see Chapter 5). Gathering a complete history allows the discovery of low-incidence disorders and diseases that students and parents are unlikely to mention because they are unaware of possible connections between the conditions and memory and learning functions.
4. Documenting the course of the disorder or disease is critical. Age at onset is often a particularly important variable. Some memory impairments, such as those resulting from childhood diabetes, will not arise until the disease has progressed for a period of time. A review of medical records should provide much relevant information.
5. In-depth, parental interviews are important. One component of the interview should address everyday memory issues.
6. Extending intervals to a day or a week before testing long-term recall allows the determination of forgetting rate and effectiveness of consolidation.

Table 4.2 Prenatal, developmental, and health factors that suggest hippocampal damage

Premature birth	Below average APGAR score
Prenatal cocaine exposure	Prenatal alcohol exposure
Prolonged neonatal jaundice	Deprivation of oxygen at birth
Head injuries	Viral infections of the brain
Brain tumors	Childhood diabetes
Childhood stroke	Physical or sexual abuse
Sleep apnea	Witnessing a traumatic event

7. Memory difficulties will often go undetected during early childhood but emerge when the child begins formal schooling, or perhaps when the academic bar is raised in middle or high school.

8. The reasons for referral will often not include memory. The evaluator needs to consider the possibility that select memory deficiencies may underlie the reported problems.

9. Practitioners who evaluate children and adolescents for learning disabilities should add memory tests to their usual assessment battery, keeping in mind that there is considerable variation in terms of which aspects of memory are involved with any specific type of learning disability.

10. Evaluators should not presume that an at-risk child or adolescent has a memory impairment (also known as hypothesis confirmation bias). For each at-risk group, there's a considerable range of individual differences in memory performance and profiles of strengths and weaknesses. This is another reason why an assessment is essential.

11. Evaluators need to take comorbidity into account; for example, ADHD frequently co-occurs with memory problems and is difficult to disentangle.

12. Formal, standardized testing should always take precedence over informal procedures. On the other hand, there are times when standardized test results are misleading, as they can overestimate or underestimate real-world functioning.

13. The typical standardized memory tests may not measure the types of memory dysfunction that are the most troublesome. For example, prospective memory and episodic memory for everyday functioning are not tapped by traditional scales. Also, forgetting over extended time periods is not assessed by measures that only include 30-minute intervals between learning and delayed recall.

IMPLICATIONS FOR INTERVENTIONS AND CLASSROOM INSTRUCTION

1. Many memory performance problems originate with poor encoding. Consequently, interventions and instruction should focus on supporting

encoding through methods that focus attention, create dual modality encoding, elaborate on the material, and attach cues that will enhance retrieval.

2. When the hippocampus has been damaged but frontal lobes are intact, interventions and instruction should strive to enhance the memory functions of the frontal lobes. For example, improving metamemory, self-monitoring, and utilization of effective memory strategies can help to compensate.

3. Children with retrieval deficits under free recall conditions but significantly stronger recognition performance should be provided with test items in true-false, matching, and multiple-choice formats so that they can access the knowledge they have learned.

4. In cases of severe amnesia, such as severe head trauma, children can still learn and retain new procedures and knowledge through implicit learning and memory. In such instances, implicit training methods, such as errorless learning, may be necessary (see Chapter 8).

5. Upon their return to school, TBI victims, even those with a mild TBI or concussion, should be provided with accommodations for their memory problems because the most debilitating interval will be within the first few days and weeks. Those with memory problems that persist beyond three months should be provided with appropriate memory interventions.

6. For children and adolescents with mental disorders, memory problems may temporally increase when they are experiencing a clinical episode, for example, students with a depressive disorder who are in a state of depression or children with bipolar disorder who are in a manic state.

5 Long-Term Memory Assessment Strategies

"Jane" was an 11-year-old fifth grader when her parents called to inquire about testing. Jane had been receiving speech and language therapy since the age of 3 and educational services for a learning disability since first grade. In fifth grade, Jane was struggling with verbal expression, oral comprehension, written expression, and reading comprehension. Her abilities and skills had been tested several times, and her school would continue to evaluate her on a regular basis. Previous examiners had reported IQ, language, and academic scores and had identified Jane's language and learning disorders. Yet, her parents, who studied with her every evening at home, were dissatisfied with the assessment information. They wanted to understand why Jane was experiencing learning problems, her learning strengths and weaknesses, and how to teach her. As her father summed it up, they wanted "answers to the riddle" so that they could more effectively help Jane learn and succeed in school. The parents wanted some answers before Jane entered middle school in a few months.

These parents and others like them have expectations for psychoeducational assessment that are often unmet. Sometimes, evaluators in medical and educational settings focus too much on making a diagnosis or disability placement and don't provide parents, teachers, and students with answers to the questions that initiated the referral. Often evaluators use a standard battery for each case instead of adapting the assessment to the specific referral questions and hypotheses. Traditionally, an IQ test has been part of the standard battery when children are referred for learning problems. But an IQ score alone provides very little information about the learner's cognitive strengths and weaknesses and at best answers only one of the "why" questions. For instance, Jane's Full Scale IQ was reported to be a 91 (at the low end of the average range) when she was tested in first grade. Knowing this "fact" about Jane provided teachers and parents with little insight as to how to teach and work with Jane. When this author was a young school psychologist, an assertive parent challenged his use of a standard assessment battery. The parent insisted that she did not want an IQ score reported. Instead, she wanted to know about her child's specific cognitive abilities. Her request (in effect, a request for a cross-battery assessment) led to the use of three different cognitive scales and a better understanding of why the child was struggling in school. Basically, the traditional cognitive assessment battery is too limited in scope. One of the crucial cognitive factors omitted is long-term memory.

A psychological or educational assessment involves the gathering of information and data through informal methods and the use of standardized tests. The data are used to make informed decisions about a diagnosis, an educational placement, interventions, accommodations, and a variety of services. The ultimate goal of psychological and educational evaluations is to meet the needs of the learner. For this goal to be accomplished, the assessment needs to produce answers. Perhaps an effective way for an evaluator to frame a cognitive assessment is to consider it an investigation. The primary goal of the investigation is to understand what is causing (or underlying) the child's learning problems. Like a detective, the evaluator may begin the investigation by reviewing the existing information, interviewing informants, and observing the subject. From the initial round of investigation, the evaluator will generate hypotheses that are likely to account for the problems and then proceed to test these hypotheses through formal and informal procedures. During this second stage of the assessment, the evaluator may uncover clues that lead to additional hypotheses and further investigation along particular avenues. After all the relevant information has been gathered, the investigator interprets the data, explains why the problems are occurring, and makes the case for appropriate treatment or interventions. For example, a child's presenting problem may be poor homework completion. The usual suspects may be lack of motivation, poor study skills, behavior problems, or lack of basic academic skills. After the usual suspects have been eliminated, the astute evaluator may hypothesize other possibilities, such as slow processing speed, poor attentional control, or subaverage intellectual ability. While testing intellectual ability the investigator may discover poor digit span performance, which leads to a further investigation of memory and the uncovering of a deficit in verbal episodic memory. Overall, the main benefit of framing an evaluation as an investigation is that it is more likely to be thorough and to identify the reasons for the difficulties the child or adolescent is experiencing. A complete and successful investigation that produces answers to referral questions and confirms some hypotheses leads to the selection and design of interventions more likely to succeed than interventions selected without in-depth knowledge of the individual who needs help. If an investigative assessment is to identify underlying cognitive and memory deficiencies and implicate effective interventions, it must be comprehensive and personalized.

A COMPREHENSIVE EXPLICIT MEMORY ASSESSMENT

A comprehensive explicit memory assessment should investigate several memory dimensions. First, short-term and working memory should be tested whenever long-term memory is being evaluated (see Dehn, 2008, for details on short-term and working memory assessment). Second, the two explicit memory systems—episodic and semantic—should both be assessed. Third, the memory processes of encoding, consolidation, retention, and retrieval should be considered. Finally, metamemory and strategy development should be investigated. A fundamental distinction in memory assessment is product versus process. The product is the observable performance, such as how many words an examinee can recall after a 30-minute delay. Underlying the product or performance are several memory processes. The purpose of identifying memory processing strengths and weaknesses is to determine the specific deficits that underlie subaverage performance in memory domains and structures. For example, knowing there is a verbal memory impairment is rather straightforward information, but knowing why there is a verbal memory impairment is even more helpful, especially when interventions can be pursued. Thus, a comprehensive assessment includes efforts to identify strengths and weaknesses among memory processes even though this task is not easily accomplished. The assessment also should incorporate measures of related cognitive processes, such as attention, language, and executive functions. Testing related cognitive functions will allow the evaluator to determine the extent of influence these cognitive functions may be having on memory performance. Those who question the need for comprehensive testing should remember that the main purpose of a memory assessment is to guide treatment. Given different etiologies of observed memory performance deficits, the same intervention may not be equally effective. For example, interventions that facilitate short-term retention may not be effective for facilitating long-term retrieval. Consequently, the more thorough the assessment, the greater the probability of selecting appropriate interventions and accommodations.

Is a Neuropsychological Assessment Necessary?

Some memory experts recommend an assessment by a neuropsychologist whenever there are referral concerns about memory (Wilson, 2004). However, this may be necessary in only the most extreme cases, such as when amnesia results from a head injury (Baron, 2004). Clinical and school psychologists are qualified to administer and interpret memory scales as long as they have been adequately trained to administer the scales, and they study and practice the material appropriately. In fact, many memory measures are embedded in the intellectual and cognitive scales routinely used by clinical and school psychologists. Nonetheless, practitioners who work in schools and clinics need to approach memory assessment from a neuropsychological perspective, such as the approach advocated by Miller (2007, 2010). That is, memory assessment should be conducted in a selective, cross-battery fashion with the neurological foundations of memory in mind. Consequently, evaluators should possess basic knowledge in the neurobiological mechanisms involved in memory, with the caveat that their brain-based interpretation of assessment results should not exceed their level of expertise.

Components and Processes to Consider Assessing

This section highlights reasons for testing specific long-term memory components and processes, summarizes the typical measurement tasks employed (see Chapter 6 for details on recommended tests), and mentions additional types of memory and cognitive processing that should be tested when there is subaverage performance in a long-term memory component (see Table 5.1 on page 134). The purpose of this section is to provide practitioners with a review and reminders before they plan and conduct an individualized, comprehensive memory assessment. For more in-depth information on memory components and processes, the reader should refer to Chapters 2 and 3 or Dehn (2008).

Phonological Short-Term Memory   Phonological (auditory) short-term memory is highly related with language development, basic reading skills, and spelling. When phonological short-term memory span is below average, opportunities for encoding information into long-term memory are diminished and learning may be slower. Phonological span can be quickly tested with a forward digit span, letter span, nonword span, or another simple span task (Dehn, 2008). When phonological span scores are subaverage, follow-up testing should include encoding, learning, and phonological processing, as well as an informal assessment of strategy development, especially basic rehearsal strategies.

Visuospatial Short-Term Memory   With the exception of early arithmetic development, visuospatial short-term memory has relatively weak relations with academic learning compared with the phonological component. Nonetheless, there is value in testing the visuospatial component to determine whether it is a strength that may be tapped when using mnemonics. The visuospatial component can be readily tested with numerous subtests found in traditional intellectual and cognitive batteries (see Dehn, 2008, for details). Such tasks typically require the examinee to recall objects and locations after a brief presentation. When assessing visuospatial short-term memory, the examiner should always consider whether the task involves mainly visual memory (memory for objects), spatial memory (memory for location), or both. When visuospatial scores are subaverage, visuospatial processing without memory requirements should be tested.

Verbal Working Memory   Verbal working memory capacity is highly related with reading comprehension, written expression, and mathematics computation and reasoning. It should be tested anytime there are concerns about explicit memory. Verbal working memory tasks are frequently contained in contemporary cognitive scales. The tasks, known as complex span tasks, include processing of information while trying to retain the same or different information. Examples include backward digit span and the last word task (see Dehn, 2008, for more details). When verbal working memory is subaverage, testing of fluid reasoning and executive functioning should be considered, as well as inquiry into the development of metamemory and memory strategies.

Visuospatial Working Memory   Visuospatial working memory is more complex than visuospatial short-term memory in that it involves mental rotation and processing of information while trying to retain stimuli. It is perhaps more important for everyday functioning than for academic learning. It is fortunate that there is little need to assess it because there are very few subtests specifically designed to measure it (Dehn, 2008). The Automated Working Memory Assessment (Alloway, 2007) is one scale that contains recently designed visuospatial subtests that include rotation and additional processing.

Prospective Memory   Although prospective memory is difficult to measure and has a low correlation with retrospective memory, an informal assessment of prospective memory should be considered for two reasons. First, it has high face validity with examinees because individuals referred for memory testing report prospective memory problems more than any other kind of memory problem (Wilson, 2009). Second, it has some functional relevance to academic performance, such as remembering to complete homework on time. It can be assessed through interviews and by arranging tasks for the examinee to complete at some future time. When prospective memory seems to be problematic, executive functions, especially planning, should be assessed.

Verbal Episodic   The learning and recall of orally presented material in the classroom is initially dependent upon verbal episodic memory. Markers of verbal episodic deficits are an unusually rapid forgetting rate, poor performance on classroom exams, and poor memory for autobiographical information. Most memory batteries contain more than one measure of verbal episodic memory, testing it approximately 30 minutes after the material was introduced. Examples include recall for narratives, word lists, paired associates, and learning tasks. Some tests only present stimuli once and measure immediate recall, whereas others provide a few learning trials with corrective feedback. The best measures of episodic memory functioning control for learning level by including a controlled learning task that has multiple trials and feedback. Assessment of verbal episodic memory should also include collection of data on classroom performance (see the section "Collecting Classroom Examination Data" later in this chapter), and everyday functioning because standardized tasks are not always a good match with real-world demands. Subaverage verbal episodic test performance is justification for testing phonological short-term memory, verbal working memory, and semantic memory. Also, a planned effort should be made to differentiate the influences of encoding, consolidation, and retrieval on the individual's performance.

Table 5.1 Additional components and processes to assess when performance on a memory component is subaverage

Phonological STM	Visuospatial STM	Verbal WM	Visuospatial WM	Prospective	Verbal Episodic	Visuospatial Episodic	Semantic	Retrieval	Recognition	Learning	Metamemory	Strategies
Verbal WM; Semantic; Phonological processing; Learning; Strategies; Processing speed	Visuospatial WM; Visuospatial episodic; Visuospatial processing	Semantic; Fluid reasoning; Executive processes; Metamemory; Strategies; Processing speed; Phonological STM	Visuospatial processing; Visuospatial episodic; Visuospatial STM	Planning; Executive processes; Verbal episodic	Phonological STM; Verbal WM; Semantic; Auditory processing; Learning; Strategies	Visuospatial STM; Visuospatial WM; Visual processing	Verbal WM; Verbal episodic; Retrieval; Recognition; Learning; Metamemory; Strategies; Fluid reasoning	Processing speed; Recognition; Semantic; Strategies	Retrieval; Semantic; Verbal episodic; Fluid reasoning	Phonological STM; Verbal WM; Metamemory; Strategies; Verbal episodic; Attention	Executive processes; Strategies; Fluid reasoning	Metamemory; Executive processes; Verbal WM; Fluid reasoning

Visuospatial Episodic Visuospatial recall of learning events may serve to cue verbal information, but visuospatial episodic memory has a weaker relationship with academic learning than does the verbal aspect. Visuospatial memory dysfunctions are more evident in everyday functioning. For example, an individual may have difficulty recalling the location of common objects, navigating in familiar surroundings, or recalling the appearance of acquaintances. Most memory batteries contain delayed recall of visuospatial material. Examples include reproduction of designs, memory for faces, memory for objects, and memory for locations. To reduce the influence of verbal mediation when testing visuospatial memory, the items should be abstract and difficult to name or all the items should belong to the same category, such as a picture with different types of houses. Visuospatial measurement tasks differ from verbal tasks in that the majority do not require uncued recall. Both the immediate and delayed recall tasks involve recognition; for example, the examinee need only select the correct face from a page of four faces. Thus, when there are deficits in the visual aspects of memory, it's important to include an uncued recall task, such as drawing designs from memory. When designs are reproduced from memory, the influences of planning and motor control need to be taken into account. Also, visual processing and visuospatial short-term and working memory should be assessed whenever visuospatial episodic memory performance is deficient.

When assessing visuospatial episodic memory, the most important consideration is the distinction between visual memory (memory for objects) and spatial memory (memory for location). In addition to location, spatial memory includes information about orientation, distance, and direction (Smith, 2008). Spatial memory enables humans to remember scenes and to navigate in their environments (Smith & Cohen, 2008). Although these two subtypes of explicit memory are integrally related, they are easily distinguished, and they are stored separately in the brain. During assessment, visual and spatial memory performance should be differentiated and contrasted whenever possible. Some measurement tasks involve both in a manner that is difficult to separate. However, newer memory scales offer separate scoring of the visual and spatial components. For example, the Wechsler Memory Scale®-Fourth Edition, (Wechsler, 2009) provides separate standard scores and norm-referenced procedures for determining significant discrepancies between visual and spatial performance. Examining the difference between visual and spatial performance is especially important when the overall visuospatial memory score is below average.

Semantic Concerns about a student's ability to learn and acquire knowledge implicate semantic memory. Although the long-term retention of semantic information is one of education's primary goals, direct standardized measurement of semantic memory functioning is difficult to achieve. The main confounding variables are the lack of control over degree of initial learning and the inability to determine when episodic memories became consolidated as semantic memories. Memory batteries typically do not include semantic memory subtests. Only tests that can be completed without reference to the original learning episode or context are considered measures of semantic memory. Consequently, examiners must use tests of knowledge, information, and vocabulary found on other types of scales (see Chapter 6 for details). Fortunately, performance on classroom exams, especially those administered a week or longer after the last relevant learning event, may provide a more valid estimate of semantic memory functioning than standardized tests. Another option is to question the examinee about prominent historical events that occurred during the examinee's school years. Only events that were reported repeatedly by news media and attracted the attention of nearly every child in the United States should be used. A sample question might be "In what city were the Twin Towers that were destroyed by terrorists on September 11, 2001?" These informal items could be in a free recall or recognition format. Most measures of semantic memory are verbal, which is consistent with the belief that semantic memory is primarily a verbal memory system. The visual aspects of semantic memory are challenging to measure. Subtests known as "Famous Faces" that contain photographs of public figures, such as U.S. presidents, have been used but performance can be heavily influenced by degree of exposure, cultural differences, and interests. With younger children, "Picture Vocabulary" types of tests tap visual and verbal semantic memory concurrently. Measures of visual semantic memory should avoid the use of autobiographical stimuli, such as old family photographs, because these are usually classified as remote episodic memories. (This is another reason why visual semantic memory is not singled out for assessment.) When there are concerns about semantic memory, the assessment should include measures of working memory, episodic memory, and learning. There should also be an effort to differentiate the influences of encoding, consolidation, and retrieval. For example, recognition could be tested and compared with uncued recall to determine the effectiveness of retrieval processes.

Learning and Encoding   Learning and long-term memory are interdependent and difficult to disentangle in real-world functioning. From a broad perspective, learning is associated more with encoding, and memory is associated mostly with storage and retrieval. In an assessment context, learning refers to the initial acquisition of content after repeated exposure and corrective feedback, such as presenting and recalling a word list several times. Such tasks provide an indication of how quickly and efficiently the examinee can acquire new material. There is a presumptive positive relationship between learning rate and delayed recall, but given the same rate and level of initial learning, delayed recall performance varies across individuals. One reason for the variability is that learning task performance depends on both short-term memory and strategy use. Rapid learning may occur when short-term memory is strong, but commensurate long-term retention and recall require strategies that bind information to related information or attach cues that facilitate retrieval. Learning efficiency is also affected by the timing and amount of feedback. Immediate corrective feedback during learning tests with multiple trials is extremely important to prevent the child from learning errors. When errors are not corrected the child assumes that they are correct. Then the child will repeat the errors on subsequent trials, thereby reinforcing and learning the wrong information. Standardized learning tasks tend to be verbal or visual-verbal, but examiners can improvise if they wish to isolate visual learning. One procedure for which there are no published norms is known as the *span plus two task*. For example, after the examinee's visual span has been established with a Corsi block-tapping task, the examiner can add two to the span and repeat the sequence until it is correctly reproduced (Wilson, 2009). Most individuals can learn a span plus two in three trials. Poor performance on a standardized learning task leads to several hypotheses that should be pursued. Among these are poor metamemory development, lack of sophisticated strategies, inadequate short-term memory, poor attentional control, and brain-based encoding difficulties (see Table 5.1).

Retrieval Fluency   Obviously, retrieval from long-term memory stores is involved whenever information is recalled. However, attempts to isolate retrieval can be worthwhile when there is a desire to identify specific underlying memory impairments. For example, sometimes encoding and storage systems are functioning normally but retrieval is slow and ineffective. When retrieval is impaired, the desired information may still be stored in memory; it just can't be quickly accessed on demand. In contrast, when an examinee can quickly and efficiently retrieve basic information, practitioners can infer that retrieval functions are normal. The most direct measures of retrieval efficiency are tasks that measure associational fluency, such as the when the examinee must quickly name items from a well-known semantic category. Another activity to include in assessment of retrieval fluency is rapid automatic naming (RAN), where the examinee is directed to quickly name pictures of common objects or other well-known stimuli. Naming is typically a less-demanding retrieval activity than recalling semantically related items, especially when naming involves a limited class such as colors. Consequently, RAN performance is an indication of poor retrieval speed more so than inefficient search mechanisms. When retrieval fluency performance is subaverage, semantic knowledge and delayed recognition should be tested, as well as general processing speed.

Recognition   Recognition is a type of retrieval in which cues facilitate the delayed recall of information. Whenever the examinee's uncued (free) recall is lower than predicted from his or her initial learning, the recognition tasks included in most memory scales should be completed. The purpose of recognition testing is to parse out retrieval from storage. If the individual's recognition is significantly higher than free recall (recognition is normally higher than recall), than retrieval instead of storage is the likely underlying deficiency. A classroom performance clue that this is the case is significantly better performance on recognition-type exams (e.g., multiple-choice) over free recall formats. Whenever standardized recognition performance is superior, unrelated retrieval fluency tasks should be administered to determine whether retrieval speed is a factor.

Metamemory Learning problems, inconsistent memory performance, limited strategy use, and poorly developed executive functions are reasons for investigating the child or adolescent's development of metamemory. As there are no standardized instruments for youth, the examiner must rely mainly on interviewing (see the "Metamemory" section later in this chapter). The evaluator will need background knowledge on developmental expectations (see Chapter 3) to appropriately appraise metamemory. Information about the examinee's metamemory level is not so much for diagnosing impairment but rather for planning and implementing memory interventions. When metamemory development appears delayed, other executive and metacognitive functions should be investigated along with inquiry into strategy development.

Strategies As children approach adolescence, the acquisition and application of memory strategies largely account for improved long-term memory performance. Learning problems, poor retention of new information, and delayed metamemory development are arguments for assessing strategy development and usage. Although some memory scales, such as the California Verbal Learning Test, Children's Version (Delis et al., 1994), provide qualitative information on strategy use, most of strategy appraisal needs to be conducted through interviewing and observation. In preparation, evaluators should review information about the normal developmental sequence of fundamental memory strategies (see Table 5.3 on page 173). When strategy development appears delayed or application is minimal, further investigation should include metamemory, executive functioning, and working memory capacity.

Related Cognitive Processes A comprehensive assessment of memory should also include testing of related cognitive processes. Some examinees who appear to be struggling because of memory deficiencies may actually have impairments in related processes. Cognitive processes that influence performance on memory tasks include attention, visual processing, auditory processing, phonological processing, planning, processing speed, fluid reasoning, and general executive processing (see Chapter 3 for details). A cross-battery, selective testing approach to assessing cognitive processes is delineated in Dehn (2006).

PLANNING A PERSONALIZED ASSESSMENT

Although a thorough memory evaluation is recommended whenever memory deficits are suspected, the practitioner should not adopt a standard memory assessment battery. To do so is not only inefficient but may fail to uncover some of the examinee's important strengths and weaknesses. Assessment batteries should be individualized based on the referral concerns or presenting problems and the examiner's hypotheses that are thought to account for the concerns. Age, developmental level, and severity of the problems should also be taken into account in selecting tests. Accordingly, the evaluator or evaluation team should take some time to plan the assessment. The planning process includes identification of referral concerns, the generation and selection of hypotheses, determination of formal and informal methods, designation of memory batteries/tests, and selection of the memory subtests that will be used. The *Memory Assessment Plan* form designed to facilitate this process is in Appendix A, and a completed example is in Table 5.2 on page 141.

Hypothesis Testing Approach

The crucial element in the assessment planning process is the generation and selection of hypotheses. Assessment hypotheses are potential explanations for the presenting problems. Hypotheses should get at the suspected deficit or underlying cause of a problem. For example, when the presenting problem is poor performance on classroom exams, one appropriate hypothesis is that the student has a retrieval deficit, and the assessment-related prediction is that the examinee will perform poorly on all retrieval fluency subtests. Of course, hypotheses might involve any domain: behavioral, social, academic, or cognitive. However, the focus in this text is on memory and related cognitive processing hypotheses. Selecting hypotheses is an important first step because it provides direction for assessment and testing. The hypothesis-testing approach to cognitive and memory assessment is a common practice in several fields of psychology and has been recommended in several texts (e.g., Hale & Fiorello, 2004).

The generation and selection of logical memory and processing hypotheses begins with a careful examination of the referral concerns and presenting problems. The student and the teacher or parent making the referral may have some hypotheses of their own. Their hypotheses should be elicited, given consideration, and, if appropriate, reframed from a memory and processing perspective. For example, a teacher may hypothesize that the student is failing a course due to lack of motivation. Such a hypothesis should be considered, but the evaluator or evaluation team should generate additional memory and processing hypotheses that also account for the behavior. Simply relying on the initially stated referral concerns is not enough because the individual making the referral often fails to report important behaviors, performance problems, or relevant risk factors. Consequently, some preliminary assessment procedures—reviewing records, interviewing to clarify concerns, gathering a developmental and medical history, and observing the examinee—should be completed to identify all potential concerns. For example, information from the child's history may reveal risk factors, such as juvenile diabetes, that point toward likely memory impairments. Once the preliminary steps are completed, assessment hypotheses can be generated and selected. The generation phase may involve a brainstorming process, but once evaluators have acquired expertise in memory assessment, generating appropriate hypotheses should be a relatively straightforward process. Only those hypotheses that have the most direct connections with the presenting problems should be selected. Knowledge of neurological functions, risk factors, and evidence-based relations should all be taken into account. For example, when the referral is for academic learning problems, the memory hypotheses should focus on the components and processes that have the strongest relationships with the specific academic areas of concern. For example, whenever basic reading skills are a concern, memory hypotheses would include deficits in phonological processing, phonological short-term memory, and semantic memory.

Completing the Planning Process

After logical and empirically based hypotheses worthy of investigation have been selected, the next step is to determine the best assessment procedure for testing each hypothesis. The assessment procedure should allow collection of data directly related to the hypothesis so that a data-based decision can be made about the validity of the hypothesis upon completion of the assessment. In many cases, an informal procedure, such as an observation, will provide enough data to test one or more hypotheses. For other hypotheses, standardized testing will be necessary. In most cases, one instrument, such as a comprehensive memory scale, can be used to test several hypotheses. For some hypotheses, a single subtest will provide enough data; however, the use of two subtests provides a more reliable sampling of the component or process under investigation. Selection of a specific subtest should be based on the extent to which the subtest measures the memory component or process thought to account for the problem (see Tables 6.1 and 6.10). For example, a list-learning subtest might be used to measure verbal episodic memory ability, a vocabulary test might be used to measure semantic memory ability, or a retrieval fluency test might be used to measure retrieval speed. See Table 5.2 for an example of a completed Memory Assessment Plan.

Caveats and Concerns Regarding the Hypothesis Testing Approach

After hypotheses that could account for the problems have been selected, it may be necessary to expand the assessment further. One drawback to limiting testing to the areas of concern is that potential strengths are ignored. Assessing potential strengths produces a balanced view of the individual and allows the identification of assets that can be utilized during interventions. Another limitation of restricting testing to potential deficits is that it will be difficult to determine intra-individual weaknesses when overall cognitive and memory functioning is underestimated because only weaknesses have been tested. Fortunately, many functions hypothesized to be deficient turn out to be normal if not strengths. There are also instances when not enough is known about the individual's difficulties, as in the case of a young child. In such cases, a more comprehensive assessment that goes beyond the initial hypotheses is warranted. Nonetheless, standard assessment batteries and redundant testing should still be avoided. In instances where the information is so limited that it is difficult to select any plausible hypotheses, it may be best to begin with screening. In such cases, a broad-based but brief measure with high predictive validity will serve

Table 5.2 Memory assessment plan (example)

Student: ___Abby___ **DOB:** _____ **Age:** ___16:4___ **Grade:** __10__ **School:** _____
Date of Referral: _____ **Form Completed By:** _____ **Date:** _____

Referral Concerns	Hypotheses*	Assessment Methods	Memory Batteries/Tests	Memory Subtests
Poor performance on classroom examinations	Has an impairment in verbal episodic memory	Observation; Interviews; Testing	WMS-IV	Logical Memory II; Verbal Paired Associates (VPA) II
	Has an impairment in retrieval	Classroom examination performance; Testing	WJ-III COG WMS-IV	Retrieval Fluency VPA II Recognition
Poor reading comprehension	Has an impairment in fluid reasoning	Testing	WJ-III COG	Fluid Reasoning Subtests
	Has an impairment in verbal working memory	Testing	WAIS-IV	Working Memory Subtests
Difficulty learning new concepts	Has an impairment in learning (encoding)	Observation; Interviews; Testing	WMS-IV WJ-III COG	VPA I Visual-Auditory Learn.
	Has an impairment in semantic memory	Classroom examination performance; Testing	WAIS-IV WJ-III COG	Vocabulary Academic Knowledge
History of cocaine use by birth mother	Has an impairment in visuospatial explicit memory	Testing	WMS-IV	Designs II; Visual Reproduction II

*Types of memory to consider: Phonological Short-Term, Visuospatial Short-Term, Verbal Working, Visuospatial Working, Prospective, Verbal Episodic, Visuospatial Episodic, Semantic, Retrieval, Recognition, Metamemory, Strategies, Learning

the purpose. For instance, a digit span task is ideal as it has a robust relationship with learning and memory.

From a scientific perspective, the main purpose of generating hypotheses before collecting and analyzing data is to increase the objectivity of the investigation and the interpretation of results. When using a hypothesis testing approach to assessment, it is critical that evaluators keep an open mind and avoid hypothesis confirmation bias (Hale & Fiorello, 2004). Confirmation bias leads to ignoring data that do not support a hypothesis while focusing on data that support it. The data for and against a hypothesis should be carefully weighed before reaching any conclusion. The best way to counteract confirmation bias is to assume that the hypothesis is false unless there is considerable convergent evidence supporting it. Another option for examiners who dislike or have concerns about the hypothesis testing approach is to frame the hypotheses as referral questions. For example, the referral question "Does the examinee have an impairment in consolidating information?" could be used in lieu of the hypothesis "The examinee has an impairment in consolidation."

When hypotheses are selected prior to assessment, they are known as *a priori hypotheses*. As data are collected and analyzed, new insights often arise and more hypotheses are added. Also, when the test results are inconsistent or are not what was predicted from the hypotheses, it is often necessary to generate new hypotheses that account for the unexpected findings. These new hypotheses are referred to as *a posteriori hypotheses.* When additional hypotheses are considered, the examiner should cycle back to an earlier step in the planning and assessment process. Follow-up testing may be necessary. In some instances, a posteriori hypotheses can be evaluated by reexamining already existing assessment data.

Basing memory evaluations on hypothesis testing serves several functions and has several advantages. First, explicitly generating and selecting hypotheses forces the examiner or multidisciplinary evaluation team to carefully think about and consider the referral concerns and how best to assess them. Each hypothesis should be one possible explanation for *why* the individual is experiencing a specific problem. Second, the hypothesis testing approach can increase the evaluator's understanding of the learner even before assessment begins. Third, following a hypotheses testing approach truly individualizes the assessment, forcing the evaluator to abandon a standard battery approach and adapt to the unique concerns of each case. Fourth, following the hypothesis testing method, coupled with selective testing, results in an efficient, time-saving assessment that avoids redundancies while measuring all of the processes that need to be assessed. In summary, the hypothesis testing approach results in an individualized, comprehensive, and efficient assessment that ultimately provides direction for subsequent interventions.

CROSS-BATTERY AND SELECTIVE TESTING

Hypothesis-driven assessment always involves selective testing and frequently involves cross-battery assessment. Selective testing refers to the selection and administration of individual tests or subtests from a particular battery without administering the entire battery or scale. Cross-battery testing occurs when more than one scale is used to assess the areas of concern. Cross-battery testing is often necessary because a single scale seldom addresses all of the hypotheses that need to be tested. For instance, when the primary scale excludes measures of visuospatial memory, the practitioner will need to select visuospatial subtests from another scale to supplement the primary battery. Informal cross-battery assessment is a common practice. Psychologists and special educators have always mixed tests and batteries when conducting psychoeducational, neuropsychological, and achievement evaluations. However, a systematic method of cross-battery cognitive assessment has only recently been advocated by Flanagan, Ortiz, and Alfonso (2007). Their approach is framed within the context of the Cattell-Horn-Carroll (CHC) theory of cognitive abilities (Carroll, 1993), but their recommended procedures can be applied to any cross-battery testing. The approach to analyzing cross-battery test scores recommended in this text (see Appendix B) is an adaptation of the cross-battery model proposed by Flanagan et al. (2007).

The cross-battery method involves administering a compilation of subtests from different batteries. It can actually be time saving and efficient even though more than one scale is utilized. From the cross-battery perspective, evaluators should not administer an entire battery just because it contains some desired subtests. Rather, they should administer only those subtests that measure the memory components and cognitive processes selected during assessment planning. Redundant testing should be avoided. For example, if the entire Wechsler Memory Scale®-Fourth Edition (WMS®-IV; Wechsler, 2009) has been administered and then is supplemented with another scale, there is no need to measure visuospatial working memory again. Administering only selected factors and subtests is acceptable, unless a test's authors specifically state that the entire scale or a certain subset must be administered for the results to be valid. A battery's subtests each have their own scaled score that can be used independently to determine an individual's functioning in the ability or process measured by that subtest. Nevertheless, cross-battery testing should be as restrained as possible. For instance, the number of batteries involved should be restricted to three at the most. Restricting the amount of battery crossing serves to maintain the reliability and validity of the resulting scores, as well as keeping the interpretation manageable (see Flanagan et al., 2007, for additional best practices in cross-battery assessment).

Although the cross-battery method is well suited for assessment of memory components and processes, a cautious interpretation of cross-battery results is necessary because of the inherent weaknesses of the method. The lack of cross-battery norms is the main concern. When conducting an intra-individual analysis, subtest and "clinical" factor scores representing cognitive components are usually compared to a cross-battery mean computed by averaging the scores of the subtests involved. There are no norms for these cross-battery means because they can be derived from numerous combinations of subtests. Also, there are no statistical tables for determining significant discrepancies between the cross-battery mean and individual factor or subtest scores. Flanagan et al. (2007) recommend using a one standard deviation discrepancy as the criterion for significance, but the number of points necessary for a statistically significant difference actually varies. Furthermore, the composite, factor, and subtest scores obtained from different batteries are based on standardization samples, distributions, and norms unique to each test. Measurement error can be reduced somewhat by using tests that were normed about the same time. Also, more caution is necessary when a specific memory component is assessed with subtests from more than one scale. Despite these concerns, structured, systematic cross-battery analysis procedures are preferable to a completely clinical approach.

MEMORY ASSESSMENT CHALLENGES

As practitioners plan and conduct a comprehensive and personalized memory evaluation, some of the challenges involved in memory assessment become evident. These challenges and some potential remedies include:

1. It is difficult to differentiate between a deficient memory system or process and the ineffective application of memory strategies. An in-depth assessment of strategy development and usage is helpful but indeterminate because there are no structured or norm-referenced methods. Testing the limits after standardized testing is completed may provide some data on how much difference the application of strategies could make. For example, after suggesting a strategy, the examiner can re-administer items that were failed during formal administration.

2. Some individuals perform well on structured, standardized memory scales but have significant memory problems in real-world functioning, either in a formal academic environment or everyday activities. The reverse also can occur; examinees may perform poorly on tests but not experience everyday problems. Thus, interpretation of assessment results should always consider non-test data.

3. Standardized memory scales typically check long-term retention after a 20- to 30-minute interval. Some examinees perform well at such short retention intervals but have unusually high rates of forgetting for longer intervals, such as a day or a week (Martin et al., 1991). Only the Visual-Auditory Learning test of the Woodcock-Johnson® III Cognitive battery (Woodcock, McGrew, & Mather, 2001b) has norms for retention intervals as long as eight days.

4. Poor performance on a memory scale may be due to related cognitive dysfunctions, such as a language impairment or slow processing speed, rather than to a specific memory deficit. Consequently, related cognitive processes should also be tested.

5. Memory deficits that impair the acquisition and long-term retention of knowledge may be due to semantic rather than episodic memory limitations. Yet, memory and cognitive batteries do not directly assess semantic memory ability. Therefore, evidence of semantic memory functioning should be gathered from the scholastic setting, and semantic memory should be tested with appropriate cognitive and achievement subtests.

6. When attempting to measure semantic memory functioning with a vocabulary or information subtest it is impossible to equate learning opportunities or determine the initial level of learning. Gathering data on the examinee's classroom exam performance can provide additional information about semantic memory.

7. Most individuals with memory problems are not able to accurately self-appraise their memory abilities. Thus, examinee interview and self-report data often lacks validity. Examinee-provided information should be corroborated by teachers and parents, as well as test data.

8. Reports of memory functioning problems in school and home environments may be widely divergent, often because the reporters are observing different types of memory. Task analysis may serve to identify the situational

demands on memory, but standardized testing is most likely to elucidate the actual memory problems.

9. When follow-up testing is administered, practice effects are a concern because most standardized measures have only one version. One solution is to have more than one memory battery available.

10. The tasks, subtests, and factors across memory scales vary considerably in what they are specifically measuring, thereby creating planning and interpretative challenges. Use of the tables found in Chapter 6 should be helpful in selecting and aligning measures.

11. The labeling of subtests and tests may be misleading. Typically, subtest names describe the task instead of the memory domain or function it measures. For example, a subtest labeled as "Logical Memory" may be primarily testing verbal episodic memory (see Chapter 6 for classification of subtests). Fortunately, the names of the composites to which the subtests are assigned are easier to connect with memory components and processes.

12. It is difficult to parse out and differentiate encoding, consolidation, and retrieval influences on memory performance. Even after completing a comprehensive memory assessment, statements about the effectiveness of these processes often must remain hypothetical.

COLLECTING MEDICAL, DEVELOPMENTAL, AND ACADEMIC HISTORY

When evaluating children and adolescents for possible memory impairments, the collection of a thorough developmental, medical, and academic history is essential. The methods used to obtain this data include reviewing records and interviewing informants and examinees. Many memory impairments are either present at birth or acquired in early childhood; the remaining are acquired later as the result of injuries or medical conditions. Initially, the evaluator should check for any medical conditions or disorders that might have caused damage to the hippocampus, prefrontal cortex, or related memory structures or put the examinee at-risk for such damage (see Table 4.1). The age at onset, occurrence, or diagnosis should be noted for all conditions or disorders that might be associated with learning and memory problems. Next, the evaluator should review the child or adolescent's developmental and learning history, paying attention to behaviors that are markers for long-term memory problems. Practitioners should be aware that some memory deficits will not surface until the demands on memory become high, such as in later elementary years. Other memory problems may be content or situation specific. When reviewing school records, the examiner should be alert for reports of behaviors associated with memory difficulties (see the "Interviewing" and "Observation" sections for examples of memory-related behaviors). For instance, a teacher's comment that a child is having difficulty memorizing arithmetic facts is a red flag for memory problems. When previous assessment records are available, it is important for the evaluator to reexamine, reanalyze, and reinterpret the test scores instead of relying on the analysis and interpretation found in the existing report(s). The primary reason for this is that previous examiners may have been uninterested or unaware of the memory measures embedded in the scales they used. For example, an achievement test might have included a measure of oral expression that actually involved the delayed retelling of a story (verbal episodic memory).

The following list is a sampling of important history that needs to be investigated through a review of records, interviews, or completion of a medical and developmental history form.

1. Prenatal factors: extent of prenatal health care; term of pregnancy; and maternal illnesses, injuries, medications, stress level, alcohol consumption, tobacco use, chemical abuse, and medical and mental disorders.
2. Perinatal factors: asphyxia, anoxia, and extended labor, as well as the Apgar score.
3. Postnatal conditions: genetic disorders and excess bilirubin (jaundice).
4. Infant and early childhood health: hospitalizations, surgeries, high fevers, injuries, sleep disorders, physical disorders, and other medical conditions.
5. Early childhood development: speech and language.
6. Any stage of development: head injuries, concussions, medical disorders, mental disorders, exposure to trauma, chronic high levels of stress, and developmental disabilities.
7. School years: diagnosed learning or behavioral disorders, grade retention, scores on state examinations, ability to pay attention, ability to complete tasks on time, ability to remember information, motivation for school learning, school attendance, performance on classroom exams, frustration with learning, and evidence of learning and memory problems in the school or home environment.

INTERVIEWING TEACHERS, PARENTS, AND STUDENTS

Effective clinical interviews are another crucial memory assessment procedure. Interviews provide an opportunity to clarify concerns, gather history, obtain details on current memory problems, and collect data on metamemory and strategy development, as well as on everyday memory functioning. Unfortunately, structured and semi-structured interview formats seldom include more than a few items specifically related to memory functions. Thus, the interviewer must independently develop and accumulate interview items that provide relevant data on various aspects of memory, keeping in mind that the primary purpose is to assess the functional difficulties caused by memory problems (Middleton, 2004). Regardless of their age or developmental level, children should always be interviewed and their memory functions should be directly addressed through language they can understand. Both teachers and parents should also be questioned about the child or adolescent's memory functions. Information obtained from interviewing should never be used alone to confirm hypotheses or reach diagnostic decisions, although it may be used for intervention planning. Interview data needs to be corroborated by other assessment data before their accuracy is accepted. What follows is a sampling of suggested interview items that address all of the memory assessment categories advocated in this text. The teacher interview items also may be used with parents and children, after they have been adapted for language and circumstances. Of course, most of these items require follow-up questions, such as asking the interviewee to describe the behavior or provide examples. See Dehn (2008) for interview items related to short-term and working memory.

Teacher Interview Items

General

- Have you noticed the student having any memory problems?
- How well does the student remember information?
- What kind of memory does the student seem to struggle with?
- What types of information does the student have difficulty remembering?
- Have any of the student's memory abilities changed recently?
- Does the student seem to forget information faster than other students?
- Does the student exhibit frustration when memorization is required?
- Has the student been slow to acquire arithmetic or other basic facts?
- How often does the student tell you that he or she can't remember?
- Why do you think the student has difficulty remembering information?

Verbal Episodic

- Does the student quickly forget written information?
- Does the student have noticeable difficulty remembering oral presentations?

Visuospatial Episodic

- Does the student display signs of forgetting events or experiences?
- Does the student forget where he or she placed personal possessions or where classroom materials are usually stored?

Semantic

- Does the student require periodic reviews to prevent forgetting material that most students remember for weeks and months?
- Does the student have difficulty associating new information with prior knowledge?

- Does the student recognize categories to which specific items belong?
- Does the student recognize pictures of well-known historical figures, such as George Washington?

Retrieval

- Is the student slow to find the words for a thought he or she is trying to express?
- Is the student slow to recall information he or she obviously knows?

Recognition

- Does the student perform noticeably better on multiple-choice test questions than on supply-the-answer questions?
- Does it help the student remember when you provide cues?

Metamemory

- Does the student seem to be aware of his or her memory problems?
- Does the student often think he or she knows the material but doesn't actually know it?

Strategies

- Does the student display normal memorization techniques, such as repeating a list over and over?
- Does the student demonstrate more advanced memorization strategies, such as grouping information before memorizing it?

Learning

- Is the student slower than normal students at memorizing a simple list of information?
- Does the student require lots of repetition to learn new material?

Prospective

- Does the student frequently fail to complete tasks on time?
- Does the student forget to do prearranged activities, such as remembering to take something to the principal's office immediately after the daily announcements?

Additional Parent Interview Items

- When did you first notice that your child was having problems remembering?
- Does your child have difficulty remembering events?
- Does your child have more difficulty remembering events that happen at home or information that is taught at school?

- Does your child forget details of his or her daily routine?
- Has your child ever gotten lost finding his way around the neighborhood?
- Does your child have difficulty remembering the names of people he or she has met before?
- Does your child fail to recognize familiar people?
- Does your child seem to know studied material really well but then forget most of it as early as the next day?
- Does your child know how to study and how to memorize?
- What memorization methods does your child use independently?
- Does your child talk about problems remembering things?
- Why do you think your child is having difficulty learning and remembering?

Additional Child and Adolescent Interview Items

- Do you forget a lot of information that you thought you knew after you studied it?
- How often do you have problems remembering something even though you know that you know it?
- How often do you forget to do something on time?
- What type of information is easier for you to remember: something you hear or something you see?
- Do you have difficulty remembering where you put things at home?
- What courses or types of material are the most difficult for you to remember?
- Describe the methods you use to memorize information.
- Why do you think you are having difficulty learning and remembering information that you need for school?

OBSERVATION

Observation of behavior is a fundamental assessment method that should be included in every assessment of memory. Deriving information about memory functions from specific classroom or home behaviors is challenging because many cognitive abilities and other factors come into play during any given behavior. To decipher relative influences, the observer may need to analyze the task and determine which memory functions are required for successful performance. To increase the reliability and validity of observational data, the observer also needs to be familiar with the intricacies of memory and the behaviors that are indicative of deficits and impairments. Until the observer becomes versed in age-appropriate memory expectations, it is helpful to compare the subject's behavior with that of one or more random peers. For example, when a third grader can't remember a new arithmetic procedure taught the day before, peers can be observed for the same behavior. To increase the opportunities to observe memory functions in action, the observations should take place while the student is engaged in tasks that place high demands on long-term memory.

What follows below is a list of observable behaviors that can be associated with long-term memory problems. The reader is encouraged to use these items with the caveat that their reliability and validity is unknown. Moreover, many of the behaviors are also characteristic of other cognitive and behavioral problems. Consequently, the occurrence of any of these behaviors should mainly be used to generate hypotheses for further investigation. Also, evaluators need to be cautious about making inferences from observed behaviors because of the lack of one-to-one correspondence between specific behaviors and memory components and processes. Therefore, hypotheses and inferences drawn from observational data should be supported by standardized test results. Suggested behaviors for short-term and working memory are listed in Dehn (2008).

Behaviors Indicative of Long-Term Memory Problems

- Difficulty recalling and completing multistep procedures that have been practiced previously.
- Difficulty completing tasks on time because the task or deadline was forgotten.
- Difficulty finding personal possessions that the child put away.
- Difficulty remembering the location of objects and possessions that are typically stored in the same location.
- Telling fanciful stories that have only a semblance of truth.
- Difficulty remembering rules of games that have been played previously.
- Rapid forgetting of information that has been studied.
- Displaying frustration during learning and memorization.
- Difficulty organizing information on a semantic basis.
- Difficulty comprehending the connection between new information and related prior knowledge.
- Difficulty remembering school rules and other routine information, such as the daily schedule.
- Frequently knowing material one day and not knowing it the next.
- Difficulty recalling information that has been repeatedly studied and reviewed.
- Difficulty automatically acquiring factual information about the world.
- Falling further behind peers as the demands for retention of information increase.

- Learning new material at the expense of losing prior learning.
- Repeatedly making the same mistakes.
- Knowing isolated facts but not being able to connect them with related concepts.
- Difficulty remembering events from the day before.
- Difficulty with delayed recall of directions, especially when no cues are available.
- Copying the activities and responses of other students.
- Difficulty learning new routines or procedures.
- Not volunteering to respond to teacher questions about subject matter.
- Becoming anxious and frustrated when no social or environmental retrieval cues are available.
- Exhibiting high test anxiety.
- Complaining of memory problems.
- Recognizing the answers to questions much better than freely recalling them.
- Difficulty remembering nursery rhymes and other cultural folklore that every child knows.
- Difficulty remembering details in stories.
- Difficulty remembering the sequence of events.
- Difficulty remembering the source of information.
- Difficulty telling jokes because part of the joke or the sequence is forgotten.
- Difficulty remembering the names or appearance of people who are encountered on a regular basis.
- Difficulty acquiring and remembering factual information that needs to be mastered, such as arithmetic facts.
- Getting lost or having difficulty navigating in familiar surroundings.
- Difficulty providing a reliable account of the day's activities.
- Frequently forgetting what was said during conversations.
- Frequently repeating things said previously.
- Finding a story's plot difficult to follow.

During Testing

Observations during the administration of standardized tests can also provide valuable clinical information about the examinee's memory strengths and weaknesses. Most of the typical behaviors exhibited during testing are related with short-term and working memory. Nonetheless, there are some behaviors indicative of long-term memory functioning. Relevant behaviors can be displayed during any type of testing, not just memory testing. Several of the behaviors suggested for classroom observation should also be observable during testing. What follows is a list of testing behaviors, along with a memory hypothesis that might account for each.

- Slow retrieval of words, names, and known facts—has a weakness in retrieval.
- Increased anxiety and frustration when the task involves delayed recall—has a weakness in episodic memory.
- Comments that over- or underestimate recall performance—has a weakness in metamemory.
- Begins to respond before the directions or item is completed as if fearful of forgetting—has a weakness in episodic memory or has poor strategy development.
- Repeating information subvocally, observed as whispering or moving of lips—is using a rehearsal strategy.
- Displays chunking or clustering of information—has well-developed strategies.
- Describing an item instead of naming it—has a weakness in retrieval.

ASSESSMENT OF METAMEMORY AND STRATEGY DEVELOPMENT

As discussed in Chapter 3, improved retention of information in later childhood is heavily dependent on normal development of metamemory and memory strategies. For instance, a child with poorly developed metamemory will not understand how to effectively manage his or her memory functions. The metamemory knowledge and regulation of children can vary considerably, even among those who struggle with learning. Some students with academic problems have already learned how to maximize their memory functioning. Sometimes they've developed advanced strategies because the strategies were necessary for their academic survival. Either from direct instruction or a trial-and-error process, they have discovered effective memory strategies that they utilize on a regular basis. On the other hand, students with average or higher abilities often have poorly developed understanding and regulation of their memory.

Because of its pivotal role, metamemory development should be assessed whenever there is documentation of memory problems and especially when there will be an opportunity for memory interventions. Despite the importance of assessing metamemory, a structured and normed approach designed for children and adolescents has yet to be published. Examples of metamemory items can be found in adult research (e.g., Dixon, Hultsch, & Hertzog, 1988), and Pierce and Lange's (2000) article on metamemory assessment includes items on general memory knowledge, specific strategy knowledge, and memory monitoring. Appropriate items will come to mind more easily if the reader reviews the section on metamemory development in Chapter 3 before conducting a metamemory assessment.

Suggested Metamemory Interview

This section highlights essential components of an interview designed to informally assess a student's metamemory development. Depending on the child's age, terminology may need to be adapted and discussion points may need explanation. Begin the assessment by stating that people have different abilities in what they remember and that each person has unique memory strengths and weaknesses. Also, state that everyone forgets things no matter how hard he or she tries to remember. If after a few questions it is apparent that the child has minimal understanding of memory, the evaluator might stop and explain the basic memory structures and processes. When doing so, it is helpful to use a visual to illustrate how memory consists of short-term and long-term memory and how it can be divided into visual and verbal memory (see Figure 5.1 on page 155). Then discuss the processes of taking in information (encoding), holding on to it (storage), and recalling it later (retrieval). Here are the key areas to address, along with sample questions or an activity for each topic:

1. *Knowledge of different types of human memory:* Does the child know that memory is divided into short-term and long-term, verbal versus visual, and personal memories versus general knowledge? Begin with the open-ended question, "Tell me what you know about how memory works." Follow up with, "What are the different kinds of memory that people have?"

2. *Knowledge of personal memory functioning and an awareness of strengths and weaknesses:* What is the child's appraisal of his or her overall memory functioning? Begin with, "Tell me about your memory" or "Do you have a good memory?" Proceed with a discussion of memory strengths and weaknesses. Ask, "Which kinds of memory are strong and weak for you?" After the child's response, specifically ask about each structure and process not mentioned. If the child is not very responsive, offer forced choices such as, "Which is easier for you to remember, words or pictures?" Consider whether the child has identified plausible strengths and weaknesses (check these for accuracy after the assessment is complete).

3. *Knowledge and beliefs about how to remember information:* Does the child realize that effort and strategies make a difference but interest and desire do not?

4. *Knowledge of forgetting and the limitations of human memory:* What does the child know about the limitations of short-term memory or how much information is normally forgotten over longer periods of time? Does the child know that what is remembered in the short term is not necessarily going to be remembered in the long term?

5. *Beliefs regarding the ability to monitor and regulate memory functions:* Does the child believe that he or she can influence memory performance? Ask for examples. If the child is reluctant to respond, say, "If people have a weak memory, is there anything they can do to make it better?"

6. *Awareness that learning and recall are affected by the difficulty level of the material:* Does the child study difficult material differently than easy material?

7. *The accuracy of judgments of learning (predictions of performance):* Give the child a minute to memorize a list of 15 words. Then ask the child to predict how many will be recalled 5 minutes later. Compare the prediction with performance.

8. *The selection of memory strategies and mnemonics:* Ask the child to describe the methods he or she uses to memorize material. Does the child use different methods for different situations and material?

9. *Anxiety about and frustration with memory performance:* Questions include "How often do you worry that you will forget something?" and "How often do you get upset because you can't remember something?"

Assessment of Memory Strategies

Assessment of memory strategy development should be completed along with the metamemory interview. To begin, the practitioner needs to recall the developmental sequence of strategy development. Table 5.3 summarizes the developmental expectations (see Chapter 3 for more details). With middle school and older students, the evaluator should also inquire into the use of self-testing, advanced mnemonics, and distributed practice. Given the lack of a normed procedure for assessing strategy development it's probably best to use a criterion referenced approach. Inquire about and check off the use of strategies listed in Table 5.4 and ask the child to demonstrate any strategies he or she claims to use (see Chapter 7 for details on specific strategies). Here is a sampling of general questions to ask:

- What methods do you use when you are trying to memorize information?
- Do you use different methods for different situations? Explain.
- Do some methods work better than others?
- If you want to remember something for a long time (more than a week), which of your memorization methods works best?
- Are there some memorization techniques that you used when you were younger but seldom use now?
- What is the latest memorization technique that you learned to use?
- Is cramming the best way to study information that you need to know for a comprehensive exam?
- Do you ever try to picture things in your mind so that you can remember them better?
- Do you ever test yourself when you are trying to memorize something?
- How many times do you typically study or review in preparation for an upcoming test?

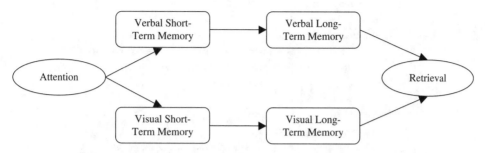

Figure 5.1 Illustration of memory functions for metamemory interview

In addition to questioning the child, the practitioner may need to conduct some informal testing of the child or adolescent's knowledge of particular strategies. For example:

- Ask the child to demonstrate how he or she will remember a list of words that you are going to read. If the child exhibits rehearsal, note whether it is rote repetition or cumulative rehearsal.
- Provide the child with a list of names that must be memorized for a quiz tomorrow, and ask the child to demonstrate the memory technique he or she will use.
- Show the child a list of a dozen items that can be grouped into three basic categories, such as food, animals, and clothing. Then tell the child that he or she could memorize them by reviewing the list several times or by grouping them by category and then reviewing them. Ask the child which method he or she thinks would be most effective.

Table 5.3 Ages by which memory strategies are usually acquired

Age Range	Strategies
3–6	Rote rehearsal
6–10	Cumulative rehearsal
8–12	Basic mnemonics
8–12	Integrating strategies
9–12	Semantic clustering
10–14	Elaborative rehearsal

Table 5.4 Memory strategies checklist

—Rote repetition

—Cumulative rehearsal

—Written repetition

—Elaborative rehearsal (rehearsing information that includes associations)

—Semantic rehearsal (putting information in a sentence or story)

—Chunking (grouping items into units, such as "43" for "4" and "3")

—Acronyms

—Acrostics

—Imagery (creating mental images)

—Chaining (linking each item in a sequence with the succeeding item)

—Semantic clustering (grouping information by category)

—Elaboration (linking new information with related prior knowledge)

—Self-testing

—Distributed study or practice

—Pegword (see Chapter 7)

—Keyword (see Chapter 7)

—Loci (see Chapter 7)

—Dual encoding (encoding information both visually and verbally)

—Integrating strategies (using more than one strategy at a time)

—Self-cuing during retrieval (thinking of cues that might elicit a memory)

—Use of external memory aids

—Arranging cues for prospective memory

—Other mnemonics or strategies

COLLECTING CLASSROOM EXAMINATION DATA

Because standardized memory tests are sometimes at odds with real-world memory performance, data on classroom examination performance is an important component of memory assessment. Classroom exam performance is an ideal source of data because classroom exams are direct measures of how much recently learned information the student can retain and recall over time. Here are the recommended steps for collecting and analyzing this data:

1. Select two core academic courses, one that the student performs poorly in and the other a course that the student does well in. Do not limit the data collection to the course that is the most challenging for the student because lack of background knowledge and other factors may be influencing memory performance.

2. Collect all of the available test data for each course, from the beginning of the course on. Record the scores and dates of the exams and ask the teacher to identify which exams were initial quizzes and which were summative or final exams. Ask the teacher or student for copies of the student's exams so that item responses can be reviewed.

3. Compare quiz performance with final exam performance, and consider whether the student consistently performs better on quizzes than on final exams. Quizzes are typically a day after new material has been covered; exams are typically administered after completing a unit or when a week or more has elapsed since the material was initially learned. For example, an initial spelling quiz is usually administered a day after the new words are introduced and the final test on the words is usually administered on Fridays. Consider these hypotheses when quiz performance appears significantly better than final exam performance: (a) the student's encoding procedures are ineffective because encoding is too passive or superficial and not enough cues are attached; (b) the student is forgetting much information over time because the information is not being consolidated; and (c) the student is not reviewing the material between the quiz and the summative exam.

4. Compare the student's average on recognition types of items with supply-the-answer items. For example, are multiple-choice scores consistently higher than fill-in-the-blank scores? Is so, there's a possibility that the student has problems with retrieval.

5. Compare assignment performance with exam performance. In doing so, first determine how much assistance the student usually receives with assignments. If the student usually completes assignments independently, proceed with the comparison. If exam performance is significantly lower, potential memory problems are indicated, especially when the student seems to be making every effort to prepare for exams.

6. If classroom test performance data are unavailable, conduct an experiment by teaching some new facts to the examinee and then testing delayed recall. Teaching some social studies facts (about 20) on a topic unfamiliar to the student is more helpful than having the examinee memorize a list of words. Elaborate when teaching the facts just like an instructor would. Go over the material until the examinee has 90% or better immediate recall. Then test delayed recall at one-day and at one-week intervals.

GUIDELINES FOR ADMINISTERING STANDARDIZED MEMORY TESTS

Standardized tests provide examiners with all of the details necessary for administering and scoring each subtest. Nonetheless, examiners can increase the reliability and validity of memory test results by providing some additional guidance before and during subtest and individual item administration. Of course, any additional guidance needs to be within the confines of the standardized procedures, but there are several things the examiner can say and do without violating the procedures.

Applying the recommendations below will increase the likelihood of obtaining the student's best performance and reduce the likelihood of examiner errors that might spoil a subtest.

1. Every effort should be made to complete administration of a memory scale in a single testing session, unless the scale allows for extended delayed recall intervals. The main reason for this requirement is that delayed recall conditions must be administered during the same sessions as the related immediate memory tasks.

2. Precise timing is critical. The presentation of most memory items has time limits that must be strictly adhered to. For example, allowing any extra time provides more opportunity for encoding and rehearsing the stimuli. More challenging for the administrator is the pacing of verbal items. For instance, the directions might be to pronounce words at the rate of one per second with a two second interval between them. Examiners should practice this pace while viewing the seconds tick off on a stopwatch. Even experienced examiners should occasionally check their pacing. Also, remember to record the time immediate memory tasks are completed so that proper intervals elapse between the immediate and delayed recall tasks. In some instances, it may be necessary to take a break to ensure adequate elapsed times.

3. When introducing the task, examiners should say nothing that might encourage or discourage strategy use. After all testing is complete, examiners should question examinees about their use of strategies during the test. Such questioning should not be done between subtests, as it may prompt the examinee to apply strategies on subsequent subtests.

4. No item or part of any item should be repeated unless allowed. When testing students who seem overly dependent on assistance, it's a good idea to inform them in advance that repetition of verbal items is not allowed and that they may not look back at visual stimuli.

5. Know when corrective feedback must be provided and when it is not allowed. Be extremely careful not to provide any cues as to the correctness of the examinee's responses. Behaviors such as nodding the head, saying "yes" to correct responses, and only marking incorrect responses can provide the examinee with subtle cues. Unintentional feedback can reinforce responses and influence performance on subsequent delayed recall of the same material.

6. Be sure to have the examinee's attention before presenting each item so that lack of attention does not confound the results. If necessary, ask "Are you ready?" or say "Here's the next one." Eye contact is a good indicator of attention.

7. When a learning or immediate memory subtest will be re-administered later as a delayed recall subtest, do not tell the examinee that this will occur unless the administration rules specifically state so.

8. After completing the entire battery, more information about the examinee's memory functioning can be gleaned from testing the limits. This method involves returning to a subtest and conducting some informal testing. For example, the clinician might suggest that the examinee try subvocal rehearsal during a span subtest. Then administer additional items to determine if the strategy makes a difference.

GENERAL GUIDELINES FOR INTERPRETATION OF TEST RESULTS

After all the assessment data has been gathered, evaluators must review, analyze, integrate, and interpret the data. During this process evaluators must draw from several areas of expertise, including knowledge of learning disabilities and knowledge of memory functions and processes. Most psychologists are adept at actuarial-based, statistical analysis of standardized test scores. Interpreting the meaning of the test scores and the discrepancies among them is the most challenging part of interpretation. Ultimately, the practitioner must rely on scientific, professional, and clinical judgment when ascribing meaning and making data-based decisions. Interpretation of test results is facilitated when: (a) interpretation involves testing of hypotheses; (b) interpretation is theory-based; (c) in-depth understanding of the examinee has been acquired; (d) testing has addressed all of the referral concerns; (e) the focus is on the individual instead of the test scores; and (f) non-test assessment data is integrated with test results.

Hypothesis Testing

After data collection is complete, the evaluator, or evaluation team, should refer back to the hypotheses selected during assessment planning and decide whether each hypothesis can be confirmed, lacks support, or needs further investigation. Hypothesis testing involves objective weighing of all the evidence for and against each of the a priori hypothesis pertaining to memory components and related processes. The evidence consists of test scores and relevant data collected through other methods. For example, subaverage short-term memory scores, subaverage learning subtest scores, and reports of significantly improved retrieval when prompts are provided all support confirmation of a hypothesis that the examinee's encoding is impaired or ineffective. Even when the data clearly support a hypothesis, oral and written conclusions should be stated cautiously. For some hypotheses, the data will be inconclusive and the evaluator will not be able to reach a decision. In instances where results are inconclusive or unexpected and answers are still sought, the evaluator should generate a posteriori hypotheses and investigate these through further assessment.

Theory-Based Interpretation

Theory-based interpretation increases everyone's understanding of what the test results mean. A theory or model provides the examiner with a logical structure that facilitates organization and integration of the data. It also allows teachers, parents, and students to grasp the meaning of the test results. Conducting interpretation from test-based structures can be confusing, especially when multiple tests have been administered. Practitioners can select from several memory models or develop one of their own. For interpreting memory functions and performance some options include Baddeley's theory (Baddeley, Eysenck, & Anderson, 2009), Anderson's (2000) theory, general information processing theory, or a neuropsychological theory that emphasizes brain structures (Miller, 2010). This author uses an information-processing model with some brain-based structures tied in. An example of a graphic that can be used to illustrate an information-processing model of memory is in Figure 5.2. When interpreting results orally, the evaluator should first present the graphic, using it to describe how memory works, and then discuss the examinee's ability or performance in each area. It's probably best to sequence the explanation according to the flow of information, discussing perception, attention, and short-term memory first and ending with long-term memory and retrieval.

Focusing on the Individual

Meaningful and beneficial interpretation is focused on the individual, not the test scores. Because the goal of assessment is to better understand the individual's strengths and weaknesses and why that individual is experiencing problems, simply reporting scores, reviewing data, and documenting symptoms is insufficient. One way of keeping the focus on the individual is to primarily address referral concerns instead of discussing test scores. Another approach is to organize the interpretation by cognitive and memory domains instead of test-by-test (see Chapter 9). Throughout the interpretation the focus should be on how the test scores and other data apply to the individual. Any given test score does not have the same meaning for everyone.

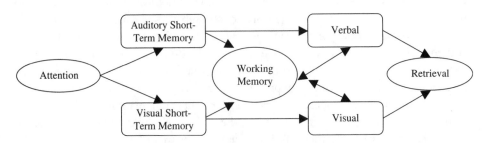

Figure 5.2 Illustration of memory model for oral interpretation

The meaning of performance in any given area is dependent on the individual's overall functioning and levels of functioning in related memory components and processes. For instance, a person with a deficit in episodic memory might still function and learn well if he or she has highly developed metamemory and effectively utilizes advanced memory strategies.

Integrating Assessment Data

Another way to ensure that interpretation of assessment results is understandable for all the parties involved is to integrate related data. The traditional interpretative model proceeds method-by-method and test-by-test. Traditionally, oral and written discussion is divided into background information, interview data, observational data, and then test-by-test reporting. The problem with this approach is that most recipients of the information don't have the expertise to integrate the data on their own. Ideally, the evaluator should pull together all information that pertains to each memory component or process as it is discussed. Structuring the report on a domain-by-domain basis rather than a method-by-method basis encourages integration. Another benefit of integrating the data is that it enhances evaluation of the a priori hypotheses. Here is an example of how information might be integrated in a written report:

> Jane appears to have an impairment in the consolidation and storage of verbal episodic information in long-term memory. On the WMS-IV, her auditory delayed recall score of 76 is significantly lower than her auditory immediate recall score of 93. With no significant difference between her recall and recognition scores, her difficulty does not seem to lie with retrieval. Also consistent with an impairment in consolidation and storage are: teacher reports that Jane rapidly forgets information; parental reports that Jane could not recall nursery rhymes as a preschooler; Jane's poor performance on classroom exams after extensive study; and previous assessment reports of poor performance on delayed recall tests.

Clarifying Strengths and Weaknesses

When discussing the examinee's strengths and weaknesses across memory components and processes there are always three perspectives that can be taken. First, the examinee's performance can be compared to what is normal for his or her age group (normative comparison). Second, the examinee's performance can be compared with his or her overall cognitive ability (ipsative comparison). Third, performance in one area of functioning can be compared with another logically related ability (pairwise comparison). Consequently, when discussing strengths and weaknesses, the evaluator always needs to specify what they are relative to. For example, it might be stated that the examinee has an ipsative weakness in verbal episodic memory relative to his or her overall cognitive ability even though his or her verbal episodic performance is within the average range. This text defines the average range of functioning as encompassing the middle 50% of a standard normal distribution instead of any score within one standard deviation of the mean. This means that for standard scores with a mean of 100 and standard deviation of 15, a normative weakness is any score below 90 and a normative strength is any score above 109. Significant ipsative differences require a discrepancy of approximately one standard deviation from the mean or global score they are being compared with. Pairwise comparisons require a discrepancy of approximately 20 points. In this text, when both a normative and ipsative weakness are present, it is referred to as a *deficit*. When the examinee has a deficit, the likelihood of an actual neurological impairment is high. Although a memory deficit is clearly cause for concern, an ipsative or normative weakness alone may also significantly interfere with the acquisition, retention, and retrieval of information. Thus, all ipsative and normative weaknesses should be examined closely, with pertinent informal assessment data taken into account.

Unitary Versus Non-Unitary Factors

When two or more subtests are aggregated and represented by one score, that score is referred to as a *factor* score. Depending on the extent of testing or the battery used, the functioning level of some memory components and processes will be represented by factor scores rather than by individual subtests. In such instances, it is important to compare the subtest scores that comprise each factor. When the difference between the highest and lowest subtest scores within a factor is extreme, the factor is said to be *non-unitary*. The criterion for this determination is an approximate discrepancy of 1.5 standard deviations, or approximately a 23-point difference with traditional standard scores. The occurrence of non-unitary factors could be due to measurement error or the fact that the two subtests are measuring two separable processes that are functioning at different levels. When a non-unitary factor arises, the clinician should examine the subtests involved and generate hypotheses that account for the discrepancy, taking testing behaviors and other evaluation data into account. For instance, an examinee may perform poorly on one verbal episodic memory subtest but not the other. Examining the content of the two subtests and the narrow abilities that they measure may reveal an explanation. For instance, the low-score subtest might have involved the retention of a word list while the high-score subtest involved a narrative. One hypothesis might be that the examinee lacks the ability to make associations among isolated words. Any hypotheses can be investigated through further testing and assessment. In the cross-battery model (Flanagan et al., 2007) the recommended solution is to administer an additional subtest that measures the same component or process but in a different way. This approach will provide a broader sampling of the memory factor. If no additional testing is conducted, the non-unitary factor score should be interpreted cautiously because it may not be a good representation of the component or process it purports to measure. Nonetheless, non-unitary factors and the subtests they comprise can still be included in profile analysis, as long as the inconsistency within the factor is reported. However, pairwise comparisons with non-unitary factors should be avoided.

ANALYSIS OF MEMORY TEST SCORES

When memory testing has been completed with a single instrument, the examiner should first follow the test score analysis procedures found in the scale's manual and then review the advice found in Chapter 6. The analytic and interpretative advice in Chapter 6 often suggests clinical analysis procedures and interpretations not found in the scale's manual. If the testing was conducted using more than one instrument, then the examiner will need to conduct a cross-battery analysis of scores. This section recommends procedures for a cross-battery analysis using the *Analysis of Memory Testing Results* worksheet found in Appendix B. After testing is complete, the worksheet is ideal for combining scores into one comprehensive analysis, as opposed to a test-by-test analysis. The primary purpose of the worksheet is to identify memory strengths and weaknesses, but additional related cognitive processes, such as processing speed, can also be incorporated. In using the worksheet, practitioners should apply clinical judgment and not feel bound by the suggested statistical criteria. For instance, when a memory component is compared with a global score, a discrepancy of 15 points is ideal because a standard deviation of difference is almost always statistically significant. However, an examinee with only a 12-point discrepancy may still have an ipsative weakness and possible deficit and impairment. To determine the significance and meaning of the 12-point discrepancy, related assessment data should be weighed.

Comparisons With a Global Score or Mean

To determine whether the examinee has ipsative weaknesses and strengths among memory functions, memory scores should be compared with a score that estimates general intellectual ability, overall cognitive processing, or general memory functioning. Using a Full Scale IQ score to predict memory performance is appropriate, given the high correlation IQ has with most forms of memory. In fact, memory scales are often co-normed with IQ tests or cognitive batteries (see Chapter 6). In these instances, the IQ composite should certainly be used to determine discrepancies. When an IQ or other cognitive composite is unavailable, a cross-battery mean of all administered subtests (memory and cognitive) should be used as the predictor. This is a less reliable approach for determining the significance of discrepancies but nonetheless is appropriate for clinical interpretation. Another drawback is that the cross-battery mean may not reveal many ipsative strengths and weaknesses when only potentially deficient memory components have been tested. Of course, in cases of subaverage intellectual ability, discrepancies between IQ and memory are also less likely to occur. A third method is to conduct an analysis limited to memory functions. This is particularly useful when a comprehensive memory assessment including working and short-term memory was completed. With this approach, a mean of all the memory subtest scores is computed and used to determine specific memory strengths and weaknesses. Ideally, the examiner should do two separate ipsative analyses, one using a mean based only on memory scores and the other using a cognitive composite or mean.

Pairwise Comparisons

Sometimes the profile analysis procedures that use a mean or composite do not yield any significant discrepancies that are indicative of ipsative strengths and weaknesses. That's why following up with pairwise comparisons is an essential part of the analysis. Differences are more likely to emerge during pairings (for a suggested list of pairings see Table 5.5). For example, verbal episodic memory may not be discrepant enough from a cross–battery mean but when contrasted with visuospatial episodic memory it becomes clear that it is a relative weakness. As indicated on the worksheet, to achieve statistical significance, a larger point discrepancy is required between pairs than between a mean and a component.

Table 5.5 Logical Pairings of Memory Components and Processes

—Phonological short-term memory versus verbal episodic memory

—Visuospatial short-term memory versus visuospatial episodic memory

—Verbal working memory versus verbal episodic memory

—Visuospatial working memory versus visuospatial episodic memory

—Visuospatial episodic memory versus verbal episodic memory

—Semantic memory versus verbal episodic memory

—Semantic memory versus visuospatial episodic memory

—Semantic memory versus fluid reasoning

—Semantic memory versus executive processing

—Learning versus attention

—Learning versus phonological short-term memory

—Learning versus semantic memory

—Learning versus verbal episodic memory

—Learning versus retrieval

—Retrieval versus processing speed

—Retrieval versus recognition

—Recognition versus fluid reasoning

—Any verbal memory component versus verbal ability

—Any verbal memory component versus auditory processing

—Any visuospatial component versus visuospatial processing

*For more comparisons involving short-term and working memory, see Dehn, 2008.

Procedures for Completing a Cross-Battery Analysis of Scores

The procedures for completing the *Analysis of Memory Testing Results* worksheet are described below, using the completed worksheet in Table 5.6 as an example (an abbreviated set of instructions is also found on the blank worksheet in Appendix B).

1. *In the lower cells of the first column, the Memory Component column, write in any related cognitive processes that were tested:* The main memory components are already entered on the template with the understanding that not all components need to be tested. In the case illustrated in Table 5.6 pre-assessment hypotheses led to the inclusion of fluid reasoning and processing speed.

2. *Write the name of the test battery in the second column:* This is the name of the scale or battery from which the subtests measuring that component were drawn. In instances where subtests from different batteries were used to measure the same component, enter the names of both batteries, with their subtests and scores in the same row (see the LTM Semantic row in Table 5.6).

3. *In the third column, write the name of the subtests or factors used to measure the memory components:* Classification of memory subtests is found in Tables 6.1 and 6.10. Enter the battery's factor name and use the battery's factor score only when all of the subtests comprising that factor are classified as measures of that memory component and when enough subtests were administered to compute the factor score.

4. *For each subtest or factor, calculate standard scores and enter these in the fourth column:* Scaled and standard scores found in the test's manual should be used. However, all subtest scores that do not have a mean of 100 and a standard deviation of 15 will first need to be transformed to scores that have such a mean and standard deviation, using the table in Appendix C. In Table 5.6, see the Vocabulary subtest score in the semantic row for an example.

5. *In the fifth column, enter a subtest or factor score for each memory component:* For components that were assessed with subtests from different factors or batteries, compute the mean and round to the nearest whole number. These component means are considered to be *clinical factor* scores. In Table 5.6, see the Semantic row for an example of clinical factor computation. Clinical factor scores should be interpreted more cautiously than the factor scores provided by test manuals.

6. *In the next column, enter a cognitive composite or cross-battery mean:* In general, this score should represent overall cognitive processing ability, overall memory functioning, or a combination of memory functioning and related cognitive processes. The preferred option is to use an IQ or other global cognitive score. In the top cell of the column indicate which is being used (see Table 5.6). In cases where a cross-battery mean must be computed, add up all of the subtest scores that are part of the analysis. To ensure proper

weighting of scores use only subtest scores, not factor scores. For example, in Table 5.6 the Verbal Working Memory factor score of 92 should not be used to compute a mean but rather the two individual subtest scores that comprise the factor. This means obtaining the scaled scores from the original protocol and then transforming them to standard scores that have a mean of 100 and a standard deviation of 15. The cross-battery mean should be rounded to the nearest whole number.

7. *Calculate and enter difference scores in the "Difference" column:* Subtract the composite or mean from each component score and enter the difference with a + or −.

8. *Determine normative strengths and weaknesses:* In the "Normative S, W, or A" column, enter an *S* (strength) for component means that are above 109. Enter a *W* (weakness) for component means that are below 90. For scores in the average range (90 to 109), put an *A*. For the sake of consistency and identification of likely weaknesses and strengths, classify all scores on this basis, even scores from tests that describe the average range as 85–115.

9. Determine intra-individual strengths and weaknesses and enter an *S* or *W* in the appropriate cells of the "Ipsative S or W" column. Enter a *W* for weakness when the memory component mean is 12 or more points lower than the individual's cognitive composite or mean, and enter an *S* for strength when the memory component mean is 12 or more points higher than the individual's cognitive composite or mean. If neither exists, leave the cell blank. A 15-point discrepancy, roughly a difference of one standard deviation, is ideal because a standard deviation of difference between two scores is very likely to be statistically significant at the .05 level or less. However, a discrepancy as low as 12 points should be considered as evidence for a weakness, especially when there is corroborating information.

10. *Determine processing deficits and assets and enter in the last column:* Enter "Deficit" for components that have both a normative and ipsative weakness. Enter "Asset" for components that have both a normative and ipsative strength.

11. *Determine whether each component is unitary:* Using standard scores that have a mean of 100 and a standard deviation of 15, compare subtest scores within each component. When the difference is greater than 22 points, consider the factor to be non-unitary. Non-unitary factors should be included in the profile analysis, but interpreted cautiously. Non-unitary factors should not be included in pairwise comparisons.

12. *Conduct comparisons of logically related pairs (see Table 5.5) in the lower portion of the worksheet:* When both components are represented by single subtest scores from the same scale, check the statistical tables in the scale's manual to determine discrepancies necessary for significance. When such tables are unavailable or when clinical factors have been calculated, use a 20-point

Table 5.6 Analysis of memory testing results (completed example)

Examinee's Name: Abby   DOB: _____   Age: 16:4   Grade: 10   Dates of Testing: _____

Memory Component	Battery Name	Subtest/Factor* Name	Subtest/Factor Scores	Component Mean	Composite or Mean	Difference	Normative S, W, or A	Ipsative S or W	Deficit or Asset
Verbal Episodic	WMS-IV	Logical Mem II / Verbal Paired Associates (VPA) II	(10) 100 / (5) 75	88	WAIS IV IQ 89	−1	W	–	–
Visuospatial Episodic	WMS-IV	Designs II / Visual Reproduction II	(7) 85 / (4) 70	78	89	−11	W	–	–
Semantic	WAIS-IV / WJ-III ACH	Vocabulary / Academic Knowledge	(11) 105 / 94	100	89	+11	A	–	–
Retrieval Fluency	WJ III COG	Retrieval Fluency	76	76	89	−13	W	W	Deficit
Recognition	WMS-IV	VPA II Recognition	>75 Cum %	–	89	–	–	–	–
Learning	WMS-IV / WJ III COG	VPA I / Visual-Auditory Learning	(5) 75 / 77	76	89	−13	W	W	Deficit
Verbal WM	WAIS-IV	WORKING MEMORY	92	92	89	+3	A	–	–
Visuospatial WM	WMS-IV	VISUAL WM	83	83	89	−6	W	–	–
Phonological STM	WJ III COG	ST MEMORY	92	92	89	+3	A	–	–
Visuospatial STM	WMS-IV	Designs I / Visual Reproduction I	(7) 85 / (3) 65	75	89	−14	W	W	Deficit
Processing Speed	WAIS-IV	PROCESSING SPEED	89	89	89	0	W	–	–
Fluid Reasoning	WJ III COG	FLUID REASONING	85	85	89	−4	W	–	–

Component and Score		Difference Between Pairs	Significant Difference: Y/N
Semantic (100)	Retrieval (76)	24	Y
Semantic (100)	Learning (76)	14	N
Learning (76)	Phonological STM (92)	16	Y
Verbal WM (92)	Visuospatial WM (83)	9	N

*Factors are set in all capital letters; subtests are set initial capped.

Directions: (1) Convert all subtest scores to standard scores with a mean of 100 and an SD of 15. (2) For each memory component, compute the mean of the subtest scores and round to the nearest whole number. (3) Enter a cognitive composite, such as a full scale IQ, or compute the mean of all available memory components. (4) Subtract the composite or mean from each memory component mean and enter amount in Difference column. (5) Indicate whether the memory component is a normative weakness, strength, or average (90–109 is average). (6) Using a criterion of 12–15 points, determine intra-individual strengths and weaknesses. (7) Determine deficits and assets. A deficit is both a normative and intra-individual weakness; an asset is both a normative and intra-individual strength. (8) Determine which factors are non-unitary. Factors are non-unitary when the two subtests involved are discrepant by more than 22 points. Non-unitary factors should be interpreted cautiously and should not be used in pairwise comparisons. (9) Compare logical pairs of components, using a 15–20 point difference as an indication of a significant discrepancy.

167

discrepancy as indicative of significance and infrequency. However, a discrepancy as low as 15 points should be considered as evidence for a weakness, especially when there is corroborating information.

SPECIFIC GUIDELINES FOR INTERPRETATION OF MEMORY ASSESSMENT RESULTS

As described in the previous section, cross-battery profile analysis encourages close examination of individual test scores and their meaning. Completing the interpretative process requires putting all the information together, not just integrating data but describing how the examinee's memory systems function from input to output. Putting all the pieces together should allow the evaluator to understand how the examinee's memory systems interact and how the individual's memory functions relate to his or her academic learning and daily living. Additional goals of a memory assessment interpretation include: (a) identification of specific memory strengths and weaknesses; (b) identification of underlying impairments in memory and cognitive processes; (c) testing hypotheses and answering referral questions; (d) determining the influence of cognitive and other factors; (e) and identifying intervention needs.

Interpretation of Long-Term Memory Components and Processes

This section provides interpretative suggestions, considerations, and hypotheses for each memory component and process. See Table 5.7 on page 172 for a list of possible interpretative hypotheses that might account for poor performance in each memory component and process.

Verbal Episodic Memory Deficits in verbal episodic memory are mainly indicated by poor test performance on delayed recall tasks involving verbal material. Standardized tasks include word lists, paired associates, and narratives. Other indicators of a verbal episodic deficit include poor performance on classroom exams, anecdotal reports of forgetting information, and observations of poor recall. The most extreme cases of verbal episodic memory impairment, where little to nothing of new learning is retained, can be diagnosed as anterograde amnesia or developmental amnesia. Moderate dysfunction is probable when delayed recall is significantly lower than what is predicted from a learning or immediate memory subtest. For instance, when a learning subtest score is normal and delayed recall is subaverage, episodic memory dysfunction is likely. Ipsative weaknesses are indicated when delayed verbal episodic performance is lower than overall cognitive ability.

The processes underlying the weakness vary. Poor encoding is implicated when phonological short-term memory is similarly low, working memory is weak, learning rate is slow, and strategy development appears delayed. Ineffective encoding (or learning) can influence consolidation and storage because of weak associations and can impair retrieval because cues are not attached during encoding. Given adequate initial learning, consolidation and storage impairments are probable when forgetting is unusually rapid. The influence of retrieval can be checked by testing retrieval fluency and recognition. Significant deficits in verbal episodic memory that cannot be attributed to poor strategy development or retrieval problems are most likely due to impaired hippocampal functioning. Regardless of the level of episodic functioning, it is essential that testing include a controlled learning task and delayed recall of that learning. The learning task functions as a baseline or pretest that predicts how much information should be recalled later. Some individuals are slow learners and don't learn as much, but they have excellent retention of what they do learn. In such instances, verbal episodic long-term memory is not the problem; the impairment lies with learning.

Visuospatial Episodic Memory   In cases of amnesia both verbal and visuospatial episodic memory are usually similarly affected. Otherwise, individuals, with and without memory impairments, often exhibit differential episodic abilities. For instance, students with a learning disability often display a strength in visuospatial episodic memory relative to verbal episodic. Usually, this difference is part of a broader visual–verbal disparity in which all processing and retention involving verbal material is weaker than that for visual material. Interpretation of visuospatial episodic performance basically follows the same logic and procedures used in interpreting the verbal component; however, there are more challenges involved. First, pure visual learning tasks are seldom available; the tasks almost always incorporate verbal information, at least in the directions. Second, some tasks encourage verbal mediation by presenting easily named stimuli instead of abstract objects. Third, most scales don't distinguish visual from spatial aspects, requiring the examiner to analyze the measurement task. Non-test assessment data that supports an impairment in visuospatial episodic memory includes difficulty navigating in familiar surroundings and forgetting the location of commonly used objects.

Semantic Memory   The determination of a potential deficit in semantic memory is quite challenging, given all the potential confounds. Some influences that must be considered include language development, English language proficiency, opportunities to learn, adequate instruction, study habits, memory strategies, diversity of experiences, and learning ability. Analyzing school examination performance (see the section "Collecting Classroom Examination Data") that occurred over an extended period of time is an essential part of semantic memory assessment. When episodic functioning is significantly better than semantic, it's appropriate to hypothesize an impairment in consolidation, as consolidation is involved in transferring information from episodic to semantic structures. The influences of encoding, learning, and retrieval can be evaluated in the same ways they are for verbal episodic memory.

Learning   Students with learning impairments typically have more difficulty with the first learning trial than students without learning impairments. Lower than normal acquisition in the early trials is indicative of encoding difficulties, inattention, or deficient short-term memory. Also, an unusually high number of intrusions (incorrect responses) on a learning task is indicative of inattentiveness. To control for these influences, it is critical that memory testing include a multiple-trial learning task. When there is only one opportunity to learn the material, such as when a story is read only once, the delayed recall performance may underestimate actual long-term memory ability. For instance, if the examinee's performance on tasks with multiple learning trials is significantly higher than with single-trial tasks, then the problem lies more with encoding and learning than with long-term retention. In such cases, examinees remember material once they have had adequate opportunities to learn it; they just have difficulty initially learning the material. Also, learning that plateaus after one or two trials is an indication the examinee is not using a strategy or benefitting from feedback.

Encoding   Poor performance on learning tasks is perhaps the most direct indication of an encoding impairment. Also, difficulty with retrieval is an indication that encoding is not functioning effectively, especially when cued recall is significantly better than uncued. Subaverage short-term memory span and limited working memory capacity are influences because encoding involves the transfer of information from short-term to long-term stores. Failure to benefit from basic strategies, such as cumulative rehearsal and elaboration, is a strong indication of a neurological basis (namely, an impaired hippocampus) for the deficient encoding. As with other memory domains, verbal and visual performance can be compared.

Consolidation and Storage   As stated previously, consolidation and storage deficits are indicated by poor performance on both free recall and recognition, as well as unusually fast rates of forgetting over time. Examinees who display normal retention of facts and episodes for about a day following learning but then have an abnormally fast rate of forgetting afterwards most likely have a problem consolidating memories. That is, initial storage in the hippocampus is normal, but subsequent storage is not being transferred to cortical regions (Mayes, 2004).

Retrieval   Retrieval deficits are indicated by difficulty accessing information at the time it is desired. In such instances, individuals can state that they know the information but can't actually recall it. Also, retrieval problems are indicated when retrieval is slow but accurate, such as poor performance on rapid automatic naming or retrieval fluency tasks.

The most reliable evidence of a retrieval but not a storage problem is when the examinee's retrieval improves when some kind of cue is provided. Recognition tasks such as multiple-choice are an extreme form of cuing. A retrieval deficit is indicated whenever recognition is significantly higher than free recall (keeping in mind that everyone does better on recognition tasks). Mild retrieval deficits are probable when general cues, such as semantic cues, also improve recall, whereas, severe retrieval deficits are likely when cued recall is no better than uncued but recognition tasks produce dramatic improvement (Duchnick, Vanderploeg, & Curtiss, 2002). When neither cuing nor recognition improve performance, a storage deficit is implicated. Poor encoding can confound the determination of a retrieval deficit. To prevent this confound, it is important to ensure that mastery of the new material has taken place before delayed recall is attempted.

Recognition   When the individual's level of recognition is not significantly better than uncued retrieval, poor retrieval performance is probably due to forgetting, not retrieval per se. In contrast, when there is significantly better cued (recognition) than uncued recall, impairments in attention, encoding, and retrieval are all implicated. Caution is urged when interpreting recognition scores because of their inherent statistical limitations, namely their restricted score ranges (Sheslow & Adams, 2003). Because of the true-false formants, nearly perfect performance is obtainable by almost everyone, causing the score distributions to be negatively skewed. Thus, score precision is lacking for average to above average performance. As a result, above average performance should not be emphasized. However, individuals with re-cognition deficits can still be accurately identified. Failure to recall information after a prompt (a recognition deficit) is a strong indication of a serious problem with storage. For example, recognition does not help amnesiacs because the sought after infor-mation is not in storage.

Metamemory   The validity of informal metamemory assessment is low; for example, self-rated ability to remember telephone numbers correlates .4 with digit span and correlations with word list recall are even lower or nonexistent (Cohen, 2008a). Inaccurate self-appraisals of memory may result from distorted self-images, lack of self-awareness, denial, or simply forgetting past memory performance. Consequently, evaluators should interpret the information cautiously and seek corroborating information. Interview and rating information that is in gross conflict with other assessment data is still useful. At least it demonstrates that the examinee lacks awareness or is in denial regarding problems. Regarding reliability, self-appraisals of memory ability have proved to have high reliability; they are consistent across time (Cohen, 2008a). Despite the challenges of interpreting metamemory information, there are some profiles that are consistent with delayed metamemory development. Poorly developed metamemory awareness is indicated by: (a) denial of memory problems; (b) self-reports of memory functioning that are not corroborated by teachers and parents; (c) poor judgments of learning, such as extreme overestimates of delayed recall; (d) limited knowledge of human memory functioning; and (e) immature use of memory strategies. Poorly developed metamemory regulation is indicated by: (a) the belief that nothing can be done to improve memory

Table 5.7   Interpretative hypotheses for poor performance by memory component

Verbal episodic memory

- The examinee has an impairment in verbal episodic memory functioning.
- The examinee has anterograde amnesia.
- The examinee has an impairment in auditory processing.
- The examinee has an impairment in phonological short-term memory.
- The examinee has a language impairment.
- The examinee has subaverage verbal abilities.
- The examinee has an encoding impairment.
- The examinee has an impairment in consolidation and storage.
- The examinee has an impairment in retrieval.
- The examinee has a verbal learning impairment.
- The examinee has poorly developed memory strategies.
- The examinee has a deficit in auditory acuity.
- The examinee has severe problems with attention.

Visuospatial episodic memory

- The examinee has an impairment in visuospatial episodic memory functioning.
- The examinee has anterograde amnesia.
- The examinee has an impairment in visuospatial short-term memory.
- The examinee has an impairment in visuospatial processing.
- The examinee has an encoding impairment.
- The examinee has an impairment in consolidation and storage.
- The examinee has an impairment in retrieval.
- The examinee is not verbally recoding visuospatial information.
- The examinee has a visual acuity deficit.
- The examinee has severe problems with attention.

Semantic memory

- The examinee has an impairment in semantic memory functioning.
- The examinee has an impairment in explicit memory functioning that includes both semantic and episodic memory.
- The examinee has an impairment in encoding.
- The examinee has an impairment in consolidation.
- The examinee has an impairment in retrieval.
- The examinee has subaverage verbal abilities.
- The examinee has limited English language proficiency.
- The examinee has a language impairment.
- The examinee has an impairment in learning.
- The examinee's metamemory development is delayed.
- The examinee does not use effective memory strategies.
- The examinee has had limited opportunities to learn.
- The examinee has not received adequate instruction.
- The examinee has an impairment in fluid reasoning.

Learning

- The examinee has a learning disability.
- The examinee has an impairment in attention.
- The examinee has an impairment in encoding.
- The examinee has an impairment in short-term memory.
- The examinee has an impairment in working memory.
- The examinee does not use effective memory strategies.
- The examinee's metamemory development is delayed.

Encoding

- The examinee has an impairment in encoding.
- The examinee has an impairment in attention.

- The examinee has an impairment in learning.
- The examinee has an impairment in short-term memory.
- The examinee does not use effective memory strategies.
- The examinee has slow processing speed.

Consolidation and storage
- The examinee has developmental amnesia.
- The examinee has an impairment in consolidation.
- The examinee has an impairment in storage.
- The examinee has an impairment in encoding.
- The examinee has an impairment in learning.
- The examinee has an impairment in retrieval.

Retrieval
- The examinee has an impairment in retrieval.
- The examinee has an impairment in encoding.
- The examinee has an impairment in consolidation.
- The examinee has an impairment in storage.
- The examinee has slow processing speed.
- The examinee does not use effective memory strategies.

Recognition
- The examinee has an impairment in explicit memory.
- The examinee has amnesia.
- The examinee has an impairment in storage.
- The examinee has an impairment in retrieval.
- The examinee has an impairment in consolidation.
- The examinee has an impairment in semantic memory.
- The examinee has an impairment in fluid reasoning.

Metamemory
- The examinee has delayed metamemory development.
- The examinee has an impairment in executive functioning.
- The examinee has an impairment in fluid reasoning.
- The examinee has an impairment in working memory.
- The examinee has poorly developed memory strategies.

Strategy development
- The examinee has acquired strategies but does not use them effectively.
- The examinee has delayed metamemory development.
- The examinee has an impairment in executive functioning.
- The examinee has an impairment in fluid reasoning.
- The examinee has an impairment in working memory.

Prospective memory
- The examinee has an impairment in executive functioning.
- The examinee has an impairment in planning.
- The examinee has an impairment in verbal episodic memory.
- The examinee has an inability to tell time.

performance; (b) not adapting study methods to the difficulty level of the material; and (c) not being aware that a memory failure has occurred.

Strategy Development Because the application of strategies during memory testing will influence performance, the examinee should be observed for strategy use during testing and then questioned about strategy use after administration of all memory tests is complete. Complete lack of strategy use by older children is an indication that full memory potential has yet to be realized. Nonetheless, the assessment of strategy development and usage is primarily for intervention purposes (see Table 5.4). Strategy assessment data collected through interviews, self-ratings, and informal experimentation should be interpreted cautiously because even poor strategy users tend to intuitively select the better strategies and pretend that they use these strategies all the time (Schneider, 2010).

Determining the Influence of Related Cognitive Factors

The majority of children and adolescents with memory problems will have other cognitive deficits as well. Consequently, related cognitive processes (see Chapter 3) should be included in a memory assessment. When analyzing memory test scores it is important to include cognitive processing scores in the analysis and contrast those that are closely related, such as pairing processing speed with retrieval fluency (see Table 5.5 for suggested pairings). It is often difficult to distinguish memory deficits from other underlying cognitive impairments. For example, differentiating attention problems from actual encoding problems can be a challenge. If the cognitive process is as low as the memory score, then the likelihood of influence is high. For instance, a low processing speed score coupled with slow retrieval fluency is an indication that processing speed underlies or is contributing to the deficit. On the other hand, if the cognitive score is high relative to the memory score then that cognitive process is not likely contributing to the memory problem. Sometimes, cognitive influences are considered more broadly. For instance, if all cognitive abilities in the verbal domain are deficient, verbal memory deficits can certainly be attributed, at least in part, to a general verbal or linguistic impairment. However, it should never be presumed that all functions in the same domain are equivalent. For example, verbal IQ and language development levels can be significantly higher than verbal memory performance, cases of amnesia being a prime example.

Interpretation of Performance on Specific Assessment Tasks

List Learning   List learning is a classic memory assessment task that involves rote memorization of a word list over two to six trials. Immediate recall of the words is dependent on phonological short-term memory span, whereas long-term retention requires effective verbal encoding. Although the total score from all trials is informative, it is important to also examine the rate of learning across trials. The immediate recall from each trial can be used to plot a learning curve. Normal learning curves display rapid improvement at first and then a more gradual rise. A rapid rise in the learning curve results from repeated exposures and from basic rehearsal strategies. Although some students may utilize a strategy other than subvocal rehearsal, it is unlikely because the words are presented quickly and the trials immediately follow each other. Performance on list-learning tasks has direct implications for academic learning because academics demand constant memorization of material, much of which is accomplished in a rote fashion. The ability to memorize information through rote rehearsal is highly related to academic success, especially in earlier grades. Thus, examinees who perform poorly on list-learning tasks are likely to have difficulty memorizing information, such as multiplication tables. For examinees who do not gain much more information through repetition (when there's no rapid rise in the learning curve), it is important to determine whether in fact they are using subvocal rehearsal. When they are not, they should be taught basic rehearsal strategies. When examinees are using a basic rehearsal strategy, deficits in verbal episodic memory are implicated, and rote memorization will not be an effective learning strategy for them. Such students should be taught strategies that encourage deeper processing of information or mnemonics that associate the rote information with familiar memory representations. Some list-learning tasks introduce a distractor list so that the examinee's susceptibility to interference can be assessed. On such measures, evaluators need to examine how much confusion there is between lists and how much loss of the original list results from introducing another list. When the examinee is easily affected by interference, presentation of new, similar material reduces recall of previously learned information.

Paired-Associates Learning   Another common verbal measurement paradigm is paired-associates learning in which examinees must learn a list of paired words over a few trials. The task is similar to list learning, only more complicated in that interference, corrective feedback, and semantic knowledge can have more influence on performance. Paired-associates tasks usually consist of some logically related pairs and some unrelated pairs. Examiners should contrast examinee performance on these two different types of pairs. Significantly better performance on related pairs indicates that the examinee is capitalizing on semantic knowledge to learn new information. In contrast, better performance on unrelated pairs implies that semantic knowledge is limited or that the examinee has difficulty recognizing common associations. Performance on paired-associates has direct implications for academic learning, especially vocabulary learning, as vocabulary acquisition depends on associating words and their definitions.

Visual-Auditory Learning   Visual-auditory learning is a measurement paradigm that involves learning the association between a visual stimulus and its verbal label across several trials with corrective feedback. Several components of memory become involved in this complex but very realistic learning task. The central executive aspect of working memory is especially important for success because it plays a crucial role whenever visual and auditory information must be integrated. Performance on visual-auditory learning tasks is highly related with the development of early language and also the development of early reading skills.

Memory for Narratives Memory for a narrative is one of the most direct and natural measures of verbal episodic memory. Performance on such tasks reveals the ability to recall meaningful, integrated information rather than abstract or isolated stimuli. Consequently, some examinees may perform significantly different on narratives than they do on random lists of information.

Those who perform significantly better on narratives should be taught elaborative rehearsal methods, such as embedding a list of words or facts within a story. Narratives also provide the opportunity to contrast memory for gist with memory for details. More mature learners are better at recalling gist and are able to infer details from the gist. Those who remember details better than gist may benefit from strategies that emphasize identification of main ideas. Regarding academic implications, memory for narratives is highly related with oral language comprehension, reading comprehension, oral expression, and written expression.

CASE STUDY

This section provides an explanation of the cross-battery analysis results found in Table 5.6, along with some appropriate interpretative hypotheses. The test data is from the case of Abby, who was introduced at the beginning of Chapter 2. A partially completed memory assessment plan for Abby can be found in Table 5.2 (only some of the referral concerns are included). A comprehensive written interpretation of Abby's test results is in Chapter 9. This section begins with a row-by-row explanation of Table 5.6 and ends with some conclusions that integrate the test results.

Verbal Episodic. A deficit in verbal episodic memory was hypothesized because of Abby's difficulties with learning new concepts and with classroom examination performance (see Table 5.2). Abby's overall verbal episodic test performance (component mean of 88) is a normative weakness (because it's below 90) but not an ipsative weakness. However, this factor is not unitary because of the extreme difference between the two subtests. Consequently, no general conclusion about verbal episodic memory can be drawn. When the two subtest tasks are examined, it appears that Abby has normal ability for delayed recall of narrative (Logical Memory II) but very deficient recall of less connected information, such as a list of word pairs (Verbal Paired Associates II). Because Verbal Paired Associates I is a learning task and Logical Memory I is not, a learning impairment is implicated.

Visuospatial Episodic. Visuospatial explicit memory (includes both episodic and semantic) was suspected of being impaired because of Abby's prenatal exposure to cocaine (see Chapter 4). Only the episodic dimension of visuospatial explicit memory was actually tested, not the semantic aspect. Because her performance on the subtests is quite different, the factor is borderline non-unitary. Spatial versus visual ability might account for the difference, as Designs has a spatial component and Visual Reproduction does not. The significantly below average component mean of 78 is indicative of an impairment even though it's not quite a significant ipsative weakness.

Semantic. The difficulties with school learning led to an impairment hypothesis regarding semantic memory. However, the semantic memory component score, bolstered by high vocabulary development and average verbal abilities, is one of Abby's highest areas of functioning. Nonetheless, this borderline strength does not seem to carry over to ready acquisition of school-based semantic knowledge. Comparison of her quizzes and summative examinations reveals that she does worse on summative examinations.

Retrieval. Her poor performance on classroom examinations led to a hypothesized retrieval impairment. Her Retrieval Fluency score of 76 appears to represent a deficit (and likely impairment), as it is both a normative and ipsative weakness.

Recognition. Recognition was tested to separate retrieval from storage. A direct score comparison is impossible because the WMS-IV only provides a cumulative percentage range (of the population) that Abby performed better than. Given her high performance when recognition cues are provided, it appears that retrieval rather than storage is the problem, as least in the verbal realm.

Learning. Given Abby's academic learning problems, learning (encoding) is certainly implicated. Her performance on the two selected subtests is commensurate and well below average, indicating a deficit and possible impairment.

Phonological STM and Verbal WM. Verbal working memory was hypothesized to be a deficit to account for Abby's low reading comprehension. Phonological short-term memory was investigated because of its relationship with learning and encoding. Both components appear to be average.

Visuospatial STM and WM. Visuospatial short-term and working memory were assessed with the WMS-IV because of their relationships with visuospatial episodic memory. Her scores on the visuospatial short-term, working, and episodic memory tasks are all commensurate. The WMS-IV subtests use abstract stimuli, thereby preventing Abby from using her verbal strengths to mediate her visuospatial performance.

Processing Speed. Processing speed was tested because of its relationship with retrieval fluency. In this case, processing is equivalent to overall cognitive processing and much higher than retrieval fluency, indicating that processing speed is not contributing to Abby's slow and ineffective retrieval.

Fluid Reasoning. Abby's fluid reasoning ability was assessed because of its relationship with reading comprehension and the role it plays integrating information stored in semantic memory. Abby's fluid reasoning level is a normative weakness and thus may be contributing to her learning and memory performance problems.

Pairwise Comparisons. The first significant pairing—semantic versus retrieval—reveals that semantic storage does not seem to be the problem. The second pairing—learning versus phonological STM—indicates that learning difficulties are not due to a short memory span or a problem processing phonological information.

Conclusions. Overall, Abby's verbal learning and memory abilities appear to be stronger than her visuospatial learning and memory abilities. Nonetheless, learning and retrieving verbal material that is not inherently organized or connected (such as a narrative) is difficult for her. Her learning and subsequent retrieval problems seem to be primarily due to an impairment in encoding, perhaps aggravated by her delayed development of memory strategies. Her high semantic memory scores are somewhat inconsistent with her acquisition and remote recall of academic knowledge. However, a review of Abby's history reveals that her semantic knowledge is acquired after a tremendous amount of study and review. See Abby's report in Chapter 9 for a more in-depth discussion.

6 Assessing Long-Term Memory With Standardized Tests

A high school senior, given the pseudonym of "Kim," came to the tutoring center ostensibly seeking assistance with test-taking skills so that she could improve her ACT college entrance examination scores. Kim had a grade point average of 3.1, but all three of her ACT Composite scores had fallen below the national mean. Tests, in general, had always been challenging and frustrating for her. During course exams Kim seemed to "forget everything" she had studied. Although Kim admitted to being anxious during exams, it was her hypothesis that she did poorly because she couldn't remember the information. As the interview progressed, Kim reported having had three concussions during soccer competitions. The first concussion, four years earlier, was severe enough to cause her to miss two weeks of school. The other two events also resulted in concussion syndrome but were less severe. Given this history and Kim's beliefs that she could not remember semantic information, a memory assessment was conducted. The Wechsler Memory Scale-Fourth Edition (WMS®-IV; Wechsler, 2009) was administered, along with verbal working memory subtests from the Wechsler Adult Intelligence Scale®-Fourth Edition (WAIS®-IV; Wechsler, 2008). Also, the School Motivation and Learning Strategies Inventory (SMALSI; Stroud & Reynolds, 2006), a self-rating scale, was used to evaluate Kim's study skills and level of test anxiety. As it turned out, none of the memory hypotheses were supported. With the exception of low average verbal working memory, all of Kim's memory components were in the mid-average range or higher. The cause of Kim's poor examination performance seemed to be a high level of test anxiety. On the SMALSI, her level of self-reported test anxiety was at the 90th percentile, in the clinically significant range. Kim's case is used in this chapter to illustrate two assessment strategies that were introduced in Chapter 5. First, even though the entire WMS®-IV scale was administered, supplemental testing with WAIS®-IV was necessary. Second, additional analytic and interpretative procedures (beyond those found in the WMS®-IV manual and record form) were necessary to fully profile Kim's memory strengths and weaknesses. Kim's completed *Analysis of Memory Testing Results* worksheet can be found in Table 6.9. Interpretation of her test results can be found at the end of the WMS®-IV section.

This chapter provides information on contemporary measurement instruments that are suitable for memory assessment. The chapter begins with comprehensive memory and neuropsychological batteries designed primarily for children and adolescents. It continues with advice on how to use the memory subtests that are embedded in intellectual, cognitive, and achievement batteries. The chapter concludes with brief reviews of some specific memory scales that can further augment memory assessment. To be selected for inclusion, the memory scales must have child or adolescent norms, been published or revised since 1990, provide evidence of adequate reliability, and include validity studies with clinical populations known for having memory problems. As for which scales evaluators should use in any given case, it really depends on the referral concerns and which memory components need to be tested. Tables 6.1 and 6.10 should prove helpful in selecting primary and secondary scales, as they display scale-by-scale classification of subtests by memory component. All memory scales contain short-term (immediate) memory subtests that introduce information the examinee is required to recall later. Only the short-term memory subtests that have delayed recall versions are discussed in this chapter. For details on the remaining short-term memory and working memory subtests, the reader should peruse Dehn (2008).

CALIFORNIA VERBAL LEARNING TEST—CHILDREN'S VERSION (CVLT-C)

The CVLT-C (Delis, Kramer, Kaplan, & Ober, 1994) is one of the most frequently used children's measures of verbal episodic learning and memory. The CVLT-C (see Table 6.2) is essentially a list-learning task that assesses various quantitative and qualitative aspects of learning and memory, with an emphasis on processes and strategies. This scale, which assesses memory within the context of an everyday task, has been shown to be particularly sensitive to the severity of TBI (Mottram & Donders, 2005; Wilde, Boake, & Sherer, 1995) and memory problems in children (Duchnick, Vanderploey, & Curtiss, 2002).

Technical Properties

The norms are based on a sample of 920 children divided into 12 age groups. Given the scale's restricted content and semantic relatedness, traditional internal consistency estimates of reliability may have limited value. Nevertheless, most of the reliability statistics presented in the manual indicate modest levels of reliability, though some test-retest coefficients are extremely low (Delis et al., 1994). Validity evidence in the manual is minimal, but the CVLT-C has been used extensively in neuropsychological research with brain-injured populations (e.g., Mottram & Donders, 2005), and the findings have supported the validity of the scale, at least in regards to populations with memory impairments. Also, the structure of the CVLT-C has been the subject of

Table 6.1 Classification of memory battery subtests by memory component

Memory Component	CMS	CVLT-C	NEPSY II	RBMT-C	TOMAL2	WRAML2	WMS-IV
Verbal Episodic	Stories Delayed; Word Pairs Delayed; Word Lists Delayed	List A: Long-Delay Free-Recall Trial; List A: Long-Delay Cued-Recall Trial	List Memory Delayed; Memory for Names Delayed*		Memory for Stories Delayed; Word Selective Reminding Delayed	Story Memory Delay Recall; Verbal Learning Delay Recall; Sound Symbol Delay Recall*	Logical Memory (LM) II; Verbal Paired Associates (VPA) II
Visuospatial Episodic	Dot Locations Delayed; Faces Delayed; Family Pictures Delayed		Memory for Designs Delayed; Memory for Faces Delayed	Remembering a new route (delayed)		Design Memory Recognition; Picture Memory Recognition	Designs (DE) II; Visual Reproduction (VR) II
Semantic							
Prospective				Hidden belonging; Remembering an appointment; Delivering a message			
Retrieval Fluency							
Recognition	Stories Delayed Recognition; Word Pairs Delayed Recognition	List A: Long-Delay Recognition Trial	Narrative Memory			Story Memory Recognition; Verbal Learning Recognition; Design Memory Recognition; Picture Memory Recognition	LM II Recognition; VPA Recognition; DE Recognition; VR Recognition
Learning	Dot Locations; Word Pairs; Word Lists	List A: Immediate Free Recall Trials	List Memory; Memory for Designs; Memory for Names		Word Selective Reminding; Object Recall; Paired Recall; Visual Selective Reminding	Verbal Learning; Sound Symbol	Verbal Paired Associates I

*This task also involves visuospatial episodic memory because the information consists of visual-verbal associations.

CMS = Children's Memory Scale; CVLT-C = California Verbal Learning Test-Children's Version; NEPSY II = A Developmental Neuropsychological Assessment, Second Edition; RBMT-C = The Rivermead Behavioural Memory Test for Children; TOMAL2 = Test of Memory and Learning, Second Edition; WRAML2 = Wide Range Assessment of Memory and Learning, Second Edition; WMS-IV = Wechsler Memory Scale-Fourth Edition.

Table 6.2 California Verbal Learning Test—Children's Version (CVLT-C)

Authors:	Dean C. Delis, Joel H. Kramer, Edith Kaplan, and Beth A. Ober
Publisher:	The Psychological Corporation
Publication Date:	1994
Age Range:	5–16

several factor analytic studies. After conducting a confirmatory factor analysis of the CVLT-C by reanalyzing scores from the standardization sample, Donders (1999) suggested that the scale measures five factors: attention span, learning efficiency, free delayed recall, cued delayed recall, and inaccurate recall. In contrast, Mottram and Donders found no support for separating delayed recall into free and cued factors when they identified a four-factor model: attention span, learning efficiency, delayed recall, and inaccurate recall.

Subtests

The test uses a hypothetical shopping list of 15 words that consist of three categories of items (fruit, clothing, and toys). No corrective feedback is given as the examinee recalls the words after each presentation. After the fifth trial, an interference list consisting of two semantic categories (food and furniture) is presented and then the examinee is asked to recall the interference list. After recalling the interference list, the examinee must recall the original list again, first freely and then cued by semantic category. It's then necessary to take a 20-minute break before the delayed recall tasks are administered. During this break no other tasks involving lists of words should be undertaken. Rather, the break may be an ideal time to test visuospatial memory. When CVLT-C administration resumes, the child first recalls the words without any prompting. Then the examiner cues the child by providing the semantic categories to which the words belong. Finally, recognition is tested with a list of 60 words that include target words and interference words, with non-list distracters consisting of phonemically similar words, words from the same semantic categories, and words that are unrelated to the target words.

Interpretation

From the learning and recall of just one 15-word list, the test quantifies numerous memory variables, including immediate recall, short- and long-delay recall, free and cued recall, recognition, rates of learning and forgetting, semantic clustering, serial position effects, interference, and error types. The scoring and analysis on the record form is cumbersome and difficult to follow, with no less than 23 scaled scores to compute, 6 of which cannot be easily computed without the scoring software. Not only is the hand-scoring time consuming, but analysis and interpretation of so many variables is challenging, especially when intra-subtest and error analysis is emphasized. For example, a Discriminability Index is computed by comparing the number of target words correctly identified with the number of false positives endorsed. Also, the number of non-list words recalled throughout the procedures is summed to produce an Intrusion Errors score, and word repetitions are tallied as Perseverations. Nevertheless, the time invested reaps an abundance of clinical information about the child's memory functions, such as: (a) the child's rate of learning, (b) the child's ability to inhibit interference from the learning of another list, (c) the child's use of a semantic clustering strategy, and (d) recognition ability compared with cued recall. Sifting through all this information will provide insights regarding the examinee's learning, encoding, storage, retrieval, and strategy abilities. Furthermore, the manual (Delis et al., 1994) provides excellent interpretative details and neuropsychological implications for each memory variable it quantifies. Because the CVLT-C measures only verbal episodic learning and memory, it will be necessary to supplement it with tests of visuospatial episodic memory. When the CVLT-C is part of a cross-battery analysis, it's suggested that evaluators include only those scores identified in Table 6.1, as the other CVLT-C diagnostic scores are too specific to align well with the memory components in Table 6.1.

The opportunity to evaluate and quantify strategy use, particularly semantic clustering, should be taken full advantage of. The diagnostic value of semantic clustering usage arises from the fact that it is below normal in nearly all clinical populations that have memory impairment (Delis et al., 1994). Semantic clustering, an important strategy for academic learning that most children acquire between 9 and 12 years of age, is judged to occur on the CVLT-C when the examinee consecutively recalls words from the same category. Poor delayed recall performance may be caused by failure to use semantic clustering. Failure to use a semantic clustering strategy suggests that there is a frontal lobe deficit contributing to the memory problem (Baldo, Delis, Kramer, & Shimamura, 2002). However, some strong learners may not use semantic clustering because they are better able to recall the items in serial order. Also, it is normal for semantic clustering to increase during the long-delay recall trials, perhaps because the categories are suggested during the preceding short-delay cued recall trial. Inability to benefit from the semantic cues provided by the examiner while benefitting from recognition cueing is an indication of a severe retrieval deficit.

Critique

Despite its usefulness with brain-impaired populations, the CVLT-C may be less helpful in identifying mild to moderate memory problems in older children, mainly because the tasks are too easy. It also has limited value as a measure of progress or recovery because it lacks parallel forms. Nevertheless, the CVLT-C can uncover some valuable qualitative information not afforded by traditional memory batteries, particularly the use of semantic clustering, the type and extent of interference, and the differentiation of retrieval into uncued, cued, and recognition levels. Consequently, data gathered with the CVLT-C is helpful when generating specific treatment recommendations.

CHILDREN'S MEMORY SCALE (CMS)

The CMS (Cohen, 1997) is a broad memory scale with two forms, one for children ages 5 to 8 and the other for ages 9 to 16. The battery divides memory into verbal and visual domains, with immediate and delayed measures of each. It also includes measures of verbal delayed recognition. In addition to a General Memory Index, the CMS yields several index scores (see Table 6.3). The General Memory Index adequately represents global memory functioning, as it includes immediate and delayed subtests in both the visual and auditory domains. The CMS is also unique in its provision of standardized scores for gist recall and detail recall.

Table 6.3   Children's Memory Scale (CMS)

Author:	Morris J. Cohen
Publisher:	The Psychological Corporation
Publication Date:	1997
Age Range:	5–16
Structure:	

Verbal Immediate Index
     Stories
     Word Pairs
Visual Immediate Index
     Dot Locations
     Faces
Verbal Delayed Index
     Stories Delayed
     Word Pairs Delayed
Visual Delayed Index
     Dot Locations Delayed
     Faces Delayed
Attention/Concentration Index
     Numbers
     Sequences
Learning Index
     Dot Locations
     Word Pairs
Delayed Recognition Index
     Stories Delayed Recognition
     Word Pairs Delayed Recognition
Supplemental
     Family Pictures
     Word Lists
     Picture Locations

Technical Properties

The CMS was standardized on a sample of 1,000 U.S. children divided into 10 age groups. Subjects at risk for a memory impairment were excluded from the sample (Cohen, 1997). Mean split-half reliability coefficients for the indexes range from .76 to .91. Coefficients for the subtests range from .54 to .91, with an average value of .78 for the six core subtests. Interrater reliability has a mean value of .99. The CMS's validity is supported by moderate, positive correlations with IQ, academic skills, language skills, and executive functioning. For example, the correlation between the CMS General Memory Index and the Wechsler Intelligence Scale for Children®-Third Edition (WISC®-III) Full Scale IQ is .58. Studies with clinical populations indicate that the CMS is sensitive to memory dysfunctions in children with neurological disorders.

Subtests

Dot Locations and Dot Locations Delayed In this measure of visuospatial episodic learning and memory, the examinee is required to learn and recall the spatial locations of dots on a grid. The immediate condition consists of three learning trials and one interference trial, followed by recall of the original dot array. After all the remaining immediate subtests are completed, Dot Locations Delayed is administered.

Stories, Stories Delayed, and Stories Delayed Recognition This verbal episodic narrative memory task involves recall of meaningful and semantically related verbal material. Two stories are read by the examiner, and the examinee is asked to retell the stories. Credit is given for story units recalled verbatim (literal recall) and also for correctly recalled thematic units (gist recall). After about 30 minutes, the delayed recall component is administered and followed by a yes-no recognition task.

Faces and Faces Delayed This subtest assesses a distinct dimension of visuospatial episodic memory. The examinee is shown a series of faces one at a time. After all the stimuli have been presented, another series of faces is presented and the examinee must state whether each face was one of the faces in the initial series. Delayed recall is tested after several intervening subtests have been completed.

Word Pairs, Word Pairs Delayed, and Word Pairs Delayed Recognition This subtest is a traditional paired-associate learning task with three learning trials. The 10- or 14-item list consists of both semantically related and semantically unrelated pairs. It is later followed by delayed recall and a yes-no delayed recognition task.

Family Pictures and Family Pictures Delayed In this measure of visuospatial episodic memory, scenes of family members engaged in various activities are presented for 10 seconds each. Then another card with the characters missing is displayed and the examinee is asked to recall which characters were in each scene, where the characters were positioned, and what they were doing. Later in the administration the delayed counterpart is completed.

Word Lists and Word Lists Delayed   This subtest is multiple-trial word list learning activity. The immediate condition consists of four learning trials and one interference trial, followed by recall of the original list. The delayed recall condition is followed by a yes-no recognition task.

Interpretation

The ability-memory discrepancy analysis found in the CMS record form is of little use because the ability scores that can be used to predict memory performance come from the WISC®-III and the Wechsler Preschool and Primary Scales of Intelligence®-Third Edition (Wechsler, 2002), test versions that are obsolete. However, practitioners can use tables in the CMS manual to evaluate discrepancies between logical pairings of CMS Indexes, such as Visual Delayed versus Verbal Delayed. The test record also includes a normed learning curve analysis for each of the three learning subtests. To conduct a memory profile analysis at the index level, each memory index can be contrasted with the General Memory Index, using a 12-point discrepancy as an indication of significance (the manual does not contain critical values for these comparisons). When the Visual Delayed Index is a normative or ipsative weakness, the practitioner should compare visual and spatial recall to determine whether one might be more responsible for the poor performance. Dot Locations Delayed is a relatively pure spatial measure that can be contrasted with the spatial-free Faces Delayed subtest (consider a scaled score difference of 3 or more points to be significant). Likewise, the subtests comprising the Verbal Delayed Index should be contrasted. The Stories subtest includes contextual information and allows gist recall, whereas Word Pairs has neither. Because the CMS structure matches up well with the memory components in Table 6.1, there is no need to calculate clinical factor scores. There is also no need to conduct a cross-battery analysis with the worksheet in Appendix B unless other cognitive processes or memory components have been tested.

Critique

Although the CMS provides comprehensive measurement of episodic memory, verbal recognition, and learning, it doesn't offer the range of diagnostic and qualitative information provided by more contemporary memory and neuropsychological scales, except for the unique verbatim versus gist scoring. Nevertheless, its structure matches well with the memory assessment model proposed in this text, and the information it provides is easy to analyze and interpret.

THE NEPSY II

The NEPSY II (Korkman, Kirk, & Kemp, 2007) is a broad neuropsychological battery developed specifically for children ages 3 to 16:11. NEPSY is an unusual acronym because it's simply taken from the word "neuropsychology." The NEPSY II consists of 32 subtests and four delayed tasks divided into six domains: attention and executive functioning, language, sensorimotor, visuospatial processing, social perception, and memory and learning (see Table 6.4). (This review is limited to the battery's memory and learning domain.) When the NEPSY (Korkman, Kirk, & Kemp, 1998) was recently revised the most significant changes were the removal of domain scores, the addition of new subtests, and an upward extension of the test to 16 years, 11 months.

Technical Properties

The normative sample, which excluded children with neurological disorders, consisted of 1,200 subjects divided into 12 age groups. Examiners may feel confident in administering parts of the NEPSY-II in a flexible, selective testing manner because four record forms, with subtests in different order, were used during standardization. The intent was to minimize the influence of partial battery administration on the normative data and promote the use of NEPSY-II subtests as supplements to other scales. Reliability coefficients vary by age and subtest. At 7 to 12 years of age, the

Table 6.4   NEPSY-II

Authors:	Marit Korkman, Ursula Kirk, and Sally Kemp
Publisher:	The Psychological Corporation
Publication Date:	2007
Age Range:	3–16:11
Structure:	

  Attention and Executive Functioning

  Language

  Sensorimotor

  Social Perception

  Visuospatial Processing

  Memory and Learning

    List Memory and List Memory Delayed

    Memory for Designs and Memory for Designs Delayed

    Memory for Faces and Memory for Faces Delayed

    Memory for Names and Memory for Names Delayed

    Narrative Memory

    Sentence Repetition

    Word List Interference

range across the memory and learning subtests is from .62 to .91, with the majority of coefficients in the .80s. There is an adequate amount of evidence supporting the validity of the NEPSY-II. However, the correlations between select NEPSY-II memory subtests and CMS Indexes are lower than one might expect. Several disability group studies were conducted, including children with learning disabilities and TBI. Generally, memory and learning scores were consistent with predictions; for instance, students with a mathematics disorder had a significantly lower ($p < .01$) Memory for Designs Total Score mean than matched controls.

Subtests

List Memory and List Memory Delayed List Memory assesses the ability to recall what is learned through rote repetition. It measures the ability to actively memorize verbal material and the ability to inhibit interference. The task involves learning a word list over five trials, followed by administration and recall of an interference list. Approximately 30 minutes later, the child is asked to recall the original list.

Memory for Designs and Memory for Designs Delayed Memory for Designs is a four-trial learning task that measures overall visuospatial episodic memory, as well as spatial versus visual recall. After viewing a page with 4 to 10 designs on a grid, the examinee selects designs from a set of cards and places the cards in the same locations on a grid. Delayed recall is administered approximately 20 minutes later. This visual analogue to List Memory is unique because nearly all standardized learning tasks are verbal or a combination of visual and verbal. Consequently, this subtest is recommended when evaluating children with suspected visuoperceptual or visuospatial processing deficits, such as those referred for a mathematics learning disability. To reduce verbal mediation, the subtest uses abstract visual stimuli that are very difficult to name.

Memory for Faces and Memory for Faces Delayed Memory for Faces is a unique dimension of visuospatial memory that is related more to social functioning than academic learning. For example, children with Autism and Asperger's Disorder typically have difficulty with memory for faces. Memory for Faces is not a multi-trial learning task, as the faces are only presented once. As an attention-focusing device, the examinee is asked to identify the gender as each face is presented. The photographs have been cropped to reveal only the faces and to eliminate nonfacial characteristics that might distinguish the faces. Delayed recall is administered approximately 20 minutes later.

Memory for Names and Memory for Names Delayed Memory for Names is a three-trial, visual-verbal paired-associate learning task, with delayed recall required approximately 20 minutes later. The examinee is shown cards with drawings of children while being told each child's name. Then the cards are shown again and the examinee is asked to recall each name. For younger children, this subtest is related to language development and early reading skills.

Narrative Memory Although Narrative Memory does not have a delayed recall component, its use is recommended for comparing free recall, cued recall, and recognition conditions. In Narrative Memory, the examinee listens to a story and then is asked to repeat the story (free recall), followed by answering questions about the story (cued recall). The recall conditions are immediately followed by a recognition condition.

Interpretation

The NEPSY-II manual (Korkman et al., 2007) provides excellent interpretative advice and hypotheses for all of the subtests and numerous available scores. The learning and memory interpretation section also compares performance with disability group profiles and discusses implications for scholastic learning. Here is a sampling of memory and learning subtest and intra-subtest comparisons and their corresponding interpretative hypotheses.

- When the Narrative Memory score is significantly higher than the List Memory score, the difference may be due to the student's dependence on context.
- When a delayed recall score is significantly higher than an immediate recall score, the unexpected improvement might be occurring because the child needs time to consolidate information in long-term memory.
- When interference is high (a high number of words from the interference list while recalling the original list), limited working memory and poor inhibition are indicated.
- Contrasting visual content and spatial scores may reveal a specific weakness underlying visuospatial episodic memory performance.
- Examinees who perform poorly on both the immediate and delayed components of Memory for Faces have a pervasive social perceptual problem.
- Better performance on Narrative Memory recognition than on free and cued recall might be caused by an expressive language deficit rather than a retrieval deficit.
- When oral language functioning is normal, a weak semantic memory system may underlie poor Narrative Memory performance.

The manual provides contrast scores, which have a mean of 10 and standard deviation of 3, for evaluating the significance of discrepancies between logically related pairs of subtests. Contrast scores allow determination of the child's relative ability to perform a task, controlling for the child's ability on a component that is required to perform that task. For example, when the degree of learning is controlled and used to predict delayed recall, contrast scores can be used to evaluate retention. A contrast score of 7 or lower would indicate retention is significantly lower than expected, given the level of learning that was attained.

After completing the analytic procedures suggested in the scale's manual, practitioners should evaluate broader memory functions by completing the work-sheet found in Appendix B while referring to the subtest classifications found in Table 6.1. For example, List Memory Delayed and Memory for Names Delayed can be combined to produce a clinical factor score representing verbal episodic memory. If subtests from other batteries have been administered, these should be included in the cross-battery analysis.

Critique

The NEPSY-II is the premier battery for the neuropsychological assessment of children and adolescents. To aggregate all of the neurological domains typically tested into one comprehensive, research-based battery is a notable accomplishment. Within the memory domain alone, the NEPSY-II provides several unique scores and contrast scores. An additional benefit is that the NEPSY-II allows direct score comparisons of memory with related processes, such as attention, executive processing, language, and visuospatial processing. Furthermore, the NEPSY-II's interpretative advice connects subtest performance with academic functioning, enhancing the battery's usefulness in school settings.

THE RIVERMEAD BEHAVIOURAL MEMORY TEST FOR CHILDREN (RBMT-C)

The RBMT-C (Wilson, Ivani-Chalian, & Aldrich, 1991), designed for use with brain-injured children, assesses memory abilities necessary for adequate functioning in everyday activities. Moreover, the RBMT-C is the only memory test that explicitly tests prospective memory in children. Developed and normed in the United Kingdom (Aldrich & Wilson, 1991) this neuropsychological memory scale (see Table 6.5) is an adaptation of the Rivermead Behavioural Memory Test (RBMT), designed for adults with nonprogressive brain injury and originally

Table 6.5   The Rivermead Behavioural Memory Test for Children (RBMT-C)

Authors:	Barbara A. Wilson, Rebecca Ivani-Chalian, and Francis Aldrich
Publisher:	Pearson
Publication Date:	1991
Age Range:	5–11

released in 1985 (Wilson, Cockburn, & Baddeley, 1985). To adapt the scale for children, items were rewritten to make them easier, more related to school, and age-appropriate (Wilson, Ivani-Chalian, Besag, & Bryant, 1993). The RBMT-2, a revision of the adult scale, (Wilson, Cockburn, & Baddeley, 2003) can be used with examinees above the age of 11 years, but the focus herein is on the children's version, which has norms for ages 5 to 11. Adolescents 16 years of age and older can be assessed with the recently released RBMT-3 (Wilson et al., 2008), which has updated and improved norms and easier tasks than the second edition. Those 16 years and older can also be tested with an extended version of the RBMT, released in 1999. The extended version was created to make the scale more sensitive to mild memory deficits. One of the unique features of the RBMT-C is that it has four parallel versions, making it suitable for monitoring recovery of memory after a head injury.

Technical Properties

The RBMT-C was normed on 335 children with normal intelligence and memory functions from nine schools in southern England. Wilson et al. (1993) report adequate coefficients for parallel forms reliability (.55 to .89), test-retest reliability, and interrater reliability. Much of the validity evidence for the RBMT-C comes from adult studies with the original RBMT. In Wilson's (2009) review of several RBMT validity studies, she reported: (a) a significant correlation of .75 between RBMT scores and therapist's observations of everyday memory problems; (b) the RBMT is a better measure of everyday memory than the Wechsler Memory Scale®-Revised (WMS®-R); (c) the RBMT discriminates between patients and controls as well as the WMS®-R; (d) the RBMT is a good predictor of independence; (e) the children's version of the RBMT discriminates between adolescents born prematurely and matched controls; (f) the children's version of the RBMT discriminates between children and adolescents with and without PTSD (Moradi, Doost, Taghavi, Yule, & Dalgleish, 1999); and (g) poor performance on the RBMT-C is associated with hippocampal volume reduction.

Subtests

The RBMT-C consists of tasks analogous to everyday situations that are especially troublesome for individuals with acquired brain injury. The 12 tasks are these: remembering a first name, remembering a surname, remembering a hidden belonging, remembering an appointment, recognizing pictures, remembering a newspaper article, recognizing faces, remembering a new route (immediate), remembering a new route (delayed), delivering a message, knowing the date, and orientation. The three prospective memory tasks are remembering where a belonging is hidden and asking for it to be returned, asking for the next appointment time when an alarm sounds, and delivering a message. The scores from all of the tasks are summed to produce an overall profile score.

Interpretation

Children with subaverage performance on the RBMT-C almost certainly have substantial memory problems in everyday life. However, norm-referenced interpretation of the RBMT-C profile score for U.S. examinees is not recommended because the norms are from the United Kingdom, the norms are based on a very small sample, and the norms are dated. Nonetheless, because the RBMT-C measures memory functions not included in traditional scales, it might be used to augment traditional memory batteries, provided RBMT-C performance is viewed as qualitative information. Furthermore, because of the RBMT-C's sensitivity and parallel forms, improved performance on the scale can be interpreted as an indication of memory improvement. On the other hand, RBMT-C performance and improvement may be unrelated to academic learning; for example, examinees who obtain a normal score may still have memory problems related to academic learning. Perhaps the best use and interpretation of the RBMT-C is as a screener for episodic memory impairments.

Critique

The RBMT-C offers a rare opportunity to assess everyday memory functioning and prospective memory with standardized procedures. Unfortunately, this unique ecological instrument lacks adequate norms, especially for U.S. purposes. Although the scale has good face validity and some evidence of differentiating TBI children from uninjured children, the manual provides very little data regarding reliability. Another of its shortcomings is a lack of sensitivity at both the high and low ends of memory functioning. Nonetheless, the RBMT-C is suitable as a screener and as a method of measuring recovery.

TEST OF MEMORY AND LEARNING, SECOND EDITION (TOMAL-2)

The TOMAL-2 (Reynolds & Voress, 2007), a revision of the TOMAL (Reynolds & Bigler, 1994), is a test of memory for individuals age 5 through 59. The scale, which emphasizes the distinction between verbal and nonverbal memory, is comprised mainly of attention, learning, and immediate memory tasks. There are only two subtests, both verbal, that measure long-term retention and recall. The minimal inclusion of long-term memory tasks is acknowledged by the authors when they state, "The test does not assess long-term memory . . . although the delayed recall tasks may be related to these components . . ." (Reynolds & Voress, p. 17). The TOMAL-2 is comprised of eight core learning and immediate memory subtests whose scores contribute to a Composite Memory Index, Verbal Index, and a Nonverbal Index. The battery also offers five supplementary indexes and several optional subtests (see Table 6.6).

Table 6.6   Test of Memory and Learning, Second Edition (TOMAL-2)

Authors: Cecil R. Reynolds and Judith K. Voress
Publisher: PRO-ED
Publication Date: 2007
Age Range: 5–59:11
Structure:
 Verbal Memory Index
  Memory for Stories
  Word Selective Reminding
  Object Recall
  Paired Recall
 Nonverbal Memory Index
  Facial Memory
  Abstract Visual Memory
  Visual Sequential Memory
  Memory for Location
 Verbal Delayed Recall Index
  Memory for Stories Delayed
  Word Selective Reminding Delayed
 Attention/Concentration Index
  Digits Forward
  Letters Forward
  Manual Imitation
  Digits Backward
  Letters Backward
 Sequential Recall Index
  Visual Sequential Memory
  Digits Forward
  Letters Forward
  Manual Imitation
 Free Recall Index
  Facial Memory
  Abstract Visual Memory
  Memory for Location
 Associative Recall Index
  Memory for Stories
  Paired Recall
 Learning Index
  Word Selective Reminding
  Object Recall
  Paired Recall
  Visual Selective Reminding

Technical Properties

Because no new items were introduced when the TOMAL (Reynolds & Bigler, 1994) was revised, the TOMAL-2 (Reynolds & Voress, 2007) norms are based mostly on the normative sample from the TOMAL. Only 579 new individuals were added to the norming sample, mainly to address the extension of the age range. Similarly, much of the validity evidence cited for the TOMAL-2 was acquired during development of the original scale. One of the TOMAL validity studies with clinical populations consisted of children with reading disabilities. As predicted, the reading disabled students scored lower on all of the TOMAL subtests, when compared with IQ-matched controls. The problem with the older validity data is that much of the concurrent validity is obsolete, as most scales the TOMAL was correlated with have since been revised. In contrast, reliability studies were conducted with the TOMAL-2 itself. Median internal consistency reliability coefficients are exceptional, ranging from .90 to .98 for the indexes, with all but one of the subtests having coefficients of .86 or higher.

Subtests

Memory for Stories and Memory for Stories Delayed

During Memory for Stories, examinees are required to recall two short stories read by the examiner. To receive credit, some story elements, such as names, need to be repeated verbatim, but synonyms are accepted for most of the elements. The delayed recall version should be administered 30 minutes after the immediate subtest is completed. Although associations with semantic memory may cue recall, the task is primarily a measure of verbal episodic memory.

Word Selective Reminding and Word Selective Reminding Delayed

Word Selective Reminding is a list-learning task that continues until 100% mastery is achieved or until six trials have been completed. After the examinee attempts to repeat the 8- or 12-word list, he or she is reminded of words left out and given another opportunity to repeat the entire list. Intrusions should be recorded, but they are not pointed out to the examinee. The delayed recall version, administered 30 minutes later, has a free recall condition, a cued verbal recall condition, and a cued visual recall condition. Only words omitted during free recall are administered during the verbally cued task. For the verbal cuing, the examinee is shown cards containing the first two letters of the words from the list. For any words still not recalled, the examinee is shown cards containing three pictures, one of which illustrates a word from the list. The Word Selective Reminding Delayed score is based only on the number of words recalled during the free recall condition.

Object Recall

Object Recall is an auditory-visual learning task in which the examiner presents a series of pictures, names them, and then has the examinee verbally recall them. The examinee has up to five trials to correctly recall all of the pictured items. No corrective feedback is provided while the examinee is recalling the items. There is no delayed recall version of this learning task.

Paired Recall   Paired Recall is a verbal paired-associate learning task comprised of easy pairs that are semantically related and difficult pairs that have no logical connection. Corrective feedback is provided as the examinee recalls each item. Although the task is primarily measuring learning, semantic memory facilitates immediate recall of the easy pairs.

Visual Selective Reminding   Visual Selective Reminding, a nonverbal analogue to Word Selective Reminding, requires the examinee to tap dots the examiner has touched. Unlike a Corsi block-tapping task, the dots need not be recalled in the correct sequence and extra dots may be touched. Similar to the other TOMAL-2 learning tasks, corrective feedback is provided, and trials continue until mastery is achieved or five trials have been completed. Visual Selective Reminding performance essentially depends on spatial processing and recall.

Interpretation

Interpretation of the TOMAL-2 should follow the procedures and tables found in the manual (Reynolds & Voress, 2007). After computation of the subtest and index scores, the examiner should complete the qualitative learning curve analysis by plotting the learning curves for each of the four learning subtests. Raw scores for each trial can be plotted and then compared with the learning curve from the normative sample (broken down by age). Although the scaled scores for the learning subtests indicate how the examinee's learning compares normatively, visual analysis of the plots can also be informative. Learning curves normally have a steep positive slope from the first to second and third trials and then continue to rise gradually. When the plots reveal slower learning, ineffective encoding, short-term memory deficits, and poor use of basic strategies are implicated. Profile analysis at the factor level can be completed by using the manual's (Reynolds & Voress) table for paired comparisons among the three core indexes and the table for comparing each of the supplementary indexes with the Composite Memory Index. Statistics are provided for the most important pairings: Verbal Memory versus Nonverbal Memory and Verbal Memory versus Verbal Delayed Recall. Of the four subtests that comprise the Verbal Memory Index, three are learning tasks, essentially making it a verbal learning index. Creating a cleaner verbal learning factor can be accomplished by averaging only the three verbal learning subtest scores. This clinical factor should then be compared with Verbal Delayed Recall (using 12 points as a criterion for significance). If Verbal Delayed Recall is significantly weaker, then an unusual amount of information is being forgotten or is not being retrieved, given how well the material was mastered only 30 minutes earlier. Because the TOMAL-2 does not include any recognition tasks, it will be difficult to determine whether poor delayed performance can be attributed to retention or retrieval problems. Memory strengths and weaknesses can also be explored through a subtest profile analysis, using a table provided in the manual. The authors (Reynolds & Voress) also discuss the clinical and neuro-psychological relevance of low scores for the indexes and for each of the subtests.

Critique

The excellent theoretical, clinical, psychometric, and neuropsychological information provided in the manual enhances effective utilization and interpretation of the TOMAL-2. One of the main advantages of using the TOMAL-2 is its extensive sampling and analysis of learning and immediate memory. Unfortunately, there is minimal sampling of long-term recall. Specifically, there are no visual delayed recall subtests and there are no recognition tasks.

WIDE RANGE ASSESSMENT OF MEMORY AND LEARNING, SECOND EDITION (WRAML2)

The WRAML2 (Adams & Sheslow, 2003) is a comprehensive memory scale with norms from age 5 to 90. It is intended for use in a variety of settings, including schools, clinical practice, hospitals, and rehabilitation units. Its predecessor, the WRAML (published in 1990), was one of the first standardized scales designed to assess memory problems in children. The WRAML2 authors have structured the scale in a manner that conforms to contemporary concepts of memory without binding it to a particular model. Numerous aspects of memory are incorporated into the scale: visual and verbal memory; immediate and delayed recall; working memory; sustained attention; short-term memory; recognition and retrieval; primacy and recency effects; semantic versus acoustic memory errors; verbatim versus gist recall; incremental trial learning; retention; and rate of learning (Adams & Sheslow). With the inclusion of all these memory dimensions, the WRAML2 affords in-depth analysis of specific memory functions. The core battery consists of six subtests, two for each of the three main factors (see Table 6.7). In addition to the core subtests, the WRAML2 offers 11 optional subtests, seven of which are delayed recall and recognition subtests. Despite its comprehensiveness, the battery does not offer a delayed recall index. Moreover, its composite score, the General Memory Index, does not include any delayed recall subtests.

Technical Properties

The WRAML2's norms are based on a national sample of 1,200, resulting in only 80 subjects being allocated to each of the 15 age groups. The median internal consistency reliability coefficients for the Verbal Memory and Visual Memory Indexes are .92 and .89 respectively. For the subtests, the coefficients are mostly

Table 6.7　Wide Range Assessment of Memory and Learning, Second Edition (WRAML2)

Authors:　　　　　　Wayne Adams and David Sheslow

Publisher:　　　　　Wide Range

Publication Date:　　2003

Age Range:　　　　　5–90

Structure:

　Verbal Memory Index

　　　Story Memory Subtest

　　　Verbal Learning Subtest

　Visual Memory Index

　　　Design Memory Subtest

　　　Picture Memory Subtest

　Attention-Concentration Index

　　　Finger Windows Subtest

　　　Number/Letter Subtest

　Delayed Recall Subtests

　　　Story Memory Delay Recall

　　　Verbal Learning Delay Recall

　　　Sound Symbol Delay Recall

　Recognition Subtests

　　　Story Memory Recognition

　　　Verbal Learning Recognition

　　　Design Memory Recognition

　　　Picture Memory Recognition

　Optional Subtests

　　　Sentence Memory

　　　Sound Symbol

　　　Verbal Working Memory

　　　Symbolic Working Memory

in the .8 range. Only the two visual recognition tasks have substandard reliability (.40 and .52). The division of the test into visual, verbal, and attention factors is supported by exploratory and confirmatory factor-analytic studies. Validity studies reported in the manual (Adams & Sheslow, 2003) found expected correlation levels with other related scales. For example, the correlation between the General Memory index and the WAIS®-III Full Scale IQ is .67. Studies of subjects with memory and learning disorders confirm the diagnostic utility of the WRAML2. Compared with matched controls, a TBI group of adults obtained significantly lower scores on all nine indexes. In another standardization study, a sample of 29 children with learning disabilities obtained significantly lower scores on all of the WRAML2 indexes when compared to a matched control sample.

Subtests

Story Memory, Story Memory Delay Recall, and Story Memory Recognition Story Memory Delay Recall measures verbal episodic memory for extended and meaningful information (see Table 6.1). The examiner reads two short stories and the examinee is asked to immediately recall as many parts as possible. Delayed recall is assessed approximately 15 minutes later. Although the responses need not be in correct order, it is recommended that examiners record the sequence in which they are recalled. Some parts must be recalled verbatim while others can be phrased differently (gist responses), as long as the meaning is preserved. The dual scoring allows the examiner to distinguish verbatim from gist recall. For example, someone who remembers relevant themes but forgets details will obtain a higher gist than verbatim score. A multiple-choice recognition subtest is administered immediately following the delayed recall subtest. During the recognition task, items that were recalled correctly during delayed recall need not be readministered (credit is given for these items). The Story Memory Recognition score may be combined with Verbal Learning Recognition to produce a Verbal Recognition Index. Analysis options include the computation of retention (the difference between performance on immediate and delayed recall), comparison of performance on the two stories (scaled scores are available for each story), and comparison of verbatim and gist scaled scores.

Verbal Learning, Verbal Learning Delay Recall, and Verbal Learning Recognition Verbal Learning is a list-learning task that allows four trials for the examinee to learn a list of either 13 or 16 words. The Delay Recall subtest is administered about 10 minutes after the last trial is completed. There should be another 10-minute interval between Delay Recall and the yes–no Recognition subtest. Analysis options include normed-referenced comparisons of the examinee's performance on each of the four trials; computation of a learning slope (the rate of learning from Trial 1 to Trial 4); calculation of how much is retained between the learning task and delayed recall (retention); comparison of semantic versus phonological errors on the recognition task; and tallying and analyzing the number of intrusion errors (words not on the list).

Design Memory and Design Memory Recognition The immediate version of Design Memory consists of exposing geometric designs for five seconds and than having the examinee draw them from memory. Because there is no delayed recall version of the task, long-term visuospatial episodic memory can only be assessed via a yes–no recognition subtest. The Recognition score can be combined with Picture Memory Recognition to produce a Visual Recognition index.

Picture Memory and Picture Memory Recognition In Picture Memory, the examinee is shown four common but visually complex scenes for 10 seconds, then shown an alternate scene and asked to identify the elements that have moved, changed, or been added by marking each part of the picture that is different (no verbal response is required). Because of the transformations involved, this task is more challenging than usual visuospatial measures. The only qualitative analysis option is computation of commission errors (elements that are erroneously marked). After several intervening subtests have been completed, the yes-no Picture Memory Recognition task is administered.

Sound Symbol and Sound Symbol Delay Recall   For children 5 through 8 years of age, Sound Symbol is a four-trial, paired-associate learning task in which the examinee must recall sounds associated with various abstract symbols. Because the task combines visual and auditory material, the episodic memory involved in Delay Recall cannot be classified as either verbal or visuospatial. Similar to the Verbal Learning subtest, additional analyses can by conducted by computing normed-referenced performance for each trial, calculating a learning slope, and determining the amount of long-term retention.

Interpretation

The WRAML2 is such a comprehensive memory scale that there is little need for cross-battery assessment, other than sampling some related cognitive processes. When all or most of the core, delayed recall, and recognition subtests have been administered, examiners should first follow the analytic procedures described in the manual. The first step in using the manual's tables is to compare index pairs, such as verbal (episodic) memory versus visual (episodic) memory. The second step is to compare immediate recall with performance on its corresponding recognition task. The third step is to examine descriptive statistics for the amount of new learning that is retained over time by subtracting the immediate recall score from the delayed recall score. Finally, the manual (Adams & Sheslow, 2003) provides descriptive statistics or scaled scores for the several optional analytic procedures described in the previous Subtest section. When the manual's recommended analyses are completed, evaluators should proceed with an ipsative analysis using the *Analysis of Memory Testing Results* worksheet found in Appendix B. This clinical procedure is necessary because the manual doesn't include tables for identifying overall memory strengths and weaknesses. When conducting this supplemental analysis, examiners should not use the WRAML2's General Memory Index as representing overall memory ability because it is based only on learning and immediate memory subtest scores. Rather, scores from all of the administered subtests should be used to calculate a mean. Alternative composites include IQ or global cognitive scores (see Chapter 5 for more explanation). Despite the in-depth and multimodal sampling of recognition, including provision of a General Recognition Index, the WRAML2 is unusual in that it does not offer statistical comparisons between delayed recall scores and corresponding recognition scores. Instead, tables are provided for contrasting recognition scores with immediate memory scores. Evaluating the difference between uncued recall and recognition can be accomplished by contrasting delay recall scores with recognition scores, used a scaled score difference of 3 points as an indication of significance. Also, a retrieval problem is indicated when the WRAML2's retention raw score (delayed recall versus immediate recall) is significantly lower than the population mean while the difference between the immediate memory and recognition scaled scores is not significantly different.

Critique

The WRAML2 is an ideal instrument for comprehensively assessing memory functions in children and adolescents. With adequate technical properties and sufficient validity evidence, evaluators can feel confident in the diagnostic conclusions derived from analyzing the examinee's performance. Most commendable about the WRAML2 are its numerous qualitative analysis options that allow evaluators to differentiate among the influences of encoding, storage, and retrieval. Additional qualitative analyses provide information on inhibition, gist recall, types of errors, and progress over learning trials. Other benefits include a memory screening option, adult norms, a measure of attention, two structured learning tasks for children younger than 9, scaled scores for many of the intra-subtest calculations, and a well-written, easy-to-follow, manual. Among the drawbacks are the lack of a composite score that includes delayed recall, the absence of a delayed recall index, the omission of visual uncued recall tasks, and the inability to directly compare delayed recall and recognition scores.

WECHSLER MEMORY SCALE®-FOURTH EDITION (WMS®-IV)

Though it's designed primarily for adults, the fourth edition of the WMS® (Wechsler, 2009) is recommended for memory testing with adolescents who are 16 years of age and older. The research directors for development of the WMS®-IV have acknowledged contemporary memory research in their design of the scale. For example, visual stimuli are very abstract so that examinees can't name them and store the information verbally. The result is a battery with strong theoretical underpinnings and an empirically based structure. Like all memory batteries, the WMS®-IV is primarily a measure of episodic memory because the information is novel and contextually bound by the testing situation. The scale is divided into two batteries, one for ages 16 to 69 and a shorter version for ages 65 to 90. (This review covers only the 16 to 69 battery.) The 16 to 69 battery contains seven subtests, four with both immediate and delayed conditions (see Table 6.8). There is a recognition component in each delayed recall subtest, and one of the visual subtests produces content (visual) and spatial scaled scores. In addition to memory measures, there is a brief cognitive status exam. The structure of the scale has changed from that of its predecessor, the WMS®-III. There is no longer a division of auditory and visual memory into

Table 6.8 Wechsler Memory Scale®-Fourth Edition (WMS®-IV)

Author:	David Wechsler
Publisher:	Pearson
Publication Date:	2009
Age Range:	16–69 and 65–90
Structure:	

Auditory Memory Index
    Logical Memory I
    Verbal Paired Associates I
    Logical Memory II
    Verbal Paired Associates II
Visual Memory Index
    Designs I
    Visual Reproduction I
    Designs II
    Visual Reproduction II
Immediate Memory Index
    Logical Memory I
    Verbal Paired Associates I
    Designs I
    Visual Reproduction I
Delayed Memory Index
    Logical Memory II
    Verbal Paired Associates II
    Designs II
    Visual Reproduction II
Visual Working Memory Index
    Spatial Addition
    Symbol Span

immediate and delayed components because this division of the WMS subtests has not been supported by factor analysis due to high correlations between immediate and delayed memory (Wechsler, 2009). For example, the Auditory Memory Index contains both short-term and long-term measures.

Technical Properties

The WMS®-IV, which was co-normed with the WAIS®-IV (Wechsler, 2008) and the CVLT-C (Delis et al., 1994), is based on a national normative sample of 1400, 100 for each age band. Any subjects with disorders or conditions that could impact memory performance, such as having experienced a traumatic brain injury or being diagnosed with substance abuse, were excluded from the sample. Reliability coefficients for the indexes range from .93 to .96 and for the subtests from .74 to .97. There is an abundance of convincing validity evidence in the manual (Wechsler, 2009). The correlations between WMS®-IV indexes and the WAIS®-IV Full Scale IQ range from .57 to .71. Several clinical populations were included in the validity studies. For example, for an adult TBI group, all of the index means were more than one standard deviation lower than the means from a matched control group.

Subtests

Logical Memory I and II   The Logical Memory tasks measure the ability to listen to a narrative, recall the information immediately, and then retrieve it again after a 20- to 30-minute interval. Unlike the WMS®-III, both stories are presented only once. Logical Memory II assesses verbal episodic memory through free recall and a yes–no recognition task, with only free recall contributing to the subtest's scaled score. Like other verbal episodic measurement tasks, semantic memory representations play a role. For instance, a low score on Logical Memory II indicates difficulty recalling verbal information that is conceptually organized and semantically related.

Verbal Paired Associates I and II   Verbal Paired Associates, a classic multiple-trial learning task, contains 14 pairs of both semantically related and semantically unrelated items. Four trials are administered to everyone regardless of performance. Corrective feedback is provided during the immediate but not the delayed task. Scores from the CVLT-C may be substituted for Verbal Paired Associates scores but may not be used in subtest discrepancy analysis.

Designs I and II   The Designs tasks assess both memory for visual details and for spatial location. In Designs I, pages with abstract stimuli are displayed for 10 seconds each. To respond, the examinee selects designs from a set of cards and places them in a grid. The orientation (rotation) of individual cards has no bearing on the score. Designs I and II are unique in that the visual (correct stimulus) and spatial (correct location) components are scored separately. That is, credit is given for correct content even when the items are placed in the wrong locations, and credit is awarded for correct location even when incorrect items are placed. Bonus points are added when both aspects are correct for any given stimulus within the item. Later, the visual and spatial process scores can be contrasted to assess relative abilities.

Visual Reproduction I and II   Visual Reproduction requires the examinee to view a design and then draw it from memory, immediately and 20 to 30 minutes later. After the recognition task is completed, there is a copy option in which the examinee draws the designs while looking at them. The intent of this procedure is to rule out the possibility of visual-motor integration problems affecting performance. The Symbol Span (working memory) subtest should never be administered between

Visual Reproduction I and Visual Reproduction II, as exposure to Symbol Span symbols may cause interference with the Visual Reproduction designs.

Interpretation

Interpretation should begin by completing the discrepancy analyses on pages 2, 3, and 4 of the record form. When comparing index scores, subtest scores, and process scores (e.g., recognition scores), contrast scores are used instead of critical values. Contrast scores indicate the examinee's ability in a particular component, relative to the level that is predicted from a related component. For example, performance on an immediate task is used to predict performance on the delayed task with the same material. This approach is more accurate than traditional discrepancy analysis because the examinee's level of acquisition is taken into account when judging delayed recall. Contrast scores have a mean of 10 and a standard deviation of 3. Thus, contrast scores from 8 to 12 indicate equivalent performance, whereas 7 and lower indicate significantly lower than expected performance, given the level attained on the predictor. Subtest differences within indexes are still determined using traditional critical values. On page 4 of the record form, WMS®-IV index comparisons with WAIS®-IV indexes are made with both contrast scores and critical values. Curiously, there are no tables for the WAIS®-IV Full Scale IQ. Only the WAIS®-IV's Verbal Comprehension Index, Perceptual Reasoning Index, and General Ability Index (GAI) can be used. (The WAIS®-IV GAI is comprised of the three verbal comprehension and three perceptual reasoning subtests.) The contrast score tables in the WMS®-IV manual also include subtest comparisons with recognition performance despite the fact that only cumulative percentages are available for the recognition tasks. Another unique set of scores are the scaled scores provided for distinguishing visual from spatial memory ability. After completing the record form, the practitioner should do a clinical analysis of the scores that divides the auditory and visual domains into immediate and delayed factors. For example, the standard scores from Logical Memory II and Verbal Paired Associates II should be averaged (see Table 6.9) and used to represent auditory delayed memory. The immediate and delayed components for each modality should then be contrasted, using a 12-point discrepancy as an indication of significance. When a delayed component is significantly lower than the immediate component, problems with consolidation and storage are indicated, unless recognition is significantly higher than uncued recall. Computation and analysis of these clinical factors is especially necessary when there is a significant discrepancy between the WMS®-IV Auditory and Visual indexes or between the Immediate and Delayed indexes.

Critique

The WMS®-IV is a masterful work of psychometrics that faithfully applies contemporary memory theory and research. Hopefully, its methods will soon be applied

Table 6.9 Case study with WMS-IV

Examinee's Name: ___Kim___   DOB: _____   Age: __17__   Grade: __12__   Dates of Testing: _____

Memory Component	Battery Name	Subtest/Factor Name	Subtest/Factor Scores	Component Mean	Composite or Mean	Difference	Normative S, W, or A	Ipsative S or W	Deficit or Asset
Verbal Episodic	WMS-IV	Logical Memory (LM) II Verbal Paired Associates (VPA) II	(9) 95 (12) 110	103	(Cross-Batt. Mean) 105	−2	A	–	–
Visuospatial Episodic	WMS-IV	Designs (DE) II Visual Reproduction (VR) II	(14) 120 (14) 120	120	105	+15	S	S	Asset
Visual Episodic	WMS-IV	DE II Content	(13) 115*	115	–				
Spatial Episodic	WMS-IV	DE II Spatial	(13) 115*	115	–				
Verbal Recognition	WMS-IV	LM II Recognition VPA II Recognition	26–50 Cum. % >75 Cum. %	–	–				
Visuospatial Recognition	WMS-IV	DE II Recognition VR II Recognition	>75 Cum. % >75 Cum. %	–	–				
Learning	WMS-IV	VPA I	(9) 95	95	105	−10	A	–	–
Verbal WM	WAIS-IV	WORKING MEMORY	89	89	105	−16	W	W	Deficit
Visuospatial WM	WMS-IV	VISUAL WORKING MEMORY	108	108	105	+3	A	–	–
Phonological STM									
Visuospatial STM	WMS-IV	DE I VR I	(13) 115 (11) 105	110	105	+5	S	–	–

*Not included in computation of cross-battery mean.

Component and Score		Difference Between Pairs	Significant Difference: Y/N
Visuospatial Episodic (120)	Verbal Episodic (103)	17	Y
Visuospatial WM (108)	Verbal WM (89)	19	Y
Verbal Episodic (103)	Verbal WM (89)	14	N
Visuospatial Episodic (120)	Visuospatial WM (89)	31	Y

Directions: (1) Convert all subtest scores to standard scores with a mean of 100 and an SD of 15. (2) For each memory component, compute the mean of the subtest scores and round to the nearest whole number. (3) Enter a cognitive composite, such as a full-scale IQ, or compute the mean of all available memory components. (4) Subtract the composite or mean from each memory component mean and enter the amount in the Difference column. (5) Indicate whether the memory component is a normative weakness, strength, or average (90–109 is average). (6) Using a criterion of 12 to 15 points, determine intra-individual strengths and weaknesses. A deficit is both a normative and intra-individual weakness; an asset is both a normative and intra-individual strength. (7) Determine deficits and assets. A deficit is both a normative and intra-individual weakness; an asset is both a normative and intra-individual strength. (8) Determine which factors are non-unitary. Factors are non-unitary when the two subtests involved are discrepant by more than 22 points. Non-unitary factors should be interpreted cautiously and should not be used in pairwise comparisons. (9) Compare logical pairs of components, using a 15- to 20-point difference as an indication of a significant discrepancy.

to the memory assessment of children younger than 16 years. The in-depth interpretative advice in the manual is extremely helpful in understanding the meaning and neurological implications of relative strengths and weaknesses among the memory components and processes sampled by the battery. The only drawback is the project directors' decision to omit indexes that divide short-term and long-term recall into modality-specific factors.

WMS®-IV Case Study

The WMS®-IV and WAIS®-IV scores for Kim, who was introduced at the beginning of this chapter, are analyzed and explained in this section. A cross-battery and clinical analysis of scores (see Table 6.9) was necessary because more than one scale was used and because clinical factor scores that divided delayed memory into auditory and visual were computed. The clinical factor analysis was thought to be necessary because there was a significant discrepancy (119 versus 101) between Kim's Auditory and Visual Indexes. To compute the clinical scores, the subtest scaled scores were first transformed into a metric with a mean of 100 and standard deviation of 15 (see Appendix C and the Subtest/Factor scores column in Table 6.9). The clinical factor and other component scores were compared with a cross-battery mean based on all the administered subtests from both scales. No IQ score was available, as only the working memory subtests on the WAIS®-IV had been administered. The recognition scores could not be compared with the cross-battery mean because they are only available as cumulative percentages (however, they can be contrasted in the WMS®-IV record form). The completed profile analysis (see Table 6.9) reveals that Kim has a normative strength in long-term visuospatial episodic memory that is also an intra-individual strength relative to her overall memory functioning and compared with long-term verbal episodic memory. Although, verbal episodic memory is weaker than visuospatial, it should not be construed as a deficit or impairment because it is within the average range and commensurate with Kim's overall memory functioning. The more accurate interpretation is to emphasize that visuospatial memory is her strength. Also, her verbal episodic recall is not significantly lower than her level of learning. She appears to retain what she learns and can retrieve the information without cueing. (Recall is not significantly lower than recognition.) However, the analysis does indicate that Kim has a deficit in verbal working memory, consistent with the pattern exhibited with her long-term memory systems. This deficit may in part account for her relatively lower verbal episodic performance.

COGNITIVE, INTELLECTUAL, AND ACHIEVEMENT BATTERIES

There are several reasons for including long-term memory subtests from cognitive, intellectual, and achievement batteries in the assessment of long-term memory. First, these embedded subtests are reliable and valid measures of long-term memory components and processes. Second, because psychoeducational evaluations routinely include these batteries, using the already administered memory subtests saves time. Third, some of the subtests are unique activities that are seldom found in traditional memory scales. Fourth, these batteries are necessary for formal assessment of semantic memory. The subtests recommended for semantic memory assessment are generally tests of verbal abilities, including vocabulary, verbal comprehension, and general knowledge (see Table 6.10). Under the CHC theory of intelligence (Carroll 1993; Flanagan, Ortiz, & Alfonso, 2007), knowledge and verbal ability subtests are classified as crystallized intelligence. The definition of crystallized intelligence—"the breath and depth of a person's accumulated knowledge of a culture and the effective use of that knowledge"—is very consistent with the type of information stored in semantic memory. However, crystallized intelligence subtests assess only the content of semantic memory, not the actual functioning (or processes) of semantic memory. Consequently, examiners can only make inferences about semantic memory functioning, based on the extent of knowledge stored therein. If the level of semantic knowledge is normal, then there is a presumption of normal semantic memory functioning. On the other hand, below average performance on tests of verbal abilities (given adequate opportunities for learning) are thought to be mediated by some type of memory dysfunction (Kovacs, Ryan, & Obrosky, 1994). An alternative, perhaps more direct, approach to appraising semantic memory functioning is to track learning and long-term retention (over weeks if not months) in a challenging academic course. Because this may not be feasible, verbal ability subtests are the next best option, despite the fact that it's impossible to determine the extent to which the examinee ever learned the material initially. Also, some individuals have had more opportunities to acquire the tested vocabulary and culturally loaded knowledge than others. Consequently, knowledge and verbal ability subtests alone should not be used to make judgments about semantic memory functioning.

The information on each of the batteries in this section is briefer than that provided on the memory batteries. Technical properties are not reviewed because the norming, reliability, and validity of these widely used instruments are known to be reputable. (For formal reviews of any scale, the reader should consult the *Mental Measurements Yearbook* reviews found online at http://buros.unl.edu/buros/jsp/search.jsp.) Specific interpretative suggestions are incorporated into the general information on the battery and subtests. A general approach to analyzing and interpreting semantic memory testing is outlined in the following section. Also, there is no longer a critique subsection because recommendations and evaluative comments are embedded in the overview. Readers seeking information about working and short-term memory subtests found in these scales should consult Dehn (2008).

General Guidelines for Using and Interpreting Intellectual Scales

Table 6.11 provides an example of how to incorporate intellectual subtest and factor scores into a broad analysis of memory. When using intellectual and cognitive scales

Table 6.10 Classification of cognitive and achievement battery subtests by memory component

Memory Component	DAS-II	KABC-II	KTEA-II	SB5	WAIS-IV	WISC-IV	WISC-IV Integrated	WPPSI-III	WJ III ACH	WJ III COG*
Verbal Episodic		Atlantis Delayed**; Rebus Delayed**							Story Recall Delayed	Visual-Auditory Learning; Delayed**; Memory for Names Delayed**
Visuospatial Episodic	Recall of Objects Delayed									
Semantic	Naming Vocabulary; Picture Similarities; Verbal Similarities; Verbal Comprehension; Word Definitions	Expressive Vocabulary; Verbal Knowledge; Riddles		Nonverbal Knowledge; Verbal Knowledge	Vocabulary; Similarities; Information; Comprehension	Similarities; Picture Concepts; Vocabulary; Comprehension; Information; Word Reasoning	Multiple Choice Versions of: Similarities, Vocabulary, Comprehension, Information, Picture Vocabulary	Information; Similarities; Vocabulary; Comprehension; Receptive Vocabulary; Word Reasoning; Picture Concepts	Academic Knowledge	Verbal Comprehension; General Information
Retrieval Fluency	Rapid Naming		Associational Fluency Naming Facility (RAN)					Picture Naming		Retrieval Fluency; Rapid Picture Naming
Recognition							Multiple Choice Versions of: Similarities, Vocabulary, Comprehension, Information, Picture Vocabulary			
Learning	Recall of Objects Immediate	Atlantis; Rebus								Visual-Auditory Learning; Memory for Names

*Includes the Diagnostic Supplement to the Tests of Cognitive Abilities

**This task also involves visuospatial episodic memory because the information consists of visual-verbal associations.

DAS-II = Differential Ability Scales-Second Edition; KABC-II = Kaufman Assessment Battery for Children, Second Edition; KTEA-II = Kaufman Test of Educational Achievement, Second Edition; SB 5 = Stanford-Binet Intelligence Scales, Fifth Edition; WAIS-IV = Wechsler Adult Intelligence Scale-Fourth Edition; WIAT-III = Wechsler Individual Achievement Test-Third Edition; WISC-IV = Wechsler Intelligence Scale for Children-Fourth Edition; WJ III ACH = Woodcock-Johnson, Third Edition, Tests of Achievement; WJ III COG = Woodcock-Johnson, Third Edition, Tests of Cognitive Abilities.

Table 6.11 Example of memory assessment with cognitive scales

Examinee's Name: Jane   DOB: _____   Age: 11-6   Grade: 6   Dates of Testing: _____

Memory Component	Battery Name	Subtest/Factor Name	Subtest/Factor Scores	Component Mean	Composite or Mean	Difference	Normative S, W, or A	Ipsative S or W	Deficit or Asset
Verbal Episodic	CMS	VERBAL DELAYED	95	95	WJ III COG GIA = 93	+2	A	–	–
Visuospatial Episodic	CMS	VISUAL DELAYED	85	85	93	–8	W	–	–
Semantic	WISC-IV	Vocabulary / Information	9 (95) / 8 (90)	93	93	0	A	–	–
Retrieval Fluency	WJ III COG	Retrieval Fluency / Rapid Picture Naming	78 / 83	81	93	–12	W	W	Deficit
Recognition	WISC-IV Integrated	Vocabulary Multiple Choice / Information Multiple Choice	10 (100) / 8 (90)	95	93	+2	A	–	–
Learning	WJ III COG	Visual-Auditory Learning	82	82	93	–11	W	–	–
Visuospatial WM	WISC-IV Integrated	Spatial Span Backward	(11) 105	105	93	+8	A	–	–
Verbal WM	WISC-IV	WORKING MEMORY	94	94	93	+1	A	–	–
Processing Speed	WISC-IV	PROCESSING SPEED	80	80	93	–13	W	W	Deficit

Component and Score		Difference Between Pairs	Significant Difference: Y/N
Semantic (93)	Recognition (95)	2	N
Visuospatial WM (105)	Visuospatial Episodic (85)	20	Y
Verbal Episodic (95)	Learning (82)	13	N
Processing Speed (80)	Retrieval (81)	1	N

Directions: (1) Convert all subtest scores to standard scores with a mean of 100 and an SD of 15. (2) For each memory component, compute the mean of the subtest scores and round to the nearest whole number. (3) Enter a cognitive composite, such as a full-scale IQ, or compute the mean of all available memory components. (4) Subtract the composite or mean from each memory component mean and enter the amount in the Difference column. (5) Indicate whether the memory component is a normative weakness, strength, or average (90–109 is average). (6) Using a criterion of 12 to 15 points, determine intra-individual strengths and weaknesses. (7) Determine deficits and assets. A deficit is both a normative and intra-individual weakness; an asset is both a normative and intra-individual strength. (8) Determine which factors are non-unitary. Factors are non-unitary when the two subtests involved are discrepant by more than 22 points. Non-unitary factors should be interpreted cautiously and should not be used in pairwise comparisons. (9) Compare logical pairs of components, using a 15- to 20-point difference as an indication of a significant discrepancy.

208

as part of a memory assessment battery, there are some caveats and some specific recommendations for analysis and interpretation:

1. An effort must be made to evaluate the influence of oral expression on performance. One option is to contrast subtests that require elaborated expression with those that require simple or one-word responses, such as naming pictures. An alternative is to compare subtests with nonverbal responses (e.g., pointing to the correct stimulus) with those requiring some kind of verbal response. Also, data on language development may be gathered. For instance, if language functioning is normal, then learning and memory problems most likely underlie subaverage performance on verbal ability tests.
2. When a student is known to have a language impairment or limited English proficiency, only subtests that rely on visual semantic memory should be utilized.
3. The student's academic and personal history should be reviewed to determine whether there have been adequate opportunities to learn general knowledge and vocabulary. The degree of assimilation into mainstream U.S. culture can also affect performance, as verbal subtests are all culturally loaded.
4. When interpreting memory results from an intellectual battery, scores representing semantic memory, retrieval fluency, and learning should first be analyzed with the statistical tables provided by that battery. Analysis should then proceed at the cross-battery level, following the guidelines on the *Analysis of Memory Testing Results* worksheet found in Appendix B and the procedures for the worksheet found in Chapter 5.
5. For a thorough profile analysis of memory, it may be necessary to compute clinical factor scores, based on the classification of subtests found in Table 6.10. For example, the Wechsler Vocabulary and Information scores could be averaged to represent semantic memory (see Table 6.11).
6. Although comparing retrieval fluency scores with recognition scores from another subtest is intuitively appealing, it should be avoided because the tasks do not involve recall of the same material. Only the WISC®-IV Integrated presents an opportunity to compare recognition with uncued responses on the same items.

Differential Ability Scales®-Second Edition (DAS-II)

The DAS-II (Elliott, 2006) is a CHC-aligned cognitive abilities battery designed to measure reliable profiles of specific cognitive strengths and weaknesses. In addition to its primary composites—Verbal Ability, Nonverbal Reasoning Ability, and Spatial Ability—the scale provides three optional diagnostic clusters: Working Memory, Processing Speed, and School Readiness. At the subtest level, the DAS-II offers a well-rounded assessment of memory, with several working and short-term memory

Table 6.12 Differential Ability Scales®-Second Edition (DAS-II)

Author:	Colin Elliott
Publisher:	PsychCorp
Publication Date:	2006
Age Range:	2:6–17:11

Long-Term Memory Subtests:

  Naming Vocabulary

  Picture Similarities

  Verbal Similarities

  Verbal Comprehension

  Word Definitions

  Rapid Naming

  Recall of Objects Immediate

  Recall of Objects Delayed

subtests (see Dehn, 2008), as well as measures of learning, retrieval fluency, semantic memory, and visuospatial episodic memory (see Table 6.12). The DAS-II Verbal Ability composite can be used to represent semantic memory content and functioning. (There's no need to compute a clinical factor score.) The remaining memory analysis, within the DAS-II or from a cross-battery perspective, should consist of individual subtest scores.

Naming Vocabulary and Word Definitions Naming Vocabulary, which requires the examinee to name pictured items, involves visual-verbal associations. A higher level of vocabulary and expressive language ability is tapped by the Word Definitions subtest in which the examinee must tell the meaning of individual words. Naming Vocabulary is a core verbal ability test for those under age 7 and Word Definitions is for those over 7 years of age. Both are appropriate measures of the verbal knowledge stored in semantic memory.

Picture Similarities and Verbal Similarities Similarities subtests require the examinee to understand how words or pictures are associated semantically. These tasks not only reveal the depth of semantic knowledge but have implications for how well the examinee's memory representations are organized and interconnected on a semantic basis. Picture Similarities, which is a visual analogue of Verbal Similarities, is classified as a nonverbal reasoning subtest on the DAS-II. Picture Similarities is only administered to children under age 7. The traditional Verbal Similarities subtest for those older than 7 requires the child or adolescent to describe how three things go together. Because similarities activities involve reasoning, poor performance due to weak reasoning may underestimate the examinee's semantic fund of information.

Verbal Comprehension   Administered to children up to 7 years of age, this test of receptive vocabulary allows sampling of verbal semantic knowledge without requiring oral expression. Correctly following instructions for the early items requires understanding of basic verbal concepts. The subsequent multiple-choice items have increasingly complex verbal material; for example, the examinee needs to understand sequencing and be able to make predictions in order to select the correct pictures.

Rapid Naming   Rapid Naming is the classic rapid automatic naming (RAN) task that relies on retrieval speed and the association of visual symbols with names. There are three item types: color naming, picture naming, and color-picture naming. This basic type of retrieval fluency, administered to all ages, is highly related with early reading skill development.

Recall of Objects Immediate and Recall of Objects Delayed   Recall of Objects begins with the immediate condition in which the child must reproduce an abstract figure after it is removed from view. Recall of Objects Immediate is also a learning activity because there are three trials. The Delayed condition involves visuospatial episodic memory. To evaluate the rate of forgetting, the Immediate and Delayed scores should be compared, using the critical values provided in the DAS-II manual (Elliott, 2006).

Kaufman Assessment Battery for Children, Second Edition (KABC-II) and Kaufman Test of Educational Achievement, Second Edition (KTEA-II)

The KABC-II (A. S. Kaufman & N. L. Kaufman, 2004a) is a unique cognitive assessment instrument with five factors: knowledge, planning, learning, sequential processing, and simultaneous processing. The test is based on Luria's neuropsychological theory but also aligns with CHC theory and contemporary research on memory. The KABC-II has a reputation for child-friendly tasks that engage examinees. It is one of the few cognitive scales that include learning and delayed recall subtests (see Table 6.13) in addition to the usual crystallized intelligence (knowledge) subtests. The KABC-II manual (A. S. Kaufman & N. L. Kaufman, 2004a) emphasizes that the crystallized/knowledge factor assesses only the content of memory, and it defines crystallized ability as "culture-based knowledge" and "the breadth and depth of the specific information that has been stored." In contrast, the learning and long-term retrieval factor measures memory processes, specifically the efficiency of encoding, storage, and retrieval. Retrieval fluency tasks are found on the KTEA-II (Kaufman & Kaufman, 2004b), which was co-normed with the KABC-II. The KABC-II's emphasis on memory assessment is evident in the manual (Kaufman & Kaufman, 2004a), where pairwise comparisons among the Learning, Knowledge, and Delayed Recall (the manual provides a table for computing a supplemental Delayed Recall scale) factors are recommended. For more information on the use of the KABC-II, see A. S. Kaufman, Lichtenberger, Fletcher-Janzen, and N. Kaufman (2005).

Table 6.13 Kaufman Assessment Battery for Children, Second Edition (KABC-II) and Kaufman Test of Educational Achievement, Second Edition (KTEA-II)

Authors:	Alan and Nadeen Kaufman
Publisher:	Pearson AGS
Publication Date:	2004
Age Range:	KABC-II: 3:0–18:11; KTEA-II: 4:6–25:11

Long-Term Memory Subtests:

Atlantis*

Atlantis Delayed*

Rebus*

Rebus Delayed*

Expressive Vocabulary*

Verbal Knowledge*

Riddles*

Associational Fluency**

Naming Facility (RAN)**

*KABC-II subtest
**KTEA-II subtest

Atlantis and Atlantis Delayed   Atlantis is a cumulative, visual–verbal learning task in which the child learns the nonsense names of sea creatures. After being introduced to each name, the examinee selects the correct figure from an array but not before identifying previously learned pictures. The scoring of this activity is unique in that 1 point can be earned for an incorrect figure that is the same category (type of sea creature) as the correct figure (which is worth 2 points). Essentially, this is giving credit for making semantic associations and is similar to recalling gist. Immediate corrective feedback is provided to prevent the learning of errors. After an interval of approximately 15 to 25 minutes, Atlantis Delayed is used to measure the examinee's retention of the associations that were learned. The Delayed subtest score should be combined with Rebus Delayed to form a Delayed Recall factor score. The Atlantis Delayed subtest score should also be contrasted with the Atlantis score to evaluate the extent of forgetting. Because the KABC-II does not provide statistics for comparing the Delayed score with an expected score, direct comparisons of standard scores is the only option. Typically, a drop of 12 or more standard score points is a strong indication of poor retention.

Rebus and Rebus Delayed   This visual–verbal, associative learning task is a rebus reading activity in which each drawing represents a word or concept. Some of the symbol-word associations have a logical link; other symbols are abstract. Some words, such as those with a suffix, are represented by two rebuses. The learning is cumulative, and each symbol is taught twice to provide the child with feedback. After an interval of 15 to 25 minutes, Rebus Delayed is administered. The interpretative recommendations for Atlantis Delayed also apply to Rebus Delayed.

Semantic Subtests   In general, the knowledge subtests on the KABC-II do not require much verbal expression, thereby providing a more direct measure of semantic memory than most verbal ability subtests found on intellectual scales. Expressive Vocabulary, which requires the naming of a pictured object, is a core Knowledge subtest for ages 3 to 7 that draws on verbal knowledge stored in semantic memory. Knowledge of the objects selected for the subtest is usually acquired through general experience rather than schooling. Verbal Knowledge is a traditional receptive vocabulary measure for students aged 7 to 19. The examinee need only point to the correct picture of the spoken word. Consequently, Verbal Knowledge is a recognition task that assesses the contents of semantic memory while eliminating the potential confounds of verbal expression and retrieval problems. In the Riddles subtest, the examinee points to a picture of the correct item after receiving several clues. Riddles bring in the element of verbal reasoning, as well as indications of how effectively the child makes semantic associations.

Associational Fluency and Naming Facility (RAN)   These two retrieval fluency tasks are optional subtests found in the KTEA-II. Associational Fluency consists of three 30-second rounds of rapidly retrieving items from a familiar semantic or phonological category. When there are long strings of variants of the same sub-category, only the first two responses receive credit. A Naming Facility round follows each Associational Fluency round (each pair of rounds is separated by administration of other subtests). The stimuli for this RAN task consist of objects, colors, and letters. The KTEA-II uses Associational Fluency and Naming Facility to compute an Oral Fluency composite. Practitioners should view this composite as representing retrieval fluency and compare it with memory scores derived from other scales, using the analysis form found in Appendix B.

Stanford-Binet Intelligence Scales, Fifth Edition (SB5)

From a CHC perspective, the SB5 (Roid, 2003) measures five factors: fluid reasoning, crystallized intelligence, quantitative reasoning, visual-spatial process-ing, and short-term memory. The crystallized factor, labeled as "Knowledge" on the SB5, can be used to assess the level of knowledge stored in semantic memory. The SB5 attempts to measure the verbal and nonverbal dimension of each factor; thus, there is a Verbal and Nonverbal Knowledge subtest (see Table 6.14). Among the cognitive batteries, the SB5 has the least to offer in regards to long-term memory assessment.

Verbal Knowledge   The Verbal Knowledge subtest, a measure of vocabulary, is used as the routing test (the score determines the entry level for remaining verbal

**Table 6.14   Stanford-Binet Intelligence Scales,
Fifth Edition (SB5)**

Author:	Gale Roid
Publisher:	Riverside Publishing
Publication Date:	2003
Age Range:	2:0–85+
Long-Term Memory Subtests:	
Verbal Knowledge	
Nonverbal Knowledge	

subtests). The early childhood items include pointing to body parts, selecting named toys, and explaining what is happening in pictures. The remaining items require an oral definition and are scored on a 1- and 2-point basis.

Nonverbal Knowledge   The Nonverbal Knowledge subtest, which reduces demands on oral expression, begins with asking the child to demonstrate everyday actions and then proceeds with Picture Absurdities that require the child to point to or explain what is silly in a picture. This task involves verbal reasoning, not just accessing a knowledge base. The first activity in the subtest seems to be a more direct measure of visual semantic memory than Picture Absurdities, but the two tasks cannot be scored separately.

The Wechsler Intelligence Scales

All psychologists are familiar with the widely used Wechsler intelligence scales. The three different versions (see Table 6.15) cover the life span, from 2 years, 6 months through 89 years of age. The subtests that address semantic memory—Vocabulary, Similarities, Comprehension, and Information—are basically the same across the three different versions, with difficulty levels adjusted to make them age appropriate. Of course, these subtests are primarily measures of verbal ability and only indirect measures of semantic memory functioning. The two Wechsler subtests that provide the best measure of semantic memory are probably Vocabulary and Information because they do not require as much verbal reasoning as the others. In accordance with this claim, some Wechsler interpretation experts (e.g., Flanagan & Kaufman, 2004) have recommended computation of a clinical long-term memory factor composed of the Vocabulary and Information subtests. Depending on the Wechsler battery, some subtests are supplemental and not routinely administered when obtaining an IQ is the goal. With the exception of the preschool version, the scales also test working and short-term memory (see Dehn, 2008).

Vocabulary   This classic measure of verbal intelligence requires the examinee to name pictured words or define words. Knowledge of words and their meaning is a

Table 6.15 Wechsler Intelligence Scales

Scales: Preschool and Primary Scales of Intelligence®-Third Edition (WPPSI®-III)
              Wechsler Intelligence Scale for Children®-Fourth Edition (WISC®-IV)
              Wechsler Adult Intelligence Scale®-Fourth Edition (WAIS®-IV)

Author: David Wechsler

Publisher: The Psychological Corporation/Pearson

Ages: WPPSI®-III: 2:6–7:3
              WISC®-IV: 6:0–16:11
              WAIS®-IV: 16:11–90:11

Long-Term Memory Subtests:

      Vocabulary (WPPSI®-III, WISC®-IV, WAIS®-IV)

      Similarities (WPPSI®-III, WISC®-IV, WAIS®-IV)

      Comprehension (WPPSI®-III, WISC®-IV, WAIS®-IV)

      Information (WPPSI®-III, WISC®-IV, WAIS®-IV)

      Picture Concepts (WPPSI®-III and WISC®-IV)

      Word Reasoning (WPPSI®-III and WISC®-IV)

      Receptive Vocabulary (WPPSI®-III)

      Picture Naming (WPPSI®-III)

---

fundamental semantic memory ingredient. Consistent with the concept of semantic knowledge, definitions that connect the word with its appropriate semantic category automatically earn maximum credit (2 points). Of course, a weakness in verbal expression may result in an underestimate of the individual's depth of verbal knowledge. When this is a potential confound, evaluators should follow up with the multiple-choice version of Vocabulary found in the WISC®-IV Integrated (see the next section).

Similarities   The Similarities subtest depends on verbal reasoning ability as well as verbal knowledge. Examinees are asked to state how two words are alike. Recognition of semantic categories is key to success on this activity. When performance on the Vocabulary test is significantly higher (3 or more scaled score points higher) practitioners might hypothesize that the examinee has an adequate verbal knowledge base but either lacks reasoning ability or has a verbal knowledge base that is not organized and interconnected on a semantic basis. Similarities are an important subtest to include in semantic memory assessment because it taps the actual structural organization of semantic memory. Accordingly, erroneous responses should be analyzed to determine whether the examinee has a fundamental misconception about how the two words are related.

Comprehension   The Comprehension subtest items tap a dimension of semantic knowledge that is less related with language development and academic learning. Correct responding to these items depends on common sense, experience, social perception, and social skills. To formulate a socially appropriate answer, examinees might rely on recall of remote episodic memories, as much as general principles stored in semantic memory. Thus, Comprehension seems to be a less direct sampling of acquired knowledge than the other three core Wechsler subtests.

Information   Of the Wechsler subtests, Information affords the most direct assessment of the examinee's depth of knowledge without depending heavily on verbal expression and verbal reasoning. As suggested by Flanagan and Kaufman (2004) Information should be combined with Vocabulary to produce a clinical long-term memory factor. Of course, performance on Information is influenced by academic learning opportunities and cultural background. On recent Wechsler revisions Information has been relegated to supplementary subtest status.

Picture Concepts   Picture Concepts, in which the examinee chooses pictures that form a group with a common characteristic, is a visual analogue of Similarities that requires reasoning and recognition of semantic relationships. Although the child may solve the item through verbal mediation, it is more of nonverbal task (the Wechsler scales classify it under the Perceptual Reasoning Index). Thus, to some extent, Picture Concepts taps visual aspects of semantic memory as well as verbal. Certainly, its score should be contrasted with the Similarities score. If Picture Concepts is significantly higher, then either limited verbal expression is influencing Similarities performance or visual semantic memory is stronger than verbal semantic memory. If Picture Concepts is significantly lower, visuospatial subtests from a memory scale might be administered to determine if there is a global visuospatial memory deficit.

Word Reasoning   Word Reasoning is another Wechsler subtest in which the examinee's performance depends partly on the ability to recognize semantic relationships. The task requires the examinee to identify a common concept being described by a series of clues. Presumably, performance is enhanced when examinees possess memory representations that are structured and interconnected on a semantic basis. For semantic memory assessment, Word Reasoning might be administered in lieu of Similarities, especially if elaborated verbal expression is a concern. If both are administered, they can be combined to form a verbal reasoning clinical cluster, as suggested by Flanagan and Kaufman (2004).

Receptive Vocabulary   Unique to the WPPSI®-III, Receptive Vocabulary offers a more direct and age-appropriate appraisal of semantic memory contents than subtests that involve uncued recall and verbal expression. Visual semantic memory and recognition each play a role as children select the pictured items representing the words spoken by the examiner. Certainly, Receptive Vocabulary performance should be contrasted with Vocabulary to judge whether expressive language ability is having an impact on performance.

Picture Naming Picture Naming is very similar to Receptive Vocabulary, except that the child must name the pictured item instead of selecting the correct picture. Contrasting scores from these two subtests should uncover any potential retrieval problems, as Receptive Vocabulary is a recognition task while Picture Naming places more demands on recall. In the event Picture Naming is significantly lower, the practitioner should follow up with the administration of rapid automatic naming task to quantify retrieval speed (the WPPSI®-III Picture Naming subtest is untimed).

WISC®-IV Integrated

The WISC®-IV Integrated (Kaplan, Fein, Kramer, Delis, & Morris, 2004) is the combination of the standard WISC®-IV battery (Wechsler, 2003) and 16 supplemental process subtests. The purpose of the Integrated is to provide an opportunity for in-depth assessment of suspected cognitive processing and memory weaknesses. Because each WISC®-IV standard subtest involves more than one cognitive process, following up with Integrated process subtests allows the examiner to distinguish among the cognitive processes involved, potentially leading to identification of the subprocess that underlies the examinee's poor performance on the standard WISC®-IV subtest. Most of the process subtests are derivations of the standard WISC®-IV subtests; only the scoring procedures or the presentation formats have changed. In addition to offering in-depth assessment of working and short-term memory (see Dehn, 2008), the Integrated offers retesting of the verbal ability subtests in a format that allows differentiation of recall and recognition, as well as distinguishing verbal expression from verbal knowledge (see Table 6.16). The interpretative section in the WISC®-IV Integrated manual (Kaplan et al., 2004) provides succinct explanations of the processes involved, as well as interpretative hypotheses for discrepancies between standard and process subtest scores.

Table 6.16 WISC®-IV Integrated

Authors:	Edith Kaplan, Deborah Fein, Joel Kramer, Dean Delis, and Robin Morris
Publisher:	The Psychological Corporation
Publication Date:	2004
Age Range:	6:0–16:11

Long-Term Memory Subtests:

    Similarities Multiple Choice

    Vocabulary Multiple Choice

    Comprehension Multiple Choice

    Information Multiple Choice

    Picture Vocabulary Multiple Choice

Multiple Choice Versions of Core Wechsler Subtests   The WISC®-IV Integrated provides a solution to the interpretative quandary created when an examinee performs poorly on the standard WISC®-IV verbal subtests. In such instances, any of the verbal subtests can be readministered in a multiple-choice format. The multiple-choice subtests consist of the same items, facilitating a direct comparison with the standard versions. Even the two-point and one-point scoring is preserved. Consequently, contrasting the scores allows the practitioner to determine whether there is a potential retrieval problem. When comparing performance, the Integrated scores should be aggregated to produce a clinical factor score and then compared with the mean of their standard version counterparts (see Table 6.11 for an example). Significantly improved performance on the multiple-choice subtests may also occur because of verbal expression weaknesses or delayed language development. To parse out this potential influence, Picture Vocabulary Multiple Choice can be contrasted with Vocabulary Multiple Choice and the results of any language assessment should also be taken into account. Interestingly, the interpretative section in the WISC®-IV Integrated manual (Kaplan et al., 2004) suggests that the multiple-choice format facilitates performance in children with memory retrieval difficulties to a greater degree than those with deficits in oral expression. Naturally, some students will perform worse on the process version of the verbal subtests. Hypotheses that account for this pattern of performance include impulsive responding and confusion recognizing the correct response when the distracters are semantically related to the target word.

Picture Vocabulary Multiple Choice   The pictured version of vocabulary further reduces the language demands, making the task a receptive vocabulary test that also requires visual-verbal associations and thus some visual semantic knowledge. The same vocabulary items are used again, but there is only 0- or 1-point scoring. The examiner reads the word and then the examinee points to one of four pictures that best depicts the definition. The pictured version may be especially appropriate for children with auditory processing deficits, as their visual abilities may provide an alternative retrieval route to the word knowledge they have stored in semantic memory.

Woodcock-Johnson® III

The Woodcock-Johnson® III Tests of Cognitive Ability (WJ III COG; Woodcock, McGrew, & Mather, 2001b) battery is known for its measurement of several cognitive processes that are closely related with academic learning. In addition to sampling seven Cattell-Horn-Carroll (CHC) broad cognitive abilities, the scale measures several cognitive processes and memory components, including working and short-term memory. The WJ III COG also includes subtests of learning, retrieval fluency, and semantic memory (see Table 6.17). Its controlled, associative learning task is unique in that delayed recall of the learning can be tested after extended intervals of up to eight days. Overall, the WJ III COG is an efficient tool

Table 6.17   Woodcock-Johnson® III

Authors:	Richard Woodcock, Kevin McGrew, and Nancy Mather
Publisher:	Riverside Publishing
Publication Date:	2001
Age Range:	2:0–90+

Long-Term Memory Subtests:

Verbal Comprehension

Visual-Auditory Learning

Visual-Auditory Learning Delayed

General Information

Retrieval Fluency

Rapid Picture Naming

Memory for Names*

Memory for Names Delayed*

Story Recall**

Story Recall Delayed**

Academic Knowledge**

*From the Diagnostic Supplement
**From the WJ III ACH

for comprehensive memory assessments that include testing of related cognitive processes. Moreover, it is ideally suited for selective, cross-battery testing, including using it as a supplement to other scales. Subtests from the Woodcock-Johnson® III Diagnostic Supplement to the Tests of Cognitive Abilities (Woodcock, McGrew, Mather, & Schrank, 2003) can be combined with subtests from the WJ III COG to form some unique clusters (factors), such as the Associative Memory cluster. Two of the 11 subtests in the Diagnostic Supplement appraise memory: Memory for Names and Memory for Names Delayed. The Woodcock-Johnson® III Tests of Achievement battery (WJ III ACH; Woodcock, McGrew, & Mather, 2001a) samples semantic memory with a knowledge test and verbal episodic memory with narrative recall. Although the WJ III ACH classifies Story Recall, the immediate narrative condition, as a test of oral expression, it is also a measure of verbal immediate memory. One advantage of the WJ III ACH subtests is that teachers with appropriate training are qualified to administer and interpret them. Another advantage is that the WJ III ACH was co-normed with the WJ III COG. Thus, these WJ III ACH tests can be directly compared with memory scores from the cognitive battery.

Verbal Comprehension and General Information   Verbal Comprehension is essentially a vocabulary and verbal reasoning measure that draws from semantic storage. It includes four parts: Picture Vocabulary, Synonyms, Antonyms, and Verbal Analogies. General Information is another test of verbal knowledge that involves semantic associations. The WJ III COG's Comprehension-Knowledge factor is comprised of these two subtests. In conducting a cross-battery analysis using the form in Appendix B, the examiner can transfer this factor score into the Subtest/Factor Scores cell for semantic memory.

Visual-Auditory Learning and Visual-Auditory Learning Delayed Visual-Auditory Learning is a learning activity in which the examinee is taught to associate words with pictorial representations (rebuses) and then must read sentences composed of the rebuses. The task is cumulative, with a few new symbols added at a time. Corrective feedback is provided as the examinee reads each page. The cued delayed recall condition can be administered after 30 minutes or can be delayed for as long as eight days. Longer delays (a day or more) are recommended to allow enough time to realistically assess consolidation and the rate of long-term forgetting. If testing must be completed in one session, examiners should avoid administering Visual-Auditory Learning Delayed until the end of the session. The WJ-III Compuscore® or Report Writer program will contrast the amount of information retained, controlling for the amount learned and the length of the interval. If the resulting z-score is greater than -1.00 then the examinee is forgetting significantly more information than normal.

Retrieval Fluency and Rapid Picture Naming The Retrieval Fluency subtest allows the examinee 1 minute to name as many examples of a basic semantic category as possible. As these are well-known categories, most children know numerous items. Therefore, poor performance is thought to represent difficulty speedily retrieving information on demand, which could arise from slow retrieval speed, inefficient searching of stores, or information that is not organized well by semantic categories. Rapid Picture Naming, a RAN task that requires the naming of pictures, assesses retrieval speed. The scores from these two subtests might be averaged and used as a clinical factor score to represent long-term memory retrieval fluency.

Memory for Names and Memory for Names Delayed Memory for Names is an auditory-visual, controlled learning task in which unfamiliar names must be associated with drawings of space creatures. This task eliminates verbal expression, as the examinee is only required to point to the correct response. Again, the cued delayed condition can be administered as long as eight days later. When comparing the learning and delayed recall conditions, the interpretation of the computer generated z-score is the same as for the Visual-Auditory Learning subtests. Compuscore® will also combine Memory for Names and Visual-Auditory learning to produce a Visual-Auditory Learning factor score, and combine the two delayed scores to create an Associative Memory Delayed factor score. When verbal expression is thought to be a concern, Memory for Names should be contrasted with Visual-Auditory Learning. If Memory for Names is significantly higher (a 12-point or greater difference), verbal expression might have influenced performance on Visual-Auditory learning.

Story Recall and Story Recall Delayed   Story Recall consists of paragraph-length stories that are not as long as most narratives used to assess memory. The number of stories administered depends on when the examinee reaches a ceiling. The examinee is expected to recall only the completed stories during the delayed condition. Some of the information must be recalled verbatim while gist recall suffices for the remaining information. However, separate scoring of these two types of recall is not provided. Story Recall Delay can be administered any time between 30 minutes and eight days later. Similar to the analysis of the cognitive subtests, Compuscore® can be used to contrast the delayed and immediate components. Again, standard deviation discrepancies of greater than -1.00 indicate the examinee is forgetting a significant amount of information that was initially recalled. The main difference between this measure of delayed recall and the ones on the cognitive battery is that the cognitive tasks involve recall of multiple-trial, visual-auditory learning.

Academic Knowledge   The WJ III ACH Academic Knowledge test is one of the best standardized measures of semantic knowledge available because it directly assesses factual knowledge instead of verbal ability. The test is similar to the Information subtest found on the Wechsler scales but actually has many more items. The items are grouped into Science, Social Studies, and Humanities sections but standardized scores for these three sections are unavailable. The Academic Knowledge score can be compared with the Verbal Comprehension score from the WJ III COG to evaluate how general knowledge compares with vocabulary development. It should also be contrasted with the WJ III COG verbal episodic measures (see Table 6.10).

OTHER SCALES WITH LONG-TERM MEMORY MEASURES

Children's Auditory Verbal Learning Test, Second Edition (CAVLT-2)

The format of the CAVLT-2 (Table 6.18; Talley, 1993), which assesses auditory learning and memory abilities, is very similar to that of the CVLT-C. The test begins with the learning of 16 common words over five trials, followed by an interference list and then recall of the original list. After a 15- to 20-minute delay, retention of the first list is assessed, first with free recall and then with recognition.

Table 6.18   Children's Auditory Verbal Learning Test, Second Edition (CAVLT-2)

Author:	Jack L. Talley
Publisher:	Psychological Assessment Resources
Publication Date:	1993
Age Range:	6:6–17:11

Table 6.19   Children's Category Test

Author:	Thomas Boll
Publisher:	The Psychological Corporation
Publication Date:	1993
Age Range:	5:0–16:11

Children's Category Test (CCT)

The CCT (Table 6.19; Boll, 1993), designed to assess nonverbal learning and memory in children with neurological injury or deterioration, requires neither a verbal nor motor response. It might be administered as the visual counterpart to a memory assessment involving the CVLT-C, with which it is co-normed. The CCT appears to be primarily a measure of learning rather than long-term memory.

ImPACT® Neurocognitive Test Battery

ImPACT®, which stands for Immediate Postconcussion Assessment and Cognitive Testing, is a computer-based neurocognitive test battery specifically designed for assessing the cognitive and memory effects of a sports-related concussion. Recently, some high schools and colleges have begun utilizing ImPACT® to pretest all athletes. Thus, when an injured athlete is retested after a concussion occurs, there is an established level of premorbid functioning the athlete must recover before being allowed to return to athletic activities (Van Kampen et al., 2006). The test, which measures attention, memory, processing speed, and reaction time, can create numerous alternate forms by randomly varying the stimulus array for each administration, thereby reducing practice effects during multiple re-tests. Regarding memory assessment, the scale seems to primarily tap visuospatial working and short-term memory. When there are injury-related decrements in working and short-term memory, long-term memory functioning is usually affected as well. Athletes should be referred for a neurological assessment that includes long-term memory testing when ImPACT® scores do not quickly return to normal or when there are persistent post-concussion symptoms (see Chapter 4). More information on ImPACT® testing can be found at www.impacttest.com.

Leiter International Performance Scale-Revised (Leiter-R)

The Leiter-R (Roid & Miller, 1998) is a strictly nonverbal test of intelligence that is administered through pantomimed instructions and requires only nonverbal responding. It is mainly intended for special populations, such as hearing impaired, language impaired, and English-as-a-second-language students. One of its two batteries—the Attention and Memory battery—includes two delayed recall activities

Table 6.20 Leiter International Performance Scale-Revised (Leiter-R)

Authors:	Gale H. Roid and Lucy J. Miller
Publisher:	Stoelting
Publication Date:	1998
Age Range:	2:0–20:11
Long-Term Memory Subtests:	
Associated Pairs and Delayed Pairs	
Immediate Recognition and Delayed Recognition	

(see Table 6.20). Associated Pairs is a visuospatial short-term memory task. Performance on its Delayed counterpart relies on visuospatial episodic memory. It appears that Delayed Recognition is no more of a recognition task than is Delayed Pairs; they both involve cued retrieval. The two delayed subtest scores might be used to calculate a clinical delayed recall factor representing visuospatial episodic memory functioning.

Rey Complex Figure Test and Recognition Trial (RCFT)

Although it's primarily an adult scale, the RCFT (Table 6.21; Meyers & Meyers, 1995) has norms for children aged 4 to 16 years. The test consists of one complex geometric figure with 18 scoring elements. After a copy trial, there is a 3-minute immediate recall trial, followed 30 minutes later by a delayed recall trial and a recognition trial. The RCFT is useful in capturing children's ability to recall complex abstract visual material. Those who draw it piecemeal or who first draw the outline, thereby distorting the general figure, tend to have greater recall difficulty than those who draw the main components (Middleton, 2004). In a factor analysis of this scale, two memory factors emerged: visuospatial recall memory and visuospatial recognition memory. The test's delayed recall and recognition scores provide an opportunity to compare uncued recall and recognition purely within the visual domain.

Table 6.21 Rey Complex Figure Test and Recognition Trial (RCFT)

Author:	Randolph Christopher
Publisher:	The Psychological Corporation
Publication Date:	1998
Age Range:	4:0–89

7 Interventions for Memory Problems

A high school sophomore, herein referred to as "Harry," was brought in for assistance with mathematics and study skills. Harry's scholastic achievement levels had declined after he entered middle school, and he was now performing poorly in about half of his courses. After a cognitive and educational assessment (which did not include long-term memory testing), it was determined that Harry had normal learning aptitudes and average basic skills but deficient academic applications in reading comprehension and math reasoning, as well as poor study skills and organizational habits. Harry's parents enrolled him in math tutoring and study skills tutoring. Although Harry welcomed the assistance in math, he was resistant to the study skills training, mainly because he believed he knew how to study. When basic memorization methods were addressed, Harry was asked to explain how he memorized material for classroom examinations. Using Spanish vocabulary as an example, he demonstrated how he copied the term and its English definition five times on a sheet a paper. The trainer followed Harry's demonstration with the comment that this was a basic method of memorization and a good place to start but that there were other memorization strategies that were more efficient and more effective for long-term retention. Harry bristled and stated that this method worked just fine for him and that he had no interest in learning another approach. The trainer subsequently got Harry to agree to an "experiment" in which Harry memorized some random words and recalled them, and then later Harry memorized words grouped by semantic categories and recalled them. Although Harry's recall nearly doubled with the semantically clustered items, he remained unconvinced. He could see no academic application of this strategy and wasn't interested. Harry continued his resistance to training in advanced study skills and memory techniques until his parents agreed to let him drop the tutoring.

Harry's case illustrates several of the challenges involved in attempting to teach memory strategies to students, challenges that are addressed in this chapter. This intervention was doomed from the beginning because of initial steps omitted by the trainer. First, the trainer should have taught Harry about how human memory works and what sorts of techniques enhance its performance. This should have been followed by some goal setting that involved Harry; for instance, Harry should have specified his academic goals and identified types of study skills and memory performance he would like to do better at. Finally, the trainer failed to demonstrate to Harry the relevance of the memory strategies to academic material. Harry's contributions to the intervention's failure were his denial of any problems, his overestimation of what he could recall, and his unwillingness to learn something new. He remained convinced that his simple rehearsal strategies were completely effective and were all that he would ever need. Overall, Harry's case illustrates that memory interventions need to be well thought out before training is attempted. That is, practitioners and educators who conduct memory interventions need to do more than follow cookbook-style directions. The challenges and best practices regarding memory interventions must first be understood. The first part of this chapter addresses these concerns before the methods are discussed in the latter part.

The interventions discussed in this chapter are intended primarily for children and adolescents who have memory problems that range from mild to severe. Although a student with average memory performance can also use and benefit from many of the recommended methods, the focus of this chapter is on addressing the needs of individuals with identified memory deficits that impede academic learning or affect daily functioning. This population includes both those who have a memory deficit but otherwise normal cognitive abilities and those whose low memory functioning is just one of several below average cognitive abilities. Given these parameters, there is sizable number of students among the K–12 student population that might benefit from memory interventions. Realistically, schools don't have the resources to offer individual or group memory training to such a large number of students. Consequently, individual treatment for memory problems has generally been reserved for those with severe impairments, such as children and adolescents who suffer amnesia following traumatic brain injury. However, conducting evidence-based memory interventions with a wider range of students may reap some worthwhile educational benefits for those students. In particular, the neediest students are those receiving special education services for a learning disability, language impairment, or other related disorder, as well as those who remain outside of special education but have an identified memory deficit or impairment. Given memory's direct link with learning and the scientific evidence for memory strategies and mnemonics, including such training in a special education student's individual educational program (IEP) seems entirely appropriate. Students without an IEP but who have documented memory problems might be served through modifications to classroom instructional methods, such as the "mnemonic classroom" approach discussed in Chapter 8.

The interventions reviewed in this chapter mainly consist of teaching memory strategies and mnemonics that enhance retention and recall of information. Although the popular press may claim that there are mental exercises that can strengthen long-term memory, there is no empirical evidence that such activities benefit children's long-term memory functioning (Wilson, 2009). The only activities with some research support for expanding a child's memory capacity involve working memory (Klingberg, 2009). In contrast, there is extensive scientific support for memory strategies and mnemonics. Memory strategies and mnemonics are very similar. Both are approaches to making information more memorable, mainly by supporting encoding, consolidation, and retrieval processes. The main distinction between the two is that mnemonics transform input or associate input with other information that serves to cue recall, whereas memory strategies generally do not utilize unrelated memory structures to mediate recall.

Most of the interventions in this chapter are not new or unheard of. It is only the empirical evidence supporting them that is relatively recent (within the past 50 years). A few of the recommended mnemonics have been used since ancient Greek and Roman times. In fact, mnemonics were widely practiced until the invention of the printing press and an increasingly literate population reduced the need for them. Interest in the study of memory and methods of enhancing it revived with the advent of psychology at the end of the 19th century. In the early 20th century educational researchers identified instructional practices, such as spaced review, that increased the amount of knowledge students retained. Teachers have traditionally taught verbal mnemonics, such as acrostics, or used rhyme and music to help students remember important material. Of course, nearly all instructors regularly repeat and review content with students. However, more involved memory-enhancing methods have never really caught on in the educational environment. Perhaps, it's because the empirical evidence and detailed methodology has never reached educators. Historically, most memory research has been conducted by experimental psychologists, and most interventions have been conducted in medical settings. Consequently, much of the information and evidence has not reached educators, school psychologists, clinical psychologists, and others who instruct or work with youth who have learning and memory problems. Even when a highly effective method has been studied in an educational setting, the majority of educators remain unaware of its applications. This chapter and the next are this author's attempt to help bridge this gap between scientific research and real-world applications.

DESIRABLE OUTCOMES FOR MEMORY INTERVENTIONS

Sometimes there's no argument about whether a child or adolescent would benefit from a memory intervention. The student and the other parties involved might all agree that there's a significant memory problem and that there are evidence-based procedures to address the problem. Often, the issue is whether the outcomes will justify the investment of resources and everyone's time. Students will usually make an effort to learn and apply strategies if they believe the strategies will make them more efficient at learning and remembering. Parents and teachers are usually interested if they believe the interventions will lead to improved academic performance. So, before deciding whether to implement an intervention, it's best to review desirable outcomes. Only some of these outcomes will actually be achieved by any given student, but stating them establishes the range of possibilities. Also, some of these outcomes may be selected by students as their personal goals (see section on goal setting later in this chapter). Desirable outcomes include:

1. The improvement in performance will be permanent.
2. The trainee will learn to more effectively utilize his or her memory abilities.
3. The trainee will be able to succeed at more activities that require effective memory functioning.
4. The trainee will be able to perform the memory strategies independently.
5. Academic learning will improve as a result of learning new memory strategies.
6. The trainee will acquire greater self-awareness of memory functions.
7. The trainee will acquire greater control over memory functions.
8. The trainee will be motivated to seek out and learn additional memory strategies.
9. The trainee will apply the newly acquired strategies to untrained situations and material.
10. The trainee will be able to task-analyze a situation, recognize what is required, and then select and apply a relevant memory strategy.

FACTORS RELATED TO SUCCESS

Another issue to consider before committing to an intervention is the likelihood of success and the variables that contribute to success. Several factors play a role in determining how well an intervention succeeds (Miller, 1992). Some are within the child or adolescent, some are characteristics of the trainer, some depend on the quality of the training, and others are environmental variables:

1. The trainee has adequate cognitive resources for learning, applying, and maintaining new memory strategies. For instance, very slow processing speed or limited fluid reasoning ability may make it difficult to utilize complex strategies. In particular, the trainee needs adequate working memory resources because learning and applying a new memory strategy will impose demands on working memory. The initial learning of a strategy will be particularly demanding but once the strategy is mastered and automatized its use will require fewer working memory resources. In cases where there are known deficits in working memory, success depends on starting out with simple, easily implemented strategies.
2. The trainee understands that successful acquisition and use of a strategy will take practice, and the trainee engages in enough practice to master the strategy.

3. The trainee understands that it may take time for the benefits of the new strategy to become evident. For example, course grades may not immediately improve upon adopting a new memorization technique.

4. The trainee is a good strategy user. The characteristics of a good strategy user include the ability to monitor performance to determine if the goal is being achieved, the ability to select a strategy that matches the task at hand, the ability to coordinate several goal-specific strategies, and the ability to modify techniques for specific situations and materials.

5. The personal efficacy of the strategy becomes apparent to the trainee. If the trainee does not believe in the efficacy of the strategy, he or she will not invest much effort during training and will not persist when the training ceases. The best way to prove personal efficacy is to show the student performance data and to attribute the improvement to use of the new strategy.

6. The trainee is able to generalize and apply the strategy to different situations and materials. Failure to generalize may not be a student problem but may be due to insufficient generalization training. Thus, training should include specific generalization procedures, such as conducting the training with a variety of materials and in a variety of settings.

7. Parents and teachers support and reinforce the trainee's efforts to learn and apply new memory strategies. Parents can become extremely influential once they understand how a strategy works, what it applies to, and its efficacy. This author gets parents involved by inviting them to observe during the training sessions, discussing how students can practice at home, and showing parents data on how the new strategy is improving student performance. Similar communication with teachers will also merit their support.

8. The trainer follows the training procedures with integrity. If interventions are to succeed, the trainer needs to adhere to general guidelines for teaching strategies, as well as the specific training steps for each strategy.

9. The training incorporates metamemory training that increases the trainee's self-awareness of memory functions and memory strengths and weaknesses. Also, the metamemory training includes training in self-management of memory functions.

10. The methods and materials are age appropriate, or adapted to make them age appropriate.

11. The methods and materials are new and challenging. Simply reinforcing basic methods already employed by the trainee is unlikely to make a difference.

12. The methods involve deep, associative processing of information, rather than simple, surface processing. For example, simple rote repetition of information does little to enhance long-term recall, whereas consciously making

associations between the target information and prior knowledge improves retention and recall.

13. Regarding academic learning success, the memory interventions are functionally integrated with the learner's typical assignments and study. Any trained memory strategy needs to have a counterpart in academic study.

14. Interventions that specifically address the learner's memory weaknesses and deficits, as well as take strengths into account, increase the likelihood of success.

CONCERNS ABOUT MEMORY INTERVENTIONS

Before attempting a memory intervention with a child or adolescent, it is important to convey to the student and his or her parents that the memory intervention will not increase global memory capacity or fix or cure a memory impairment. What can be accomplished through a memory intervention is more effective utilization of some specific memory abilities. More effective use of existing memory functions should result in better performance (i.e., the student will be able to remember more information for longer periods of time). In effect, the student's memory performance may improve because he or she has learned to cope with, manage, bypass, and compensate for memory problems. However, better memory performance does not guarantee that the brain's memory functioning has actually changed or that improved performance will occur with all types of memory and materials. In other words, no one can promise to remediate or rehabilitate memory (Glisky & Schacter, 1986). As world-renowned memory rehabilitation expert Dr. Barbara Wilson reported in 2009, "at present we can do little to restore memory functioning" (p. xiii).

Wilson (2009) and other cognitive rehabilitation experts (e.g., E. L. Glisky & M. L. Glisky, 2002) are talking mainly about severe memory impairments that have been acquired through brain injury, surgery, and other medical conditions. Their subjects have often received intensive long-term intervention and been studied for years. In some cases, there is evidence of brain-based improvements in memory functions. However, these researchers remain skeptical about treatments actually changing the brain. When the brain does change, it may simply be natural healing and restorative processes at work. Despite limited evidence of a treatment effect, there is some evidence of brain plasticity in regards to memory. Neurological investigations have discovered that the brain compensates for functional loss by using other brain regions to perform cognitive functions not normally associated with those regions (Berninger & Richards, 2002; Wilson, 1987). The fact that associated brain structures are sometimes able to perform the function of a damaged or poorly developed structure is testimony to the plasticity of the brain (Shaywitz, 2003). For example, the semantic learning ability of children with developmental amnesia (see Chapter 4) might be explained by parahippocampal structures performing some of the functions of a disabled hippocampus. The bottom line is that not enough is currently known about the brain's response to memory interventions. It may very well be that some interventions prompt the brain to compensate, thereby improving functioning. Regardless, the important fact is that there is empirical evidence that memory interventions can significantly improve memory performance. Furthermore, most individuals are satisfied with the perspective that improved performance is due to more effective use of existing memory capabilities.

A related concern about teaching memory strategies and mnemonics is that many are applicable only to certain situations and types of information. Consequently, using a method that enhances performance with particular material does not necessarily improve performance with other types of material. For instance, there is the frequently reported case of a college student who devised a mnemonic strategy for increasing his digit span. After several months of practice he could recall over 80 digits in correct order after only one exposure. A day after accomplishing this feat, the undergraduate was asked to recall strings of letters instead of digits. Surprisingly, he could only recall a normal adult span of seven letters, indicating that his strategy and improved performance did not automatically transfer to other material. The lack of transferability seems to be an inherent characteristic of many strategies and mnemonics; they are only effective with certain kinds of content. This problem can be addressed by teaching different strategies for different situations. However, even when strategies, such as elaborative rehearsal, are broadly applicable across a range of content and tasks, children and adolescents are unlikely to transfer the skill to different situations (Franzen & Haut, 1991). In such instances, methods that enhance generalization need to be incorporated into the training. Regardless of the cause, the effects of practice, strategy learning, and improved performance are usually limited to the same materials and contexts used during training (E. L. Glisky & M. L. Glisky, 2002).

Another issue is whether interventions should attempt to strengthen deficient memory components and processes or to utilize memory strengths in a compensatory manner. By focusing on strengths, compensatory approaches bypass the deficient components and processes (E. L. Glisky & M. L. Glisky, 2002). For example, visual mnemonics are often used to circumvent verbal memory deficits. Compensatory approaches typically involve strategy training, but they may also include external aids, accommodations, or substitute methods of reaching the same goal. Compensatory methods also include practices that modify instruction and other aspects of the learning environment. Although compensatory interventions are likely to be more effective than remedial interventions that target only weaknesses, most practitioners and researchers believe that a combined approach has the best chance of success (Work & Choi, 2005). With the combined approach, the goal of the intervention is to optimize the functioning of deficient components and processes while utilizing and enhancing memory strengths.

Finally, the reality is that many interventions, regardless of the quality of training, will fail, at least in the short run. Failure often consists of trainees correctly using a new strategy without achieving any improvement in performance (known as a production deficiency). In a review of 76 memory-training conditions, 51% of the subjects displayed evidence of a production deficiency, with the deficiencies being more common with younger children (Bjorklund, 1997). Luckily, some children believe enough in the efficacy of the strategy to persist in spite of failure. For some of these children, the strategy use may prove successful in the long run.

SELECTING AND DESIGNING INTERVENTIONS

There is not a single memory intervention that addresses any and all types of memory impairments. Moreover, indiscriminate use of common memory techniques is unlikely to produce any lasting improvements. Consequently, memory interventions should be selected and designed on the basis of the individual's weaknesses and strengths. (The memory strategies and mnemonics recommended for specific types of memory impairments can be found near the end of this chapter.) Obviously, a comprehensive memory assessment that includes formal testing is necessary to validly determine individual strengths and weaknesses. Informal inquiry into the strategies already used by the trainee can also help in selecting strategies for the intervention (see Table 5.4). Other factors, such as the student's goals, areas of academic deficiency, and general cognitive ability, also need to be considered. Once enough is known about the student, an individualized set of strategies, mnemonics, and other methods can be selected. After the selection, some methods may need to be adapted for the student's developmental level and some may need to be adapted for the type of academic material the student wishes to memorize. At times, a creative combination of mnemonics may produce the best results. Of course, with any intervention, adjustments and modifications to the plan are often necessary once the student's initial response to the training can be evaluated.

In addition to incorporating specific memory strategies and mnemonics, there are some general and fundamental procedures that should be included in every intervention. These include:

1. Encouraging development of metamemory awareness and regulation.
2. Demonstrating how the methods are personally effective for the trainee.
3. Teaching how organizing information, such as clustering items semantically, improves recall.
4. Teaching how to recode items to produce dual encoding, such as recoding visual information into a verbal code.
5. Teaching visual mnemonics that link new information to images that can easily be recalled.
6. Teaching methods, such as elaborative rehearsal, that require the trainee to process information more deeply.

SETTING GOALS AND MEASURING PROGRESS

Prior to initiating a memory intervention, student-centered, specific, reasonable, and measurable goals should be agreed on and put in writing. Involving the student and parents in a goal-setting meeting is one of the keys to intervention success, as a properly conducted goal-setting meeting can give the student a sense of ownership that will increase motivation and effort. In fact, setting goals is so important that the act of goal setting itself has been shown to improve performance (Locke & Latham, 2002). Ideally, goal setting follows an assessment results meeting in which the student learns more about his or her memory problems and accepts the need for improvement. Confident, informed, and articulate students should be directly questioned about their goals. With students unable to express what they would like, the practitioner or educator should make suggestions and ask if the student agrees with them. Obviously, many student-formulated goals will need to be reframed and refined to meet the criteria for appropriate goals. For example, when a student's goal is "Being able to remember stuff better," the material and the degree of improvement will need to be specified, lest the student and parents expect global changes in memory. Or, when the student says, "Be able to see something and be able to remember it when needed," the goal will need to be adjusted to make it realistic. Memory goals should also be relevant to academic learning and performance, as this is what is most important to parents and students. In addition to being clear, specific, realistic, and student-centered, the goals must also be measurable. Well-written goals that specifically describe the behavior or performance that will occur when the goal is reached facilitate measurement of progress and determination of success (E. L. Glisky & M. L. Glisky, 2002). Here are a couple examples of goals linked with academic performance:

- After studying for Spanish vocabulary tests by self-testing with flash cards, Jane will improve her test scores an average of 10% over an eight-week period.
- After using visualization methods to memorize material for science tests, Jane will improve her test scores by 5% over a three-month period.

Here are some examples of more general long-term memory goals:

- After eight sessions of memory training, John will identify his memory strengths and weaknesses with 90% accuracy.
- After eight weeks of memory training, John will correctly demonstrate the procedures for three new memory strategies.
- By the end of eight weeks of memory training, John will improve his recall of word lists by 20%.

For more suggestions on goal setting for memory interventions, see Wilson (2009).

Unless there is an intensive memory intervention over a period of several months, standardized tests seldom are good measures of progress. Even when there is meaningful improvement, standardized test scores seldom shift significantly. There is also the problem of practice effects when standardized tests are used repeatedly. The most direct measure of progress is to track recall of the actual material used during training. Similar to curriculum-based measurement, a baseline should be determined before a new memory method is introduced and then repeated measures taken to assess progress. An alternative measurement approach with memory interventions is to periodically conduct recall tests of information learned without applying a memory strategy and contrast the recall scores with similar information learned strategically (see Chapter 9 for case study examples).

Finally, there is the option of goal attainment scaling (GAS; Kiresuk & Sherman, 1968), especially when progress towards memory goals is difficult to quantify. GAS is essentially a rating system that ranges from -2 to $+2$. With GAS, a realistically expected outcome level, and varying degrees of positive and negative outcomes are specified. When the treatment or intervention is concluded, the trainee's performance is rated according to these terms: $0 =$ expected outcome; $+1 =$ better than expected; $+2 =$ even better than 1; $-1 =$ worse than expected; and $-2 =$ even worse than -1. Wilson (2009) suggests that GAS has been used successfully to assess progress and treatment effectiveness in medical settings and that GAS applies well to evaluating memory improvement.

GENERAL MEMORY STRATEGY TRAINING RECOMMENDATIONS

Regardless of which specific memory strategies are selected for an intervention, there are many important general training practices that will increase the likelihood of a successful intervention:

1. Strategy training and practice should be intensive over an extended period of time until the correct use of the strategy becomes automatic.
2. Even easily acquired methods should be reviewed and practiced over the course of several sessions.
3. The training should be divided into brief, focused sessions held at least a couple times weekly over a period of several weeks.
4. The intervention should begin with a simple, easy-to-use strategy.
5. The directions for each strategy should be simple, clear, and concise. The same wording should be used each time they are presented.
6. When introducing a strategy, the trainer should model all of the steps and components of the strategy while thinking aloud.
7. After introducing and initially practicing a strategy, the trainee should be asked to paraphrase the directions and explain the procedure.

8. Each step in the strategy procedures should be explained, demonstrated, and taught in detail, with special attention to the steps that are difficult to understand.

9. The trainee should be provided with a written rubric to check when he or she forgets any steps in the procedure. An alternative is a mnemonic, such as an acronym, that can be used to facilitate recall of the procedures.

10. Using the trainee's own practice data, the efficacy of a strategy should be repeatedly demonstrated throughout the intervention.

11. The trainee should be taught the purpose and rationale for each strategy, including why, when, and how to use each strategy.

12. The trainee should be provided with scaffolding as needed. With memory training, the purpose of scaffolding is to reduce the load on working memory. For example, the trainer should repeat the directions as many times as necessary so that the learner can focus on the strategic process.

13. The trainee should be encouraged to monitor and evaluate strategy use outside of the training sessions.

14. The trainee should be encouraged to attribute his or her improved performance to strategy use.

15. Generalization should be developed by discussing diverse applications of the strategy and practicing the strategy with different materials and under different situations.

16. Trainer support should be gradually withdrawn to encourage independent application of each strategy.

METAMEMORY: THE CORNERSTONE OF THE INTERVENTION

Because metamemory plays a crucial role in the management of memory functions and strategies (see Chapter 3), it is an essential component of any long-term memory intervention. Without adequately developed metamemory, children and adolescents will not use strategies wisely, even when they know the strategic procedures. No assumptions should be made about the trainee's level of metamemory development, as even intelligent students with normal memory performance may have poor self-awareness and self-regulation of memory components and processes. Thus, if no metamemory assessment has occurred, it should be conducted during the first training session (see Chapter 5 for details). Metamemory instruction can begin immediately following the informal assessment. The key ingredients of metamemory instruction and training are: (a) how human memory works; (b) the trainee's memory strengths and weaknesses; (c) conditional knowledge about memory strategies; (d) self-monitoring of learning and memory; and (e) management of memory strategies. Topics "a" and "b" should be addressed during the first session; the remaining topics should be incorporated into all of the sessions.

How Memory Works

Age-appropriate direct instruction about the workings of human memory should occur during the first session. Begin by explaining the differences between short-term and long-term memory (the concept of working memory can be added for adolescents), followed by discussing how information is taken in, stored, and retrieved. Always ask the student how long he or she believes information is held in short-term memory. (The majority believe it extends for many minutes if not hours.) It is important to impress upon students that short-term memory usually lasts for 20 seconds or less, and emphasize that any information recalled after that interval is being retrieved from long-term memory. Proceed with the major divisions of long-term memory: prospective versus retrospective, visual versus verbal, and personal (episodic) versus factual (semantic). A graphic that illustrates the major divisions of memory, such as the one in Figure 6.1, should be used.

Personal Strengths and Weaknesses

Immediately following the explanation of memory systems and how they work, ask the student to identify his or her memory strengths and weaknesses. If the student is unsure, have the student identify which is stronger: visual or verbal, short-term or long-term, and personal or factual. Younger students might be allowed to color in the graphic used to represent memory functions, with one color representing strengths and another representing weaknesses. When a student's perceptions are incongruent with memory assessment results, review what the test results indicate about the personal strengths and weaknesses. At this point, it might be fruitful to review the goals for the intervention that address the areas of weakness.

Conditional Knowledge

Strategy knowledge consists of declarative, procedural, and conditional components. Conditional knowledge refers to knowing the types of material the strategy applies to, knowing how to use the strategy in different situations, knowing about the effectiveness of the strategy, and knowing how much effort is required (Paris, Newman, & McVey, 1982). Basically, conditional knowledge consists of knowing when, where, why, and how to use a strategy. The greater the conditional knowledge, the more likely the strategy will be maintained and applied to a variety of tasks. Students naturally acquire declarative and procedural strategy knowledge from learning and practicing a strategy, but it should not be assumed that conditional knowledge will be learned without explicit instruction. O'Sullivan and Pressley (1984) found that explicit conditional knowledge instruction produced greater strategy transfer, and that this explicit and elaborated instruction is especially important with children. Essentially, children need explanations that allow them to understand the connection between the means and the goals. When they understand the conditional factors and the usefulness of a strategy, their motivation to continue using the strategy will be increased. Consequently, imparting conditional knowledge should be embedded into strategy training and reiterated regularly.

Self-Monitoring of Learning and Memory

As discussed in Chapter 3, the majority of children lack accurate appraisals (judgments of learning) for delayed recall of material they have just studied or learned (Brown & Sproson, 1987). Overestimating learning and subsequent retention and recall is a problem because it is associated with early termination of memorization efforts and satisfaction with ineffective strategies. Consequently, procedures for improving self-monitoring of learning and memory should be embedded in all of the strategy training sessions. Given what is known about judgments of learning, self-monitoring training should be a continual effort to demonstrate discrepancies between judgments of learning and future performance, not in a manner that discourages students but in a way that encourages more realistic self-appraisal. Emphasizing the difference between short-term and long-term memory is another way of encouraging more accurate self-appraisals. During this discussion, trainers should explain how quickly everyone forgets information so that the student does not assume forgetting is a personal shortcoming. Once students realize that immediate recall does not guarantee delayed recall, they begin to lower their estimates and act accordingly. Also, training self-monitoring is important because not all children, especially younger ones, will make the connection between strategy use and changes in performance. Furthermore, this type of training is important because not all strategies work equally well for all students. Although the trainer can usually identify which strategies are working best, it is important for the child or adolescent to come to the same realization.

Whenever content is being memorized (with or without effective strategies) the trainer should have the student estimate how much information he or she will remember when tested later. When doing so, always specify the interval, for example, five minutes, an hour, or a day. After the testing is complete, compare the student's prediction with the actual performance level. An alternative is to have trainees study material (using a memory strategy) until they believe they will be able to recall it with 90 to 100% accuracy. The purpose of predicting subsequent recall is to encourage more self-monitoring while using strategies and also to improve the accuracy of the student's metamemory judgments, as improved accuracy will lead to better allocation of study time and better selection of strategies. Additionally, self-monitoring during strategy usage affords an opportunity to evaluate the strategy's effectiveness and make adjustments as necessary. At times, monitoring will lead to abandonment of an ineffective strategy and selection of another. Strategy monitoring training in young children has been shown to bring about appropriate changes in strategic behavior. Essentially, self-monitoring training teaches children to monitor and understand the relationship between their strategic behavior and their performance.

Improving self-monitoring of learning is related to understanding the relative efficacy of strategies (see this chapter's section on demonstrating efficacy). Even when students detect improved performance following use of a new strategy, they will not necessarily attribute the improvement to the efficacy of the new strategy, failing to make the connection due to weak monitoring of learning and memory. Simply telling students that a strategy improves performance has been shown to make students more likely to apply the strategy to a task similar to the training situation (Pressley, Borkowski, & O'Sullivan, 1984). However, it is even more effective to have the student predict subsequent delayed recall any time a strategy is used to learn material. These predictions should then be compared with actual performance. During subsequent lessons, check to determine whether the student has improved the accuracy of judgments of learning by practicing with both old and new strategies and having the student predict performance for each. In summary, having the trainee predict performance each time information is memorized is an appropriate metamemory training method that not only improves self-monitoring of learning and memory, but also makes students realize the relative efficacy of strategies. Additional benefits of self-monitoring training include greater generalization, greater maintenance, more frequent strategy use, and increased metamemory knowledge. For more details on strategy monitoring training, see Ghatala, Levin, Pressley, and Lodico (1985).

Students should also be taught how to monitor learning and memory outside of the intervention sessions. Basically, they should be taught to self-test after extended delays of an hour up to a week, depending on the circumstances. Self-testing after delay is one of the most trainable and direct ways of encouraging and improving memory monitoring. Self-testing allows individuals to independently determine the state of their knowledge. Even early elementary-age children can be taught a self-testing strategy. For instance, Leal, Crays, and Moely (1985) taught third graders a self-testing strategy, emphasizing that if not all items were recalled, this meant that the material had not been learned and additional study was necessary. The 12 sessions of training increased the extent and efficiency with which the students self-monitored their study. Moreover, there was good evidence of generalization and maintenance.

Management of Memory Strategies

A high level of metamemory knowledge and strategy expertise is of little value if the individual does not possess good strategy management skills. Younger children in particular have difficulty accurately evaluating their memory functioning and performance and recognizing when strategies are making a difference (Pressley, Levin, & Ghatala, 1984). Directing them to use particular strategies and providing them with ongoing feedback is helpful, but ultimately they need to learn how to independently manage memory strategies. Self-monitoring of learning is one aspect of managing memory strategies; other aspects include selecting strategies for the task at hand, modifying strategies as needed, and integrating strategies.

Learning to effectively select, monitor, and integrate strategies will be especially effective once trainees have mastered more than one strategy. At that point, children can be taught to monitor their performance under different strategies and compare one strategy with another (Lodico, 1983). The best training is to actually have students apply two different strategies to the same task and then compare performance. When this comparative training begins, students should be reminded that there are many ways to remember information and that some ways are better than others. To learn and remember well, they must select the method that allows them to perform best. After material has been studied, the trainer should pose questions like, "Do you think you remembered more with the first method or the second method?" As training progresses, the trainee should be allowed to select a strategy before studying the material and then asked why he or she selected one strategy over another. In the Lodico study approximately 75% of the second-grade subjects could do the following: correctly assess when they remembered more items, attribute their better performance to the correct strategy, select the best strategy in succeeding practice, and indicate that they chose the strategy because it was more effective. Training in each of these elements is essential; for example, even when children realize differential strategy effects, they often do not use this information in subsequent strategy selection. In other words, monitoring performance, something most children do spontaneously, is not enough. Training is necessary in how to use strategy-efficacy knowledge in strategy selection.

For older children and adolescents who possess a repertoire of memory strategies, some training may be directed towards modifying and integrating strategies. Ongoing monitoring may make the learner aware that the standard application of a particular strategy may not be succeeding. Accordingly, students should be taught to stop and modify the strategy or select another. With sufficient metamemory and strategy expertise, students should be able to creatively adapt and combine strategies when the situation requires more than a standard application (Shaughnessy, 1981). The integration of strategies can be encouraged by teaching trainees how to apply multiple strategies to the same learning and memorization task.

DEMONSTRATING THE EFFICACY OF MEMORY STRATEGIES

Either before or immediately following the initial metamemory discussion with the trainee, the instructor should use a semantic clustering example to illustrate the efficacy of memory strategies. The purpose of this activity is to hook the student on the potential benefits of learning and using memory strategies, thereby gaining the student's interest and cooperation. For students about fifth grade and higher, here are the steps involved in demonstrating the benefits of adopting memory strategies:

1. Present the student with a list of 16 randomly ordered, common words that comprise four concrete categories, such as food and clothing. Tell the

student he or she will have 60 seconds to memorize the words without copying them.

2. After 60 seconds has elapsed, remove the list and engage the student in a conversation for at least two minutes. Then have the student write down the words he or she can recall, check the responses, and compute the percentage correct.

3. Next, explain to the student that you will now present him or her with a list of similar but different words, but only this time the words will be grouped into four categories. Again, the student will have 60 seconds to memorize the words without writing them down. Advise the student to first memorize the names of the four categories before reviewing the individual items.

4. After 60 seconds has elapsed, remove the list and engage the student in a conversation for at least two minutes. Then have the student write down the words he or she can recall. Finally, check the responses and compute the percentage correct.

5. Show the student the scores from each round. Typically, students will recall 40 to 60% of the unorganized words and 90% or more of the semantically clustered words. Emphasize the dramatic improvement, attributing the difference to the organization of the material. Point out that in the future, the student should organize information into categories and that this procedure will improve memory for that information.

For early elementary students, use the following procedure to illustrate the benefits of memory strategies:

1. Direct the student to try to remember the list of words that will be read. Then read a list of 15 names for common objects. Pause for about three seconds between each word. After a two-minute conversation or interference task, have the student orally recall the words and tabulate the number correct.

2. Then inform the student that a different list of words will be read. Only this time the student should imagine a picture of each object as its name is read. Again, after a two-minute conversation or interference task, have the student orally recall the words and tabulate the number correct.

3. Show the student the improvement in performance between the first and second word lists. (Nearly all students will improve their recall when they visualize the named objects.) Emphasize the improvement with the student, attributing the difference to visualizing the words. Explain how using such visualization strategies can help the student remember more information.

After such a demonstration, most students are now hooked and believe in the potential efficacy of the strategies they are about to learn. Convincing them of the efficacy of memory strategies serves to increase their motivation, effort, and maintenance. The efficacy discussions should continue throughout the intervention by showing the student improvement data and reminding him or her that the improvement is due to strategy use. The younger the student, the more clearly strategy efficacy must be communicated. Elementary school children are more likely to abandon new strategies unless they are explicitly and repeatedly informed of how the strategy improves their performance (Lodico, 1983). Older students are more likely to understand the connection and continue using a new strategy. Children who continue to receive feedback about the efficacy of a new memory strategy are more likely to continue using it (Kennedy & Miller, 1976).

PROMOTING GENERALIZATION AND MAINTENANCE

Unfortunately, individuals often do not apply well-learned memory strategies and mnemonics to other applicable materials and situations. Moreover, they often do not maintain the use of strategies after the intervention ends. Consequently, directed efforts towards generalization and maintenance are a critical element of all memory interventions. Overall, the acquisition of conditional knowledge surrounding the strategy may have the most impact. That is, knowing when, where, why, and how to use a strategy is the best insurance against limited use. Realizing the personal efficacy of the strategy further promotes generalization and maintenance. Personal efficacy can be so influential that a single exposure may be all that is required. For instance, in the first session of a memory intervention, this author discovered that the struggling high school student was already using a semantic clustering strategy on a regular basis. When asked why, the student reminded the author that he had briefly introduced the strategy to her during a study skills lesson two years earlier. She was immediately convinced of its effectiveness and had been using it ever since.

The literature on memory strategy training supports these procedures for increasing generalization and transfer:

1. The training needs to be intensive enough for the strategy procedures to be completely mastered.
2. The training should include periodic review and practice of the strategy.
3. The training should be conducted with a variety of materials and in different situations, as well as discussion about other situations and events in which the strategy would be effective.
4. The training should include conditional knowledge instruction: details on when, where, why, and how to use a strategy.
5. The trainee should continually be presented with data documenting the personal efficacy of the strategy by comparing performance with the strategy to performance without the strategy.

6. The trainee should be taught to attribute successful memory performance to strategy usage.

7. The trainee should be presented with different learning scenarios and then be required to select the best strategy for the task.

LENGTH OF TRAINING

The number of training sessions per strategy should vary depending on several factors, such as age, cognitive ability, severity of the memory impairment, motivation, and opportunities to apply the new skill. Trainees who need more elaborated instruction and more practice sessions include children who are younger, have a moderate to severe TBI, have a weakness in working memory, and have less motivation to learn and apply a new strategy. For example, in a study of strategy training with preschoolers who were taught semantic clustering, Lange and Pierce (1992) conducted seven training sessions with direct, detailed, and explicit instructions, followed by demonstrations and lots of practice. The training also included meta-cognitive instruction about when, why, and how to use the new strategy. The results indicated that younger children need a highly embellished instructional procedure over several sessions to produce maintenance and transfer of a newly learned strategy. Older children and adolescents who see the relevance of the training and faithfully attempt to apply the procedures outside of training sessions can master strategy use with fewer training sessions. Older students can also handle instruction and practice in more than one strategy at time; for example, during each session a few minutes might be spent reviewing a previously learned strategy before introducing and practicing another strategy. The degree of parent and teacher support is another variable that determines the length of the intervention training.

MEMORY STRATEGIES

Memory strategies are effortful, goal-directed, conscious cognitive operations used to improve memory performance. With instruction, children and adolescents can learn to use these strategies independently (what others can do to support memory is found in Chapter 8). Many of the recommended methods in this section are general strategies that can be adapted for different situations and content. These methods are distinct from well-known mnemonics in that mnemonics typically have lock-step procedures. Underlying each of the recommended strategies is one or more memory principles that have been derived from research. It is important for trainers and trainees to understand "why" the strategy works. Understanding why facilitates generalization and adaptations that are consistent with the empirically supported principle. The suggested procedures under each strategy include the typical, basic steps. The trainer will need to incorporate general training practices recommended previously in this chapter, such as metacognitive instruction, collecting data, and ongoing practice and review.

Organizational Strategies: Semantic Clustering

Cognitive psychologists have long promoted a memory model that emphasizes the inherent organization of memory. For example, semantic knowledge is thought to be arranged in schemas, and episodic memories are thought to be associated with scripts. The strong neurological connections among related pieces of information are supported by brain-based research. For example, an individual can retrieve a word in the same semantic category as a previously retrieved word more quickly than an unrelated word. Numerous applied studies have consistently found that encoding of organized information produces improved retention and recall. Thus, a primary memory principle is that organized input is retained and retrieved better than disorganized or random input. The information becomes even more memorable when the individual organizes the information in ways that personally make sense. The best example of an organizational strategy is semantic clustering, a robust method of memorization that many children discover prior to adolescence. Semantic clustering consists of recognizing and grouping information according to meaningful categories.

Training Procedures

1. Explain to the trainee that memory performs better when input is organized and that one of the best ways to organize input is to group information into categories.
2. With younger children, use pictures of objects that can be easily sorted into three to five basic semantic categories like animals, tools, clothing, and so on. Each item should be solidly colored and the number of colors limited to five. Tell the trainee to organize the cards into groups that go together. If the child organizes by color, explain that color is not an effective way to remember the items, and provide guidance until the trainee is able to group them by higher-level characteristics.
3. With older children, present a list of words that can be grouped into four to five semantic categories like animals, tools, clothing, and so on. Tell the trainee to reorganize the list into groups that go together. If the trainee begins to organize by first letter or some other non-semantic characteristic, explain that such organization is not effective for remembering the information and provide guidance until the semantic groupings are formed.
4. Teach the student how to encode information that is semantically clustered. It is vital that the student learn to focus on the organization rather than rehearsing individual elements (Parente & Herrmann, 1996). So, direct the student to first memorize the number of categories, the name of each

category, and the number of items in each category before rehearsing individual items one category at a time.

5. Finally, teach the trainee to follow the same sequence during retrieval. First, the trainee should recall the number of categories, the name of each category, and number of items in each category. Then, the trainee should recall as many items under each category as possible. To retrieve missing items, teach the trainee to mentally run through exemplars of the semantic category in an effort to recognize missing items.

Applications　In subsequent sessions, apply the semantic clustering to course content the student needs to learn. For instance, the method can be applied when studying for a history test. Typically, historical information is presented to the student in chronological order. The student might reorganize period facts into categories such as important people, locations, events, changes, and so on. Science is another academic subject that lends itself to organizing information into clusters of related information. Organizational methods, other than semantic clustering, will also enhance memory. For example, historical information could all be written on a time line, or graphic organizers could be used to study a narrative.

Verbal Association Strategies: Elaboration

Elaboration, sometimes referred to as elaborative rehearsal, is a powerful associative learning method that increases consolidation and recall, especially for semantic learning. Elaboration is the effortful process of connecting new information from a learning event with related prior knowledge. In general, elaboration occurs when individuals reflect on how new information is related to already known facts, concepts, and events. Elaboration during encoding serves to integrate new content with prior knowledge, thereby facilitating understanding, consolidation, and subsequent retrieval. At the neurological level, elaboration creates additional pathways between related memory traces (Hunt & Einstein, 1981). In effect, elaboration develops alternate retrieval routes and facilitates inferential, reconstructive processes when a response is not completely retrieved. The elaboration strategy is based on the principle that information that is associated with related knowledge is more memorable, whereas unrelated information is forgotten more quickly (Hockley, 1992). Classroom teachers can also provide elaboration for learners (see Chapter 8). However, capable students should be taught to elaborate independently because self-generated elaborations, even when they are not sophisticated or entirely accurate, are more effective than those provided by an instructor (Grier & Ratner, 1996).

Training Procedures

1. Explain to the trainee that elaboration is the processes of linking new facts with already known facts and that elaboration makes remembering easier

because the new facts can be recalled by thinking about the already known related information. This author often uses the analogy of needing to open a word processing file stored on a computer before new information can be added to the file. Stopping to think about how new and existing information is related opens up the brain's file on the topic, thereby ensuring that the new information will be stored in the correct file.

2. Present the trainee with some new facts from a science or social studies topic. Direct the trainee to verbalize some information that he or she already knows about that topic, and then to think about and explain how the new information is connected with the prior knowledge. For example, a new science fact might be that ocean levels will rise because of global warming. After thinking about it, the student might make the connection between rising temperatures, melting ice, and rising sea levels. Once the connection is made the student should write it down as "rising sea levels—melting ice produces more water."

3. After the student understands the process, practice by having the student read some expository text, stopping to write down each important fact gleaned from the text. A related known fact should be written alongside, even if the student is unsure of the exact connection. Specific links are better than vague or general links.

4. After the student understands the purpose, process, and efficacy of elaboration, teach the student to use a standard prompt that will cue related knowledge. The research identified prompt is, "Why does this new fact make sense?" The student should then be directed to frame the associated information as the answer to a question and write down something like "sea levels will rise because melting ice produces more water."

5. For students who have difficulty elaborating independently, the trainer might model the process through thinking aloud or remind the student of already known related information.

Applications   Elaboration has numerous applications because the method can be applied to almost any academic course or type of learning. Generalization is relatively easy once the student understands the value of stopping to think about what is already known and how the new information is related. Elaboration can be conducted while reading text, studying notes, or listening to a presentation. Students should be encouraged to apply the method to material they study outside of the training sessions and then report back on what they did and the resulting performance.

Rehearsal Strategies: Cumulative Rehearsal

Rehearsal refers to any self-directed repetition of material. Rehearsal might involve repeated reading, repeated writing, oral repetition, or subvocal repetition. Ask anyone to commit something to memory and the first course of action typically will be rehearsal. Most people, including educators and psychologists, believe that rote rehearsal improves retention and recall of information. Unfortunately, rote rehearsal does more for short-term memory than it does for long-term memory (E. L. Glisky & M. L. Glisky, 2002). In fact, simple rehearsal is relatively ineffective when the goal is to permanently store information. Craik and Watkins (1973) came to the stunning conclusion that when there is only one study period consisting of just rote rehearsal, there seems to be no relationship between number of repetitions and amount learned (Craik & Watkins). Furthermore, there is no evidence that practicing rehearsal strategies improves long-term memory functioning among individuals with long-term memory impairments. In reality, simply repeating material is not a particularly effective learning strategy for individuals with memory deficits (Wilson, 2009). Rote rehearsal is ineffective because material learned by passive, rote procedures forms a separate memory representation that is not interwoven with related knowledge (Emilien et al., 2004). Although rote rehearsal does not improve free recall, it does increase the amount of information that can be recognized (Gardiner, Gawlik, & Richardson-Klavehn, 1994). Thus, training students in cumulative, subvocal rehearsal should be limited to those who are developmentally delayed or have processing speed, short-term memory, or working memory impairments, in addition to long-term memory impairments. Cumulative rehearsal consists of adding each new time as it is presented and then repeating the entire list from the beginning. The underlying principle is that more information can be encoded when information is maintained in short-term memory for a longer interval.

Training Procedures

1. Explain to the trainee how whispering information over and over can extend how long information will be retained in short-term memory and might increase how well it will be remembered after a delay.

2. After the student has been directed to repeat the information in a whispering mode, slowly read a list of words to the student, pausing a few seconds between each word. Teach the student to add new words to the rehearsal in a cumulative fashion. For example, if the words are "cow, tree, door," the student should repeat "cow" until "tree" is introduced and then say "cow, tree" until "door" is added and then say "cow, tree, door." Many young students have a tendency to only rehearse the most recent item, such as saying "tree, tree, tree" and dropping "cow" when the second item is added.

3. For students with low verbal episodic memory but strong visuospatial episodic memory, a more interesting and challenging variation is to add a visual component during the cumulative rehearsal. For example, an n-back procedure can be used with a regular deck of cards. In n-back, the trainee is to remember the card that was displayed n number of cards back. In 2-back for example, if the sequence of cards individually displayed and removed is 6-King-4-8-2. The trainee should say "6" when the 4 is displayed, "King"

when the 8 is displayed and so on. This task will be very challenging without using a cumulative rehearsal strategy. For example, a cumulative rehearsal strategy that works is to keep repeating "6-King" until the 4 is flipped up, then say "6" followed by the repeating of "King-4" until the 8 is turned over. Essentially, this is an ongoing cumulative rehearsal strategy in which the no-longer-needed item is dropped as another is added. N-back practice has been shown to improve working memory performance (Jaeggi, Buschkuehl, Jonides, & Perrig, 2008).

Applications   First, basic rehearsal strategies apply to functional everyday memory situations. For example, an individual with poor verbal episodic memory might successfully complete four-step directions by using rehearsal to maintain the sequence in working memory. For instance, maybe the individual is learning to fry an egg and the steps are, "Put butter in the pan, turn the heat to medium, put in the egg, and put a lid on the pan." The sequence might be repeated over and over, dropping each step as it is completed. In the classroom, students might use subvocal rehearsal to maintain instructions, words, or ideas until they can write them down on paper.

Dual Coding Strategies: Recoding Information

Dual coding refers to encoding information in both visual and verbal formats. During learning activities it's not something that happens automatically. Usually, a conscious, direct effort is required before individuals will encode information both ways. Dual coding requires that information received in one format be recoded into the other. Humans display a distinct preference for verbal coding. The preference is so strong that children over 8 years of age usually recode visually perceived information into verbal information. However, verbal to visual recoding is less common. Consequently, students seldom recode verbal content into visual code unless directed to do so. This ingrained behavior is unfortunate because dual coding research has established the increased memorability of information that is encoded both verbally and visually. Dual coding is thought to improve recall because an additional retrieval route is created.

Training Procedures

1. Explain to the student that recoding means that words should be pictured and viewed objects should be named. Add that recoding creates two ways of remembering. So, if a person can't remember the words, he or she might remember the pictures and by that means arrive at the correct response.
2. Practice recoding visual input by first having the student name objects that have been displayed. Proceed with having the student practice describing a pictured scene.

3. Practice recoding of verbal input by first having the student pause to visualize each word read from a list. Proceed with having the student pause to visualize a detailed scene after reading a paragraph in a narrative.

4. Remind the student that when reviewing content in preparation for a test to think about the information in both the verbal and visual modes. Ask the student to keep a study log and indicate in the log each time information is recoded.

Applications   The dual coding principle and recoding strategy applies to any and all perceived information but is especially beneficial when trying to commit verbal academic material to memory. To achieve the dual coding advantage, no specific mnemonic procedure is necessary. When listening to or studying verbal information, students can picture it any way they like. Regardless of how they visualize the information, the probability of recall will be increased (Roediger, Gallo, & Geraci, 2002). Naturally, recoding of information is critical for children and adolescents with an impairment in one or the other mode. For instance, children with normal visuospatial memory but deficient verbal memory should be taught to visualize verbal input.

Retrieval Strategies: Self-Testing

Another prominent memory principle is that consolidation, long-term retention, and retrieval is strengthened each time a memory is retrieved. The retrieval principle accounts for the fact that testing improves learning and retention. Consequently, actually retrieving information is much more effective than just reviewing it. A straightforward approach to ensuring that retrieval occurs is self-testing.

Training Procedures

1. Explain to the student that the act of remembering strengthens memories, especially when the student must come up with the answer or correct information. Add that reading over information and rehearsing it is not as effective as self-testing.

2. Using a review sheet with questions and answers, have the student practice covering up the answers while reading the question and retrieving the answer, followed by checking to see if the response is correct. With younger children who have spelling words, the words should be covered while the student attempts to retrieve the correct spelling. With older elementary students, study cards can be created and used to practice self-testing.

3. Ask the student to keep a study log and record every time self-testing is used.

Applications   Using retrieval to strengthen memories applies well to nearly every form of academic and semantic learning. Self-testing also enhances performance on subsequent classroom exams because of the encoding specificity principle. That is, when information retrieved during self-testing is re-encoded as the answers to specific questions, similar test questions in the future will serve as cues for the stored information.

Spaced Practice Strategies: Planning a Review Schedule

Another well-known memory principle is that spaced and expanding interval practice and review is much more effective than massed practice or studying material only once. Ideally, students should first review material the day after it was first encountered, such as reviewing class notes a day after they were written. Intervals between follow-up study sessions can then become longer and longer. The review schedule should approximate the typical forgetting curve; for example, most forgetting occurs within the first 24 hours after content is first learned. However, getting older students to independently follow a regular review schedule is unrealistic. Perhaps, the best approach is to train students to start studying for exams well in advance.

Training Procedures

1. Explain to the student that waiting until the night before an exam to study for a test is not an effective way of memorizing material, especially if the material needs to be recalled again after the exam. Continue to explain how test performance will improve if the material is studied on at least three different occasions.
2. Select an academic subject the student is struggling in and devise a spaced review plan that includes these strategies: reviewing notes and readings one day after they were first written or read; reviewing the material a second time a few days later; and studying a third time the night before the exam. Have the student enter specific dates, times, and content covered into an assignment calendar.
3. Monitor the student's adherence to this plan, attributing improved test performance to the spaced review strategy.

Applications   This strategy particularly applies to content and procedures that must be mastered for a lifetime of use, such as learning grammar rules, learning another language, and learning the rules of the road for a driver's license examination. Ideally, expanded intervals occur between multiple reviews, such as reviewing after one day, one week, two weeks, one month, three months, and six months. Another reason spaced reviews are effective is that they reduce the interference caused by studying too much material at one time.

Reducing Interference Strategies: Study Before Sleeping

The research on the benefits of sleep (reviewed in Chapter 2) leads to an obvious strategy: Material that needs to be remembered the next morning should be studied in the evening shortly before going to sleep. Although unconscious nocturnal consolidation processes may strengthen memories, a sleep cycle also enhances recall by preventing retroactive interference. Consequently, this strategy may be helpful for students whose recall is especially vulnerable to retroactive interference.

Training Procedures

1. Inform the student about how information studied in the evening will be recalled better the following day than material that is studied several hours before going to sleep. However, be certain to clarify that the student should not wait until late in the evening to begin studying, as fatigue may undue any benefits from sleep. Rather, the student should study at normal times but do a final review of the material before retiring for the evening. The critical factor is that the content that needs to be remembered is the last content studied that day. The trainer should also emphasize that an adequate amount of sleep is required for the effect to take place.
2. This procedure cannot really be practiced during memory training sessions. Consequently, the student might be assigned to keep a log of which subjects are studied last each day and compare the study pattern with performance on tests administered the following day.

Applications   Obviously, this strategy applies to nearly any academic course of study. In everyday functioning, an example might be the need to remember to complete a sequence of activities the following morning. In such instances, the details should be reviewed before retiring for the evening.

Retrieval Strategies: Using Context Cues

Remembering personal perceptions and the context of the learning event has been found to enhance retrieval of factual information. Students who are tested in environments different from those where the learning occurred don't perform as well as students tested in the same environment. When the learning environment is unavailable, trying to recall the episodic details about the learning environment is a useful mnemonic technique (Smith, 1979). This simple retrieval strategy is based on the principle that contextual cues facilitate retrieval of factual information.

Training Procedures

1. Explain to the student that trying to remembering what was happening when factual information was being presented or learned may help recall of the factual information. For example, remembering the scene, action, or personal feelings that occurred during a science class might help the student remember the science facts and concepts that were taught at that time.

2. In an interactive fashion, similar to a classroom lesson, complete a brief science or social studies lesson with the student.

3. Two to seven days later, administer a quiz on the content covered in the lesson. Before the student answers the questions, direct the student to envision the scene, as well as the interactions and perceptions that occurred during the lesson.

4. Direct the student to use this strategy during an upcoming classroom quiz or exam and report back on what contextual information was recalled and whether that might have reminded the student of some factual information.

Applications   This strategy can be applied to nearly every situation in which material is presented or studied in one setting but needs to be recalled in another setting. An everyday example might occur when a child or adolescent can't remember what a parent told him or her to bring home from school. Recalling the scene at the breakfast table that morning might help jog the memory.

MNEMONICS

Mnemonics are specialized memory techniques that enhance encoding, retention, and retrieval. They are based on the principle that the effectiveness of encoding determines the success of retrieval (Mastropieri & Scruggs, 1998). Whereas mnemonics and memory strategies both involve manipulation and transformation of information, mnemonics are distinct in that they usually involve memory representations that bear little or no relation to the conceptual content of the material being committed to memory (Bellezza, 1981). Mnemonics create unique cuing structures, usually in the form of visual images, sentences, or rhymes, that mediate retrieval. During retrieval the cue is accessed first, and this in turn leads to recall of the desired information. The characteristics that make mnemonic structures successful include meaningfulness, organization, association, visualization, and interest. Mnemonics also improve retention and retrieval through creating additional memory codes, such as construction of a visual image to associate with auditory information. Over the past 30 years, an abundance of empirical evidence has supported the use of mnemonic strategies to improve learning and memory (Eslinger, 2002; Levin, 1993; Mastropieri & Scruggs, 1991). For example, in a meta-analysis of 34 studies involving the use of mnemonic strategies with students who have learning disabilities, the overall effect size was a very strong 1.62 (Mastropieri, Sweda, & Scruggs, 2000).

Essentially, mnemonics consist of strategies for associating relatively difficult to remember input with images or words already well established in long-term memory, thereby making retrieval easier. Mnemonics are particularly beneficial when they are used to associate meaning with information that initially has little meaning for the learner. That is, mnemonics are needed most when the learner doesn't possess a schema that allows for easy assimilation of new, unfamiliar information. In such instances, mnemonic devices create a simple artificial structure to which the new information can be attached. Research has indicated that mnemonics function like a temporary bridge between new learning and established memory structures. Each time the information is retrieved, new associations with related schemas are formed, eventually obviating the need for the mnemonic aid. For example, students may initially depend on the acronym *HOMES* to recall the names of the Great Lakes, but after numerous associations have been made, the use of the mnemonic declines (Bellezza, 1981).

Most mnemonics involve the use of mental imagery to meaningfully link difficult to remember verbal information with images that are readily recalled. Imagery is a form of elaborative processing that creates new and unique associations between items to be remembered. Examples include the keyword, pegword, and loci methods (discussed in the next subsections). The effectiveness of imagery mnemonics, especially for concrete information, has been well documented in numerous studies. For instance, imagery has been used to effectively improve recall in individuals with mild to moderate acquired brain injury. TBI victims typically have problems with the spontaneous use of mental imagery, but with imagery training and trainer-provided images, their retention improves, as long as some prompting is provided (Richardson, 1995). There are also countless studies documenting the efficacy of imagery for learning and retaining academic knowledge. There are two explanations as to why imagery is effective: (a) converting verbal information into visual images is dual-encoding that creates more retrieval pathways, and (b) mental imagery creates a single integrated memory representation. Whereas, the recoding of visual stimuli into verbal information tends to develop naturally, the reverse does not seem to be true. Children and adolescents seldom report the use of imagery to remember verbal content but they will use imagery when directed to do so. Consequently, even students without memory problems will benefit from instruction and training in visual mnemonics.

Older children benefit more from elaborate imagery mnemonics than younger children. Thus, training in more involved imagery techniques is best reserved for children older than 8 years of age. Although children younger than 8 automatically construct imaginal representations of what they hear (Foley, Wilder, McCall, & Van Vorst, 1993), they have difficulty deliberately creating images that make memorable associations. Consequently, they perform better when associative pictures are provided. However, producing pictures for younger children may not be worth the additional time and effort because young children have difficulty retrieving images even when pictures are provided during learning. It seems that younger children have more difficulty retrieving the imagery mediators, such as the cues that bring the interactive images to mind (Pressley & Levin, 1980). Consequently, they will need retrieval cues, sometimes even the picture itself, to retrieve the image and make the association (Ryan, Ledger, & Weed, 1987).

Keyword

Keyword is a mnemonic that combines verbal information with visual imagery. The process of forming and retrieving a keyword mnemonic consists of several stages: the first stage is the acoustical link stage in which the learner thinks of a word (the keyword) that sounds like the target word; in the second stage the learner creates an image with the keyword that makes the meaning of the target word apparent; and in the final stage the learner first retrieves the keyword and then recalls the image with the keyword that leads to the correct response. For example, if a student wants to remember that the Spanish word "pato" means "duck," the student might first think that "pato" sounds like "pot" and then create an image connecting pot and duck, such as a duck splashing in a pot of water. The more unique, ridiculous, personal, and interactive the images, the easier they are to recall. With young children and those who have learning disabilities, the trainer or teacher might need to provide the keywords and images (see Chapter 8).

Of all the school-relevant mnemonics, the keyword technique is the most researched and the most robust. Consistently high effect sizes have been reported. In a meta-analysis of 34 studies involving LD students, Scruggs and Mastropieri (1990) found an extremely high effect size of 1.62. Such high effect sizes translate into a 50 to 100% improvement in learning (Mastropieri & Scruggs, 1991; Pressley, 1982). Mastropieri and Scruggs report that LD students who learn material with the keyword mnemonic consistently outperform students who don't use keyword or who fail to use metamemory strategies. In a study with 64 12-year-old LD students, Condus, Marshall, and Miller (1986), found that students who learned vocabulary with the keyword method significantly outperformed students using all other methods. Although the students in other learning conditions tested well initially, they were unable to maintain their new knowledge across two- and eight-week intervals, whereas those learning with keywords were. In another study with four third-grade LD children (Uberti, Scruggs, & Mastropieri, 2003), students who received keyword-linked vocabulary instruction recalled 75% of the content, while those with nonmnemonic instruction remembered only 37%. Mastropieri and Scruggs (1998) also emphasize how well students with cognitive disabilities can remember state capitals when the keyword method is used.

Training Procedures

1. Say a word and have the student tell you another word (a keyword) that sounds like the target word. Emphasize that the keyword need only sound like the first part of the target word. For example, if the target word is "Madison," the keyword could be "mad." Practice this procedure with a variety of words: some familiar and some unfamiliar; some short and some long; and some concrete and some abstract.

2. Once the student can proficiently generate a keyword for most target words, teach the student how to create images in which the keyword is interacting with the response associated with the target word. For example, if the task is to remember that "pato" means duck, then the image should combine "pot" (the keyword) with duck. It's important to model this step for the trainee.

3. Have the trainee describe the image he or she has created and provide feedback on the quality of the image. Emphasize that the best images are interactive, as interactive images are more effective than static images. Also, be sure that details unrelated to the concept are left out of the image. Younger children and those who have difficulty with verbal expression should be required to draw the image.

4. Practice the retrieval steps while always requiring the trainee to first state the keyword and then describe the image before expressing the response.

Applications   The keyword method can be used when learning a variety of semantic material like science and social studies facts, but it is especially effective when learning new English vocabulary words or when learning another language. For some linked information, such as the names of state capitals, it works best to create a keyword for each name and then bind the two keywords together in one image (see example in Chapter 8). That way, starting with either name leads to the image with the answer. Another variation of keyword, the Paired Associates Strategy, has students write the target word and keyword pairs on study cards, draw the image with the keyword in it, and then do a self-test (Bulgren, Hock, Schumaker, & Deshler, 1995).

Pegword

Pegword is a visual imagery mnemonic that incorporates rhyming and numbers. The "pegs" consist of the numbers 1 to 10 or 20 paired with easily pictured rhyming words, such as "one is a bun, two is a shoe, and three is a tree." A peg is something that can be remembered automatically and to which to-be-remembered information can be attached. The learner creates an image that pairs each item to be learned with the predetermined images associated with particular numbers. For example, the first item to be memorized is visually linked with a bun, the second with a shoe, and so on.

Training Procedures

1. First, the student must select and memorize the pegs. Together with the student, select a rhyming word for each number, making sure the rhyme is a common word that is easily visualized. Write down the rhyming pegs and have the student rehearse them until they are memorized. If necessary, a picture of each peg can be created.

2. For each item to be memorized, the student is directed to create an image in which the item is paired with the peg. For example, if the first item on a shopping list is carrots, an image of carrots sticking out of a bun would suffice.

3. As each image is created, have the student describe the image and give feedback on its memorability. Associations that are funny, unusual, and interactive with no unrelated imagery work best. Make suggestions when the student has difficulty generating useful associations.

4. Have the student practice retrieving the information by first reciting each numbered, rhyming peg in order. Saying "one is a bun" will certainly recover the image of a bun. As the image of a bun is retrieved, the item depicted with it should automatically be recalled.

Applications   The pegword method is ideal for remembering material that needs to be recalled sequentially, but it can also be used effectively with unordered content. It can be applied to nearly any set of items that needs to be memorized, as long as the number of items does not exceed the number of pegs. In everyday functioning, it might be used to remember a shopping list. In addition to using numbers to recall the pegwords, other familiar sequences or groups, such as days of the week or names of family members, can be used.

Loci

Another evidence-based mnemonic known as loci involves associating items with a sequence of familiar objects or locations. For instance, a student might associate information to be learned with furniture and objects in his or her home. The home objects are a fixed arrangement of elements that the memorizer already knows. To remember an item, the student creates an image in which each item to be remembered is associated with a different object or location. For example, when a student needs to memorize that the Spaniards, French, and English were the main European nations to explore North America, the student might create an image of each group associated with each of the three primary objects in his or her bedroom. The first image might consist of an armored Spaniard on a horse standing on the student's bed; the second image might include a Frenchman wearing a beret working at the student's desk, and the third image could be a character dressed like a Pilgrim sitting on the student's dresser. During retrieval, the student pictures the bedroom objects, recalls the associative image, and recognizes the response.

Training Procedures

1. The first step is to have the student identify the objects in his or her bedroom in clockwise or counterclockwise order. If the items being studied out-number bedroom objects, then have the student proceed through other rooms in the house until there are enough objects.

2. Proceeding in order through the room or rooms, have the student create an image that pairs the household object with the item being learned. If the student needs to recall the items sequentially, then the first item is paired with the first item in the room and so on. When items need not be recalled sequentially, the student should still visualize and use the household objects in order so that nothing is omitted during retrieval.

3. Have the student describe the image he or she has created and provide feedback on the quality of the image. Explain that the best images are unusual or funny and that details unrelated to the concept should be left out.

4. Have the student practice retrieving the information. Household objects should be visualized one at a time in the order they are arranged in the house. Once the student has pictured the well-known object, he or she should try to recall the item that was paired with the object. Successful recall of the image should automatically produce the correct response.

Applications   Although the loci mnemonic works well for remembering sequential information, it can also be used with unordered content. The method is suitable for nearly every set of academic facts, concepts, or procedures that needs to be memorized. It could also be used to remember everyday information, such as remembering a list of chores that needs to be completed. If loci is used extensively, a different sequence of objects or locations should be used occasionally to reduce the interference that will result from making too many associations with the same objects.

Verbal Mnemonics

Nearly every student is familiar with verbal mnemonics because they have traditionally been taught in the classroom. Verbal mnemonics include the following: acronyms in which the first letters of target words are combined to form a word or phrase; acrostics in which the first letters of target words are used as the first letters of words in a sentence; and sentences or stories that incorporate the target words. Unfortunately, acronyms, acrostics, or sentences can be very difficult to create and can be forgotten because they are not always associated with an automatically retrieved memory representation. Moreover, single letters make poor retrieval cues; for example, *HOMES* might be retrieved but what the *H* stands for might not be. Not surprisingly, first-letter mnemonics are not supported empirically despite their popularity (Levin, 1993). Training in the use of verbal mnemonics is particularly ill advised for children and adolescents who have broad verbal abilities deficits, a verbally related learning disability, or an impairment in verbal episodic memory.

COMPUTERIZED INTERVENTIONS

Computer-directed practice can increase learning and delayed recall. For instance, in a study of at-risk middle school students, Metcalfe, Kornell, and Son (2007) found that computer-directed study can produce significantly more learning and recall than self-directed study. The experiment was a success because the program incorporated highly effective memory strategies: elaborative processing, encoding specificity, multiple tests, and spaced practice. By providing realistic feedback, the computer program also reduced inaccurate judgments of learning, thereby encouraging additional study. In contrast, software that employs an interesting game format to elicit rehearsal strategies has not produced positive results. For example, Oyen and Bebko (1996) discovered that a computer context can bring about a large increase in the number of children using rehearsal. Unfortunately, increased overt rehearsal did not result in significantly improved recall. Of course, computers can be extremely helpful as external aides (see the section on external memory aides). Not only can they remind individuals with severe prospective memory impairments to perform actions on time, but they can also support brain-injured amnesic individuals by storing memory notebooks and checklists.

Most of the research-based, innovative computerized training that is available commercially is designed for children and adolescents with working memory and attentional disorders (Gray, Robertson, Pentland, & Anderson, 1992). For example, *Cogmed* offers an Internet-based program (found at www.cogmed.com) that incorporates working memory practice in a game format. The software program was supported through several studies (reviewed in Klingberg, 2009) before it was released commercially. Research on this program indicates that it can increase working memory performance and improve attention. *Jungle Memory* is another Internet-based program that can boost working memory performance (found at www.junglememory.com).

There are several advantages to using computers to provide or support training of effective memory strategies: (a) these tools offer endless practice opportunities at low cost; (b) the programs can automatically vary the content; (c) they can monitor performance and provide feedback that encourages sufficient study time; and (d) they can collect data and inform the student of strategy efficacy. On the other hand, it may be difficult to design software that can successfully impart metamemory knowledge, and computer games may interfere with encoding because they introduce additional processing requirements beyond trying to remember.

HOME INTERVENTIONS

Regardless of the child's age or the severity of the memory impairment, parents can play an important role in the success of memory interventions. Even without their knowing, most parents have already played a crucial role in the development of their children's memory functions. For instance, early childhood research has confirmed that many mothers naturally teach their children memory strategies before their children begin formal education. In a study with 3-year-olds, Larkina, Guler, Kleinknecht, and Bauer (2008) found that children's memory is enhanced when mothers verbally and physically sort items into categories and name the categories. In addition to emphasizing grouping and organization during encoding, mothers also encouraged retrieval by categories, and this behavior also improved the preschooler's performance. Furthermore, mothers have been observed encouraging elaboration through using an elaborative style when conversing, talking about an ongoing event, and recalling episodic memories. The frequency of questions asked by mothers during conversations is also positively correlated with children's recall and consistent with the finding that retrieval is more difficult for young children than is encoding. Finally, even basic parent-child conversations about past events can improve young children's abilities to recall past experiences. Thus, ordinary parent-child social interactions can influence the development of memory functions and strategies.

With school-age children who have mild to moderate impairments, parents are willing to support interventions that advance academic learning. A key to enlisting parental support is sharing effectiveness data and helping parents understand why particular strategies work. Ideally, parents might observe some of the memory training sessions or occasionally meet with the trainer. Alternatives include good written communication and detailed step-by-step written instructions for implementing strategies. Once they are informed, parents can reinforce memory strategy practice and encourage the child to adhere to the procedures.

In severe cases where children have amnesia or prospective memory impairments, actual in-home interventions are necessary. In such cases, more extensive consultation and training with parents is necessary so that they not only understand what the child must do but also learn to modify their interactions with the child. Home interventions should begin with restructuring the environment. The purpose of restructuring the environment is to reduce memory demands. For example, frequently used objects should be stored in the same locations and daily routines should be followed. Next, external memory aides, such as timers and procedural checklists should be put in place. Finally, strategies and mnemonics should be taught, practiced, and used consistently.

EXTERNAL MEMORY AIDS

In cases of severe memory impairment, such as amnesia resulting from traumatic brain injury, teaching children and adolescents to use external memory aids is a crucial component of improving the quality of their daily functioning and learning (Kapur, Glisky, & Wilson, 2004). When memory impairments are severe, external aids are actually more effective than mnemonic strategies or rehearsal (Zencius, Wesolowski, Burke, & McQuade, 1991). Although most of the research on memory aids has been conducted with adults, the same principles and materials are appropriate for memory-impaired youth because most of the devices have as much utility with youth as they do with adults. Training to use a memory aid includes teaching children, their parents, and their teachers about the device and its features, as well as teaching children how to use the aid in everyday situations.

Memory Checklists

Creating and using a memory checklist is one method that works well in both school and home environments. Memory checklists are external aids that can help individuals with severe memory impairments to learn and remember skills and procedures (Zencius et al., 1991). A memory checklist consists of written procedural steps, along with boxes for checking off each step upon completion. Checklists can be used to teach and prompt recall of any daily function, vocational task, or academic task that involves step-by-step procedures. A checklist with the steps necessary for solving arithmetic problems is a prime academic example. Checklists are particularly beneficial because mnemonics are not very suitable for remembering daily activities and step-by-step procedures. Checklists can be developed for each specific task that needs to be recalled; thus, generalization is not a concern. Checklists also have the advantage of being constantly available. However, checklist usage need not be permanent because its use may serve to consolidate memories and strengthen retrieval. For instance, when checklists were used in the Zencius et al. (1991) study, brain-injured patients rapidly reacquired daily living skills that were otherwise difficult to remember. Furthermore, repeated use of the checklists led to at least some of the information being retained, and performance remained at 100% after the checklists were eventually withdrawn. Clearly, individuals with severe memory impairments can learn even complex tasks through the use of checklists (Kime, Lamb, & Wilson, 1996). Checklists are typically organized into what's called a "memory book" or "memory notebook" that can be kept with the individual at all times. A memory book also should include other important information and reminders that the student needs to access regularly.

Miscellaneous Memory Aids

To cope with severe memory impairments and learn to function more independently, children with severe memory impairments may need to use several memory aids. For instance, Wilson (2009) reported that adults with severe memory impairments who utilized six or more memory aids and strategies were more likely to live independently than those who employed fewer devices. When selecting memory aids, it's essential to first determine which behaviors and learning need the most support. Memory aides are mainly cuing devices or storage devices. The list of possibilities includes:

- Diaries or journals
- Memory books or memory notebooks
- Alarms and timers

- Reminders provided by computers
- Schedules and assignment calendars
- Checklists with step-by-step procedures
- Folders for organizing notes and materials
- Lists of activities that need to be completed
- Step-by-step instructions for using a strategy

PSYCHOPHARMACOLOGICAL TREATMENTS

In the future, mild to severe memory impairments in children and adolescents may be alleviated through psychopharmacological treatment. Although no such medications are routinely used with youth, the findings of some pharmacological studies and current usage with Alzheimer's patients hold promise for the future. For example, cholinesterase inhibitors are already being used with Alzheimer's patients. There have also been medication trials with subjects who have suffered hippocampal atrophy. In these studies selective serotonin reuptake inhibitors (SSRIs) have been shown to have positive effects on memory. One experiment that involved a 9- to 12-month regimen of the SSRI paroxetine improved verbal declarative memory among adult patients with PTSD and increased their hippocampal volume by 4.6% (Vermetten, Vythilingam, Southweick, Charney, & Bremner, 2003). As reviewed in Bremner and Narayan (1998), a study at Rockefeller University reported that Dilantin reversed stress-induced hippocampal atrophy. Apparently, these medications can produce positive outcomes because the neurons in the hippocampus have the capacity to regenerate themselves, yet it's still not certain that hippocampal atrophy can be reversed (Bremner & Narayan).

Other potential pharmacological treatments for memory impairments encompass a wide range of drugs that act on many different neurotransmitters. Some of these medications are classified as cognitive enhancers, designed to improve conditions ranging from normal forgetting to amnesia. For example, estrogen administered to postmenopausal women seems to affect the brain's organization for memory, leading to improved performance on verbal memory tasks (Sherwin, 1997). Emilien et al. (2004) reported that dopamine agonists may improve anterograde memory impairments. Experiments have also been conducted with a variety of other compounds. For instance, in an experiment with a compound known as donepezil, two TBI victims showed significantly improved memory function within three weeks (Taverni, Seliger, & Lightman, 1998). Another class of drugs known as ampakine drugs has been found to facilitate cellular processes involved in long-term memory encoding. For an in-depth discussion of pharmacological treatment for memory impairments see Emilien et al. (2004).

There is one psychopharmacological treatment routinely used with children and adolescents, but it is not ostensibly given for memory problems. Methylphenidate (Ritalin) is known to boost working memory performance by about 10% (Metha,

Owen, Sahakian et al., 2000). This finding is consistent with other evidence that the consumption of psychostimulants, such as amphetamines, caffeine, and nicotine, enhances memory functioning (Anderson, 2000). Glucose administration has also been shown to enhance memory in humans (Emilien et al., 2004). Even treatment with antioxidants holds promise for reducing damage and promoting recovering after a TBI (Chan, 1996). However, the popular Ginkgo Biloba offers very limited benefits for memory (Oken, Storzbach, & Kaye, 1998).

MEMORY INTERVENTIONS FOR TRAUMATIC BRAIN INJURY

After a moderate to severe traumatic brain injury, there is a period of natural recovery. Nonetheless, recommended practices in this field are to begin retraining, rehabilitation, and other interventions as soon as possible (Rohling, Faust, Beverly, & Demakis, 2009). Interventions for students recovering from moderate to severe TBI begin with environmental restructuring, accommodations, and external memory aids that help to compensate for posttraumatic amnesia (Matteer, Kerns, & Eso, 1996). Restructuring reduces the mismatches between environmental demands and residual memory abilities. Restructuring might include eliminating distractions and organizing the workspace. Academic accommodations include extended testing time and recognition types of testing. Regarding memory aids, there are many options available (see earlier section in this chapter). When memory aids are selected, it's always important to train the individual to use them effectively. After the initial interventions and some recovery of working memory functions, judicious and adapted training in select memory strategies and mnemonics may be attempted.

Empirical findings on the effectiveness of memory interventions with TBI victims have been inconsistent. Part of the inconsistency stems from variability in the extent and severity of injuries, not just to memory but to related cognitive functions like attention. Another confound is variability in the naturally occurring recovery process. The most recent meta-analysis of cognitive retraining that includes memory training (Rohling et al., 2009) concluded that cognitive rehabilitation for acquired brain injury is effective, with a modest mean effect size of 30. (Most of the studies in the meta-analysis were with adult subjects.) Some cognitive retraining efforts, especially attention training, are more successful, whereas the effectiveness of memory rehabilitation is weaker. That is, memory may be more resistant to restoration of full function than other cognitive functions (Wilson, 2000). Overall, the most sobering and consistent finding in TBI intervention research is that children and adolescents with TBI often have persistent cognitive deficits in attention and memory, despite a resumption of normal daily activities and the appearance of full recovery (Mateer, Kerns, & Eso, 1996).

Hopefully, the old myth that children recover from a TBI better than adults has been dispelled. The developmental level of the child at the time of injury is a crucial variable that determines long-term outcomes. Early, diffuse injuries tend to result in more persistent memory deficits, especially for children injured at five years of age or younger (Wright & Limond, 2004). This phenomenon is not just because memory systems are more vulnerable to damage in early life but because children have not yet acquired the knowledge and skills that adults can fall back on. It's somewhat of a catch-22: The semantic knowledge that could support a weakened memory system will be difficult to acquire because of memory impairments. Also, persistent memory impairments may not become obvious until greater demands are placed on semantic memory as the child transfers from primary to middle and high school.

In addition to structure, accommodations, and external memory aides, TBI students can benefit from learning and applying memory strategies and mnemonics that address their specific impairments and cognitive capabilities. Memory training should begin with metamemory instruction about the student's current memory strengths and weaknesses, being sensitive to the student's feelings, frustrations, and fears about his or her brain injury and current status. Not all strategies and mnemonics are practical with TBI students, especially techniques that place high demands on working memory (Richardson, 1995), such as complex imagery mnemonics. Consequently, the selection and adaptation of strategies must be individually tailored according to the student's current functional levels and evidence of existing strategy use. For example, learners with a severe TBI will need to be provided with visual images when they are unable to generate their own (Benedict, 1989). TBI students also require much more practice than students with garden-variety memory problems. Instead of allowing just a few sessions to learn a strategy, TBI students may need up to 30 sessions spaced far enough apart to require retrieval of the procedures (Ehlhardt et al., 2008). In addition, student progress with strategy implementation needs to be frequently evaluated, and there must be an emphasis on generalization training. Accordingly, TBI victims are most likely to benefit from training in:

- Attentional control
- Reducing interference
- Self-monitoring of learning
- Cumulative rehearsal
- Generalization
- Simple visual mnemonics
- Distributed study and practice
- Repeated retrieval and self-testing

Practitioners and educators need to keep in mind that mnemonic strategies are not the main focus of memory interventions with TBI students. Teaching compensatory strategies, adapting the environment, and providing memory aides are the emphasis (Wilson, 2009). Also, children and adolescents with moderate to severe TBI will require special instructional methods when they return to school (see Chapter 8).

INTERVENTIONS FOR OTHER DISABLED AND AT-RISK POPULATIONS

The more that is known about the learning and memory characteristics of students with particular disorders, disabilities, and medical conditions, the easier it is to select memory strategies, mnemonics, and accommodations that will typically match their needs. Table 7.1 is an attempt to identify methods that should be especially beneficial for students with particular medical conditions and mental disorders. The recommendations are based on what seems the most likely profile of memory strengths and weaknesses that individuals with a particular condition will display. The decisions are based on information garnered from research (see Chapter 4) and the author's personal experience. For example, if the group is known to consistently have weaknesses in short-term memory, then training in rehearsal strategies is recommended because extending short-term memory retention is thought to increase the amount of encoding. When using Table 7.1, three caveats should be kept in mind. First, the recommendations are based on expected needs, not on any impairment-treatment interaction research that specifically looked at a group's response to a particular strategy. Second, the identified groups in Table 7.1 are heterogeneous in regards to memory functions because they are not memory-disordered groups per se. Third, every child and adolescent needs to be treated on an individual basis, based on the needs identified through a memory assessment. Consequently, the table is intended as a starting point when selecting methods for intervention or consultation. It may be especially helpful when a comprehensive memory assessment has not been completed.

Of all the groups listed on Table 7.1, students with a learning disability comprise a large group that is well understood. Although this group is also heterogeneous in regards to memory strengths and weaknesses, there has been enough intervention research with LD students to realize that they will benefit from acquiring and using nearly all memory strategies (Mahan, 1993). The majority of LD students have deficits in verbal episodic and semantic memory but a strength in visuospatial memory. Accordingly, they will benefit from capitalizing on their visual strengths by learning to use dual coding and visual mnemonics to bypass their weaker verbal processes (Brady & Richman, 1994). At the same time, instruction in methods that enhance verbal encoding, such as semantic clustering and elaboration, may strengthen their weak verbal processing skills. Self-testing and spaced practice are methods that will support consolidation and enhance the weak study skills most LD students demonstrate. Finally, LD students are also in need of metamemory training as they are known to have delays in metacognitive development.

MATCHING INTERVENTIONS WITH MEMORY DEFICITS

This section provides the rationale for the interventions recommended in Table 7.2. As stated in the previous section, these recommendations are based on perceived matches

Table 7.1 Memory interventions especially recommended for specific disabilities, disorders, and medical conditions

Risk Factor	Metamemory	Semantic Clustering	Elaboration	Rehearsal	Dual Coding	Self-Testing	Spaced Practice	Reducing Interference	Context Cues	Verbal Mnemonics	Visual Mnemonics	External Aids
Traumatic Brain Injury	X			X	X	X	X	X	X		X	X
Frontal Lobe Lesions	X	X	X	X	X	X	X	X				X
Perinatal Asphyxia	X			X	X		X	X		X	X	
Congenital Hypothyroidism				X						X		
Childhood Diabetes	X		X	X	X	X	X				X	
Epilepsy	X	X	X	X	X	X	X				X	
Childhood Stroke	X	X	X	X	X	X	X				X	
Specific Language Impairment	X	X	X	X	X	X	X		X		X	
Learning Disabilities	X	X	X	X	X	X	X	X	X		X	X
ADHD	X	X	X					X	X			
Autism		X	X		X				X	X		
Developmental Amnesia	X					X	X		X	X		X
PTSD, Abuse, and Chronic Stress	X	X	X	X	X	X	X				X	
Obsessive-Compulsive Disorder	X	X	X	X	X		X				X	
Depression	X	X	X	X	X	X	X				X	
Pediatric Bipolar Disorder	X				X		X				X	
Prenatal Alcohol Exposure	X	X	X	X	X		X	X		X	X	
Prenatal Cocaine Exposure	X	X	X	X	X	X	X				X	

Table 7.2 Memory interventions especially recommended for specific memory deficits

Memory Deficit	Metamemory	Semantic Clustering	Elaboration	Rehearsal	Dual Coding	Self-Testing	Spaced Practice	Reducing Interference	Context Cues	Verbal Mnemonics	Visual Mnemonics	External Aids
Verbal Episodic	X	X	X		X	X	X				X	
Visuospatial Episodic	X				X					X		X
Semantic	X	X	X			X	X		X		X	
Encoding	X	X	X	X	X	X	X				X	
Consolidation	X	X	X			X	X	X				X
Retrieval	X	X	X		X	X	X		X		X	
Metamemory	X	X	X		X	X	X					

between needs and treatment rather than on any aptitude-treatment interaction evidence. Assuming that an assessment has identified the individual's specific memory deficits and assets, the recommended interventions should benefit the student. However, non-memory variables, such as other cognitive abilities, should also be considered. For example, elaboration and semantic clustering techniques may be too challenging for students with below average cognitive abilities. As always, working memory capacity is another important variable to take into account, as elaborate strategies may overload an already stressed working memory. For interventions recommended for specific short-term and working memory impairments, see Dehn (2008).

Verbal Episodic Memory

Students with a deficit in verbal episodic memory have difficulty consolidating and recalling verbal learning. There are three main avenues of intervention for a verbal episodic memory deficit. First, improving verbal-verbal associations through elaboration and semantic clustering can support consolidation and enhance recall. Second, spaced practice and self-testing increase the probability of retention and strengthen the pathways used during retrieval. Third, visual mnemonics and dual coding establish verbal-visual associations and alternate retrieval routes. When extremely deficient verbal abilities underlie poor verbal episodic memory performance, there will need to be a heavy emphasis and reliance on visuospatial memory functions. Such students must learn to recode all verbal information into a visual format and to utilize the visual route first when studying and self-testing. In cases where both verbal and visuospatial abilities are impaired, a unique encoding strategy, known as subject-performed tasks, might prove beneficial. In this strategy, trainees are instructed to act out a word to be remembered; for example, for the word "comb" they are told to "comb your hair." In a study with eight autistic children, subject-performed tasks improved word recall by 92% (Summers & Craik, 1994).

Visuospatial Episodic Memory

For visuospatial deficits, the first approach is to teach the trainee to recode visuospatial information into verbal code (dual coding). Learning to name objects is easy but a system for describing spatial locations may need to be devised and practiced. In cases of amnesia, objects may need labeling and locations of possessions might need to be recorded in a memory notebook (external aids). When normal verbal abilities exist, verbal mnemonics might facilitate retrieval better than visual mnemonics.

Semantic Memory

With semantic memory deficits, there are four main explanations for the deficit. First, information initially retained episodically may never reach semantic schema because of weak consolidation processes. In such instances, spaced practice and self-testing provide additional opportunities for consolidation. Second, information that is not encoded on the basis of meaning may never become associated with schemas it is logically related with. For these cases, semantic clustering and elaboration are the methods of choice. Third, if retrieving information is the challenge, recalling episodic context cues may jog recall of facts. Fourth, with the learner's limited knowledge base, schemas that can assimilate the new information may simply not exist. In such cases, visual mnemonics are ideal because they can create structure and associations that will facilitate recall of isolated information.

Encoding and Learning

Students who perform poorly on the learning subtests of memory scales usually are deficient at encoding. Oftentimes, encoding lacks proficiency because it is too superficial. In-depth encoding can be increased by learning to use semantic clustering and elaboration. Encoding can also be enhanced through the additional connections made through dual coding and visual mnemonics. Self-testing and spaced practice provide additional opportunities to re-encode forgotten material.

Consolidation and Storage

Consolidation should not be viewed as a passive or automatic process that inevitably runs its course. As Paller says, "Consolidation proceeds as the memory is actively used" (2004; p. 76). Hence, consolidation can be strengthened through strategies that repeatedly retrieve information, such as self-testing and distributed (spaced) review and practice. Increasing the depth of processing through elaboration and semantic clustering also improves consolidation and long-term storage. Studying in the evening before going to sleep (reducing interference) may also enhance consolidation processes and recall the following day.

Retrieval and Recognition

In general, strategies that reinforce encoding also augment retrieval because effective encoding attaches cues that increase access during retrieval processes. Most verbal and visual mnemonics serve to cue target information by pegging the new information to cues that cannot be forgotten. Visual mnemonics that support retrieval include keyword, pegword, and loci. Memory strategies that produce multiple pathways to stored information, such as elaboration and dual encoding, also increase the likelihood of successful retrieval. Students who have special difficulty retrieving semantic information should be taught to recall context cues as a form of self-cuing during retrieval. An alternative retrieval strategy is to recall the class or category a question brings to mind, and then mentally run through items in that group until the correct response is recognized.

Metamemory

Any deficit that is essentially metacognitive in origin can be remediated through increasing the individual's awareness, monitoring, and strategy use (see the previous section on metamemory). Fortunately, metamemory deficits are more amenable to intervention than other types of memory dysfunction. Which non-metamemory strategies are selected for intervention depends on which memory components and processes are most affected by the delayed metamemory.

A TYPICAL INTERVENTION

In this section the reader will find a suggested sequence of activities for an eight-session intervention. The suggested program includes training in methods that most trainees need. This typical intervention sequence is targeted at middle school students who have average cognitive abilities and enough motivation to practice and apply the activities outside of the training sessions. The methods and length of training will need to be adapted for the severity of memory impairments, the age of the trainee, and the cognitive abilities of the trainee, as well as for the extent to which the methods will be practiced outside of the training sessions. For younger children, those with severe memory impairments, and those who will not practice outside of the sessions, the number of sessions will need to be doubled or more. In such instances, fewer topics will be covered per session, and there will be more review and practice across several sessions.

Session 1

- Assessment of metamemory development (if not conducted earlier)
- Assessment of strategy use (if not conducted earlier)
- Setting goals
- Explanation of how human memory works
- Review of trainee's memory strengths and weaknesses
- Activity that demonstrates the efficacy of memory strategies
- Semantic clustering training
- Cumulative rehearsal training with numbers, words, and cards

Session 2

- Review of trainee's memory strengths and weaknesses
- Review of semantic clustering
- Discussion regarding applications of semantic clustering
- Review of cumulative rehearsal
- Discussion regarding shortcomings of rehearsal strategies
- Elaboration training with science and social studies facts

- Practicing judgments of learning with short-delay recall
- Predicting recall of science and social studies facts at next session

Session 3

- Test of facts learned last session without elaboration strategy
- Test of facts learned last session with elaboration strategy
- Comparison of scores and attribution of success to elaboration
- Comparison of performance with predictions from last session
- Review of elaboration strategy
- Practice the "why does that make sense" variation of elaboration
- Discussion about dual coding and recoding
- Practice recoding visual into verbal
- Practice recoding verbal into visual

Session 4

- Test of facts learned last session without "why" elaboration strategy
- Test of facts learned last session with "why" elaboration strategy
- Comparison of scores and appropriate attributions
- Discussion regarding applications of elaboration strategy
- Test of words learned last session with visual recoding
- Test of words learned last session without visual recoding
- Comparison of scores and appropriate attributions
- Keyword training with Spanish vocabulary
- Discussion of why keyword works and its applications
- Discussion regarding the benefits of study before sleeping

Session 5

- Test of vocabulary learned last session without keyword strategy
- Test of vocabulary learned last session with keyword strategy
- Comparison of scores and appropriate attributions
- Practice learning state capitals with keyword strategy
- Loci training with social studies facts
- Discussion of benefits of spaced study

Session 6

- Test of vocabulary learned two sessions ago without keyword strategy
- Test of vocabulary learned two sessions ago with keyword strategy
- Comparison of scores and appropriate attributions
- Test of facts learned three sessions ago without "why" elaboration strategy
- Test of facts learned three sessions ago with "why" elaboration strategy

- Comparison of scores and appropriate attributions
- Test of social studies facts learned last session without loci
- Test of social studies facts learned last session with loci
- Planning of spaced study for an upcoming test
- Discussion of importance of self-testing when studying
- Practice self-testing with notes and study cards

Session 7

- Review of spaced study sessions that were conducted outside of training
- Continued practice with self-testing by writing self-test questions and answers
- Practice using two strategies at the same time
- PQRST strategy training for remembering reading material (see Chapter 8)
- Practice using cumulative rehearsal with cards (n-back procedure)

Session 8

- Practice using cumulative rehearsal with cards (n-back procedure)
- Review of performance data with and without strategies
- Discussion of which strategies are preferred and most effective for trainee
- Practice selecting strategies for various tasks
- Continued practice with PQRST
- Review of progress towards goals
- Student writes reflections on what has been learned
- Student writes plan for continued use of strategies

8 Classroom Instruction That Supports Memory

A frequently expressed educational outcome for students is that they will "learn to learn." This worthy goal refers to students acquiring skills that allow them to successfully acquire knowledge on their own. Curiously, educational outcomes never refer to "learning to remember." Although the goal is not overtly expressed, most educators would say that they are certainly teaching their students how to remember, just as they are teaching them how to learn. Yet, memory skills, or what teachers might call memorization techniques, are taught like learning strategies and study skills. That is, instruction in study skills is variable and often so indirect that most older students and adults will report that they were never taught study skills in school. This circumstance is unfortunate, given the importance of well-honed and sophisticated study skills for success in post-secondary education. The missed opportunity to explicitly teach memory skills to all K–12 students is also a concern, especially in view of the fact that a child's memory development depends heavily on education. As Schneider (2010, p. 71) said, "Most of memory development is not so much a product of age but of education and practice."

Teachers are quite capable of effectively teaching critical memory strategies that will further memory development and enhance long-term memory functioning. Whether they realize it or not, they are encouraging memory development and the learning of strategies by the learning demands they place on their students. Many students will respond to the challenge by adopting tried and true memorization practices, such as repeating information over and over. Some students will go on to discover more efficient and effective strategies, such as using imagery or semantic clustering. However, the students who are most in need of sound memory strategies (those with memory problems) are least likely to discover and utilize effective strategies on their own. Consequently, the U.S. educational system could increase the amount of lifelong knowledge that students acquire by making the explicit teaching of memory strategies a priority.

The nation's hard-working teachers already have a lot on their instructional plates. Fortunately, teachers who adopt more memory-enhancing teaching techniques and incorporate memory strategy training into their instruction may reap rewards in much the same way that a teacher who improves his or her classroom management skills reaps rewards. This call for more emphasis on memory development in the classroom is not about increasing differentiated instruction. Nearly all students will benefit from learning more memory strategies and from instruction that supports memory functions. Thus, the recommendations in this chapter can be incorporated into regular classroom instruction for all students. There will be some highly capable students who don't need these methods, but they will not be harmed. Those who need these methods most, those with memory problems, will benefit the most. Only a few students, those with severe memory impairments, may need some special accommodations.

For readers who remain skeptical about the potential payoffs of this proposal, consider this anecdote. When this author was a young school psychologist, he was assigned to reevaluate a fourth-grade elementary student with below-average cognitive abilities. The student had been placed in a pull-out, special education room for most of the day where he had developed such disruptive behaviors that his academic learning was nearly at a standstill. At his IEP meeting, it was decided to conduct an experiment and return him to a full-time regular education classroom placement. When this school psychologist returned to observe the child in his new classroom, an amazing transformation had taken place. The student's behavior problems were all but gone (he still had some challenges on the playground), and his academic learning had taken off. Upon further observation and investigation, two variables emerged that accounted for the changes. First, the classroom teacher consistently used a token economy behavior management system with all of her students. At the end of the week, students could use their accumulated tokens to bid on desirable items that she auctioned off. Second, the teacher was using a very structured direct instruction program to teach literacy and arithmetic. Her students were all well behaved and were all making solid academic progress. There was no doubt that her investment in direct instruction and a token economy system was paying off for her. Much like the effective teacher in this story, teachers who increase their use of memory-enhancing, instructional strategies and who train and encourage students to use memory strategies independently will also receive good returns on their investment.

The reason for placing confidence in the practices recommended in this chapter and in Chapter 7 is that they are scientifically based practices, the majority of which have been investigated in several educational environments across a range of ages and materials. However, some of the research has been confined to experimental psychology laboratories or medical settings. There are advantages and disadvantages to lab research. The main advantage is that more variables can be controlled in lab research, whereas, in a classroom, there are numerous uncontrolled variables, such as instructional technique, degree of original learning, student ability, and study outside the classroom. Although most psychologists put more faith in the reliability and validity of lab research, educators are often skeptical about real-world applications of such research. For educators and some psychologists, applied research in classrooms has more validity than well-controlled laboratory research. Ideally, all the methods recommended in this chapter should have been tested in both educational and non-educational settings, but some have not been. Nonetheless, a few practices researched only in labs and medical settings are recommended because they address student needs and because they can easily be adapted for classroom use.

Most of the methods covered in Chapter 7 can be taught by teachers to an entire classroom of students at a time. The focus in Chapter 7 is on relatively short-term, one-on-one interventions, with the goal of students learning to use the strategies independently. Essentially, Chapter 7 is about what students can learn to do for themselves, whereas the focus in this chapter is on what others, namely teachers, can do to continually support and develop students' memory functions. In addition to teaching students memory strategies and mnemonics, teachers are being asked to incorporate memory-enhancing strategies into their regular instruction.

THE MNEMONIC CLASSROOM

The idea of a "mnemonic classroom" was first suggested by Mastropieri and Scruggs (1991), two applied researchers who conducted numerous investigations into how teachers can enhance students' memory functions. Mastropieri and Scruggs (1991, 2000) were advocates for the classroom-wide teaching of memory strategies and mnemonics. They emphasized the effectiveness of mnemonics, such as keyword, and the applications of such strategies with young and disabled children. This author is in agreement with Mastropieri and Scruggs's proposal, and suggests further expansion of the concept. In the mnemonic classroom, a focus on memory, strategies, and mnemonics should permeate all of the instruction and learning activities. Here are the components of the ideal mnemonic classroom and the characteristics of effective mnemonic teachers:

- Beginning in first grade, instruction in memory strategies and mnemonics takes place whenever students are developmentally ready for a new method. For instance, it requires only minimal instruction to teach first graders how to rehearse several items together (Ornstein, Grammar, & Coffman, 2010).
- At all grade levels, teachers speak in strategic terms and continually remind students to use their memory strategies during learning activities. When doing so, teachers explain how a strategy or mnemonic can be applied to the task at hand.
- Teachers regularly model the use of memory strategies, through thinking aloud and explaining their processing. For example, a teacher might model the process of grouping items by semantic categories.
- Memory strategy instruction and metamemory information do not stand alone, but are integrated into the regular, daily instruction of nearly every subject (Schneider, 2010).

- Students are taught about memory, how it works, and how they can control it to maximize their learning.
- Teachers regularly emphasize the efficacy of memory strategies and mnemonics, using student data as proof (see Chapter 7).
- Teachers monitor student use of memory strategies and mnemonics and provide encouragement, reinforcement, and reteaching of strategies when needed.
- Teachers embed memory strategies into their instruction. For example, they provide plenty of elaboration as they teach new concepts and facts.
- When teaching content, teachers emphasize remembering the material.
- Teachers structure content in a manner that facilitates strategy use. For example, providing highly structured materials encourages children to group them categorically.
- Teachers do more than emphasize a particular strategy. Rather, they teach the flexible use of a range of methods.
- Teachers have expertise in human memory and understand how instruction can be tailored to enhance long-term retention of valued academic skills and content.
- Teachers make an effort to apply empirically derived memory principles (see Chapters 2 and 3) to all skill and content instruction. For example, the encoding specificity principle might be applied by structuring study guides in a test-like format, or repeated testing may be used to promote learning and memory.
- In the mnemonic classroom, all memory processes—encoding, consolidation, and retrieval—are supported. For example, a mnemonic teacher provides prompts and cues when students have difficulty retrieving new knowledge.

In the mnemonic classroom, learning is maximized because the memory part of the learning equation is continually emphasized. Essentially, "mnemonic teachers" not only explicitly teach memory strategies and mnemonic devices but incorporate memory-enhancing instructional practices into all of their instruction. Teachers should strive for a mnemonic classroom because when they do students will learn effective mnemonic behaviors and their memory for academic content will improve significantly. For example, first graders taught by high "mnemonic" teachers spend significantly more time engaged in memory strategies than first graders taught by low mnemonic teachers (Ornstein et al., 2010). Also, the impact of mnemonic strategy learning is long-term; for instance, students who learn to sort materials in first grade continue the practice in second grade even when they are taught by a low mnemonic teacher (Ornstein et al., 2010). Overall, research has confirmed that mnemonic-based instruction is more effective than traditional instructional methods. Delivering academic content through mnemonic strategies can double retention and recall of information, compared with strategy-free instruction (Carney, M. E. Levin, & J. R. Levin, 1993).

METAMEMORY INSTRUCTION

As discussed previously, age-appropriate metamemory development is essential for effective utilization of memory processes and strategies. The ability to understand and control study methods and memory strategies is crucial for the optimization of long-term retention and recall of knowledge (see Chapters 3, 5, and 7 for in-depth discussions of metamemory). Teachers can play a crucial role in students' metamemory development by teaching the following:

- There are different kinds of memory: short-term and long-term; visual and auditory; and personal and academic.
- Retention and recall of information are partially under the individual's control.
- Retention and recall can be improved by employing effective strategies.
- Remembering information immediately after studying it does not mean that it will be remembered later on.
- It takes time, effort, and the use of strategies to make academic knowledge memorable.
- Remembering is easier when material is organized.
- Remembering is easier when information is encoded both visually and verbally.
- Simply desiring to remember something does not make it more memorable.
- Using effective memory strategies can actually save study time.

Teachers can further enhance metamemory development, strategy development, and memory performance by:

- Teaching conditional knowledge about strategies (see Chapters 3 and 7).
- Demonstrating the efficacy of each strategy (see Chapter 7).
- Teaching students how to monitor the relative efficacy of strategies they are using (Schneider, 2010).
- Teaching students how to select an effective strategy for the task at hand.
- Teaching students how to concurrently apply more than one strategy.
- Improving the accuracy of students' judgments of learning (see Chapters 3 and 7).

INSTRUCTIONAL PRACTICES THAT ENHANCE MEMORY

Many of the instructional practices recommended in this section are actually memory strategies. For example, elaboration is a strategy that students can learn to perform on their own. However, these strategies are easily embedded into instruction and function nearly as effectively when they are performed by teachers. Just as teachers often act as students' frontal lobes by providing structure and helping students focus, teachers can also serve a crucial role in helping students encode, consolidate, and retrieve information. Assuming this responsibility is especially appropriate for elementary and special education teachers. A teacher's support of students' memory processing is analogous to reading to students when they have not yet attained reading fluency or repeatedly demonstrating a mathematics procedure until the students have mastered it. If teachers support learners in these endeavors, why not directly support them while they are learning to effectively utilize their memory functions?

Distributed and Expanding-Interval Reviews

Every educator knows that practicing skills and reviewing subject matter strengthens learning and memory. Regular review is part of teacher lesson plans and is embedded in many published educational materials. Consequently, many educators might think that this fundamental instructional practice needs no discussion or modification. However, there is a science to reviewing that some educators may not be aware of. Convenient, random, or even regularly scheduled reviews are definitely better than no review at all but may not be the most effective and efficient. The science of distributed and expanding-interval reviews reveals that daily reviews are unnecessary and that waiting until the day before an exam to review material is ineffective. Scheduling reviews and practice so that they are consistent with memory functioning can significantly improve retention and recall of academic skills and content. In an educational setting, distributed and expanding-interval review and practice is thought to increase learning by approximately 15% (Bahrick, 2000). Such a systematic approach to reviewing is especially important when the material is something that the student should know for a lifetime.

What It Is and How It Works   The technique consists of a review shortly after learning followed by successive reviews over an extended period of time. Expanding-interval, or expanded-spacing, review is the most popular and most effective variation of distributed study. For maximum effect, distributed study episodes should occur on an expanding-interval basis. For example, reviewing material once each day for a week is no more effective than reviewing it after one day and then again seven days after initial learning. Essentially, expanding-interval review involves recalling information over progressively longer periods of time. Gradually increasing the intervals between review and study produces better recall during subsequent tests and better long-term retention beyond the tests. The critical variable for promoting long-term retention is to delay the study period until retrieval is somewhat difficult (Karpicke & Roediger, 2007a, 2007b). The idea is that effortful retrieval conditions will ultimately lead to greater long-term retention because more effortful retrieval enhances learning, a notion similar to the depth-of-processing during encoding idea.

The timing of the initial review is crucial to the success of this approach. If the interval between initial learning and the first review is too long, too much information will be irretrievably lost from memory. If the first interval is too short, recall will be too easy. The underlying variable that determines success is the difficulty of retrieval. Research has confirmed that long-term retention of information is correlated with the difficulty level of retrieval during review (Karpicke & Roediger, 2007a). Easy retrieval does not promote long-term retention; moderately challenging retrieval does. Thus, the initial review should not occur until the information has had time to transfer to long-term memory and had time to partially decay. If the initial review consists of immediately repeating something that was learned only moments ago, then there will be little long-term benefit. Accordingly, the interval between initial learning and the first review should range from a minimum of a few minutes to a maximum of one day. Because most students forget approximately 50% of new material within the first 24 hours, initially reviewing material the following day definitely requires effortful retrieval. For younger students and those with unusually rapid forgetting rates, the initial review should occur at the end of the lesson, followed by a second review a day later. End-of-lesson reviews should also be conducted when there will be no opportunity for review the next day.

After the initial review, the first few succeeding review and practice sessions should be close together in time, as the rate of forgetting is very rapid at first. As memories strengthen and forgetting slows down, the relearning episodes need not be as frequent. As knowledge becomes consolidated over time, recall during frequent evenly spaced reviews would become progressively easier, a condition that does little to further enhance long-term retention. Consequently, review sessions should be scheduled on an expanding-interval basis that allows some forgetting to occur so that effort is required to retrieve the information.

Distributed and expanding-interval review should not be confused with the overlearning approach that has often been recommended as a remedy for forgetting. Overlearning is defined as continuing to rehearse facts or practice procedures after they can be perfectly recalled or correctly completed during a learning session. Although the attainment of mastery (100% recall during a lesson) does boost long-term retention, overlearning is an inefficient way of increasing long-term retention (Rohrer, Taylor, Pashler, Wixted, & Cepeda, 2005). An example of overlearning would be a mathematics procedure that is practiced several times in class after everyone can successfully complete the procedure. In the short-term (the next day or within a few days), overlearning improves recall but when long-term retention (longer than a week) is the goal, overlearning produces no gain (Pashler, Rohrer, Cepeda, & Carpenter, 2007; Rohrer et al., 2005). Basically, time invested in multiple rounds of practice within a single learning episode is not as effective as the same amount of practice spaced out over days and weeks.

Why It Works Expanding-interval reviewing is based on the principle that effortful but successful retrieval significantly improves long-term retention. The memory process underlying improved retention is not retrieval itself; rather, it is consolidation (Litman & Davachi, 2008). A memory that has been consolidated is more likely to be retained for a long interval, if not permanently. As explained in Chapter 2, consolidation takes a considerable amount of time, and new learning is often forgotten before it becomes consolidated. Relearning sessions reactivate recent memory traces before they are completely decayed, and this reactivation provides another opportunity for consolidation. If the trace has already been consolidated, reactivation leads to a reconsolidation process that reorganizes and enhances the memory. Litman and Davachi propose waiting 24 hours before reviewing because the delay allows initial consolidation to occur before re-activation. Review sessions also establish additional memory traces and connections among memory networks. Essentially, spaced practice and review slows the rate of forgetting while supporting consolidation. Although consolidation processes are not fully understood, the spacing of memory reactivation that occurs with expanding practice and review clearly serves to strengthen synapses and neural networks.

Distributed study over an extended period of time is also crucial if fresh content is to make the transition from episodic to semantic memory (see Chapter 2). Semantic memory is the meaning-based storage where knowledge resides. Once information has been abstracted from episodic memory and incorporated into semantic memory, it becomes more enduring because episodic memories decline more rapidly than semantic memories. Review and retrieval of information can facilitate this transition, as repeated exposure to facts, rules, and concepts can help establish representations that are semantic in nature. Conway et al. (1997) concluded that students who perform well on course exams are retrieving more from semantic memory than episodic memory. Also, responses derived from semantic memory are more likely to be correct than responses constructed from episodic memory.

Apart from understanding the basic consolidation processes underlying the benefits of distributed and expanding-interval reviews, it is critical that educators realize that reviews must require students to actually retrieve the information. This crucial factor is based on the principle that retrieval is more effective than simply being re-exposed to material. That is, various forms of rehearsal, recital, and repetition are ineffective compared with actually retrieving information, such as when responding to a question. Moreover, as discussed earlier, retrieval has even more impact when it requires some effort.

The Research   The beneficial effects of distributed and expanding-interval review sessions are some of the most robust phenomena ever discovered in memory research. Memory researchers have consistently found that review and study opportunities distributed across time are more effective at promoting learning and long-term retention of information than study opportunities that are massed together or occur only once (Altmann & Gray, 2002; Bloom & Shuell, 1981; Cull, 2000). For instance, a meta-analysis by Donovan and Radosevich (1999) reported that distributed practice had a mean effect size of .46 over massed study conditions (rehearsing and practicing without rest followed by no subsequent study sessions). This "spacing effect" has been known since 1885 when Ebbinghaus published the results of his research on memory and forgetting (Dempster & Farris, 1990). Although regularly scheduled reviews are moderately efficacious, expanding-interval study sessions are even more effective than uniformly spaced study schedules (Cepeda, Pashler, Vul, Wixted, & Rohrer, 2006; Cull, 2000). For example, Landauer and Bjork (1978) reported that expanding retrieval practice produced about a 10% advantage over equally spaced retrieval practice.

The benefits of distributed practice and review have been found for nearly every form of learning and memory, including verbal learning, motor learning, and skill learning. Academic learning examples include the learning of spelling, multiplication, and a second language. In a study by Rea and Modigliani (1985) in which 44 third-grade students were taught spelling and multiplication facts, the performance of students who learned the facts and words under expanded interval practice conditions was superior to those who mastered the material during one continuous practice session. In a study of high school students learning French vocabulary (H. P. Bahrick, L. E. Bahrick, A. S. Bahrick, & P. E. Bahrick, 1993), the distributed practice group studied 20 words for 10 minutes on each of three consecutive days while the control group studied for one 30-minute session. When tested immediately after completing their study, there was little difference between the groups. However, when retested seven days later, the distributed study group recalled 15 words, whereas the massed study group could remember only 11 words. Distributed study benefits are found even when the interval between study periods is extremely long. For example, in a nine-year longitudinal study, Bahrick et al. (1993) found that 13 sessions spaced 56 days apart were as effective as 26 sessions spaced only 14 days apart when vocabulary recall was tested five years later.

Who Benefits Distributed study opportunities are particularly beneficial for students who have learning problems or long-term memory weaknesses and impairments. For example, Cull, Shaughnessy, and Zechmeister (1996) found that expanding retrieval practice benefitted college-age poor learners more than good learners. Spaced review is also a critical instructional practice for students with acquired brain injury because these students typically do not have the cognitive resources necessary for utilizing elaborate mnemonic techniques. Consequently, spaced review should be incorporated into nearly everything taught to students with TBI. Because of their extensive need for this method, brain-injured students should also be taught to use distributed practice independently. Training that culminates in self-cued, spaced review sessions has successfully been conducted with TBI victims (Schacter, Rich, & Stampp, 1985). Of course, for those with severe memory impairments, the intervals between review sessions need to be shorter than for students with normal memory abilities.

How to Apply It in the Classroom   At first glance, it may appear that incorporating more reviews into already crowded classroom instruction schedules is unrealistic. However, a well-designed expanding-interval review and practice schedule may not actually increase overall instructional time. First, time invested in the initial learning session can be reduced if there will be follow-up sessions. In fact, educational research has proved that brief learning episodes separated by at least a day are more effective than concentrating all learning into one session. For instance, three 10-minute study sessions can be more effective than one 30-minute session. Second, when review sessions are not implemented, reteaching may be necessary after poor performance on an exam reveals inadequate learning. Furthermore, not that many review sessions are necessary, and the review sessions required for any specific content will become less and less frequent.

In the classroom, an expanding-interval review schedule might look like this: (a) review at the end of the lesson, (b) review the next day, (c) review a week later, (d) review after a two-week interval, and (e) if necessary, review after a four-week interval. When information is reviewed the day after it is taught the average student will remember it very well for one week (Pashler et al., 2007). However, for individuals with memory impairments or those who demonstrate rapid forgetting, more sessions may be required, along with more gradually expanding intervals. For instance, a mid-week review may be necessary instead of waiting a full week. The optimal interval is also a function of the type and complexity of the material being learned. Effortful but successful retrieval during the review sessions is crucial. If sessions are spaced so far apart that most information cannot be retrieved, then this instructional method loses its effectiveness. Thus, review sessions should be scheduled close enough together so that learners can recall at least some of the difficult material.

Of course, more mature students and independent learners can conduct their own study, review, and practice sessions, reducing the workload for teachers. Teachers typically elicit such sessions when they provide study guides and review packets. However, the drawback to this practice is that it typically happens only once and seldom matches the typical rate of forgetting. Accordingly, instructors should teach students about the benefits of distributed practice and provide guidance in setting up appropriate review schedules. Essentially, students should be taught to study for tests over several sessions that have been spaced far enough apart to benefit from the spacing effect. In practice, this means that the majority of students need to be encouraged to conduct their first study session well in advance of an upcoming exam. Once students begin to follow an expanding-interval review schedule, they may realize that they don't know the material very well, a discovery that might reinforce further study (Bahrick & Hall, 2005). Realistically, it will be quite a challenge to get students to independently follow a distributed study schedule. Although many memory strategies are intuitively appealing to children and adolescents, distributed study is not one of them. Consequently, teachers should frequently emphasize the benefits of it, and they might encourage the behavior by providing mandatory review packets that must be completed at times consistent with the research. For instance, an initial review sheet should be provided one day after the lesson, followed by a second one a week later.

Repeated Testing

A persistent finding in memory research is that repeated testing enhances recall over long intervals more than additional study opportunities do (Carpenter, Pashler, Wixted, & Vul, 2008; Roediger & Karpicke, 2006a, 2006b). Students who complete at least one test between initial learning and a final examination perform significantly better on the final exam than students who study but are not administered an intervening test. For example, in a study by Roediger and Karpicke (2006a), undergraduate students who took two intervening tests scored 61% on a test a week after initial learning in contrast to a mean of only 40% for those who studied extensively but were not tested during the week. The beneficial effect of testing versus restudying is known as the *testing effect*. The educational implication is that tests should not be used merely to assess learning but to promote it. According to McDaniel, Anderson, Derbish, and Morrisette (2007), this robust phenomenon and its educational implications have largely been ignored by the field of education because the conventional wisdom is that studying and reviewing material promotes learning, whereas testing does not. Although repeated studying and reviewing after initial learning does improve delayed recall, repeated testing has an even stronger effect (Karpicke & Roediger, 2008). When long-term retention of material is the goal, testing is clearly more efficacious than additional study time.

What It Is and How It Works　　The timing of the initial testing, the intervals between tests, and the number of tests are important variables. The initial test should occur relatively soon after learning (Dempster, 1992). In a study with college students (reviewed in Butler & Roediger, 2007), long-term retention of lecture material was greatly enhanced by administering a brief test immediately following a class lecture. With just one short-delay quiz, the amount of information the college students recalled eight weeks later was greater than that retained after just three days without a prior test. Apparently, a single quiz immediately after presentation of the material can produce a significant improvement in long-term retention. However, when new material must be retained for at least an academic semester, weekly testing is more effective than just an immediate quiz. McDaniel et al. (2007) found that college students benefitted when administered weekly quizzes prior to a cumulative final. Nonetheless, quizzes every week are unnecessary, as it has been documented that increasingly greater intervals between subsequent tests is more effective (Cull, 2000). Given the similarities between reviewing material and completing a test, it is not surprising that an expanding-interval approach to repeated testing is the most effective method. For example, Rea and Modigliani (1985) demonstrated that school children learn spelling and multiplication facts best when there is expanding-interval testing. In effect, the spacing of testing adheres to the same principle as expanding intervals for distributed study and review. That is, tests should occur when retrieval will be effortful but mostly successful. Regardless of the age of the students, it is probably best to administer the first quiz immediately after the lesson, followed by a quiz the next day, another one a week later, and any remaining retests at more extended intervals. For older students with average memory abilities, three intervening tests should suffice.

Although summative test performance is generally better for information covered in preliminary quizzes than for omitted information, the testing effect is not limited to test items that are repeated on the final exam. That is, the testing effect emerges even when the intervening quizzes do not contain exactly the same items. The testing effect also occurs when test formats are different and when the wording of individual items is changed. Moreover, repeated testing can lead to improved test performance, as more content is recalled each time the learner is tested (Wheeler, 1995). In fact, the increased knowledge resulting from repeated testing extends beyond the specific information covered by the tests (McDaniel et al., 2007). Clearly, testing not only reduces the rate of forgetting over the first few days and weeks following initial learning but also increases the amount of information that will be retained long term (Carpenter et al., 2008).

Why It Works   When attempting to identify the memory processes and other factors that underlie the testing effect, a number of possibilities emerge. First, testing forces the learner to retrieve the recently learned skill or material. Retrieving information is an effective procedure for increasing retention and subsequent recall because retrieval strengthens memory traces, memory representations, and retrieval routes, in addition to enhancing consolidation. Evidence for retrieval being the mediator of the testing effect was reported by Carpenter et al. (2008). Their subjects who were instructed to recall the answer without outwardly producing a response benefitted as much as those who actually completed the test items. Therefore, the testing effect may be just one manifestation of the retrieval effect (Glover, Krug, Hannon, & Shine, 1990). Second, some researchers have hypothesized that additional exposure time accounts for the phenomenon; however, this contention has not been supported in the research. Third, testing reveals the facts and information that have not been sufficiently learned, leading motivated students to restudy the unknown material. Fourth, transfer-appropriate processes might account for the effect. According to this hypothesis, memory performance improves when the processes engaged during study and review overlap those required for good test performance (Roediger & Karpicke, 2006a). That is, prior testing requires students to engage in the same retrieval processes they will need to access the information later on. Also, specific retrieval cues given on intervening tests benefit retention to the extent that cues on the final test match those provided initially. For example, students perform better on final test questions that are phrased similarly than on those that are phrased differently. Finally, if testing is viewed as just another form of periodic retrieval, it supports and reinforces consolidation and reconsolidation of new learning in the same manner that distributed review does. Regardless of the exact cause, repeated testing is clearly effective as an instructional approach that promotes learning and long-term memory.

The Research   For those who are skeptical about the testing effect and believe it may simply be an artifact of more exposure, the evidence is unambiguous. When an equivalent amount of time is spent studying or testing, long-term retention benefits the most from repeated testing. In a meta-analysis of 35 classroom studies (seven at the high school level) that manipulated the number of tests administered to students during a semester, 83% of the studies found positive effects for frequent testing and the mean effect size was .23 (Bangert-Drowns, J. A. Kulik, & C. L. Kulik, 1991). For studies where the control group received no preliminary tests at all, the effect size was a strong .54. The meta-analysis concluded that giving just one preliminary test shortly after initial learning produced a significant gain relative to no prior tests at all. The study also found that subsequent repeated tests added to the gains in learning and retention. Some of the data reported by researchers is very convincing. For instance, Roediger and Karpicke (2006a) reported that undergraduate students who read a reading passage 14.2 times performed worse than students who read the passage only 3.4 times and took two intervening quizzes. In another study by Roediger and Karpicke (2006b), students who studied a word list only five times and were tested once performed better when tested a week later than students who studied the list 15 times but were not tested until a week later. Although repeated testing will itself promote learning and long-term retention, study paired with testing is even more effective (Cull, 2000). Overall, the research indicates that learners who study the material only once but are tested three times will have better long-term retention than those who study the material numerous times. Clearly, testing reduces forgetting of recently learned material, and multiple tests reduce forgetting more than a single test.

How to Apply It in the Classroom   The research indicates that the best results are obtained when there are a minimum of three quizzes or tests between the initial learning event and the summative examination. If testing is to promote learning and retention, an ideal schedule consists of (a) administering a brief quiz immediately following a presentation, lesson, or study episode; (b) administering another quiz the next day; (c) following up with a quiz one week later; and (d) progressively increasing the interval between successive tests until the unit or summative exam is administered. Other variables that enhance the effectiveness of repeated testing include: (a) using recall-type tests (e.g., short answer) instead of recognition-type tests (e.g., multiple choice); (b) incorporating some new test questions in each subsequent quiz while retaining some previous items; (c) providing corrective feedback relatively soon after testing, especially for tests on which performance is low; (d) scheduling tests in advance so that students can prepare for them; and (e) constructing challenging test items that evoke elaborative and semantic processing. If adopting these testing procedures for an entire class is infeasible, special out-of-classroom quizzes should at least be provided for students with memory impairments. However, the benefits of testing are not restricted to learning disabled or memory impaired students; all students at all ages benefit from the practice.

For students who object to frequent testing, the efficacy and efficiency of the method should be communicated to them. First, students should be informed of the improved knowledge and test performance that repeated testing produces. This explanation is necessary because students have more confidence in their knowledge after they study than after they are tested (Roediger & Karpicke, 2006b). Second, students also need to understand that preliminary testing makes learning more efficient for them because they learn without actually having to study the material. Naturally, with mature students, frequent testing encourages more study, and not just review of the items that are on preliminary tests. Teachers can increase the incentive for additional study by grading and awarding credit for each preliminary test.

Test Format   The format of the intervening test(s) influences the extent of the testing effect. Multiple-choice tests, because they only require recognition rather than full retrieval, generally are not as effective as short-answer or fill-in-the-blank tests (Butler & Roediger, 2007; McDaniel et al., 2007). The more demanding the retrieval processes required by intervening tests, the greater the long-term retention of information. Also, McDaniel et al. report that errors made on short-answer quizzes are more likely to be answered correctly on unit exams than errors made on multiple-choice quizzes. With multiple-choice, there is the risk that the incorrect responses will interfere with later recall of the correct response. Moreover, an initial multiple-choice test tends to be less effective even when the final test is in multiple-choice format (Kang, McDermott, and Roediger, 2007).

Self-Testing   When repeatedly testing new learning is impractical, instructors should teach students to self-test when studying independently. Although self-testing is not as effective as classroom exams, it is more effective than rehearsing material because it requires retrieval. Ideally, students should write questions and answers on index cards. When study cards are not created, trying to retrieve specific information before reading it will suffice. For example, a student might look at a topic heading in his or her notes and then cover up the details until the information is retrieved. Alternatives that teachers should consider are putting review sheets into a question-and-answer format or giving students take-home quizzes. When student self-testing is the only option, instructors should invest some time in teaching students how to self-test and how to use the feedback to guide additional study. One way of convincing students to use self-testing is to emphasize how it saves time. For instance, Roediger and Karpicke (2006a) reported that 5 rounds of testing were more effective than 15 rounds of study. Regular rounds of self-testing and follow-up review should come close to replicating the effects of teacher-administered tests, especially when the self-testing occurs during expanding-interval study sessions.

Retrieval

As discussed previously, the success of distributed study and repeated testing depends on effortful but successful retrieval. Actually retrieving information strengthens memories more than simply reviewing information. Also, retrieval is as effective as intentional memorization efforts, even when the retrieval occurs with minimal effort and awareness (Buckner, Wheeler, & Sheridan, 2001). This phenomenon is known as the *retrieval effect.* The retrieval effect mainly occurs because the act of retrieval modifies and strengthens memory traces and neural networks while supporting consolidation and reconsolidation. However, the act of retrieval does more than strengthen memory representations. In addition, it enhances aspects of the retrieval process itself. Successful retrieval has a powerful and beneficial effect upon retrieval strength, or the ease with which a memory trace can be accessed (Wheeler, Ewers, & Buonanno, 2003). Retrieval strength is increased by using retrieval pathways, in addition to creating multiple and elaborated retrieval routes. Regardless of the underlying processes, there's no doubt that successful retrieval provides preventive and corrective maintenance against normal forgetting and interference. The process of retrieving information not only strengthens memories but restores access to lost or partially forgotten information.

Applying this memory principle during classroom instruction can significantly boost learning and memory. The appeal of this application is that almost no additional work is required of teachers and no special training of students is needed. Teachers merely need to take advantage of more opportunities to incorporate retrieval into regular instruction and learning activities. First, teachers might use a question-and-answer format whenever they conduct routine reviews during class. Even if only one student is called upon, the others will be engaging in retrieval, provided the teacher waits long enough between posing the question and calling on a student. Second, any review materials can be structured as questions to be answered. Third, part of previously taught material could be held back until students retrieve the remaining information. For example, instead of having students recite the spelling of a word while looking at the entire word, some of the letters should be omitted so that the students are forced to retrieve the remaining letters.

Corrective Feedback

Like periodic reviews, corrective feedback is a common teacher behavior that advances learning and long-term retention. Corrective feedback augments the effects of distributed review, repeated testing, and retrieval by reinforcing correct responses and preventing the learning and consolidation of errors. Both distributed study and repeated testing will significantly increase long-term retention without corrective feedback. However, properly conducted corrective feedback can heavily influence the effectiveness of these two practices. For example, Pashler, Cepeda, Rohrer, and Wixted (2005) found a 494% increase in final retention when corrective feedback was provided during the learning of words. Certainly, corrective feedback is important during learning activities, but it is even more critical following testing (McDaniel & Fisher, 1991). Although correctly recalled learning will benefit from testing without feedback, many educational studies (reviewed in Carpenter et al., 2008) have emphasized that information not recalled during testing has almost no chance of being learned if corrective feedback is not provided. Supplying the correct response after an incorrect response significantly improves delayed retention.

For maximum impact, teachers should be aware of some variables that determine the effectiveness of corrective feedback. The first variable is thoroughness. Simply telling students that a response is right or wrong accomplishes very little. The correct response and appropriate explanation should be provided. Second, it's important to allow learners adequate time to process the feedback so that they can correct their erroneous information. Third, feedback on short-answer items has more of an impact than feedback on multiple-choice items (Kang et al., 2007). Fourth, the degree of confidence students have in the correctness of their response also determines the influence of feedback. Corrective feedback on high-confidence errors is highly arousing and facilitates the encoding and storage of the correct response (Butterfield & Metcalfe, 2001). Fifth, the benefits of feedback are not limited to specific items and responses; feedback also improves performance on related test questions found on the summative examination (McDaniel et al., 2007). In situations where teachers simply don't have time to provide feedback after tests, requiring students to look up the correct responses may suffice.

Another important variable that influences the effectiveness of feedback is the length of the interval between testing and feedback. Many studies of classroom learning and testing have found immediate feedback more effective than delayed (Kulik & Kulik, 1988). On the other hand, some studies have reported that delayed feedback is more beneficial than immediate feedback because delayed feedback is essentially another study opportunity that allows learners to correct their mistaken associations (Butler & Roediger, 2007). In a study with 144 high school students, Surber and Anderson (1975) found that withholding feedback on test items for one day was more effective than immediate feedback. It is thought that the delay reduces the interference from the incorrect response, thereby allowing relearning of the correct information. Either immediate or delayed, corrective feedback is crucial for learning and long-term retention. If test feedback is delayed, it should be no longer than one day.

Elaboration

Basically, elaboration is the process of explicitly making associations between related prior knowledge and new information. Elaboration facilitates learning and increases memorability by creating interconnections between new input and related information (Mastropieri & Scruggs 1989). When teachers introduce new concepts and facts, they should pause to elaborate so that learners can recognize the connections between the new material and what they already know. For example, when teaching young students about penguins, the instructor might point out that penguins are a type of bird because they have wings, feathers, beaks, and lay eggs.

Why It Works   In general, elaboration enhances memory because it involves deeper processing of information, compared with simply presenting information, which only requires shallow processing. At the neurological level, elaboration alters neural networks to accommodate new information and increases connections between related neural networks. Basically, elaboration increases the associative pathways between related memory traces, and these additional pathways facilitate recall. In effect, elaboration facilitates encoding and consolidation, and it develops alternate sources of retrieval. As these new retrieval routes are used repeatedly, they are strengthened and recall is facilitated even more. If the desired fact or information cannot be directly accessed, the elaborations that embellished the information might be activated and these will either cue the target information or allow the target to be inferred. Thus, elaboration especially supports recall when the response is not automatically retrieved. When a response is generated through inferential and reconstructive processes, the availability of alternate pathways that connect related knowledge increases the likelihood of producing a correct response (Walker, 1986).

The Research   Educational research has confirmed the value of elaboration as an instructional practice (Ritchie & Karge, 1996). Memory research also has found that elaboration improves long-term retention and recall of learning. Elaboration is an extremely useful strategy at any age but adolescents tend to use it more spontaneously than younger students (Suzuki-Slakter, 1988). In adults, elaboration has been found to improve learning and retention by as much as one standard deviation (Wood, Willoughby, Bolger, Younger, & Kaspar, 1993). Studies with learning disabled students have reported that they especially benefit from interrogative elaboration, such as answering questions about the new material (Scruggs, Mastropieri, & Sullivan, 1994). Elaboration seems to be a suitable strategy for the learning of basic skills and higher-level concepts, and it is effective with all types of academic content: reading, social studies, science, mathematics (Swing & Peterson, 1988), and so on.

How to Apply It in the Classroom   There are many variations of elaboration that can be incorporated into instruction. They range along a continuum from teacher-generated elaborations to student-generated elaborations. The variations include:

- Beginning a lesson with an advance organizer that elicits an appropriate schema to which the new information can be attached.

- Directly connecting new information with the appropriate schema or category, such as stating that penguins are a type of bird.
- Explaining the personal relevance the concept has for students, such as connecting a recent storm they experienced with global warming.
- Directing students to think about or reflect on a concept before proceeding with instruction.
- Directing students to write down what they already know about a topic, what they would like to learn more about, and what new information they learned (after instruction is complete).
- Providing students with several examples and non-examples of the concept.
- Paraphrasing and summarizing information.
- Drawing inferences and logically connecting concepts.
- Connecting the information through semantic mapping.
- Requiring students to answer "why" questions about the new information.
- Generating and answering questions about the topic.

A more in-depth explanation is warranted for two of the above suggestions: the interrogative approach and providing examples. In the interrogative approach, students answer *what* or *why* questions about the material. Answering these questions forces the students to process the information semantically and hence more deeply. Consequently, the interrogative approach to elaboration is very effective (Pressley, 1982). Even when the answer to the question is not entirely correct, recall of the new fact will still be enhanced, although correct and precise elaborations are more effective (Wood, Willoughby, Kaspar, & Idle, 1994). One variation of this method is to present a fact and then ask, "Why is this true?" or "Why does this make sense?" For example, suppose the fact is that the rivers in northern Europe are very polluted. The answer to the "why" question could be that polluted rivers makes sense because northern Europe is heavily populated and has a lot of industry. Answering "why" questions forces the students to draw from their own prior knowledge and construct rational explanations (Scruggs et al., 1994). Of course, one drawback to the interrogative approach is that it requires some basic prior knowledge about the topic. The provision of examples is another form of elaboration that strengthens connections. Examples work when they are representative of a category or schema. An effective set of examples should include simple examples, typical examples, unusual examples, and nonexamples (Sprenger, 2005). Having students generate their own examples also provides an opportunity to check their understanding of the material.

With younger and learning-challenged students, elaboration might include the use of pictures. Pictures can be more stimulating, and they reduce verbal processing demands. When pictures are used, the procedure consists of talking about the pictures. The process begins with the teacher elaborating on or telling a story about the first picture, which represents prior knowledge. Then the students are asked to name the picture and tell a story about it. The teacher supports this step by asking questions that enable further elaboration, such as "What do you think is happening in the picture?" Next, a second picture that illustrates the new concept is introduced to the students, and they must invent a story that links the two pictures together. Their stories should go beyond the obvious information in the pictures. In the next phase, written information is introduced along with the picture. Eventually, the pictures can be faded out and replaced by verbal or written elaboration (see Sugden & Newall, 1987, for more details).

Training Students to Self-Elaborate   Teachers should definitely provide most of the elaboration for children who are very young, have low cognitive abilities, have memory impairments, or have limited prior knowledge. For other students, teachers should offer some elaborations but also should train and encourage students to self-elaborate. In general, self-generated elaborations are more effective than those generated by a teacher, even when the elaborations are less complex and less accurate (Grier & Ratner, 1996). Student elaborations are more effective, mainly because they are personally meaningful or relevant to the learner (Levin, 1988). Teacher-generated elaborations tend to fail when they are not compatible with students' prior knowledge and not inherently meaningful to the students. Furthermore, when teachers provide the elaborations, students may or may not be actively processing them. Consequently, one educational application of elaboration involves training students to elaborate on their own. Even students as young as first grade can be taught to generate elaborative thoughts (Pressley, 1982).

Follow these steps when training a classroom of students to independently use the elaboration strategy:

1. Explain that elaboration is a process of thinking about how two things are alike or how they are connected with each other. Add that elaboration makes understanding and remembering the new material easier.
2. Model the strategy by thinking aloud, using material with which the students are familiar. When modeling, don't be a perfect model; at first, struggle with making the connections but persist until some understanding emerges.
3. Given new material, instruct students to think about what they already know about the topic and about how the new information and the prior knowledge might be related. Proceed with having them verbalize their elaborations. Encourage specific links, as opposed to general or vague links.
4. For young children and those with learning and memory difficulties, remind students of related knowledge they already know. Then allow them time to create a meaningful link. When students are unable to provide a rational elaboration, guide them to an appropriate response rather than immediately providing one.
5. For students who struggle with Steps 3 and 4, train them to ask and answer the question, "Why does this new fact make sense?"

6. Once the students can adequately generate their own elaborations, prompt them to do so each time it might be beneficial. After oral prompts, allow the students enough time to retrieve related information and to think about possible connections. Periodically, have students share their elaborations to ensure that they are producing helpful elaborations. An alternative is to have students write elaborative statements on their worksheets, in their notes, or on a separate sheet of paper.

7. Require elaboration with a variety of materials, and encourage students to use the strategy whenever they study independently.

Prior Knowledge

Memory performance is highly dependent on the extent of prior knowledge and domain-specific expertise. The amount of prior knowledge or expertise in a particular domain is a powerful determinant of the amount and quality of information that can be stored and recalled (Recht & Lauren, 1988; Schneider, 2000). In general, students with high levels of prior knowledge or expertise are able to acquire new information, retain new learning, and utilize stored knowledge more effectively than students with little prior knowledge or expertise (Cohen, 2008a). The greater the prior knowledge, the more easily new knowledge is linked with it, and the more resistant the resulting memory structure is to forgetting (Klimesch, 1994). Prior knowledge influences retention and recall more than strategy use or metamemory (Schneider, 1993), and expertise may even be powerful enough to compensate for general memory weaknesses. Moreover, increasing domain knowledge improves efficiency of memory processes, and a rich fund of information can diminish the need for strategy activation. Clearly, the level of prior knowledge is a primary source of individual differences in long-term memory performance. In scholastic learning, students with high prior knowledge about a topic will recall significantly more new information about that topic than students with low prior knowledge.

One way in which prior knowledge augments retention is that exposure to familiar material naturally stimulates elaborative processing as students think about what they already know and associate it with the new information. These elaborations produce alternate retrieval pathways and clues for reconstruction at recall. In a study with middle school students, Gagne, Yarbrough, Weidemann, and Bell (1984) found that after students read passages about familiar topics, they are able to retrieve the new information by first recalling the elaborations they thought of while reading. Consequently, students who lack prior knowledge will have difficulty remembering new information. In such cases, teachers should adapt instruction to each student's knowledge base so that the student has a framework in which to store the new learning. For learners with very limited prior knowledge, instructors should introduce concepts in a concrete manner, and they should elaborate for the students by drawing connections with basic facts, concepts, and categories the students possess.

Reducing Interference

Interference of one form or another is one of the primary causes of forgetting (see Chapter 2). In general, interference increases as the similarities between two sets of information increase. The degree of interference is also high when different sets of information are encountered too close together in time. Given the almost continual barrage of information K–12 students face for six hours per day, it is amazing that they remember as much as they do. Teachers can increase learning and retention by reducing interference through the following methods:

1. Helping students develop as much in-depth knowledge, mastery, or expertise in a subject as possible. Research has discovered that mastery of material allows that material to better withstand interference from related information.
2. Keeping lessons, presentations, and classes relatively short because long periods of instruction increase interference. Research on interference indicates that more is learned from short, spaced lessons than from very long sessions on the same subject. Most schools reduce interference in this manner by scheduling several different classes during the day.
3. Providing breaks of more than a few minutes between academic learning sessions. Research indicates that extending the intervals between lessons curtails interference, especially when back-to-back lessons contain similar types of material.
4. Increasing consistency in what is taught. When information presented on a topic is inconsistent, there is greater interference. For example, there is greater interference when a student is taught two different procedures for solving a particular type of arithmetic problem.
5. Using different contexts or settings to create more distinctions between subjects. For instance, students with a changing learning environment remember more than those who learn different material in the same environment (Anderson, 2000).

Context Cues

Academic content that will eventually become consolidated with semantic memories is primarily stored as episodic memories for the first few days and weeks after initial learning. Consequently, educators need to give serious consideration to any factors that increase retrieval of episodic memories. One of the main factors that enhance episodic retrieval is the presence of stimuli that elicit context cues that in turn facilitate retrieval of the targeted information. Contextual variables that can affect episodic recall include odors, sounds, temperature, lighting, persons present, objects present, size of room, location of room, and other physical characteristics of the learning environment (Smith, 1979). Being in a particular place reminds individuals of the contextual cues associated with that specific location. With academic learning, these episodic cues serve to remind students of associated facts they would otherwise not recall. Accordingly, memory researchers have reported evidence that students will perform better when they are tested in the same environment in which they learned the material (Cassaday, Bloomfield, & Hayward, 2002). The difference in performance has been attributed to the presence or absence of context cues. The impact of context cues on recall is significant. Memory retrieval may be as much as 30% higher when testing takes place in the same environment or context where the learning occurred (Schwabe, Bohringer, & Wolf, 2009).

Why They Work As discussed in Chapter 2, the acquisition of academic knowledge begins with specific learning episodes. Even though these episodes may ultimately coalesce into a general semantic representation, they are initially retained as episodic memories. While students are trying to learn the factual knowledge, they are simultaneously experiencing a variety of stimuli that then become associated with the new factual learning. Because these stimuli become bound (at least temporarily) to the factual information, recalling them mediates retrieval of the facts. As the material becomes consolidated and transferred to semantic memory stores (see Chapter 2), contextual details are forgotten and no longer facilitate recall. Therefore, new learning is more dependent on contextual clues than learning that has transferred from episodic to semantic storage.

The Research Godden and Baddeley (1975) were the first to report the effects of context-dependent memory on test performance. In their classic experiment, scuba divers, half of them on dry land and the other half submersed in water, learned word lists. When tested, each group performed significantly better in the environment where they had learned the words than when tested in the opposite environment. In other memory experiments (e.g., Smith, Glenberg, & Bjork, 1978) subjects have been found to recall more words when they were tested in the same room where they studied the words. Hudson and Gillam (1997) reviewed several studies of young children whose recall improved when they were able to view physical props that were present during the experience of a novel event. Mental reinstatement of the original learning environment also has been shown to improve performance. Smith (1979) found that undergraduate students can supply their own contextual retrieval cues, especially when the context can be easily recalled. Directing the students to first recall the learning environment significantly improves their word recall. In fact, the impact of context is more mental than physical. Even when recall occurs in the learning environment, the physical stimuli only serve to cue the mental cues, which in turn lead to retrieval of the desired information. Thus, Smith concluded that contextual associations in memory can be accessed mnemonically and that the physical stimuli need not actually be present.

How to Apply It in the Classroom   The finding that information is recalled better when the retrieval environment resembles the learning environment has implications for academic testing. Ideally, testing should occur in the same physical environment in which the learning took place (Koriat, 2000). For example, the common practice of pulling special education students out of the classroom for testing may actually hinder rather than enhance their performance. When testing in a different environment is unavoidable, students should be encouraged to imagine and recall the circumstances associated with the learning events. For example, students might be directed to imagine the room, the objects in it, and the persons present during the learning episodes (see Chapter 7 for more details). Students will recall information better when they can mentally recreate the contextual elements that are associated with the factual memories.

Unfortunately, the availability of contextual cues is relatively short lived. Most contextual cues are only available and helpful during the early stages of memory consolidation before memories have transitioned from episodic to semantic storage. That is, information tested a week after instruction may be primarily drawn from episodic stores, whereas a final semester exam must rely more on semantic memory. Thus, the availability and usefulness of episodic context cues will diminish as the interval between learning and testing is extended (Conway et al., 1997). Also, the teaching of the same content in different rooms can reduce the effectiveness of contextual cues because changing the learning environment introduces interference (Smith, 1979).

Organized Presentations

Educators are well aware of the importance of organized presentations, as organization is emphasized in effective teaching literature (Mastropieri & Scruggs 2007). Well-organized material not only enhances encoding but strengthens memory representations and enhances retrieval. Organization also significantly reduces the load on working memory (see section on working memory later in this chapter). Information can be organized in several different ways, from sequencing to grouping by similarities. The important variable is that the teacher's structuring of content makes sense to the students. A well-organized presentation begins with advance organizers, such as metaphors, that activate relevant background knowledge.

Visual Representations

A high proportion of students who struggle with academic learning have deficits in verbal abilities and verbal memory while possessing strengths in visuospatial processing and visuospatial memory. Traditional academic instruction puts these students at a disadvantage because it is primarily verbal. Research has clearly demonstrated that visual material, such as a picture, is particularly well remembered, especially when the learner has a meaningful interpretation of the picture (Anderson, 2000). Consequently, memory for verbal material can be improved by constructing concrete visual representations or creating mental images. For many students, independently converting verbal information into visuospatial information is too challenging. Thus, teachers should avail themselves of more opportunities to present material in a visual format along with verbal instruction. Visual representations include drawings, webs, graphs, pictures, and mind maps (Greenleaf & Wells-Papanek, 2005). For example, a history teacher might create a timeline with pictures of events and characters.

Mental Imagery

Learners benefit from mental imagery in much the same way they benefit from concrete visual representations. Mental images serve as visual representations in students' memory, thereby enhancing retention and recall of explicit learning. Although associative mental imagery is a critical component of all visual mnemonics, images need not involve structured associations to enhance retention and recall. Thus, no special training is required to capitalize on mental imagery. Basically, teachers just need to encourage students to generate images and give them time to do so. For most learners, creating mental images is relatively easy, as most learners who are reading, listening, or thinking have a natural tendency to generate mental images of the events or concepts involved. Another advantage of imagery is that it does not require much background knowledge. Distinctive images can be created even when there is limited prior knowledge. Also, imagery can support procedural learning and memory, in addition to explicit memory. For example, having students visualize themselves enacting each step in a procedure may be as effective as physical practice (Greenleaf & Wells-Papanek, 2005).

Despite the pervasive, independent use of imagery, there are some students who have difficulty creating images when directed to do so. For instance, early elementary age children or learning disabled students may not have the cognitive resources to generate and process imagery, other than simply picturing a word or action. Adequate working memory capacity is required to hold information, perform a skill such as reading, and create and process images simultaneously. Teachers might help such students by providing actual visual representations or by "painting a picture" for them. An alternative that strengthens weak images is to have students describe the details of their images. However, requiring imagery from students with learning disabilities may be counterproductive when the LD students are developmentally similar to younger children in their ability to generate effective images. For example, Rose, Cundick, and Higbee (1983) studied the reading comprehension and recall of 8-year-old LD children. Their subjects recalled more information from verbal rehearsal than they did from using a visual imagery strategy. Thus, when an imagery technique is taught in the classroom, LD students may need additional individual instruction and practice in the method, just as they do with academic skills. If imagery generation is still a challenge after additional training, then teachers should create the images and describe them to the students.

Emotions

It is a well-known fact that memories are more enduring when emotions are attached to them. The more emotional the student feels during learning or experiences, the deeper the information or episode is processed. The improved long-term retention is consistent with the principle that information is more memorable when it is processed more deeply. Also, the emotions function as cues that facilitate recall of the information associated with the emotions. Of course, overly emotional students may not be able to focus on the learning material itself (see Chapter 4). Some classroom procedures that might engage helpful levels of positive emotion include personal stories, role-playing, debates, persuasive writing, experiential learning, cooperative learning, and making the material personally relevant.

Music

Musical jingles have long been used in U.S. marketing of products because setting information to music makes it more memorable. It seems that redundancy and novelty in musical stimuli contribute to improved recall. In a scholastic environment, setting academic facts to music is easily accomplished when popular melodies are used. Educational research has confirmed that music aids the recall of students with learning disabilities (Ho, Cheung, & Chan, 2003). For example, students with learning disabilities recall significantly more multiplication facts when they use musical rehearsal instead of verbal rehearsal (Gfeller, 1986). In fact, music is so powerful that it need not be used as a mnemonic to influence memory development and functioning. Ho et al. discovered that musical training can actually improve verbal memory in children. The more music training during childhood, the better the individual's verbal memory. In order to produce this effect, music training needs to occur for at least three to six years. Also, the improvement is limited to the verbal domain; visual memory does not improve with music training.

Distinctive Learning Events

Learning and memory are enhanced whenever instruction can incorporate distinctiveness. For example, bizarre images are easier to recall than common ones. Distinctive learning events include those that are unique, unexpected, atypical, or begin with implausible information. Howe, Courage, Vernescu, and Hunt (2000) clearly demonstrated the positive impact that distinctive information and events can have on student's retention. In their study, pictures that were bizarre, colorful, or interactive were more memorable than black-and-white pictures of a single object. However, when the distinctive event contains information that is too novel and therefore difficult to associate with existing schemas, the advantage of distinctiveness may be lost. At some point during the learning episode, the information embedded in the distinctive event needs to be associated with related prior knowledge.

Strategies for Remembering Reading Material

As students mature, much of their knowledge needs to be acquired through independent reading. Regardless of their reading fluency or level of reading comprehension, many students of all ages read through masses of written material without acquiring any appreciable storage and recollection of the content. To remedy this situation, classroom teachers should consider explicit teaching of structured reading comprehension strategies. Remarkably, reading comprehension strategies not only improve comprehension but significantly increase retention and delayed recall of the content. Such strategies especially benefit students with memory problems ranging from mild to severe.

PQRST   A well-researched reading strategy that facilitates both comprehension and memory is PQRST (Preview, Question, Read, State, and Test). The PQRST technique consists of these steps: (a) previewing and skimming the passage; (b) generating at least four questions that need answers, such as who, what, when, and where; (c) actively reading the passage while seeking answers to the questions; (d) studying the information and stating the answers to the questions; and (e) self-testing on the answers to the questions. Using PQRST with reading material has been shown to improve delayed recall of passages in individuals with memory disorders (Franzen, Roberts, Schmits, Verduyn, & Manshadi, 1996; Wilson, 2009). Compared to simply rehearsing content that has been read, the PQRST approach has been found to be significantly more effective, even with TBI victims (Benedict, 1989; Wilson, 1987). PQRST seems to improve memory because it involves activating prior knowledge, elaboration, deeper encoding, self-testing, and attaching retrieval cues during encoding.

Other Reading Comprehension Strategies   Another strategy that enhances both comprehension and recall is the ARROW strategy, which stands for activate, read, reread, organize, and write. The ARROW strategy has been found to be particularly useful for increasing long-term recall of facts in expository texts, such as social studies textbooks (Wynn-Dancy & Gillam, 1997). Also, the BRIDGE strategy, which includes brainstorming, categorization, heirarchical organization, discussion, and self-questioning, has been found to facilitate comprehension and recall (Wynn-Dancy & Gillam). The primary reason for the success of both strategies seems to be the active associations made between the reading content and related schemas.

However, none of these multicomponent strategies may be necessary if the learner is able to systematically elaborate while reading (see this chapter's section on elaboration). Elaboration while reading not only enhances comprehension, but also it is an effective strategy for facilitating later recall of the passage. Teaching students to ask, "Why does this make sense?" after reading each paragraph will stimulate elaboration (see Chapter 7). An alternative is to provide readers with text that has embedded questions, or at least has questions at the end of a passage. Such questions have been demonstrated to induce elaboration and lead to better retention of passage information (McDaniel & Einstein, 1989). Embedded questions even improve recall for material not addressed by the questions. When students are reading orally, teachers may interject questions that induce elaboration.

STUDY SKILLS THAT ENHANCE MEMORY

Despite the obvious benefits of knowing how to study effectively, most children and adolescents are never formally taught higher-level study skills. In a survey of college students, 64% reported never being taught any explicit learning strategies (Willoughby, Porter, & Belsito, 1999). Left to their own devices, most individuals develop study habits that allow them to complete assignments, gather information, and prepare for examinations. However, many students never discover or systematically apply study skills that specifically support memory processes. The evidence is the common complaint from students that they can't remember information that they studied and thought they knew. Upon investigation, it's often discovered that students are not using effective encoding strategies while they study and that they don't know how to select and combine strategies for the task at hand. That is, a series of strategies or integrated strategies will improve retention and recall more than applying only one method. For example, forgetting will occur even after the deepest level of elaboration if the information is not retrieved or tested at periodic intervals (Wheeler et al., 2003). Many of the memory strategies already discussed in this chapter and Chapter 7 apply well to independent study. This section reviews a few additional study techniques that are consistent with basic memory principles.

Study Cards

Nearly every student has used study cards to memorize information. Study cards, or flash cards, have a prompt or question on one side and the correct response on the other side. The cards are typically created and used for difficult vocabulary or facts that need to be mastered, and students will periodically use the cards to rehearse the material. However, reading the cards over and over is an ineffective means of committing information to memory.

To obtain maximum benefit from study cards, there are several specific procedures to follow. First, when the items involve a question-and-answer format, students should be required to generate and write down their own questions. This recommendation is based on a memory principle known as the *generation effect*. Research has established that self-generated verbal items are retained better than verbal items that are provided. The generation effect occurs because the student is processing the information at a deeper level and because the questions generated by the student later act as retrieval cues for the correct responses (Carpenter & DeLosh, 2006). The generation effect has been observed in average individuals, and self-generation has been found to significantly improve verbal learning and memory in individuals with traumatic brain injury (Lengenfelder, Chiaravalloti, & DeLuca, 2007). Second, review of the study cards needs to be spaced, rather than massed. Rehearsing with study cards a few minutes each day is more effective than long rehearsal sessions or only reviewing the cards once before a test. Third, study cards should always be used in a self-testing fashion. This means not looking at the answer until a response has been retrieved and evaluated for accuracy. Finally, each time students review a set of study cards they should sort the cards into "know" and "don't know" piles during the first round. They should then proceed to spend more time rehearsing the "don't know" items. At the end of a study session, the "know" cards should be mixed back in so that they will be reviewed again at the beginning of the next session. The "know" items should never be permanently eliminated because they can be forgotten if not reviewed on a periodic basis (Karpicke & Roediger, 2008). Reviewing only some of the material can also create interference for the unpracticed information.

Review Sheets

When students need to remember information from textbooks, they typically highlight important information, take notes from the text, or re-read the text. An effective alternative that is similar to the study cards technique is to create and use a review sheet. These should be constructed in a question-and-answer format. The steps include the following: (a) reading the text a paragraph at a time; (b) selecting the most important facts from the paragraph; (c) generating short-answer questions for each fact; (d) writing the questions in the left-hand column and the answers in the right-hand column on a sheet of paper; (e) during reviews, covering up each answer until a response is retrieved; (f) and checking to see if the response is correct. Of course, the sheet should be reviewed periodically before taking a test on the material. This study method supports long-term memory processes through deeper processing at encoding, opportunities to reconsolidate the information, and strengthening retrieval through self-testing.

Studying Moderately Difficult Material

Even when they apply effective study methods, middle and high school students often perform poorly on classroom examinations because they have not invested enough time in studying and reviewing the more difficult material. For some students, the underlying problem is poorly developed metamemory, which results in overestimating how well they know the subject matter. Teachers might reduce this problem through metamemory instruction. For example, students need to understand that knowing something in the short term does not guarantee they will recall in the long term. At the other end of the continuum are students who invest all their study time on the most difficult material and still fail to recall it.

During study, learners with adequate metamemory development typically drop material they believe they have learned and focus further review and practice on material they have not yet learned. Allocating more time to the most difficult material makes sense and is encouraged in many popular study skills guides. However, with students who have memory problems it may not be the most productive approach because the reality is that they will not be able to recall the most difficult material even after intensive study. Perhaps, the best advice for students with memory problems is to allocate the most study time to content that is only moderately difficult to remember, not the most difficult material. Students have a better chance of learning and remembering moderately difficult content over very difficult content (Kornell & Metcalfe, 2006). Selecting the right material for further study may require some fine-tuning of judgments of learning such that content is not sorted simply into known and unknown categories, but partially learned content is also identified. For example, items that were known initially but forgotten a day later should receive more attention than very difficult items that were not understood or remembered during the first study episode.

Other Study Skills

For students with long-term memory impairments, basic study skills should be explicitly taught and reinforced. Students with memory impairments need to learn how to independently access information they cannot remember. Aside from notes, lists, and checklists, these students need to learn how to access information from textbooks, reference books, and the Internet (Rankin & Hood, 2005). Skills for accessing information from these sources include knowing how to use indexes, tables of contents, and search engines. Furthermore, students can build their own reference folders or memory notebooks that contain important and frequently needed information.

INSTRUCTIONAL METHODS FOR SEVERE MEMORY IMPAIRMENTS

Most of the instructional practices recommended in this chapter will benefit children and adolescents with mild to moderate memory impairments. For those with severe impairments, such as youth who have suffered a TBI or have developmental amnesia or a severe learning disability, most of the practices can still be effective, provided the methods are adapted and the procedures accentuated as necessary. However, there are a few methods reserved for youth with severe memory impairments. The methods reviewed in this section are primarily for these children, especially for those who suffer from persistent anterograde amnesia that makes explicit learning extremely difficult for them. For such children, the acquisition of skills and knowledge must rely more on implicit learning and memory. Although implicit memories cannot be accessed consciously, they do influence behavior and memory performance in everyone. With amnesiacs and TBI students, research has clearly documented that they are capable of learning even when they have no conscious recollection of the learning experiences (see Chapter 4). In such instances, their learning is successful because the methods are consistent with implicit memory functions. These special methods include reduction of errors, conditioning through shaping, and slower and more intensified rehearsal and practice.

Errorless Learning

The old adage about people learning from their mistakes may not apply well to children and adolescents with severe learning and memory problems. Allowing these special learners to make mistakes and errors during learning may only serve to make their mastery of the skill or material more challenging. Errorless learning is a method of instruction whereby the task is manipulated to eliminate or reduce errors. The premise is that reducing errors during acquisition promotes efficient learning and reduces forgetting. The objective of errorless learning is to prevent the student from making errors during learning. To accomplish this goal, opportunities for making errors are restricted. Usually, students are told or shown the correct information or response during a number of learning episodes. This approach is in contrast with common instructional methods where learners are encouraged to guess and are then provided with corrective feedback. Of course, guessing frequently results in erroneous responses, with the risk that the erroneous responses will be reinforced, learned, practiced, and subsequently become difficult to extinguish, especially in individuals who cannot recall learning experiences or corrective feedback.

Who Benefits Errorless learning has been demonstrated to be effective with children and adolescents suffering from moderate to severe memory impairments, including youth with pervasive developmental disorders, mental retardation, learning disabilities, and traumatic brain injuries (Mueller & Palkovic, 2007; Tailby & Haslam, 2003; Wilson, 2009). The effectiveness of errorless learning over trial-and-error learning was first documented in behavioral psychology research in the 1960s. Shortly thereafter, it was discovered that errorless instruction facilitated learning in children with intellectual disabilities. Subsequently, errorless learning methods were found to improve the learning and memory of youth with severe learning problems and disorders. Curiously, it wasn't until the 1990s that the technique was systematically applied to the treatment of memory disorders. Since then it has become clear that errorless learning is especially beneficial for students with severe memory impairments, such as those with acquired brain injury. Errorless learning has been used successfully with individuals suffering from retrograde and anterograde amnesia who do not benefit from traditional training methods and appear to have no explicit learning capabilities (Hunkin, Squires, Aldrich, & Parkin, 1998). Errorless learning techniques may also benefit individuals with less obvious memory impairments, such as those who are deficient in the metacognitive functions of monitoring performance, detecting errors, and updating knowledge on the basis of feedback. The opportunity to learn without producing errors also creates fewer processing demands on attentional and working memory resources, thereby making errorless learning an appropriate form of instruction for children with attentional disorders and severe working memory deficits. Not only does errorless learning benefit several disabled populations, but it is also very efficacious. In a meta-analysis of eight studies of errorless learning, Kessels and de Haan (2003) found a large and significant effect size of .87.

How It Works and Why It Works   Once an error has been expressed, it will become stored in memory and continue to interfere with successful performance until it's corrected. For students with significant impairments in explicit memory, unlearning errors is difficult because they can't remember the feedback that the response was incorrect. Curiously, they often don't remember making the mistake either. Yet, the mere act of making an error strengthens or reinforces that response and it's likely to persist, presumably due to implicit memory. That's because implicit memory is automatic and does not discriminate between correct and erroneous responses. Preventing erroneous responses prohibits them from being recorded in implicit memory. Eliminating errors also reduces interference from competing memory traces that would be stored in explicit memory. Consequently, it's best if errors can be prevented during learning when severe memory impairments exist.

Several researchers have reported that youth with amnesia learn better when they are prevented from making mistakes (Wilson, 2009). The initial explanation for the beneficial effects of errorless learning was that learning must be relying on implicit memory processes (Baddeley & Wilson, 1994). Because implicit memory unconsciously elicits production of the strongest response, erroneous responding during training should be avoided lest errors be strengthened through repetition. Individuals with acquired brain injury typically have such deficient episodic memory that they cannot remember skill training sessions and deny they possess the recently acquired skill even though they can perform it when prompted. However, the success of errorless learning does not seem to depend solely on implicit memory ability (Tailby & Haslam, 2003). Errorless learning has also been demonstrated to be effective with students who are capable of explicit learning. In fact, Tailby and Haslam, as well as Hunkin et al. (1998), claim that explicit memory processes and semantic memory are what actually underlie the errorless learning effect. However, it is more likely that both implicit and explicit memory processes underlie the errorless learning advantage (Clare & Jones, 2008). Consequently, errorless training methods may be an appropriate instructional choice for students with intact explicit memory and only mild to moderate memory problems.

How to Apply It in the Classroom   The benefits of errorless learning have been reported for several different types of learning materials and a broad range of tasks (Wilson, 2009). Superior performance under errorless learning conditions has been reported with the learning of word lists, word pairs, names of objects, names of people, colors, numbers, shapes, sight words, general knowledge, and multi-step skills. Errorless learning also has been used to teach basic word processing skills to amnesic patients who cannot remember being trained in the skills. In the classroom, current errorless learning techniques are similar to rote learning, as they involve repeated exposure to correct information. The classic scenario involves offering the student a choice, but the task is construed in such a manner that the student is highly unlikely to select the incorrect response. For example, after the student can identify a penny every time it is shown, a dime will be added to the scene and the student asked to select the penny. The dime is introduced in a manner that makes it unlikely to be selected, such as positioning it farther away than the penny. A variation of this approach is to preclude choosing the incorrect response by making it physically impossible to select even though it is displayed. In another option, known as "delayed prompting," the teacher initially points to the correct choice immediately and then gradually delays pointing, giving the child a chance to respond first (see Mueller and Palkovic, 2007, for implementation details). Reduction and elimination of errors during learning can also be achieved by the following: providing written instructions; modeling the steps of a procedure a little at a time; guiding the student through the task; encouraging the student to avoid guessing; immediately correcting errors; carefully fading prompts; and breaking the task into small, discrete steps (Clare & Jones, 2008). Given the extent of practice and the incremental changes required, computers with touch-screen monitors are an ideal method of delivering errorless instruction.

Errorless learning methods have successfully been combined with various memory strategies and instructional practices. For instance, errorless learning works well when combined with spaced and expanding-interval rehearsal. Elaborative rehearsal methods have also been incorporated with errorless learning, based on the presumption that increasing the level of processing during encoding will further enhance learning and retention. As predicted, adding elaborative processing was more effective than errorless learning techniques alone (Tailby & Haslam, 2003). Thus, teachers who apply errorless learning methods can incorporate active processing methods, as long as the student is not completely amnesic and the additional procedures do not increase erroneous responses.

The application of errorless learning methodology in the classroom commonly involves the use of programmed materials that use stimulus shaping and fading techniques to promote discrimination learning (Cipani & Madigan, 1986; Mueller & Palkovic, 2007). These methods typically provide special cues that reduce errors.

As learning proceeds, the special cues are gradually removed until they are completely withdrawn. For example, superimposed pictures of words, such as a picture of a cat appearing in the background of the printed word "cat," have been used to teach reading. Over five stages, the intensity of the picture decreases while the prominence of the word increases. Curricula such as *Distar Reading, Distar Arithmetic,* and *Reading Mastery* have applied stimulus shaping and fading techniques (Cipani & Madigan).

Disadvantages and Concerns   There are several drawbacks and concerns regarding the errorless learning method. First, errorless learning is restricted to certain types of skills and knowledge. Second, it does not generalize well across learning situations. Third, the learner may generate covert errors of which the teacher is unaware. Fourth, a completely errorless learning procedure is very difficult to attain. In reality, errorless learning is a managed learning condition under which there are fewer errors than normal instruction allows. Fifth, effortful learning, including making an effort to retrieve, needs to be encouraged during errorless learning because if the learner is too passive little learning will take place. Finally, for students with severe memory impairments, repeated testing may impair learning rather than enhance it, unless the testing interval is very short or the test's structure is modified to reduce errors. Because error prevention is crucial during the early stages of learning, testing without cues should be avoided until the skill or knowledge is mastered. Being allowed to make errors on a test only serves to reinforce the incorrect responses, even when corrective feedback is provided. Even a recognition type of test may be counterproductive during the early stages of learning.

Vanishing Cues

The vanishing cues method is another clinically researched approach that has applications in an educational setting, especially for learners with severe explicit memory impairments. This method is similar to errorless learning in that both methods minimize student errors and both rely mainly on implicit learning and memory. Unlike errorless learning, which can be effective with little or no explicit memory functioning, vanishing cues is more effective with individuals who have at least some explicit memory. Vanishing cues is essentially a faded cuing technique that initially provides enough information for a correct response and then progressively withdraws (or fades) parts of the information across learning trials. For example, when teaching vocabulary the full word is presented for at least 10 seconds, then the word is presented with some letters showing and blanks indicating the number of missing letters. When the learner fails to produce the correct response within 10 seconds another letter is added and so on. The first letter is a stronger cue than other letters; thus, training is more effective if the first letter is withheld until last. When teaching a procedure, vanishing cues uses a backward chaining technique. In backward chaining, the student is first guided through the entire task. Next, the student is guided through all the steps except the last one, then the last two steps in the chain are omitted, and so on. Vanishing cues may work because it is a cued-recall task and because it minimizes interference. Unfortunately, the vanishing cues method does not emphasize error prevention as much as errorless learning. Some vanishing cues methods actually encourage the learner to guess. Consequently, vanishing cues has been found to be a less effective approach than errorless learning (Kessels & de Haan, 2003). However, training that combines the two approaches is very effective.

Recognition Testing

"Recognition testing" refers to test formats, such as multiple choice, word banks, and matching, in which the learner needs to select the correct response from a group of options. Essentially, recognition formats provide response cues. The ability to recognize a response precedes the ability to freely recall and express it, much like receptive vocabulary precedes expressive vocabulary development. Thus, recognition testing is an appropriate formative type of testing that can play a role on the way to mastery. For students with significant retrieval problems, recognition testing is an accommodation that affords them the opportunity to demonstrate the knowledge they possess. However, this type of cuing may do little for students with anterograde amnesia because they usually have not been able to consolidate and store the new learning. Moreover, there are some risks associated with multiple-choice testing. For instance, the exposure to incorrect responses has the potential to create interference and the implicit learning of errors.

Incremental Rehearsal

Practicing too much new material at a time has been shown to be less effective than intermixing unknown information with known information. Burns and Boice (2009) replicated a study in which intermixing one unknown item with nine known items produced significantly better long-term retention of the new items than having students rehearse items that were 50% or 100% unknown. This method of one to nine intermixing, known as *incremental rehearsal*, can produce two to three times as much retention of new learning as traditional approaches do. Although the incremental rehearsal method takes longer for students to complete (because it includes so many already known words), the net gain in new words acquired per minute invested can be twice that of the other methods. Incremental rehearsal is recommended for students with significant learning and memory impairments.

Additional Recommendations

Additional instructional recommendations for students with severe memory impairments include:

1. Providing the students with study guides that are formatted the same as the test. For example, if vocabulary words are to be matched with their definitions on the test, then the study format should also consist of matching. The principle underlying this application is the encoding specificity principle: When the cues provided at retrieval are similar to those present during encoding (learning), recall is enhanced.
2. Using very structured, "direct instruction" curricula. Direct instruction approaches have been shown to be effective with TBI children (Glang, Singer, Cooley, & Tish, 1992; Mateer, Kerns, & Eso, 1996).
3. Using experiential learning in which students learn by doing.
4. Reducing the quantity of material to be learned at any one time, with the focus on the most important information.

ACCOMMODATIONS AND MEMORY AIDS

Whereas the needs of most children and adolescents with memory problems can be met through the instructional practices and memory strategies discussed in this chapter, some students also will require accommodations and external aids to more effectively access their learning and memory capabilities. Academic accommodations and memory aids include:

1. Providing preferential classroom seating that reduces distractions during encoding (learning).
2. Guiding the student through retrieval by providing prompts and increasingly specific cues.
3. Allowing extended time on examinations.
4. Providing the student with review and study guides as soon as the instructional unit begins (not waiting until just before the exam to provide these).
5. Allowing the student to review unit quizzes and no longer used unit examinations.
6. Providing the student with more recognition-type test items than classmates.
7. Simplifying and paraphrasing verbal information to facilitate encoding.
8. Providing the student with more elaborations than other students or helping the student to self-elaborate each time a new concept is introduced.
9. Reducing the amount of information that the student must learn for examinations.
10. Allow the student to use procedural checklists as a memory aid (see Chapter 7 for more details); for example, a checklist might contain all of the steps necessary for solving a particular type of math problem.

TEACHING MEMORY STRATEGIES

In addition to incorporating memory strategies into their instructional practices, teachers can help students with memory problems become successful, independent learners by directly teaching them how to use memory strategies. Most of the memory strategies covered in Chapter 7 can be efficiently taught in the classroom. For some strategies, only minimal instruction and prompting is necessary. For example, instructing students to sort information on the basis of meaningful categories, instead of superficial characteristics like sound or color, may be all that is necessary for them to adopt the practice of semantic clustering. On the other hand, more involved strategies like elaboration may require prolonged, direct instruction, with modeling, scaffolding, and lots of varied, guided practice.

Ideally, there should be some memory strategy instruction during each academic year. Even first graders are capable of learning basic memory strategies, such as rote rehearsal and cumulative rehearsal. Sophisticated strategies, such as elaboration, should not be taught until later elementary or middle school. Only one strategy should be taught at a time and should be practiced and reinforced until students have mastered it (see Chapter 7 for more recommendations for strategy training). One of the advantages of acquiring strategies at an early age and making sure they're mastered is that students will obtain some automaticity with them. Accruing strategies through the years also prepares students for the time when learning is complex and many facts need to be committed to memory.

Beginning in first grade, various forms of rote rehearsal should be taught. Rote rehearsal basically involves non-associative repetition, such as whispering verbal information over and over. Although rote rehearsal is effective for short-term memory, it does little to enhance long-term retention. Nonetheless, it occupies a developmental niche and needs to be mastered before students attempt other strategies. Thus, first graders and developmentally delayed children should be taught how to properly perform rote rehearsal, with more sophisticated forms of rehearsal, such as cumulative rehearsal, added as they become developmentally ready. The Chapter 3 section on memory development provides information that can be used to determine when to teach the remaining memory strategies (also see Table 5.3).

TEACHING MNEMONICS

Mnemonics differ from general memory strategies in that mnemonics consist of structured procedures for associating new content with well-established, but logically unrelated, memory representations. The well-established memory representations are easily and automatically recalled, thereby increasing the recall of the new content that has been associated with them. Mnemonics are particularly helpful when the learner lacks prior knowledge to which the new material can be connected. In such instances, mnemonics function as a scaffold until the new knowledge is consolidated (see Chapter 7 for an in-depth discussion on mnemonics). Training students to use visual mnemonics over verbal mnemonics is recommended because visual mnemonics are more effective and have broader applications than verbal mnemonics. Although visual mnemonics share properties with the general use of imagery during instruction, students will need to be trained to adhere to step-by-step procedures for visual mnemonics to work. Fortunately, such training can easily be conducted on a classroom-wide basis.

Efficacy

Teaching students how to use mnemonics has been shown to significantly improve school performance, especially for students with learning problems (Mastropieri & Scruggs, 1991). As summarized by Carney, Levin, and Levin (1993), student use of mnemonics in the classroom (a) improves students' memory for terminology and facts, (b) benefits all types of learners at all ages, (c) allows retention of information for long periods of time, and (d) enhances the ability to apply the new knowledge. Even preschoolers can benefit from mnemonics instruction (Kraft, 1990). For example, preschoolers who were taught to use the loci method (see Chapter 7) to study word lists recalled 80% of the words in the correct order, whereas controls recalled only 25% (Kraft, 1990). The children in the study were capable of generating their own associational images as long as they had an observable path to follow, and they even displayed the ability to transfer the strategy to different situations. Regarding teachers' use of mnemonics in the classroom, researchers have reported that mnemonics are flexible, can be easily combined with instructional strategies, and can be applied to most academic content (Carney et al.). For example, mnemonics have been used to remember content from social studies, science, vocabulary, foreign languages, and spelling.

Keyword

All of the mnemonics recommended in Chapter 7 are suitable for classroom training, but the keyword method seems to have the broadest applications (Mastropieri, Scruggs, & Levin, 1985; Uberti, Scruggs, & Mastropieri, 2003). Chapter 7 contains the details for step-by-step training of keyword. In addition to using keyword to learn new vocabulary and a second language (Condus, Marshall, & Miller, 1986), it has successfully been used to teach paired items such as state capitals. For example, here are the steps involved in creating and retrieving a mnemonic that will allow students to remember that Topeka is the capital of Kansas:

1. Have the class create and agree on a keyword for the state; for example, Kansas sounds like "cans."

2. Have the class create and agree on a keyword for the capital; for example, Topeka might remind a person of "toe."

3. Have the class create a unique image that combines the two keywords; for example, the image might be a row of cans with toes pictured on the cans and a label that says "Canned Toes."

4. Train the students to first think of the keyword for Kansas when they are asked, "What is the capital of Kansas?"

5. After they recall that "cans" is the keyword, train them to next recall the image with cans in it.

6. Train the students to use the information in the image to arrive at the correct response. For example, when they see toes on the cans, they should automatically recognize that "toe" is the keyword for Topeka, and therefore the correct response must be "Topeka."

7. Practice steps 4 through 6 until the students can perform them without prompts.

8. For children who have difficulty recalling images, pictures of the images should be drawn and used during the learning phase.

INSTRUCTION THAT REDUCES WORKING MEMORY LOAD

Because of the integral relationship between working memory and long-term memory, anything that supports or strengthens one enhances the other. Long-term memory enhances working memory capacity by delivering information that is well organized in schemas (see Chapter 2). Schemas support efficient processing in working memory because the large amount of information contained in a schema can often be processed as a single unit in working memory. Also, long-term memory can reduce processing time in working memory when retrieval is automatic and accurate because retrieval pathways have been strengthened through effective encoding, consolidation, and repeated retrieval. For its part, working memory supports long-term memory processes by providing enough resources for effective encoding and reconsolidation, for consciously organizing and connecting information during encoding, and for supporting retrieval when conscious searching is necessary. Thus, interventions and instructional methods that increase the efficiency of working memory also serve to support and improve long-term memory systems and processes. Consequently, classroom techniques and interventions for working memory (see Dehn, 2008) should be part of any improvement program for long-term memory.

The strong influence of working memory on academic learning is so pervasive (Dehn, 2008) that it should never be ignored, even when student long-term memory functioning is normal. With working memory in the classroom, the concern is twofold: first, all students have a limited working memory capacity, and second, typical classroom instruction is constantly overloading students' working memory. Although fully developed short-term memory can hold about seven items of information, adult working memory can only process four units of information at a time (Cowan, 2005), and children and adolescents can process only two or three units of information simultaneously (Kirschner, 2002). When working memory is overloaded, cognitive tasks are not completed, including effective encoding of information into long-term memory. Thus, efficiently utilizing working memory without overloading it leads to effective learning and long-term retention of learning.

Applying Cognitive Load Theory

Cognitive load refers to the amount of combined processing and storage that can be handled by working memory and interrelated processes. Cognitive load is created by the inherent nature of the material (e.g., degree of complexity) and by the manner in which the material is presented. Cognitive load theorists (e.g., Kirschner, 2002) assume that working memory is easily overwhelmed by too much cognitive load, especially during classroom instruction. Cognitive load theorists are concerned with reducing cognitive load during classroom instruction because learning diminishes as the load on working memory becomes excessively high (Pass, Renkl, & Sweller, 2004). Excessive loads occur during complex learning tasks where learners must simultaneously process several information elements and their interactions. Cognitive load theorists believe that instructional design can be used to keep student working memory load manageable. For example, a disorganized presentation requires much working memory processing by the learner just to make sense of the material. Therefore, instruction should be designed in a manner that allows the typical learner's working memory to adequately process the information. When the load from content and presentation is minimal, learners can engage in the conscious cognitive processing necessary for enhancing schemas and other memory representations.

A basic premise of cognitive load theory is that interactions between long-term memory and working memory play a significant role in academic learning (Clarke, Ayres, & Sweller, 2005). When working memory is overloaded, learning is impaired and the amount of information that can be effectively encoded is reduced. That is, students learn best under "low load" conditions. Given this concern about memory and learning in the classroom, cognitive load theorists have empirically identified several instructional methods that reduce working memory load (van Merrienboer, Kirschner, & Kester, 2003). Their recommendations for reducing cognitive load include:

1. Instruction should assist the learner in constructing and expanding organized schemas because an organized schema allows more information to be processed in working memory without creating an overload. Elaboration

is one method that supports construction and expansion of organized schemas.

2. Instruction and curriculum should be designed in a manner that eliminates or reduces information that is not germane to the task or to the content to be learned.

3. Completed or "worked" examples should be used to teach procedures, such as how to complete a particular mathematics operation. Worked examples reduce problem-solving search strategies that impose a heavy load on working memory. This approach allows learners to initially study the procedures and solutions to problems without having to keep all of the steps in mind. Over time, this procedure fades out the completed examples, step by step beginning with the elimination of the first or last step.

4. Similar to the worked examples approach, teaching of new skills or material can begin with partially completed items. For example, when teaching how to spell a word, some of the word's letters should be provided. As learning progresses, more and more of the item must be completed by the student.

5. When teaching a complex task, instruction should begin with subcomponents and simple applications of the task.

6. Information should be presented in both visual and verbal modes.

7. Instruction should be designed in a manner that encourages and supports the use of memory strategies; for example, material might be clustered semantically before it is presented.

8. Unnecessary wordiness and embellished materials should be avoided. Presentations should use concise wording and material should be straightforward and relevant.

9. Teachers should provide plenty of scaffolding (devices and strategies that support learning), at least during early stages of learning. Scaffolds should be embedded in the learning tasks.

10. Coaching students during retrieval reduces working memory load. Coaching includes hints, cues, prompts, feedback, and suggested search strategies.

11. Presenting information sequentially and just in time helps manage working memory load. That is, necessary information and procedures should be presented precisely when learners need them during task performance. For example, when students are analyzing data in a science class, the data would be withheld until students are ready to begin analyzing them.

12. The theory and rationale underlying a procedure should be taught before students begin practicing and applying the procedure.

13. Instructional materials should be compiled and integrated in a fashion that does not require the learner to simultaneously use two sources of material, such as shifting between printed directions and a procedure on a computer screen.

Additional Recommendations

In addition to the practices derived from cognitive load research, there are several other empirically based methods for reducing working memory load. These practices also enhance long-term memory processing and storage:

1. Basic working memory strategies, such as chunking and cumulative rehearsal (Dehn, 2008), should be taught classroom-wide in the early elementary grades.

2. All verbal communication should be linguistically simple, brief, and concise. Sentences should be syntactically simple, vocabulary should be highly familiar, and wording should be redundant and precise.

3. Tasks that require secondary processing should be avoided. Only one focused activity should be conducted at a time, and multitasking should be prevented. Information should not be presented while learners are engaged in an activity that is demanding their attention. For example, it is difficult to listen attentively and write down notes at the same time. Ideally teachers should pause while students are copying notes. In general, teachers should try to minimize competing inputs by requesting only one process or operation at a time.

4. Ample exposure, repetition, and practice should be provided at times when the demands on working memory are minimal. Directions and instructions should be repeated frequently, and students should be required to repeat information. There should also be numerous opportunities for student rehearsal.

5. Students need to be allowed enough time to process new information and retrieve prior knowledge. It can take up to a minute or more to initially process a new idea and encode it. When asking questions, teachers need to allow sufficient time for students to retrieve information and construct a response.

6. Students need to be actively involved during learning, as opposed to rote repetition or passively listening to instruction. When students are actively engaged with the material, teachers should encourage them to process it deeply by thinking and making elaborations.

7. Most of the external aids for long-term memory mentioned in Chapter 7 also serve to reduce the load on working memory. For example, a checklist of procedures to follow during mathematics problem solving reduces demands on both long-term and working memory.

8. A quiet learning environment not only reduces interference but also prevents disruptions to working memory processing. Background speech is known to reduce verbal working memory span by interfering with rehearsal functions.

9. Academic content should be presented in an integrated and organized manner. Organized presentations, a cornerstone of effective teaching, enhance long-term retention while reducing the processing load on working memory.

10. Teacher-directed elaboration and other methods of activating relevant prior knowledge, such as advance organizers, reduce the need for working memory to retrieve related information and to recognize and create connections.

For more suggestions on reducing working memory load in the classroom, see Dehn (2008) and Gathercole and Alloway (2008).

SUMMARY: LONG-TERM MEMORY PRINCIPLES AND RECOMMENDATIONS FOR EDUCATORS

By adhering to some basic long-term memory principles that relate to academic learning, many teachers will be able to intuitively and creatively apply these principles without dramatically altering their classroom environments or significantly modifying their instructional practices. Essentially, this author believes that teachers already have all the skills they need, as they are already experts at promoting learning. As they gain more expertise on the encoding, consolidation, and retrieval aspects of memory and learning, they will become even more effective at promoting long-term memory storage and retrieval. These are some key long-term memory principles and recommendations that educators should keep in mind:

1. Students remember best when information makes sense to them.
2. Students remember best when information is organized semantically.
3. Students remember best when information is presented in both a visual and verbal mode.
4. Students remember best when emotions are associated with the information.
5. Students remember best when context cues and other retrieval cues are attached to the information because successful recall depends on the availability of appropriate retrieval cues. Mnemonics are known for connecting information to retrieval cues (see Chapter 7). The student's own retrieval cues are more effective than retrieval cues provided by teachers.
6. Students remember best when information is reviewed on an expanding-interval basis. For students with memory problems, doubling the length of each succeeding interval between review sessions is ideal for increasing retention. For example, reviews could be scheduled one day, two days, one week, and two weeks after initial learning.
7. Students remember best when information is actually retrieved instead of just repeated. Delayed retrieval that requires some effort is more effective than easy retrieval that occurs after a very short delay. Effortful but successful retrieval facilitates future retrieval.

8. Students remember best when they are periodically tested on new learning. Repeated testing of the same content promotes long-term retention because it requires retrieval of the studied information. As knowledge is consolidated and retrieval pathways are strengthened, the intervals between retesting can become longer (Bahrick, 2000).

9. Students remember best when they process information at a deeper level, such as an abstract, schematic, or conceptual level, as opposed to information that is processed according to superficial characteristics, such as color or sound.

10. Students remember best when they use a memory strategy or mnemonic.

11. Students remember best when they use elaboration to make connections between new information and related concepts. Self-generated elaborations are more memorable than teacher-generated elaborations.

12. Students remember best when they have adequately developed meta-memory. Supporting the metamemory development of students will prompt and enhance development of more sophisticated memory strategies.

13. Some methods that facilitate short-term maintenance of information are ineffective at improving the retention and recall of long-term memory representations. For example, repetition works well for short-term memory but does little to ensure long-term retention of new learning.

14. For students with severe memory impairments, prevention of erroneous responses during learning is important.

15. Study is most effective when the learner must retrieve information from long-term memory rather than short-term memory.

16. The quality of rehearsal has more influence on retention and recall than does the quantity of rehearsal. For example, effortful, elaborative rehearsal is more effective than lots of easy, rote rehearsal.

17. How the information is processed is more important than whether or not the learner intends to remember the material.

18. Reduction of interference is important. Trying to learn too much material at one time is ineffective because of the buildup of interference. Recently formed memories need a chance to consolidate before more content is introduced. Also, events and material that are distinctive from previous events and other recently learned material are remembered better than similar events and closely related material because the greater the similarity, the greater the interference.

19. The success of strategy instruction is dependent on the extent to which it is supplemented by metamemory information. Maintenance, transfer, and generalization are dependent on conditional metamemory knowledge about why, when, and where to use the strategy (see Chapter 7). Moreover, strategy instruction should make the value and effectiveness of the method evident to the student.

20. Students should be tested in the same environment where the learning took place so that the environment prompts contextual cues that then mediate

retrieval of the factual knowledge. When tested in a different environment, students should be reminded to think about the context of the learning environment.

21. The more difficult the learning activity, the more it promotes long-term memory storage, even though it may slow initial learning. Techniques that make initial learning slower and more effortful usually enhance long-term retention. Fast acquisition of information does not guarantee long-term retention and retrieval. Creation of enduring, accessible memories takes time and effort.

22. The discovery, learning, and application of memory strategies are more likely to occur during less cognitively demanding learning activities because adequate working memory resources are necessary for the learning, performing, and monitoring of strategies (Waters & Kunnmann, 2010).

23. For students with retrieval problems, a teacher may support retrieval through prompts, cues, and allowing recognition responses.

24. Instruction is most effective when it is consistent with how the brain typically processes, stores, and retrieves information.

25. When applied in the classroom, the methods recommended in this chapter will help educators achieve one of the primary goals of education: the acquisition of knowledge that will be remembered for a lifetime.

Case Studies and Recommendations

ASSESSMENT CASE STUDY

The case of "Sarah" illustrates how a concussion (or mild traumatic brain injury) incurred during a school sporting event can cause memory problems that might persist for weeks or months. (A brief overview of Sarah's injury, assessment, and memory problems is at the beginning of Chapter 4.) Sarah, a high school student, experienced post-concussion syndrome after being kicked in the forehead during a soccer match. Her physical symptoms consisted of dizziness, fatigue, nausea, and severe headaches. Her memory was also affected; for example, during the first few days following the injury she displayed amnesia for certain events and facts, such as being unable to recall the combination to her school locker. Despite her debilitating physical symptoms, Sarah returned to school within a few days even though she frequently was unable to complete a full day of school. After a month, the dizziness and nausea subsided, but she was still experiencing daily fatigue and migraine-like headaches.

Within a couple of weeks of the incident, Sarah's normal grades indicated that she was not experiencing memory problems that were significantly impacting academic performance. Nonetheless, her parents suspected memory problems as they observed her and helped her study. During the first two weeks after the injury, it was obvious to her parents that Sarah was having difficulty remembering material she studied. Sarah also was having everyday memory problems, such as not remembering where she had placed objects at home. For a few days after the concussion, Sarah even displayed signs of partial temporary amnesia for skills and knowledge she had previously known, such as how to multiply. Sarah was frightened by the amnesic experiences, but after a few days she insisted that she was not having any memory problems. After learning more about the memory risks associated with mild head trauma, Sarah's parents decided to have her memory tested.

When the memory evaluation was conducted 33 days after the injury, Sarah was still experiencing daily fatigue and headaches. During the interview with her mother present, Sarah gave the impression that she was no longer having any memory problems. In contrast, Sarah's mother reported indications of minor ongoing memory problems, but Sarah disputed them all. The most interesting exchanges between Sarah and her mother involved recounting of past events, including events that happened prior to the concussion. Not only did Sarah often disagree with her mother about what had transpired, but her dates for the events were significantly off. For example, Sarah insisted that the head injury had happened on a date approximately six weeks before the actual incident. Although Sarah's mother agreed that the amnesic-like problems evident during the first week had been resolved, she was still concerned about Sarah's memory functioning.

In reviewing Sarah's history, there was no indication of any prior memory problems. There were no conditions in her medical history that would put her at risk for memory problems. Also, Sarah's academic progress had been normal and her grades in high school were average. Her only academic challenge was higher-level mathematics, for which she had been receiving some after-school assistance and tutoring. The challenge with all post-TBI and post-concussion memory evaluations is not having any pre-injury data on the child or adolescent's memory functions. Fortunately, in this case there had been some selective cognitive testing just four months earlier. At the time, the goal was to test cognitive aptitudes for mathematics reasoning and calculation. Select tests from the Woodcock-Johnson® III (WJ III) Tests of Cognitive Abilities had been administered. Although there had been little testing of long-term memory functions, Sarah's WJ III scores indicated that her memory abilities were normal. Her WJ III Working Memory (verbal) cluster score was 97 (mid-average), her Retrieval Fluency test score was 102 (mid-average), and her Spatial Relations score of 96 indicated that her visuospatial processing abilities were also average.

After the interview, Sarah was administered the entire Wechsler Memory Scale-Fourth Edition (WMS®-IV). In addition, the verbal working memory subtests from the WISC®-IV Integrated were administered. Although Sarah was not enthusiastic about being tested, she did cooperate and made an effort to perform well. During testing she displayed few observable signs of how she was processing or trying to recall the material. She seemed focused and responded at a normal rate even on the tasks that were difficult for her. Also, she displayed no signs of frustration. When prompted to continue on some tasks, she would say that she was unable to recall any more information. Given her denial of current memory problems, Sarah seemed interested in trying to demonstrate that she had no memory problems. During testing Sarah reported that she was feeling fine and she did not take any breaks when offered the opportunity.

Sarah's memory profile from the WMS®-IV and WISC®-IV Integrated testing was very clear (see her June scores in Table 9.1). Her auditory/verbal memory was average, both for short-term and long-term memory. In contrast, her Visual Memory composite, at the 5th percentile rank, was well below average, and both short-term and long-term memory performances were equally deficient. In addition, her visual working memory was at the 1st percentile, and her verbal working memory was at the 18th percentile. On the WMS-®IV Sarah was equally weak in both the visual and spatial aspects of visuospatial memory. Sarah's visuospatial test performance was consistent with her mother's reports that Sarah was having significant difficulty

Table 9.1   Sarah's WMS®-IV and WISC®-IV Integrated results

Index	Score (June)	Score (November)	Change
Auditory Memory	98	101	+3
Visual Memory	76	84	+8
Visual Working Memory	67	77	+10
Immediate Memory	81	91	+10
Delayed Memory	90	92	+2
Auditory Short-Term (Clinical)	98	103	+5
Visuospatial Short-Term (Clinical)	75	85	+10
Auditory Long-Term (Clinical)	100	100	0
Visuospatial Long-Term (Clinical)	85	88	+3
Verbal Working Memory (Clinical)	86	101	+15

remembering where she had placed objects in the home environment. Furthermore, Sarah's problems with delayed recall of visuospatial episodic memory could not be attributed to a retrieval problem, as her visuospatial recognition performance was no better than her uncued delayed recall (indicating that the visuospatial information had not been retained). It was evident that Sarah had an impairment in visuospatial episodic memory that involved all three major memory systems: short-term, working, and long-term.

Given the limited pre-injury data, it was difficult to determine whether in fact Sarah's memory deficits could be attributed to her injury. When her verbal working memory score from June was compared with prior cognitive testing, it appeared that there had been a significant decline. (When comparing within child scores, a standard score difference of 10 of more points is likely to be significant.) Her verbal working memory had dropped 11 points from a standard score of 97 (42nd percentile) to a score of 86 (18th percentile). There were no premorbid data to compare her extremely low Visual Working Memory Index of 67 and her Visual Memory Index of 76 with. However, her pre-injury WJ III Spatial Relations test score of 96 (40th percentile) indicated that any visual memory problems could not be attributed to premorbid visuospatial processing impairments. It was unlikely that her pre-injury visuospatial memory functioning had been more than a standard deviation (20 points) lower than her visuospatial processing level. Moreover, there were no preconcussion indications that Sarah's visuospatial memory was so low. Consequently, it was hypothesized that Sarah's concussion had caused some dysfunction in her visuospatial memory that was unusual because it had not cleared up within a few days of the concussion.

Given that it was June and school was out for the summer, it was decided to wait until fall and give Sarah more time to recover from her mild traumatic brain injury. Thus, no interventions were implemented over the summer. When school resumed, Sarah's parents reported that she seemed to be doing fine although they did want her retested to determine whether there had been improvement. After some cancelled appointments, Sarah returned in November, six months after the injury and five months after her initial memory assessment. Sarah reported that she was still having almost daily headaches and recently had begun experiencing severe bouts of vertigo that made it difficult for her to function in school. Her physician thought the vertigo might be due to the concussion. Her mother reported that Sarah was doing well in school and was no longer exhibiting any obvious signs of memory problems. Once again, Sarah was administered the WMS®-IV and WISC®-IV Integrated. The interval seemed to have been long enough to avoid concern over practice effects, and Sarah gave no indication of recalling any details from previous testing.

Upon retesting, Sarah maintained her average performance in verbal episodic memory while exhibiting significantly improved performance in the visuospatial domain, especially in the short-term and working memory systems (see Table 9.1). Her visual working memory score was 10 points higher, visual memory overall (both immediate and delayed recall) was up 8 points, and short-term memory improved 10 points (mainly due to the visuospatial component). When clinical factor scores were computed for visuospatial short-term memory, there was also a 10-point improvement. However, there was only a non-significant change of +3 points when clinical scores for visuospatial long-term memory were calculated. Interestingly, all of Sarah's gains in visuospatial short-term memory were due to improved visual recall, not any improvement in spatial recall. Specifically, her Designs I recall for content (visual) went from a scaled score of 3 to a scale score of 9 while her Designs I spatial recall remained at a scaled score of 5. As before, her visuospatial performance did not improve significantly under recognition conditions. Overall, Sarah's greatest gain was in verbal working memory, which improved 15 points, returning to mid-average functioning where had it had been prior to the injury. Therefore, the opportunity to reevaluate Sarah provided further evidence that she had in fact suffered some memory impairment that persisted beyond the immediate effects usually observed during post-concussion syndrome. As this text went to press there had not been another opportunity for a follow-up assessment with Sarah to determine whether she continued to recover more visuospatial memory functions.

INTERVENTION CASE STUDIES

George's Intervention

The case of "George" is used to illustrate three things: first, how extremely slow processing speed, along with subaverage short-term and working memory, can limit effective functioning of long-term memory; second, how parental involvement makes a difference in the success of an intervention; and third, how long-term memory strategies and mnemonics can improve academic learning and performance.

Background   When he was in second grade, George was diagnosed with dyslexia by a psychologist at a medical clinic. George's school district refused to recognize the diagnosis. So, George continued in regular education until fourth grade when, according to his mother, he became very frustrated with reading and academic learning, in general. At that point, his parents withdrew him from school, and his mother, a trained teacher, began homeschooling him. Near the end of seventh grade when George was 13, he and his parents came to this author seeking assistance. George's mother reported that George had such difficulty with reading fluency and reading comprehension that she frequently read academic material to him. He was also struggling significantly with handwriting and written expression to the extent that she usually functioned as his scribe. Moreover, although George wanted to succeed, he had a difficult time studying independently, especially for extended periods of time. Consequently, his mother usually guided him through worksheets and reviewed all of the material with him prior to exams. George's mother also reported that he had difficulty remembering what they studied and performed poorly on unit examinations in the curricula they were using at home. Finally, there were indications that George had difficulties with selective, sustained, and divided attention. Parents and student were frustrated. Their goal was for George to return to full-time public school when he reached ninth grade.

Assessment Results   George was administered the complete WJ III COG and WJ III ACH batteries. His WJ III COG General Intellectual Ability (GIA) score (similar to an IQ) was 101, a mid-average score. However, there were extreme differences among his cognitive abilities, with his cognitive cluster scores ranging from 74 to 134. George exhibited a profile consistent with reading and written language disabilities. First, George demonstrated that he had high average intellectual ability, as he performed very well on the two factors that load highest on general intelligence: fluid reasoning and crystallized intelligence. George's Fluid Reasoning score was 134 (99th percentile) and his Comprehension-Knowledge (crystallized) score was 105 (64th percentile). His auditory, visual, and phonological processing scores were all mid-average. Second, George had processing deficits that were impeding his academic learning. The primary deficit was George's extremely slow processing speed, a challenge that was also evident during his second-grade evaluation. His Processing Speed score of 77 was at the 6th percentile. In addition, he had subaverage abilities in phonological short-term memory (score of 84, percentile of 15) and verbal working memory (score of 84, percentile of 14). Third, George's academic skills were significantly discrepant from his overall learning aptitude, as indicated by his WJ III ACH Broad Reading score of 81 (10 percentile) and his Broad Written Language score of 76 (6th percentile). Despite these challenges, George was able to learn fundamental material at an average rate, as indicated by his Visual-Auditory Learning score of 100, and his retrieval fluency for known facts was average, as indicated by a score of 90. Given George's assessment results, it was hypothesized that: (a) his slow processing speed, coupled with short-term and working memory deficits, meant that he was losing a substantial amount of information before he could encode it into long-term memory; (b) the same processing deficits, coupled with poor reading fluency, made reading comprehension challenging; and (c) once he learned and consolidated new content, he could retain and retrieve that information without difficulty. It was decided to provide George with tutoring in reading comprehension, written expression, and study skills, along with an individualized memory intervention program.

Memory Training Sessions   One unique aspect of George's memory training was that his mother observed all nine weekly, one-hour sessions. As his mother was also his teacher, George was comfortable with her presence, and did not look to her for assistance or approval. After each of George's sessions, his mother was provided with about 15 minutes of consultation in which the procedures were reviewed, the rationale explained, and plans for home follow-up were discussed. Without the consistent practice and reinforcement at home during the week, it would not have been feasible to teach so many strategies to George in such a short period of time.

As suggested in Chapter 7, George's first session emphasized metamemory awareness and the potential efficacy of using memory strategies. With George, the session began with explanations of why and how his slow processing speed and memory challenges affected his learning. The discussion then focused on the differences between short-term, working, and long-term memory, with an emphasis on the importance of maintaining information long enough for it to be processed and then encoded into long-term memory. The whole sequence of processing was illustrated for George with a graphic that began with selective attention and that divided memory systems into verbal and visual. The metamemory instruction concluded with an emphasis on humans' ability to make their memories stronger through the use of strategies. Appropriately, this was followed by the efficacy demonstration explained in Chapter 7, in which George was able to recall a semantically clustered list of words significantly better than a random list of words. Because of George's additional difficulties with attention, there was also a discussion about focusing on the most important information and trying to filter out any information that is no longer relevant. During this conversation, George volunteered that he had problems getting rid of thoughts that interfered with what he was trying to comprehend and process. He explained that this interference became worse when he was tired, and agreed that taking regular breaks seemed to help. The session concluded with practicing basic subvocal rehearsal. Like most students with delayed metamemory, George was familiar with rote repetition, but did not use cumulative rehearsal. After a few rounds of practice, he demonstrated that he could perform and apply cumulative rehearsal.

The second training session began with a review of the previous week's content, followed by more cumulative rehearsal practice. The basic short-term memory strategy of chunking was then introduced. Curiously, George had a difficult time trying to chunk numbers, not being able to consistently pair them up without confusing the sequence or the numbers to pair. After a few attempts, it was decided that this method was not going to work for George, and there was no further attempt to teach it in subsequent sessions. The bulk of the second session focused on practicing recoding visual information into verbal information and recoding verbal information into visual images. George reported that he had not recoded information in the past, even though he seemed quite capable of doing it proficiently. The session ended by introducing the *n*-back procedure (see Chapter 7 for details) for strengthening working memory. A round of *n*-back with a regular deck of cards would be practiced at each succeeding session, with an emphasis on maintaining a rehearse-and-inhibit strategy that enhanced the ability to reach 10 correct responses in a row.

During the third session, keyword was the first new method that was introduced and practiced (see Chapter 7 for details). When using keyword, the importance of making the images personal, funny, and unique was stressed, along with the idea that making personal connections with academic material can facilitate recall. George seemed to enjoy sharing the funny images he was creating, but he had a tendency to skip the mnemonic steps and blurt out the answer during the retrieval stage. Consequently, the importance of following the steps, by first thinking of the keyword and then the image, was emphasized and the retrieval steps were practiced several times. For the remainder of the session, there was some practice using semantic maps to organize thoughts for writing assignments, a method that was expected to relieve some of the load on working memory that occurs when trying to put ideas into writing.

During the fourth session, the new strategies focused on methods that would concurrently enhance reading comprehension and long-term retention. George was taught a modified version of PQRST (see Chapter 8) that incorporated an elaboration technique. Using a school social studies textbook, George was taught to preview everything (such as pictures, headings, and review questions) but the text itself. Following the preview, George generated a few questions that he wanted to learn the answers to while reading the section. It was explained to George that previewing and questioning "opened up his files on the topics," thereby facilitating connections between the new input and prior knowledge. As he read, George was taught to stop at the end of each paragraph, pick one of the important facts or ideas in that paragraph, underline that fact or idea, ask himself "why" that fact or idea made sense, and answer the why question as best he could. Answering the "why" question was the elaborative component (see Chapter 8) added to PQRST. After the reading and elaboration strategy were completed, George first checked to see which of his questions he had learned the answers to, and then he reviewed the information by rereading the content that he had underlined. During this lesson, George's poor reading fluency and slow processing speed came into play. To cope with these challenges, George was taught to reread sentences that didn't make sense or contained a word he did not recognize. The PQRST and elaboration processes were challenging for George. Although he was successful at acquiring and retaining important information, he was fatigued by the end of the session.

After reviewing and practicing methods learned previously, the fifth session introduced new verbal and visual mnemonics. Because of George's strong verbal abilities, acronyms and acrostics were tried. Although George seemed to retain those that were provided to him, he had difficulty generating memorable acronyms or acrostics. In contrast, he was more successful when asked to create sentences that contained words and facts that needed to be memorized. To strengthen the recall of his sentences, George was taught to visualize them. In addition to elaborative sentences, George was taught the loci method (see Chapter 7) during this session. For loci, George created images that paired social studies facts with furniture in his bedroom. Again, his images were quite creative and his recall for the facts studied in this session was perfect for the next few weeks.

The sixth session was unique from the others in that the focus was on dealing with prospective and everyday memory problems. Because George was being homeschooled, he had never been required to record due dates and other information in an assignment calendar. After practicing how to use an assignment calendar, there was discussion about self-cuing, such as placing objects in a manner that prompts recall of a task that needs to be completed. Next, there was practice at creating and using "to do" lists. The other part of the session involved suggestions for reducing the load on working memory during academic tasks. First, a written rubric for editing writing assignments was created so that George could use it as a reminder when editing and revising writing assignments. Then there was practice writing down partial solutions during mental arithmetic so that they would not be forgotten while trying to complete the remainder of the problem.

The seventh session introduced some effective practices to apply when reviewing and studying information in preparation for upcoming tests. First, George practiced creating vocabulary study cards, receiving some help writing them out because of his slow handwriting. Next, he learned how to sort the study cards as he reviewed them, placing those that were quickly and easily recalled aside while continuing to rehearse the more difficult ones. Then there was a discussion about when to study and review, with an emphasis on spaced practice. This was operationalized by having George plan the times he would study for a test and enter these dates into his assignment calendar. This discussion included a suggestion to review important information just before going to bed the night before a test. Finally, there was an explanation of the rationale for self-testing, followed by practice with his study cards.

The first half of the eighth session involved review and practice of the methods introduced in the previous two sessions. The second half focused on the working memory overload that was created when George attempted to take notes while listening to instruction. Note taking was a tremendous challenge for George because of his slow processing speed, slow handwriting, and below average working memory span. After discussing the concern with George and his mother, it was decided that the best approach was for George to reduce note taking and writing demands as much as possible. The solution was for George to use abbreviations and shorthand. To increase the number of abbreviations that could be recalled, George was taught to put an abbreviation key in his notes that consisted of words that were used repetitively. For example, if the teacher was constantly referring to "global warming," George would write "GW = global warming" at the top of his notes and use "GW" whenever the teacher referred to global warming. The second aspect of succeeding at note taking was for George to learn some basic shorthand. This was accomplished outside of the training sessions by George and his mother studying shorthand and having George use it while taking notes. Reportedly, George enjoyed learning and using the shorthand, and he was able to successfully take notes in class during his next semester at school.

During the ninth and final session, there was a review of all the memory strategies and mnemonics that George had been able to successfully learn. Regarding each strategy, there was discussion of why it worked and how it could be applied to school studies. Following the review, George practiced selecting strategies for a specific task, and then practiced using two strategies to accomplish the same task. The session concluded with George writing out a list of how to "study and remember for tests." His list included these items: "difficult words—make a mind picture to help remember; study most important parts first; and review what was highlighted."

In addition to memory training sessions, George was tutored in study skills, including homework completion skills, test-taking strategies, and other reading comprehension strategies. After the memory training sessions ended, George and his mother did consistently practice and apply the new methods at home and into eighth grade. As George began eighth grade with a couple of courses in a private school, his academic performance improved significantly, his confidence grew, and his frustration abated. Although little hard data had been collected during the intervention, George and his parents needed no convincing. They were so pleased with George's progress that they announced in their family Christmas letter that the memory training had had a significant impact on George's life.

Data From Abby's Intervention

The case of Abby was first introduced at the beginning of Chapter 2. The reader may recall that Abby struggled to acquire and retain academic knowledge, often performing poorly on classroom examinations that she had studied extensively for. When assessed, it was discovered that Abby's phonological short-term and verbal working memory were at the low end of the average range (see Table 9.2). In contrast, she had subaverage abilities in verbal episodic memory, learning (encoding), retrieval fluency, and the visuospatial components of working and episodic memory. (For more details, see the Illustrative Report section later in this chapter.) Abby received individual one-hour memory training sessions, twice a week for six weeks during the summer when she was 16. During the sessions Abby learned many of the same memory strategies and mnemonics that "George" had learned (see his intervention earlier in this chapter). Consequently, there will not be a session-by-session review of Abby's intervention. Rather, the information reported on Abby will focus on unique contributions of her intervention, as well as some data on her performance.

The main objectives for the first session were to informally assess Abby's metamemory, begin metamemory training, have Abby set goals, and illustrate the efficacy of a higher-level memory strategy. The session began with Abby responding to written and oral metamemory items. Following completion of the scale, the trainer immediately reviewed the items and then asked some follow-up questions. The metamemory assessment revealed that Abby's knowledge of how memory functions was fairly typical for an adolescent. A couple of common misconceptions that she asserted were that recall "depends on what you want to remember" and short-term memory "lasts for at least an hour." On the other hand, Abby made it clear that she understood memories don't just happen when she said, "Most of my memory problems come from how much effort and energy I put in." Her understanding of self-regulation and appraisal of what works also seemed appropriate when she stated that "only you are in control of your memory" and "strategies help a lot." When asked about her own memory strengths and weaknesses, she revealed that she knew about her long-term memory shortcomings. She stated that "getting it to stick" was the hard part and that she was frustrated that she would forget so much of what she studied. In later sessions, it would also become apparent that Abby's judgments of learning were fairly accurate; she had a good sense of what she would be able to recall at a later time. Overall, her metamemory seemed well developed for her age and intellectual ability, perhaps because her memory challenges had spurred its development.

Next, there was goal-setting activity in which Abby was invited to write out her goals for the memory intervention. Her goals for improving memory were: "Being able to remember stuff faster, keep important stuff in my mind even if I don't need it, and remember what I had reviewed for a test and still have it the next day." Abby was told that her goals were appropriate and that many of the intervention's activities would be directed towards her goals and towards academic studies. The trainer then explained that his goals for Abby were (a) to increase her metamemory awareness and regulation; (b) broaden her use of effective memory strategies; and (c) improve her abilities to encode, store, and retrieve information she studied for academic subjects.

Data was kept on Abby's retention of information studied with strategies. Sometimes, her strategy-based performance was contrasted with her non-strategy-based learning of equivalent material (both sets were studied during the same session). Abby was always shown her test data to illustrate the efficacy of the strategies she was learning. Because she knew that her day-to-day retention was 50% or less, anything greater than 50% accuracy impressed her. Here are the some of the data that demonstrated strategy effectiveness:

- Spanish vocabulary was studied with and without keyword. One week later, Abby recalled 80% of the keyword items, whereas she remembered only 20% of the non-keyword items.

- For state capitals, keyword recall a week later was 75%, whereas non-keyword recall was 50%.
- When she used the "why does this make sense" elaboration technique to study social studies facts, her recall after two days was 75%, followed by 100% a week later and 100% two weeks later. (The testing effect might have accounted for the improvement without re-study.)
- When she used the pegword mnemonic to study 10 items, her recall after two days was 80%.

Throughout the sessions, Abby was given time to write down her reflections about what she was learning during the memory sessions: Here are some of her comments:

- "Memorizing words the old way was so slow and time consuming."
- "Pictures make it a lot easier."
- "Asking why is this important so that it will help trigger the fact."
- "The method I like is pictures because it's fun to create funny ones to help memorize."
- "Studying it every day is not helpful but expanding the time period on studying is more successful."
- "I like using keyword because finding what it sounds like and then creating a picture to help remember the word definitely helps."
- "When using strategies, memory is powerful."
- "My final thoughts on memory is that it can be a lot easier once you use various helpful strategies."

During the final session, Abby was asked to write up her own "Study and Memory Plan" for the fall semester. In the plan she was asked to specify the memory strategies and mnemonics she planned to use. The content of Abby's plan made it evident that she had learned several strategies and understood how to apply them. Here is Abby's plan:

1. Memory likes organization
   - Grouping when possible (Social Studies, Science)
   - Flashcards in categories
2. Picture things
   - Keyword: action picture
   - Pegword if things have to be in order
   - When reviewing a list of words, stop and picture each one
3. Putting pictures into words
   - Both picture and word
4. Other methods
   - Why does this make sense?
   - Review important stuff before you go to sleep

5. Review schedule
   - Spread review out
   - Start early—days ahead
   - Test yourself
6. Short-term memory
   - Keep repeating it to yourself
   - Group in chunks

When Abby returned to school in the fall, she was more confident than ever of her ability to study and memorize independently. Except for her continuing struggle in written language assignments, her high school grades were better than in the past. During subsequent conversations with Abby, she reported that she was continuing to use several of the memory enhancing methods she had learned over the summer. There were several reasons for the apparent success of Abby's intervention: (a) she came to all the sessions with a positive attitude, (b) she knew she had memory problems and was goal-driven to improve her memory, (c) she believed in the efficacy of the strategies and mnemonics, (d) her metamemory had reached a mature level of development, and (e) she was completely engaged in the activities throughout the sessions.

ILLUSTRATIVE REPORT

Recommendations for Report-Writing

When writing the interpretative section of a psychological report, the primary goal should be to explain the assessment results in a manner that the majority of readers can understand (see Chapter 5 for more recommendations on interpretation). Here are some recommended approaches for accomplishing this goal when writing reports that include results of memory testing:

1. The interpretation should focus on the individual, not on test scores.
2. The interpretative (or discussion) section should include an explanation of how the test results were analyzed. When there has been a cross-battery analysis of results, such as that recommended in Appendix B, the report writer needs to explain what the scores were compared with (e.g., a Full Scale IQ, cross-battery mean, etc.) when determining potential discrepancies.
3. The interpretative section of the report should be organized by domains, not by tests. Reporting and interpreting results test by test or method by method without integrating information across tests and methods makes it difficult for most readers to understand what the results mean for the examinee. For example, the interpretative report might be subdivided by cognitive processes and memory components. Then, as each component is discussed, all

relevant test scores and corroborating information are reported and explained within the subsection on that component.

4. For each cognitive process and memory component there should be an understandable definition, an example, and an application to academic learning.

5. When reporting memory strengths and weaknesses, the writer should specify whether they are normative, intra-individual, or both.

6. Corroborating information from informal assessment procedures should be included in the same paragraph as the standardized test scores.

7. An implication of the test performance in terms of real-world or academic performance should be stated.

8. When there is a deficit that is indicative of a disability or disorder, it should be indicated.

9. When applicable, the writer should indicate the extent to which the findings confirm or disconfirm the hypotheses that led to the testing of particular processes or memory components.

10. When applicable, the writer should introduce new hypotheses that account for the examinee's test performance.

The interpretative report section that follows is an attempt to illustrate these recommendations and provide a model for interpretation of memory assessment results. This report is limited to the test-results interpretative section that might be written when there has been a cross-battery assessment of memory and related processes. This report is about Abby, whose background information is at the beginning of Chapter 2 and whose analysis of test scores is in Table 5.6.

Abby's Report

A comprehensive assessment of Abby's cognitive abilities and memory functions was completed because of Abby's significant ongoing problems with academic learning and performance. First, Abby's general intellectual abilities were assessed with the Wechsler Adult Intelligence Scale-Fourth Edition (WAIS-IV). On the WAIS-IV, Abby obtained a Full Scale IQ of 89, which has a percentile rank of 23. The confidence interval associated with her score of 89 indicates that there is a 95% chance that Abby's true Full Scale IQ is within the range of 85 to 93 and that her general intellectual abilities are in the low average to average range. The two primary factors measured by the WAIS-IV are Verbal Comprehension and Perceptual Reasoning. Based on Abby's Verbal Comprehension Index of 93 (percentile of 26), it appears that Abby's ability to reason and express herself verbally is in the low average to average range. In contrast, her Perceptual Reasoning abilities (which are a combination of fluid reasoning and visuospatial processing) are well below average, as indicated by her Perceptual Reasoning Index of 73 (percentile of 4). Second, several of Abby's memory functions and specific cognitive processes were assessed. The tests and subtests used to evaluate these components were selected

Table 9.2   Abby's test results

Memory or Processing Component	Battery	Subtest or Factor	Subtest/ Factor Scores		Component Mean
Verbal Episodic	WMS-IV	Logical Memory II	(10)	100	88*
		Verbal Paired Associates II	(5)	75	
Visuospatial Episodic	WMS-IV	Designs II	(7)	85	78*
		Visual Reproduction II	(4)	70	
Semantic	WAIS-IV	Vocabulary	(11)	105	100
	WJ-III ACH	Academic Knowledge		94	
Retrieval Fluency	WJ-III COG	Retrieval Fluency		76	76**
Learning	WMS-IV	Verbal Paired Associates I	(5)	75	76**
	WJ-III COG	Visual-Auditory Learning		77	
Verbal WM	WAIS-IV	WORKING MEMORY		92	92
Visuospatial WM	WMS-IV	VISUAL WM		83	83*
Phonological STM	WJ-III COG	SHORT-TERM MEMORY		92	92
Visuospatial STM	WMS-IV	Designs I	(7)	85	75**
		Visual Reproduction I	(3)	65	
Processing Speed	WAIS-IV	PROCESSING SPEED		89	89*
Fluid Reasoning	WJ-III COG	FLUID REASONING		85	85*

*A normative weakness.
**Both a normative and an intra-individual weakness.

from three additional batteries (see Table 9.2): the Wechsler Memory Scale–Fourth Edition (WMS-IV), the Woodcock-Johnson III Tests of Cognitive Abilities (WJ III COG), and the Woodcock-Johnson III Tests of Achievement (WJ III ACH). To determine Abby's intrapersonal strengths and weaknesses, her scores on the cognitive and memory components were compared with her WAIS-IV Full Scale IQ of 89.

Fluid Reasoning   Fluid reasoning is the ability to reason and solve problems, especially during novel situations. Fluid reasoning is one of the strongest contributors to general intellectual ability and is essential for successful functioning in reading comprehension and mathematics reasoning. For example, the ability to write an algebraic equation for a story problem requires fluid reasoning. An estimate of Abby's fluid reasoning ability is provided by her WJ III COG Fluid Reasoning score of 85. Abby's low average functioning in fluid reasoning could account for the difficulty she has in academics that require logic, applications, and higher-level reasoning. For example, low average reasoning will make it difficult for Abby to understand proofs in geometry. Despite its importance, Abby's fluid reasoning ability only partially accounts for her academic learning and performance difficulties.

Processing Speed Processing speed refers to how quickly individuals process information and perform simple cognitive tasks. Processing speed plays an important role in most aspects of academic learning. When processing speed is too slow, learners may have difficulty completing tasks or lose information before it can be transferred to long-term memory. Based on her WAIS-IV score of 89 (percentile of 23), Abby's processing speed level is at the low end of the average range, consistent with her overall intellectual ability. Her processing speed seems adequate for most cognitive and learning tasks. When observed, the only sign of slow processing she displays is when she is retrieving information, but that may be primarily a function of retrieval inefficiency.

Phonological Short-Term Memory Phonological short-term memory involves the brief retention and immediate recall of auditory and verbal information. It is important for vocabulary development, basic reading skills, and spelling. Abby's phonological short-term memory capacity appears to be average, based on her Short-Term Memory cluster score of 92 from the WJ III COG. Abby's average ability in this memory component is consistent with her average verbal abilities and average scores in verbal episodic memory, semantic memory, and phonological processing skills (tested during a previous evaluation).

Verbal Working Memory Verbal working memory involves the ability to briefly retain verbal information while processing the same or other information. It is important for reading comprehension, note taking, and written expression. Abby's verbal working memory capacity is equivalent to her phonological short-term memory span, as indicated by her WAIS-IV Working Memory Index of 92. Abby's average functioning in verbal short-term and working memory is consistent with teacher reports that Abby seems to have good immediate recall during instruction and study. Although it was suspected that a deficit in verbal working memory might account for Abby's learning and performance problems, this does not appear to be the case.

Verbal Episodic Memory Verbal episodic memory involves the delayed recall of verbal information that has been recently learned. All learning of academic material is initially stored in episodic memory before it makes the transition to semantic memory. For example, when Abby takes a quiz on material learned the day before, she must rely heavily on her verbal episodic memory. Overall, Abby's verbal episodic memory functioning appears to be in the low average range, as indicated by her WMS-IV clinical score of 88 (derived from the Logical Memory II and Verbal Paired Associates II subtests). However, Abby's delayed recall for the type of material learned in a scholastic environment is well below average, in contrast with her recall for the type of verbal information encountered in daily living. For example, Abby obtained a mid-average score on the WMS-IV Logical Memory I and II subtests that involve recall of stories about everyday life events. In contrast, her below average recall of paired words on Verbal Paired Associates I and II was significantly lower. Although

Abby struggles to learn and retain facts, concepts, and abstract verbal information, she performs at an average level when the information is more familiar and easily associated, such as the contextual information in a narrative. Regardless of the content, Abby's verbal delayed recall is equivalent to her verbal immediate recall. The information that she is able to encode into long-term memory is retained at a normal level, at least over the 30-minute delay in the WMS-IV.

Visuospatial Short-Term and Working Memory Visuospatial short-term memory is the ability to briefly retain visuospatial information, whereas working memory involves the ability to briefly retain and manipulate visual and spatial information, including mental images generated by the learner. Although visuospatial working memory is not a significant individual weakness for Abby, her ability in this memory component is clearly in the low average range, as indicated by her WMS-IV Visual Working Memory score of 83. In contrast, Abby's short-term visuospatial span is a deficit for her because it is both a normative and intra-individual weakness, as indicated by her clinical visuospatial short-term memory score of 75 (derived from the WMS-IV Designs I and Visual Reproduction I subtest scores). Although visuospatial memory abilities apply more to everyday functioning than academics, they can be employed when memorizing academic content.

Visuospatial Episodic Memory Visuospatial episodic memory is the ability to remember visual and spatial information after a delay. Successful recall of visual and spatial information can serve to cue recall of abstract and verbal information. Abby's clinical score of 78, derived from her performance on the Designs II and Visual Reproduction II subtests from the WMS-IV, reveals that visuospatial episodic memory is a significant normative weakness (relative to peers) and most likely an intrapersonal weakness as well. Her deficit in this memory function seems to originate with immediate loss of spatial information in her short-term and working memory systems. There is no decrement in her visual recall of stimuli between short-term and long-term recall; what she remembers immediately, she is able to retain and retrieve later. However, there is a significant decline between her nearly average short-term spatial recall and her well-below average long-term spatial recall. Also, she performs worse when recall is completely uncued. For example, she had extreme difficulty reproducing a design from memory but performed closer to average when she could pick out the stimuli from a group of cards.

Learning/Encoding Two controlled learning tasks, Visual-Auditory Learning from the WJ III COG and Verbal Paired Associates I from the WMS-IV were used to assess Abby's ability to efficiently learn novel material when provided with corrective feedback across several trials. To succeed at these structured tasks, the examinee needs to effectively encode the new material into long-term memory. With below average standard scores of 75 and 77 on these two tasks, it appears that Abby is very inefficient at encoding new information and consequently needs more repetition and opportunities to learn than the average student. In addition to encoding being a normative weakness for Abby, it is also an intrapersonal weakness. Her deficit in encoding is not due to an inability to retain information long enough for encoding, as her short-term and working memory spans are average and significantly higher than her encoding ability. Consequently, her encoding deficit is probably related to ineffective encoding strategies or an underlying neurological impairment in the ability to transfer information from short-term to long-term memory.

Semantic Memory   Semantic memory consists of the factual, conceptual, and verbal knowledge that an individual retains on a relatively permanent basis. Learners accrue semantic memories through repeated episodic learning events. Consequently, semantic memory level can be higher than episodic memory level, provided there are abundant opportunities to learn the material. This scenario appears to be the case with Abby, whose semantic memory, as measured by the WAIS-IV Vocabulary subtest and the WJ III ACH Knowledge subtest, is in the mid-average range (with a clinical factor score of 100). Although Abby is slow to learn academic content, she does acquire an average amount of knowledge because of the extensive tutoring and guided home study that she receives. Her average semantic memory score indicates that she is able to retain information on a long-term basis once that information becomes consolidated in long-term memory.

Consolidation   Basically, consolidation consists of automated processes that transfer information from episodic storage to semantic storage. Consolidation is a relatively slow process that can take days, weeks, or longer. For consolidation to occur, information must be encoded into episodic memory and retained there long enough for automated memory processes to transfer it to more permanent storage in semantic memory. Abby's primary memory challenge seems to be that a relatively limited amount of information is initially encoded into her episodic memory. In addition to an encoding weakness, it is suspected that Abby also has problems with consolidation, meaning that information available for consolidation is not being effectively consolidated before it is forgotten. (There is also the possibility that her consolidation functions are normal, but she is forgetting information at an unusually fast rate.) Abby's consolidation abilities were not formally tested, but reports from her teachers, tutors, and parents are consistent: Abby seems to forget a lot of information that she is initially able to retain for 30 minutes, a day, or a week. For example, comparison of her daily quizzes and summative examinations reveals that she does worse on summative examinations.

Retrieval   In addition to difficulties with encoding and consolidation, Abby appears to have difficulty efficiently retrieving verbal and visuospatial information that she knows, as indicated by her below average WJ III COG Retrieval Fluency score of 76. Abby's retrieval fluency score represents a deficit (and likely impairment), as it is both a normative and intra-individual weakness. When learners have problems with retrieval, they cannot produce responses on demand even when they know the material. This appears to be the case with Abby, as her recall improved significantly during verbal and visuospatial recognition tasks on the WMS-IV.

Summary Abby has several memory weaknesses and deficits that make the acquisition, retention, and retrieval of knowledge difficult for her. First, she loses a significant amount of verbal information during the learning stage because of ineffective encoding, even though her short-term and working memory spans are adequate. It is likely that she has a neurological impairment in the ability to transfer information from short-term to long-term memory. Second, although it cannot be ascertained, it appears that she is not consolidating many of her episodic memories before they decay. Third, Abby has difficulty efficiently retrieving information that she has retained in episodic or semantic memory. Essentially, Abby seems capable of normal long-term storage once her memories become consolidated. She also has normal storage over a short delay, such as 30 minutes. Her problems lie not with storage or retention, but the processes involved in encoding, consolidating, and retrieving information. Although poor use of memory strategies can exacerbate these problems, strategy deficiencies do not appear to be the cause of Abby's memory problems, given her extensive guided study opportunities. Overall, her verbal episodic memory is stronger than her visuospatial episodic memory, but performance within each domain varies, depending on the nature of the content.

RECOMMENDATIONS FOR FUTURE RESEARCH

1. More memory research needs to be conducted with children and adolescents. To date, the majority of memory studies have been with adults.
2. More memory studies need to be conducted in educational settings, with the goal of understanding the most effective ways for children to acquire and retain information in the classroom. Traditionally, memory research has been conducted in the laboratory or an analog environment. These types of studies lack ecological validity and generalize poorly to the classroom.
3. Research in educational settings should focus on instructional methods and study techniques that have the potential to enhance retention and recall of semantic information in children with mild to moderate memory problems. Ideally, these studies would be long-term, across days, weeks, and months. Studies that track memories from initial acquisition to final test would allow for some control over encoding and other study variables that influence long-term retention.
4. Research articles by neuroscientists and neuropsychologists should discuss the implications of their findings for acquiring academic knowledge.
5. More research needs to be conducted on the mechanisms of consolidation and on how conscious efforts might influence the consolidation of memories.

6. More research needs to focus on the influence that parents and teachers have on children's memory development, including metamemory and memory strategy development.

7. All learning-related disorders should be reexamined to determine the contribution of memory impairments.

RECOMMENDATIONS FOR MEMORY TEST DEVELOPMENT

Although recent revisions of cognitive and memory scales have incorporated new subtests that take contemporary memory theories and research into account, the development of some additional tasks could enhance the value of memory testing while maintaining efficiency. Here are some suggestions:

1. An age-appropriate, long-term memory screener for preschoolers and kindergarten students could help with the early identification of students at-risk for learning and memory problems. Such a screener should include a controlled learning task, retrieval fluency, and measures of delayed verbal and visuospatial episodic memory.

2. The most serious deficiency across school-age memory batteries is the lack of a norm-referenced, extended-interval, delayed recall measure. Nearly all current batteries limit delayed recall intervals to about 30 minutes. This prohibits discovery of consolidation and retention problems in children who have normal recall for 30 minutes or so but then have rapid forgetting afterwards. Checking delayed recall at one day or a week is quite feasible in scholastic environments, as school psychologists are typically housed in schools and can conveniently access students for retesting.

3. Creating memory tests that have follow-up measures of delayed recall after extended intervals could also provide opportunities to more directly assess semantic learning and memory. For example, a controlled learning task might teach the examinee some novel facts or vocabulary, and then proceed to test the examinee's retention after a week or month when presumably the new knowledge would need to be retrieved from semantic memory stores.

4. Although its use might be limited to youth with developmental amnesia or traumatic brain injury, there is a need for a test of "everyday memory" that has U.S. norms. Such a battery would evaluate the examinee's prospective memory, along with memory abilities, such as spatial recall, that are important for everyday functioning.

5. A standardized measure of metamemory would provide useful information, especially for recommendations and interventions. Perhaps the most valid approach to metamemory assessment would be a rating scale with parent, teacher, and student forms, similar to the rating scales used to evaluate

executive functions. Such a rating scale might also encompass items about memory strategy usage, much like those items found in rating scales for study skills.

6. More scales are needed that attempt to directly assess encoding. Currently, it is difficult to parse out the influence of encoding on memory test performance.

Memory Assessment Plan

Student _____ DOB _____

Age _____ Grade _____ School _____

Date of Referral _____ Form Completed By _____

Date _____

Referral Concerns	Memory Hypotheses[*]	Assessment Methods	Memory Batteries/Tests	Memory Subtests

[*]Types of memory to consider: Phonological Short-Term, Visuospatial Short-Term, Verbal Working, Visuospatial Working, Prospective, Verbal Episodic, Visuospatial Episodic, Semantic, Retrieval, Recognition, Metamemory, Strategies, Learning

B

Analysis of Memory Testing Results

Examinee's Name: _____ DOB: _____

Age: _____ Grade: _____ Dates of Testing: _____

Memory Component	Battery Name	Subtest/ Factor Name	Subtest/ Factor Scores	Component Mean	Composite or Mean	Difference	Normative S, W, or A	Ipsative S or W	Deficit or Asset
Verbal Episodic									
Visuospatial Episodic									
Semantic									
Retrieval Fluency									
Recognition									
Learning									
Verbal WM									
Visuospatial WM									
Phonological STM									
Visuospatial STM									
Other:									
Other:									

Component and Score	Component and Score	Difference Between Pairs	Significant Difference: Y/N

Directions: (1) Convert all subtest scores to standard scores with a mean of 100 and an SD of 15. (2) For each memory component, compute the mean of the subtest scores and round to the nearest whole number. (3) Enter a cognitive composite, such as a full-scale IQ, or compute the mean of all available memory components. (4) Subtract the composite or mean from each memory component mean and enter the amount in the Difference column. (5) Indicate whether the memory component is a normative weakness, strength, or average (90-109 is average). (6) Using a criterion of 12 to 15 points, determine ipsative strengths and weaknesses. (7) Determine deficits and assets. A deficit is both a normative and ipsative weakness; an asset is both a normative and ipsative strength. (8) Determine which factors are non-unitary. Factors are non-unitary when the two subtests involved are discrepant by more than 22 points. Non-unitary factors should be interpreted cautiously and should not be used in pairwise comparisons. (9) Compare logical pairs of components, using a 15- to 20-point difference as an indication of a significant discrepancy.

C Conversion Table: Scaled Scores to Standard Scores[*]

Scaled Score (M = 10; SD = 3)	Standard Score (M = 100; SD = 15)
19	145
18	140
17	135
16	130
15	125
14	120
13	115
12	110
11	105
10	100
9	95
8	90
7	85
6	80
5	75
4	70
3	65
2	60
1	55

[*]The formula for converting t-scores to standard scores is t-score $\times$ 1.5 + 25.

References

Adams, W., & Sheslow, W. (2003). *Wide Range Assessment of Memory and Learning* (2nd ed.). Wilmington, DE: Wide Range.

Aldrich, F. K., & Wilson, B. (1991). Rivermead Behavioural Memory Test for Children (RBMT-C): A preliminary evaluation. *The British Journal of Clinical Psychology, 30*, 161–168.

Allen, L., Palomares, R., DeForest, P., Sprinkle, B., & Reynolds, C. R. (1991). The effects of intrauterine cocaine exposure: Transient or teratogenic? *Archives of Clinical Neuropsychology, 6*, 133–146.

Alloway, T. P. (2007). *Automated Working Memory Assessment.* London: Harcourt Assessment.

Alloway, T. P., & Gathercole, S. E. (Eds.). (2006). *Working memory and neurodevelopmental disorders.* New York: Psychology Press.

Altmann, E. M., & Gray, W. D. (2002). Forgetting to remember: The functional relationship of decay and interference. *Psychological Science, 13*, 27–33.

American Psychiatric Association. (1994). *Diagnostic and statistical manual of mental disorders* (4th ed.). Washington, DC: Author.

Anderson, J. R. (2000). *Learning and memory: An integrated approach* (2nd ed.). Hoboken, NJ: John Wiley & Sons.

Atkinson, R. C., & Shiffrin, R. M. (1968). Human memory: A proposed system and its control processes. In K. W. Spence (Ed.), *The psychology of learning and motivation: Vol. 2. Advances in research and theory* (pp. 89–195). New York: Academic Press.

August, G. J. (1987). Production deficiencies in free recall: A comparison of hyperactive, learning-disabled, and normal children. *Journal of Abnormal Child Psychology, 15*, 429–440.

Awad, N., Gagnon, M., Desrochers, A., Tsiakas, M., & Messier, C. (2002). Impact of peripheral glucoregulation on memory. *Behavioral Neuroscience, 116*, 691–702.

Babikian, T., & Asarnow, R. (2009). Neurocognitive outcomes and recovery after pediatric TBI: Meta-analytic review of the literature. *Neuropsychology, 23*, 283–296.

Baddeley, A. D. (1986). *Working memory*. New York: Oxford University Press.

Baddeley, A. D. (1990). The development of the concept of working memory: Implications and contributions of neuropsychology. In G. Vallar & J. Shallice (Eds.), *Neuropsychological impairments of short-term memory* (pp. 54–73). New York: Cambridge University Press.

Baddeley, A. D. (1996). Exploring the central executive. *The Quarterly Journal of Experimental Psychology, 49A*, 5–28.

Baddeley, A. D. (2000). The episodic buffer: A new component in working memory? *Trends in Cognitive Sciences, 4*, 417–423.

Baddeley, A. D. (2003). Working memory: Looking back and looking forward. *Nature Reviews: Neuroscience, 4*, 829–839.

Baddeley, A. D. (2006). Working memory: An overview. In S. J. Pickering (Ed.), *Working memory and education* (pp. 1–31). Burlington, MA: Academic Press.

Baddeley, A. D., Eysenck, M. W., & Anderson, M. C. (2009). *Memory*. New York: Psychology Press.

Baddeley, A. D., Vargha-Khadem, F., & Mishkin, M. (2001). Preserved recognition in a case of developmental amnesia: Implications for the acquisition of semantic memory? *Journal of Cognitive Neuroscience, 13*, 357–369.

Baddeley, A. D., & Wilson, B. A. (1994). When implicit learning fails: Amnesia and the problem of error elimination. *Neuropsychologia, 32*, 53–68.

Bahrick, H. P. (1984). Semantic memory content in permastore: Fifty years of memory for Spanish learning in school. *Journal of Experimental Psychology: General, 113*, 1–29.

Bahrick, H. P. (2000). Long-term maintenance of knowledge. In E. Tulving & F. I. M. Craik (Eds.), *The Oxford handbook of memory* (pp. 347–362). New York: Oxford University Press.

Bahrick, H. P., Bahrick, L. E., Bahrick, A. S., & Bahrick, P. E. (1993). Maintenance of foreign language vocabulary and the spacing effect. *Psychological Science, 4*, 316–321.

Bahrick, H. P., & Hall, L. K. (2005). The importance of retrieval failures to long-term retention: A metacognitive explanation of the spacing effect. *Journal of Memory and Language, 52*, 566–577.

Baldo, J. V., Delis, D., Kramer, J., & Shimamura, A. P. (2002). Memory performance on the California Verbal Learning Test-II: Findings from patients with focal frontal lesions. *Journal of the International Neuropsychological Society, 8*, 539–546.

Baldo, J. V., & Dronkers, N. F. (2006). The role of inferior parietal and inferior frontal cortex in working memory. *Neuropsychology, 20*, 529–538.

Bangert-Drowns, R. L., Kulik, J. A., & Kulik, C. L. (1991). Effects of frequent classroom testing. *Journal of Educational Research, 85*, 89–99.

Barkley, R. A. (1997). Behavioral inhibition, sustained attention, and executive functioning: Constructing a unifying theory of ADHD. *Psychological Bulletin, 121*, 65–94.

Baron, I. S. (2004). *Neuropsychological evaluation of the child*. Oxford: Oxford University Press.

Bauer, P. J., DeBoer, T., & Lukowski, A. F. (2007). In the language of multiple memory systems: Defining and describing developments in long-term declarative memory. In L. M. Oakes & P. J. Bauer (Eds.), *Short- and long-term memory in infancy and early childhood* (pp. 240–270). Oxford, UK: Oxford University Press.

Beers, S. R., & De Bellis, M. D. (2002). Neuropsychological function in children with maltreatment-related posttraumatic stress disorder. *American Journal of Psychiatry, 159*, 483–486.

Bellezza, F. S. (1981). Mnemonic devices: Classification, characteristics, and criteria. *Review of Educational Research, 51*, 247–275.

Benedict, R. H. (1989). The effectiveness of cognitive remediation strategies for victims of traumatic head-injury: A review of the literature. *Clinical Psychology Review, 9*, 605–626.

Benjamin, A. S., Bjork, R. A., & Schwartz, B. L. (1998). The mismeasure of memory: When retrieval fluency is misleading as a metamnemonic index. *Journal of Experimental Psychology: General, 127*, 55–68.

Bennett, D. S., Bendersky, M., & Lewis, M. (2008). Children's cognitive ability from 4 to 9 years old as a function of prenatal cocaine exposure, environment risk, and maternal verbal intelligence. *Developmental Psychology, 44*, 919–928.

Benton, D. (2001). The impact of the supply of glucose to the brain on mood and memory. *Nutrition Reviews, 59*, S20–1.

Berninger, V. W., & Richards, T. L. (2002). *Brain literacy for educators and psychologists*. San Diego: Academic Press.

Best, D. L., & Ornstein, P. A. (1986). Children's generation and communication of mnemonic organizational strategies. *Developmental Psychology, 22*, 845–853.

Beuhring, T., & Kee, D. W. (1987). Developmental relationships among metamemory, elaborative strategy use, and associative memory. *Journal of Experimental Child Psychology, 44*, 377–400.

Bjorklund, D. F. (1997). Instructing children to use memory strategies: Evidence of utilization deficiencies in memory training studies. *Developmental Review, 17*, 411–441.

Blake, R. V., Wroe, S. J., Breen, E. K., & McCarthy, R. A. (2000). Accelerated forgetting in patients with epilepsy: Evidence for an impairment in memory consolidation. *Brain*, *123*, 472–483.

Blaxton, T. A. (1989). Investigating dissociations among memory measures: Support for a transfer-appropriate processing framework. *Journal of Experimental Psychology: Learning, Memory, and Cognition*, *15*, 657–668.

Block, G. W., Nanson, J. L., & Lowry, N. J. (1999). Attention, memory, and language after pediatric ischemic stroke. *Child Neuropsychology*, *5*, 81–91.

Bloom, K. C., & Shuell, T. J. (1981). Effects of massed and distributed practice on the learning and retention of second-language vocabulary. *Journal of Educational Research*, *74*, 245–248.

Boll, T. (1993). *Children's Category Test*. San Antonio, TX: The Psychological Corporation.

Borden, K. A., Burns, T. G., & O'Leary, S. D. (2006). A comparison of children with epilepsy to an age- and IQ-matched control group on the Children's Memory Scale. *Child Neuropsychology*, *12*, 165–172.

Born, J., Rasch, B., & Gais, S. (2006). Sleep to remember. *The Neuroscientist*, *12*, 410–424.

Brady, J. V., & Richman, L. C. (1994). Visual versus verbal mnemonic training effects on memory-deficient and language-deficient subgroups of children with reading disability. *Developmental Neuropsychology*, *10*, 335–347.

Brainerd, C. J., & Reyna, V. F. (1995). Learning rate, learning opportunities, and the development of forgetting. *Developmental Psychology*, *31*(2), 251–262.

Brandt, K. R., Gardiner, J. M., Vargha-Khadem, F., Baddeley, A. D., & Mishkin, M. (2006). Using semantic memory to boost "episodic" recall in a case of developmental amnesia. *Neuroreport: For Rapid Communication of Neuroscience Research*, *17*, 1057–1060.

Bremner, J. D., & Narayan, J. D. (1998). The effects of stress on memory and the hippocampus throughout the life cycle: Implications for childhood development and aging. *Development and Psychopathology*, *10*, 871–885.

Bremner, J. D., Randall, P., Scott, T. M., Bronen, R. A., Seibyl, J. P., Southwick, S. M., et al. (1995). MRI-based measurement of hippocampal volume in patients with combat related posttraumatic stress disorder. *American Journal of Psychiatry*, *152*, 973–981.

Bremner, J. D., Randall, P., Scott, T. M., Capelli, S., Delaney, R., McCarthy, G., & Charney, D. S. (1995). Deficits in short-term memory in adult survivors of childhood abuse. *Psychiatry Research*, *59*, 97–107.

Bremner, J. D., Vermetten, E., Afzal, N., & Vythilingam, M. (2004). Deficits in verbal declarative memory function in women with childhood sexual abuse-related posttraumatic stress disorder. *Journal of Nervous and Mental Disease*, *192*, 643–649.

Briscoe, J., Gathercole, S. E., & Marlow, N. (2001). Everyday memory and cognitive ability in children born very prematurely. *Journal of Child Psychology and Psychiatry, 42,* 749–754.

Brizzolara, D., Casalini, C., Montanaro, D., & Posteraro, F. (2003). A case of amnesia at an early age. *Cortex: A Journal Devoted to the Study of the Nervous System and Behavior, 39,* 605–625.

Broadbent, N. J., Clark, R. E., Zola, S., & Squire, L. R. (2002). The medial temporal lobe and memory. In L. R. Squire & D. L. Schacter (Eds.), *Neuropsychology of memory* (3rd ed., pp. 3–23). New York: Guilford.

Brown, G., & Sproson, R. N. (1987). The involvement of memory and metamemory in the schoolwork of secondary school pupils. *Educational Studies, 13,* 213–221.

Brown, S. C., & Craik, F. I. M. (2000). Encoding and retrieval of information. In E. Tulving & F. I. M. Craik (Eds.), *The Oxford handbook of memory* (pp. 93–107). New York: Oxford University Press.

Brown, T. E. (1996). *Brown Attention-Deficit Disorder Scales.* San Antonio, TX: The Psychological Corporation.

Brown-Chidsey, R., & Steege, M. (2005). *Response to intervention: Principles and strategies for effective practice.* New York: Guilford.

Buckner, R. L., Wheeler, M. E., & Sheridan, M. A. (2001). Encoding processes during retrieval tasks. *Journal of Cognitive Neuroscience, 13,* 406–415.

Bulgren, J. A., Hock, M. F., Schumaker, J. B., & Deshler, D. D. (1995). The effects of instruction in a paired associate strategy on information mastery performance of students with learning disabilities. *Learning Disabilities Research & Practice, 10,* 22–37.

Burns, M. K., & Boice, C. H. (2009). Comparison of the relationship between words retained and intelligence for three instructional strategies among students with below-average IQ. *School Psychology Review, 38,* 284–292.

Busch, R. M., Booth, J. E., McBride, A., Vanderplog, R. D., Curtiss, G., & Duchnick, J. L. (2005). Role of executive functioning in verbal and visual memory. *Neuropsychology, 19,* 171–180.

Butler, A. C., & Roediger, H. L. (2007). Testing improves long-term retention in a simulated classroom setting. *European Journal of Cognitive Psychology, 19,* 514–527.

Butterfield, B., & Metcalfe, J. (2001). Errors committed with high confidence are hypercorrected. *Journal of Experimental Psychology: Learning, Memory, and Cognition, 27,* 1491–1494.

Cantor, J. & Engle, R. W. (1993). Working-memory capacity as long-term memory activation: An individual differences approach. *Journal of Experimental Psychology: Learning, Memory, and Cognition, 19,* 1101–1114.

Carney, R. N., Levin, M. E., & Levin, J. R. (1993). Mnemonic strategies: Instructional techniques worth remembering. *Teaching Exceptional Children*, *25*, 24–30.

Carpenter, S. K., & DeLosh, E. L. (2006). Impoverished cue support enhances subsequent retention: Support for the elaborative retrieval explanation of the testing effect. *Memory and Cognition*, *34*, 268–278.

Carpenter, S. K., Pashler, H., Wisted, J. T., & Vul, E. (2008). The effects of tests on learning and forgetting. *Memory and Cognition*, *26*, 438–448.

Carroll, J. B. (1993). *Human cognitive abilities: A survey of factor-analytic studies.* Cambridge: Cambridge University Press.

Cassaday, H. J., Bloomfield, R. E., & Hayward, N. (2002). Relaxed conditions can provide memory cues in both undergraduates and primary school children. *British Journal of Educational Psychology*, *72*, 531–547.

Cavanaugh, J. C., & Poon, L. W. (1989). Metamemorial predictors of memory performance in young and older adults. *Psychology and Aging*, *4*, 365–368.

Ceci, S. J. (1985). A developmental study of learning disabilities and memory. *Journal of Experimental Child Psychology*, *38*, 352–371.

Ceci, S. J., Ringstrom, M., & Lea, S. E. G. (1981). Do language-learning disabled children (L/LDs) have impaired memories? In search of underlying processes. *Journal of Learning Disabilities*, *14*, 159–162.

Cepeda, N. J., Pashler, H., Vul, E., Wixed, J. T., & Rohrer, D. (2006). Distributed practice in verbal recall tasks: A review and quantitative synthesis. *Psychological Bulletin*, *132*, 354–380.

Chan, P. H. (1996). Role of oxidants in ischemic brain damage. *Stroke*, *27*, 1124–1129.

Cipani, E., & Madigan, K. (1986). Errorless learning: Research and application for "difficult to teach" children. *Canadian Journal for Exceptional Children*, *3*, 39–43.

Clare, L., & Jones, R. S. P. (2008). Errorless learning in the rehabilitation of memory impairment: A critical review. *Neuropsychology Review*, *18*, 1–23.

Clarke, P. A., Ayres, P., & Sweller, P. (2005). The impact of sequencing and prior knowledge on learning mathematics through spreadsheet applications. *Educational Technology Research & Development*, *53*, 15–24.

Cohen, G. (2008a). Memory for knowledge: General knowledge and expert knowledge. In G. Cohen & M. A. Conway (Eds.), *Memory in the real world* (3rd ed., pp. 206–227). New York: Psychology Press.

Cohen, G. (2008b). The study of everyday memory. In G. Cohen & M. A. Conway (Eds.), *Memory in the real world* (3rd ed., pp. 1–20). New York: Psychology Press.

Cohen, J. (1997). *Children's Memory Scale.* San Antonio: The Psychological Corporation.

Condus, M. M., Marshall, K. J., & Miller, S. R. (1986). Effects of the keyword mnemonic strategy on vocabulary acquisition and maintenance by learning disabled children. *Journal of Learning Disabilities, 19,* 609–613.

Conway, M. A., Cohen, G, & Stanhope, N. M. (1992). Very long-term memory for knowledge acquired at school and university. *Applied Cognitive Psychology, 6,* 467–482.

Conway, M. A., Gardiner, J. M., Perfect, T. J., Anderson, T. J., & Cohen, S. J. (1997). Changes in memory awareness during learning: The acquisition of knowledge by psychology undergraduates. *Journal of Experimental Psychology: General, 126,* 393–413.

Cornoldi, C., Barbieri, A., Gaiani, C., & Zocchi, S. (1999). Strategic memory deficits in Attention Deficit Disorder with Hyperactivity participants: The role of executive processes. *Developmental Neuropsychology, 15,* 53–71.

Cowan, N. (1995). *Attention and memory: An integrated framework.* Oxford Psychology Series, #26. New York: Oxford University Press.

Cowan, N. (2001). The magical number 4 in short-term memory: A reconsideration of mental storage capacity. *Behavioral and Brain Sciences, 24,* 87–185.

Cowan, N. (2005). *Working memory capacity.* New York: Lawrence Erlbaum.

Cowan, N., Saults, J. S., & Morey, C. C. (2006). Development of working memory for verbal-spatial relations. *Journal of Memory and Language, 55,* 274–289.

Cox, B. D., Ornstein, P. A., Naus, M. J., Maxfield, D., & Zimler, J. (1989). Children's concurrent use of rehearsal and organization strategies. *Developmental Psychology, 25,* 619–627.

Craik, F. I., & Lockhart, R. S. (1972). Levels of processing: A framework for memory research. *Journal of Verbal Learning and Verbal Behavior, 11,* 671–684.

Craik, F. I., & Watkins, M. J. (1973). The role of rehearsal in short-term memory. *Journal of Verbal Learning and Verbal Behavior, 12,* 599–607.

Cull, W. L. (2000). Untangling the benefits of multiple study opportunities and repeated testing for cued recall. *Applied Cognitive Psychology, 14,* 215–235.

Cull, W. L., Shaughnessy, J. L., & Zechmeister, E. B. (1996). Expanding understanding of the expanding-pattern-of-retrieval mnemonic: Toward confidence in applicability. *Journal of Experimental Psychology: Applied, 2,* 365–378.

Cull, W. L., & Zechmeister, E. B. (1994). The learning ability paradox in adult metamemory research: Where are the metamemory differences between good and poor learners? *Memory and Cognition, 22,* 249–257.

Curvits, T. G., Shenton, M. R., Hokama, H., Ohta, H., Lasko, N. B., Gilbertson, M. W., et al. (1996). Magnetic resonance imaging study of hippocampal volume in chronic combat-related posttraumatic stress disorder. *Biological Psychiatry, 40,* 192–199.

Davidson, M., Dorris, L., O'Regan, M., & Zuberi, S. M. (2007). Memory consolidation and accelerated forgetting in children with idiopathic generalized epilepsy. *Epilepsy and Behavior, 11,* 394–400.

Deckersbach, T., Otto, M. W., Savage, C. R., Baer, L., Jenike, M. A. (2000). The relationship between semantic organization and memory in obsessive-compulsive disorder. *Psychotherapy and Psycholinguistics, 69,* 101–117.

Deckersbach, T., Savage, C. R., Reilly-Harrington, N., Clark, L, Sachs, G., & Rauch, S. L. (2004). Episodic memory impairment in bipolar disorder and obsessive-compulsive disorder: The role of memory strategies. *Bipolar Disorders, 6,* 233–244.

de Haan, M., Mishkin, M., Baldeweg, T., Vargha-Khadem, F. (2006). Human memory development and its dysfunction after early hippocampal injury. *Trends in Neuroscience, 29,* 374–381.

de Haan, M., Wyatt, J. S., Roth, S., Vargha-Khadem, F., Gadian, D., & Mishkin, M., (2006). Brain and cognitive-behavioural development after asphyxia at term birth. *Developmental Science, 9,* 350–358.

Dehn, M. J. (2006). *Essentials of processing assessment.* Hoboken, NJ: John Wiley & Sons.

Dehn, M. J. (2008). *Working memory and academic learning: Assessment and intervention.* Hoboken, NJ: John Wiley & Sons.

Delis, D. C., Kramer, J. H., Kaplan, E., & Ober, B. A. (1994). *The California Verbal Learning Test—Children's Version.* San Antonio, TX: The Psychological Corporation.

Delis, D. C., Kramer, J. H., Kaplan, E., & Ober, B. A. (2000). *The California Verbal Learning Test* (2nd ed.). San Antonio, TX: The Psychological Corporation.

DeLuca, J., Schultheis, M. T., Madigan, N. K., Christodoulou, C., & Averill, A. (2000). Acquisition versus retrieval deficits in traumatic brain injury: Implications for memory rehabilitation. *Archives of Physical Medicine and Rehabilitation, 81,* 1327–1333.

Dempster, F. N. (1992). Using tests to promote learning: A neglected classroom resource. *Journal of Research and Development in Education, 25,* 213–217.

Dempster, F. N., & Farris, R. (1990). The spacing effect: Research and practice. *Journal of Research and Development in Education, 23,* 97–101.

D'Esposito, M., Detre, J. A., Alsop, D. C., Shin, R. K., Atlas, S., & Grossman, M. (1995). The neural basis of the central executive system of working memory. *Nature, 378,* 279–281.

Desrocher, M., & Rovet, J. (2004). Neurocognitive correlates of Type I Diabetes Mellitus in childhood. *Child Neuropsychology, 10,* 36–52.

Dickstein, D. P., Treland, J. E., Snow, J., McClure, E. B., Mehta, M. S., Towbin, K. E., et al. (2004). Neuropsychological performance in pediatric bipolar disorder. *Biological Psychiatry, 55*, 32–39.

Dixon, R. A., Hultsch, D. F., & Hertzog, C. (1988). The metamemory in adulthood (MIA) questionnaire. *Psychopharmacology Bulletin, 24*, 671–688.

Donders, J. (1999). Structural equation analysis of the California Verbal Learning Test—Children's Version in the standardization sample. *Developmental Neuropsychology, 15*, 395–406.

Donohoe, R. T., & Benton, D. (2000). Glucose tolerance predicts performance on tests of memory and cognition. *Physiology and Behavior, 71*, 395–401.

Donovan, J. J., & Radosevich, D. J. (1999). A meta-analytic review of the distribution of practice effect: Now you see it, now you don't. *Journal of Applied Psychology, 84*, 795–805.

Drosopoulus, S., Schulze, C., Fischer, S., & Born, J. (2007). Sleep's function in the spontaneous recovery and consolidation of memories. *Journal of Experimental Psychology: General, 136*, 169–183.

Drosopoulus, S., Wagner, U., & Born, J. (2005). Sleep enhances explicit recollection in recognition memory. *Learning and Memory, 12*(1), 44–51.

Duchnick, J. J., Vanderploey, R. D., & Curtiss, G. (2002). Identifying retrieval problems using the California Verbal Learning Test. *Journal of Clinical and Experimental Neuropsychology, 24*, 840–851.

Dudai, Y. (2004). The neurobiology of consolidations, or, how stable is the engram? *Review of Psychology, 55*, 51–86.

Ebbinghaus, H. (1913). *Memory: A contribution to experimental psychology* (H. A. Ruger & C. E. Bussenius, Trans.). New York: Teachers College, Columbia University.

Ehlhardt, L. A., Sohlberg, M. M., Kennedy, M., Coelho, C., Ylvisaker, M., Turkstra, L., et al. (2008). Evidence-based practice guidelines for instructing individuals with neurogenic memory impairments: What have we learned in the past 20 years? *Neuropsychological Rehabilitation, 18*, 300–342.

Ellenberg, J. H., Levin, H. S., & Saydjari, C. (1996). Posttraumatic amnesia as a predictor of outcome after closed head injury. *Archives of Neurology, 53*, 782–786.

Elliott, C. D. (2006). *Differential Ability Scales* (2nd ed.). San Antonio, TX: PsychCorp.

Ellis, J. A., & Cohen, G. (2008). Memory for intentions, actions, and plans. In G. Cohen & M. A. Conway, (Eds.), *Memory in the real world* (3rd ed., pp. 141–172). New York: Psychology Press.

Ellis, N. C., & Hennelley, R. A. (1980). A bilingual word-length effect: Implications for intelligence testing and the relative ease of mental calculation in Welsh and English. *British Journal of Psychology, 71*, 43–52.

Elzinga, B. M., Bakker, A., & Bremner, J. D. (2005). Stress-induced cortisol elevations are associated with impaired delayed, but not immediate recall. *Psychiatry Research*, *134*, 211–223.

Emilien, G., Durlach, C., Antoniadis, E., Van Der Linden, M., & Maloteaux, J-M. (2004). *Memory: Neuropsychological, imaging, and psychopharmacological perspectives*. New York: Psychology Press.

Engle, R. W. (2002). Working memory capacity as executive attention. *Current Directions in Psychological Science*, *11*(1), 19–23.

Ericsson, K. A., & Kintsch, W. (1995). Long-term working memory. *Psychological Review*, *102*, 211–245.

Eslinger, P. J. (Ed.). (2002). *Neuropsychological interventions: Clinical research and practice*. New York: Guilford.

Flanagan, D. P., & Kaufman, A. S. (2004). *Essentials of WISC-IV assessment*. Hoboken, NJ: John Wiley & Sons.

Flanagan, D. P., Ortiz, S. O., & Alfonso, V. C. (2007). *Essentials of cross-battery assessment* (2nd ed.). Hoboken, NJ: John Wiley & Sons.

Flavell, J. H. (1979). Metacognition and cognitive monitoring: A new area of cognitive-developmental inquiry. *American Psychologist*, *34*, 906–911.

Foley, M. A., Wilder, A., McCall, R., & Van Vorst, R. (1993). The consequences for recall of children's ability to generate interactive imagery in the absence of external supports. *Journal of Experimental Child Psychology*, *56*, 173–200.

Frank, D. A., Augustyn, M., Knight, W. G., Pell, T., & Zuckerman, B. (2001). Growth, development, and behavior in early childhood following prenatal cocaine exposure: A systematic review. *Journal of the American Medical Association*, *285*, 1613–1625.

Franzen, K. M., Roberts, M. A., Schmits, D., Verduyn, W. & Manshadi, F. (1996). Cognitive remediation in pediatric traumatic brain injury. *Child Neuropsychology*, *2*, 176–184.

Franzen, M. D., & Haut, M. W. (1991). The psychological treatment of memory impairment: A review of empirical studies. *Neuropsychological Review*, *2*, 29–63.

Gadian, D. G., Aicardi, J., Watkins, K. E., Porter, D. A., Mishkin, M., & Vargha-Khadem, F. (2000). Developmental amnesia associated with early hypoxic-ischaemic injury. *Brain*, *123*, 499–507.

Gagne, E. D., Yarbrough, D. B., Weidemann, C., & Bell, M. S. (1984). The effects of text familiarity and cohesion on retrieval of information learned from text. *Journal of Experimental Education*, *52*(4), 207–213.

Gais, S., Lucas, B., & Born, J. (2006). Sleep after learning aids memory recall. *Learning and Memory*, *13*, 259–262.

Gardiner, J. M., Gawlik, B., & Richardson-Klavehn, A. (1994). Maintenance rehearsal affects knowing, not remembering; elaborative rehearsal affects remembering, not knowing. *Psychonomic Bulletin and Review, 1*, 107–110.

Gathercole, S. E. (1998). The development of memory. *Journal of Child Psychology and Psychiatry, 39*, 3–27.

Gathercole, S. E., & Alloway, T. P. (2008). *Working memory and learning: A practical guide for teachers*. Los Angeles: Sage Publications.

Gathercole, S. E., & Baddeley, A. D. (1993). *Working memory and language*. East Sussex, UK: Lawrence Erlbaum.

Gathercole, S. E., & Pickering, S. J. (2000). Working memory deficits in children with low achievements in the National Curriculum at seven years of age. *British Journal of Educational Psychology, 70*, 177–194.

Gathercole, S. E., & Pickering, S. J. (2001). Working memory deficits in children with special educational needs. *British Journal of Special Education, 28*, 89–97.

Gathercole, S. E., Pickering, S. J., Ambridge, B., & Wearing, H. (2004). The structure of working memory from 4–15 years of age. *Developmental Psychology, 40*, 177–190.

Geary, D. C. (1993). Mathematical disabilities: Cognitive, neuropsychological, and genetic components. *Psychological Bulletin, 114*, 345–362.

Gershberg, F. B., & Shimamura, A. P. (1995). Impaired use of organizational strategies in free recall following frontal lobe damage. *Neuropsychologia, 33*, 1305–1333.

Gettinger, M. (1991). Learning time and retention differences between nondisabled students and students with learning disabilities. *Learning Disability Quarterly, 14*, 179–189.

Gfeller, K. E. (1986). Musical mnemonics for learning disabled children. *Teaching Exceptional Children, 19*, 28–30.

Ghatala, E. S., Levin, J. R., Pressley, M., & Lodico, M. G. (1985). Training cognitive strategy-monitoring in children. *American Educational Research Journal, 22*, 199–215.

Giap, B. T., Jong, C. N., Ricker, J. H., Cullen, N. K., & Zafonte, R. D. (2000). The hippocampus: Anatomy, pathophysiology, and regenerative capacity. *The Journal of Head Trauma and Rehabilitation, 15*, 875–894.

Gilliam, R. B. (1998). *Memory and language impairment in children and adults: New perspectives*. (ERIC Document Reproduction Service No. ED421835).

Glahn, D. C., Bearden, C. E., Caetano, S., Fonseca, M., Najt, P., Hunter, K., et al. (2005). Declarative memory impairment in pediatric bipolar disorder. *Bipolar Disorders, 7*, 546–554.

Glang, A., Singer, G., Cooley, E., & Tish, N. (1992). Tailoring direct instruction techniques for use with elementary students with brain injury. *Journal of Head Trauma Rehabilitation, 7*, 93–108.

Glisky, E. L., & Glisky, M. L. (2002). Learning and memory impairments. In P. J. Eslinger (Ed.), *Neuropsychological interventions: Clinical research and practice* (pp. 137–162). New York: Guilford.

Glisky, E. L., & Schacter, D. L. (1986). Remediation of organic memory disorders: Current status and future prospects. *Journal of Head Trauma Rehabilitation, 1*, 54–63.

Glover, J. A., Krug, D., Hannon, S., and Shine, A. (1990). The "testing" effect and restricted retrieval rehearsal. *Psychological Record, 40*, 215–226.

Godden, D. R., & Baddeley, A. D. (1975). Context-dependent memory in two natural environments: On land and underwater. *British Journal of Psychology, 66*, 325–331.

Graf, P. (1990). Life-span changes in implicit and explicit memory. *Bulletin of the Psychonomic Society, 28*, 353–358.

Gray, J. M., Robertson, I., Pentland, B., & Anderson, S. (1992). Microcomputer-based attentional retraining after brain damage: A randomized group controlled trial. *Neuropsychological Rehabilitation, 2*, 97–115.

Greenleaf, R. K., & Wells-Papanek, D. (2005). *Memory, recall, the brain and learning.* Newfield, ME: Greenleaf and Papanek Publications.

Grier, L. K., & Ratner, H. H. (1996). Elaboration: The role of activity and conceptual processing in children's memory. *Child Study Journal, 26*, 229–252.

Hagen, J. W., Barclay, C. R., Anderson, B. J., Feeman, D. J., Segal, S. S., Bacon, G., et al. (1990). Intellectual functioning and strategy use in children with insulin-dependent diabetes mellitus. *Child Development, 61*, 1714–1727.

Haist, F., Shimamura, A. P., & Squire, L. R. (1992). On the relationship between recall and recognition memory. *Journal of Experimental Psychology: Learning, Memory, and Cognition, 18*, 691–702.

Hale, J. B., & Fiorello, C. A. (2004). *School neuropsychology: A practitioner's handbook.* New York: Guilford.

Hannon, B., & Craik, F. I. M. (2001). Encoding specificity revisited: The role of semantics. *Canadian Journal of Experimental Psychology, 55*, 231–243.

Hanten, G., Bartha, M., & Levin, H. S. (2001). Metacognition following pediatric traumatic brain injury: A preliminary study. *Developmental Neuropsychology, 18*, 383–398.

Harris, J. R. (1996). Verbal rehearsal and memory in children with closed head injury: A quantitative and qualitative analysis. *Journal of Communication Disorders, 29*, 79–93.

Hasher, L., & Zacks, R. T. (1979). Automatic and effortful processes in memory. *Journal of Experimental Psychology: General, 108,* 356–388.

Hayne, H. (2007). Infant memory development: New questions, new answers. In L. M. Oakes & P. J. Bauer (Eds.), *Short- and long-term memory in infancy and early childhood* (pp. 209–239). Oxford, UK: Oxford University Press.

Henry, L. A. (2001). How does the severity of a learning disability affect working memory performance? *Memory, 9,* 233–247.

Hepworth, S. L., Pang, E. W., & Rovet, J. F. (2006). Word and face recognition in children with congenital hypothyroidism: An event-related potential study. *Journal of Clinical and Experimental Neuropsychology, 28,* 509–527.

Hershey, T., Craft, S., Bhargava, N., & White, N. H. (1997). Memory and insulin dependent diabetes mellitus (IDDM): Effects of childhood onset and severe hypoglycemia. *Journal of the International Neuropsychological Society, 3,* 509–520.

Hershey, T., Lillie, R., Sadler, M., & White, N. H. (2003). Severe hypoglycemia and long-term spatial memory in children with type 1 diabetes mellitus: A retrospective study. *Journal of the International Neuropsychological Society, 9,* 740–750.

Hitch, G. J. (1990). Developmental fractionation of working memory. In G. Vallar & J. Shallice (Eds.), *Neuropsychological impairments of short-term memory* (pp. 221–246). New York: Cambridge University Press.

Ho, Y.-C, Cheung, M.-C., & Chan, A. S. (2003). Music training improves verbal but not visual memory: Cross-sectional and longitudinal explorations in children. *Neuropsychology, 17,* 439–450.

Hockley, W. E. (1992). Item versus associative information: Further comparisons of forgetting rates. *Journal of Experimental Psychology: Learning, Memory, and Cognition, 18,* 1321–1330.

Hood, J., & Rankin, P. M. (2005). How do specific memory disorders present in the school classroom? *Pediatric Rehabilitation, 8,* 272–282.

Howe, M. L. (1995). Interference effects in young children's long-term retention. *Developmental Psychology, 31,* 579–596.

Howe, M. L., & Brainerd, C. J. (1989). Development of children's long-term retention. *Developmental Review, 9,* 301–340.

Howe, M. L., Courage, M. L., Vernescu, R., & Hunt, M. (2000). Distinctiveness effects in children's long-term retention. *Developmental Psychology, 36,* 778–792.

Hudson, J. A., & Gillam, R. B. (1997). "Oh, I. remember now!": Facilitating children's long-term memory for events. *Topics in Language Disorders, 18* (1), 1–15.

Hulme, C., & Mackenzie, S. (1992). *Working memory and severe learning difficulties.* East Sussex, UK: Lawrence Erlbaum.

Hunkin, N. M., Squires, E. J., Aldrich, F. K., & Parkin, A. J. (1998). Errorless learning and the acquisition of word processing skills. *Neuropsychological Rehabilitation, 8*, 433–449.

Hunt, R. R., & Einstein, G. O. (1981). Relational and item-specific information in memory. *Journal of Verbal Learning and Verbal Behavior, 20*, 497–514.

Hupbach, A., Gomez, R., Hardt, O., & Nadel, L. (2007). Reconsolidation of episodic memories: A subtle reminder triggers integration of new information. *Learning and Memory, 14*, 47–53.

Isaacs, E. B., Lucas, A., Chong, W. K., Wood, S. J., Johnson, C. L., Marshall, C., et al. (2000). Hippocampal volume and everyday memory in children of very low birth weight. *Pediatric Research, 47*, 713–720.

Jaeggi, S. M., Buschkuehl, M., Jonides, J., & Perrig, W. J. (2008). Improving fluid intelligence with training on working memory. Retrieved from http://www.pnas.org/cgi/doi/10.1073/pnas.0801268105.

Jocic-Jakubi, B., & Jovic, N. J. (2006). Verbal memory impairment in children with focal epilepsy. *Epilepsy and Behavior, 9*, 432–439.

Jonides, J., Smith, E. E., Marshuetz, C., & Koeppe, R. A. (1998). Inhibition in verbal working memory revealed by brain activation. *Proceedings of the National Academy of Sciences, U.S.A, 95*, 8410–8413.

Joseph, M. F., Frazier, T. W., Youngstrom, E. A., Soares, J. C. (2008). A quantitative and qualitative review of neurocognitive performance in pediatric bipolar disorder. *Journal of Child and Adolescent Psychopharmacology, 18*, 595–605.

Kaemingk, K. L., Mulvaney, S., & Halverson, P. T. (2003). Learning following prenatal alcohol exposure: Performance on verbal and visual multitrial tasks. *Archives of Clinical Neuropsychology, 18*, 33–47.

Kaemingk, K. L., Pasvogel, A. E., Goodwin, J. L., Mulvaney, S. A., Martinez, F., Enright, P. L., et al. (2003). Learning in children and sleep disorder breathing: Findings of the Tucson children's assessment of sleep apnea (TuCASA) prospective cohort study. *Journal of the International Neuropsychological Society, 9*, 1016–1026.

Kane, M. J., & Engle, R. W. (2002). The role of prefrontal cortex in working-memory capacity, executive attention, and general fluid intelligence: An individual-differences perspective. *Psychonomic Bulletin and Review, 9*, 637–671.

Kang, S. H. K., McDermott, K. B., & Roediger, H. L. (2007). Test format and corrective feedback modify the effect of testing on long-term retention. *European Journal of Cognitive Psychology, 19*, 528–558.

Kaplan, E., Fein, D., Kramer, J., Delis, D., & Morris, R. (2004). *Wechsler Intelligence Scale for Children, Fourth Edition—Integrated.* San Antonio, TX: PsychCorp.

Kapur, N., Glisky, E. L., Wilson, B. A. (2004). Technological memory aids for people with memory deficits. *Neuropsychological Rehabilitation, 14,* 41–60.

Kapur, N., Millar, J., Colbourn, C., Abbott, P., Kennedy, P., & Docherty, T. (1997). Very long-term amnesia in association with temporal lobe epilepsy: Evidence for multiple-stage consolidation processes. *Brain and Cognition, 35,* 58–70.

Karpicke, J. D., & Roediger III, H. L. (2007a). Expanding retrieval practice promotes short-term retention, but equally spaced retrieval enhances long-term retention. *Journal of Experimental Psychology: Learning, Memory, and Cognition, 33,* 704–719.

Karpicke, J. D., & Roediger III, H. L. (2007b). Repeated retrieval during learning is the key to long-term retention. *Journal of Memory and Language, 57,* 151–162.

Karpicke, J. D., & Roediger III, H. L. (2008). The critical importance of retrieval for learning. *Science, 319,* 966–968.

Kaufman, A. S., & Kaufman, N. L. (2004a). *Kaufman Assessment Battery for Children* (2nd ed.). Circle Pines, MN: AGS Publishing.

Kaufman, A. S., & Kaufman, N. L. (2004b). *Kaufman Test of Educational Achievement* (2nd ed.). Circle Pines, MN: AGS Publishing.

Kaufman, A. S., Lichtenberger, E. O., Fletcher-Janzen, E., & Kaufman, N. (2005). *Essentials of KABC-II assessment.* Hoboken, NJ: John Wiley & Sons.

Kelley, C. M., & Lindsay, D. S. (1993). Remembering mistaken for knowing: Ease of retrieval as a basis for confidence in answers to general knowledge questions. *Journal of Memory and Language, 32,* 1–24.

Kennedy, B. A., & Miller, D. J. (1976). Persistent use of verbal rehearsal as a function of information about its value. *Child Development, 47*(2), 566–569.

Kessels, P. C., & de Haan, E. H. F. (2003). Implicit learning in memory rehabilitation: A meta-analysis on errorless learning and vanishing cues methods. *Journal of Clinical and Experimental Neuropsychology, 25,* 1230–1240.

Kheirandish, L., & Gozal, D. (2006). Neurocognitive dysfunction in children with sleep disorders. *Developmental Science, 9,* 388–399.

Kime, S. K., Lamb, D. G., & Wilson, B. A. (1996). Use of a comprehensive program of external cuing to enhance procedural memory in a patient with dense amnesia. *Brain Injury, 10,* 17–25.

Kipp, K. H., & Mohr, G. (2008). Remediation of developmental dyslexia: Tackling a basic memory deficit. *Cognitive Neuropsychology, 25,* 38–55.

Kiresuk, T. J., & Sherman, R. E. (1968). Goal attainment scaling: A general method for evaluating comprehensive community mental health programs. *Community Mental Health Journal, 4*(6), 443–453.

Kirschner, P. A. (2002). Cognitive load theory: Implications of cognitive load theory on the design of learning. *Learning and Instruction*, *12*, 1–10.

Kirschner, P. A., & Klatsky, R. L. (1985). Verbal rehearsal and memory in language-disordered children. *Journal of Speech and Hearing Research*, *28*, 556–565.

Klimesch, W. (1994). *The structure of long-term memory: A connectivity model of semantic processing*. Hillsdale, NJ: Lawrence Erlbaum.

Klingberg, T. (2009). *The overflowing brain: Information overload and the limits of working memory*. New York: Oxford University Press.

Knowlton, B. J., & Squire, L. R. (1995). Remembering and knowing: Two different expressions of declarative memory. *Journal of Experimental Psychology: Learning, Memory, and Cognition*, *21*, 699–710.

Kornell, N., & Metcalfe, J. (2006). Study efficacy and the region of proximal learning framework. *Journal of Experimental Psychology: Learning, Memory, and Cognition*, *32*, 609–622.

Koriat, A. (2000). Control processes in remembering. In E. Tulving & F. I. M. Craik (Eds.), *The Oxford handbook of memory* (pp. 333–346). New York: Oxford University Press.

Koriat, A. (2008). Easy comes, easy goes? The link between learning and remembering and its exploitation in metacognition. *Memory and Cognition*, *36*, 416–428.

Koriat, A., & Goldsmith, M. (1996). Monitoring and control processes in the strategic regulation of memory accuracy. *Psychological Review*, *103*, 490–517.

Korkman, M., Kirk, U., & Kemp, S. (1998). *NEPSY: A Developmental Neuropsychological Assessment*. San Antonio, TX: The Psychological Corporation.

Korkman, M., Kirk, U., & Kemp, S. (2007). *NEPSY-II: A Developmental Neuropsychological Assessment*. San Antonio, TX: The Psychological Corporation.

Kovacs, M., Ryan, C., & Obrosky, S. (1994). Verbal intellectual and verbal memory performance of youths with childhood-onset insulin-dependent diabetes mellitus. *Journal of Pediatric Psychology*, *19*, 475–483.

Kraft, R. N. (1990). *Teaching preschool children to generate and apply mnemonic strategies*. (ERIC Document Reproduction Service No. ED317321).

Kramer, J. H., Knee, K., & Delis, D. C. (2000). Verbal memory impairments in dyslexia. *Archives of Clinical Neuropsychology*, *15*, 83–93.

Kreutzer, M., Leonard, C., & Flavell, J. (1975). An interview study of children's knowledge about memory. *Monographs of the Society for Research in Child Development*, *40* (1).

Kron-Sperl, V., Schneider, W., & Hasselhorn, M. (2008). The development and effectiveness of memory strategies in kindergarten and elementary school: Findings from the Wurzburg and Gottingen longitudinal memory studies. *Cognitive Development, 23,* 79–104.

Kulik, J. A., & Kulik, C. C. (1988). Timing of feedback and verbal learning. *Review of Educational Research, 58,* 79–97.

Kurtz, B. E., Reid, M. K., Borkowski, J. G., & Cavanaugh, J. C. (1982). On the reliability and validity of children's metamemory. *Bulletin of the Psychonomic Society, 19,* 137–140.

Kurtz, M. M., & Gerraty, R. T. (2009). A meta-analytic investigation of neurocognitive deficits in bipolar illness: Profile and effects of clinical state. *Neuropsychology, 23,* 551–562.

Landauer, T. K., & Bjork, R. A. (1978). Optimum rehearsal patterns and name learning. In M. M. Gruneberg, P. E. Morris, & R. N. Sykes (Eds.), *Practical aspects of memory* (pp. 625–632). London: Academic Press.

Lange, G., & Pierce, S. H. (1992). Memory-strategy learning and maintenance in preschool children. *Developmental Psychology, 28,* 453–462.

Lansing, A. E., Max, J. E., Delis, D. C., Fox, P. T., Lancaster, J., Manes, F. F., et al. (2004). Verbal learning and memory after childhood stroke. *Journal of the International Neuropsychological Society, 10,* 742–752.

Larkina, M., Guler, O. E., Kleinknecht, E., & Bauer, P. J. (2008). Maternal provision of structure in deliberate memory task in relation to their preschool children's recall. *Journal of Experimental Child Psychology, 100,* 235–251.

Lauer, R. E., Giordani, B., Boivin, M. J., Halle, N., Glasgow, B., Alessi, N. E., et al. (1994). Effects of depression on memory performance and meta-memory in children. *Journal of the American Academy of Child and Adolescent Psychiatry, 33,* 679–685.

Leach, L., Kaplan, E., Rewilak, D., Richards, B., & Proulx, G. B. (2000). *Kaplan Baycrest Neurocognitive Assessment (KBNA).* San Antonio, TX: PsychCorp.

Leal, L., Crays, N., & Moely, B. E. (1985). Training children to use a self-monitoring study strategy in preparation for recall: Maintenance and generalization effects. *Child Development, 56,* 643–653.

Lengenfelder, J., Chiaravalloti, N. D., & DeLuca, J. (2007). The efficacy of the generation effect in improving new learning in persons with traumatic brain injury. *Rehabilitation Psychology, 52,* 290–296.

Lepine, R., Barrouillet, P., & Camos, V. (2005). What makes working memory spans so predictive of high-level cognition. *Psychonomic Bulletin and Review, 12*(1), 165–170.

Levin, H. S., Fletcher, J. M., Kusnerik, L., & Kufera, J. A. (1996). Semantic memory following pediatric head injury: Relationship to age, severity of injury, and MRI. *Cortex, 32,* 461–478.

Levin, H. S., & Hanten, G. (2004). Posttraumatic amnesia and residual memory deficit after closed head injury. In A. D. Baddeley, M. D. Kopelman, & B. A. Wilson (Eds.), *The essential handbook of memory disorders for clinicians* (pp. 37–67). Hoboken, NJ: John Wiley & Sons.

Levin, J. R. (1988). Elaboration-based learning strategies: Powerful theory = powerful application. *Contemporary Educational Psychology, 13*, 191–205.

Levin, J. R. (1993). Mnemonic strategies and classroom learning: A twenty-year report card. *Elementary School Journal, 94*, 235–244.

Levy, D. A., Stark, C. E. L., & Squire, L. R. (2004). Intact conceptual priming in the absence of declarative memory. *Psychological Science, 15*, 680–686.

Liddell, G. A., & Rasmussen, C. (2005). Memory profile of children with nonverbal learning disability. *Learning Disabilities Research and Practice, 20*, 137–141.

Litman, L., & Davachi, L. (2008). Distributed learning enhances relational memory consolidation. *Learning and Memory, 15*, 711–716.

Locke, E. A., & Latham, G. P. (2002). Building a practically useful theory of goal setting and task motivation: A 35-year odyssey. *American Psychologist, 57*, 705–717.

Lodico, M. G. (1983). The effects of strategy-monitoring training on children's selection of effective memory strategies. *Journal of Experimental Child Psychology, 35*, 263–277.

Logie, R. H. (1996). The seven ages of working memory. In J. T. E. Richardson, R. W. Engle, L. Hasher, R. H. Logie, E. R. Stoltzfus, & R. T. Zacks (Eds.), *Working memory and human cognition* (pp. 31–65). New York: Oxford University Press.

Lovell, M. R., Collins, M W., Iverson, G. L., Field, M., Maroon, J. C., Cantu, R., et al. (2003). Recovery from mild concussion in high school athletes. *Journal of Neurosurgery, 98*, 295–301.

Maguire, E. A., Vargha-Khadem, F., & Mishkin, M. (2001). The effects of bilateral hippocampal damage on fMRI regional activations and interactions during memory retrieval. *Brain, 124*, 1156–1170.

Mahan, V. (1993). Mnemonics and the learning disabled child. *B.C. Journal of Special Education, 17*, 45–53.

Malisza, K. L. (2007). Neuroimaging cognitive function in fetal alcohol spectrum disorders. *International Journal on Disability and Human Development, 6*, 171–188.

Mandler, J. M. (2007). How do we remember? Let me count the ways. In L. M. Oakes & P. J. Bauer (Eds.), *Short- and long-term memory in infancy and early childhood* (pp. 271–290). Oxford, UK: Oxford University Press.

Maneru, C., Junque, C., Botet, F., Tallada, M., & Guardia, J. (2001). Neuropsychological long-term sequelae of perinatal asphyxia. *Brain Injury, 15*, 1029–1039.

Mangels, J. A., Gershberg, F. B., Shimamura, A. P., Arthur, P., & Knight, R. T. (1996). Impaired retrieval from remote memory in patients with frontal lobe damage. *Neuropsychology, 10,* 32–41.

Maquet, P. (2001). The role of sleep in learning and memory. *Science, 294,* 1048–1052.

Martin, R. C., Loring, D. W., Meador, K. J., Lee, G. P., Thrash, N., & Arena, J. G. (1991). Impaired long-term retention despite normal verbal learning in patients with temporal lobe dysfunction. *Neuropsychology, 5,* 3–12.

Martins, S., Guillery-Girard, B., Jambaque, I., Dulac, O., & Eustache, F. (2006). How children suffering severe amnesic syndrome acquire new concepts? *Neuropsychologia, 44,* 2792–2805.

Mastropieri, M. A., & Scruggs, T. E. (1989). Reconstructive elaborations: Strategies that facilitate content learning. *Learning Disabilities Focus, 4,* 73–77.

Mastropieri, M. A., & Scruggs, T. E. (1991). *Teaching students ways to remember: Strategies for learning mnemonically.* Cambridge, MA: Brookline Books.

Mastropieri, M. A., & Scruggs, T. E. (1998). Enhancing school success with mnemonic strategies. *Intervention in School and Clinic, 33,* 201–208.

Mastropieri, M. A., & Scruggs, T. E. (2007). *The inclusive classroom: Strategies for effective instruction.* Columbus, OH: Pearson.

Mastropieri, M. A., Scruggs, T. E., & Levin, J. R. (1985). Maximizing what exceptional students can learn: A review of research on the keyword method and related mnemonic techniques. *Remedial and Special Education, 6,* 39–45.

Mastropieri, M. A., Sweda, J., & Scruggs, T. E. (2000). Putting mnemonic strategies to work in an inclusive classroom. *Learning Disabilities Research & Practice, 15,* 69–74.

Matteer, C. A., Kerns, K. A., & Eso, K. L. (1996). Management of attention and memory disorders following traumatic brain injury. *Journal of Learning Disabilities, 29,* 618–632.

Mattson, S. N., & Riley, E. P. (1998). A review of the neurobehavioral deficits in children with fetal alcohol syndrome or prenatal exposure to alcohol. *Alcoholism: Clinical and Experimental Research, 22,* 279–294.

Mattson, S. N., & Riley, E. P. (1999). Implicit and explicit memory functioning in children with heavy prenatal alcohol exposure. *Journal of the International Neuropsychological Society, 5,* 462–471.

Mattson, S. N., & Roebuck, T. M. (2002). Acquisition and retention of verbal and nonverbal information in children with heavy prenatal alcohol exposure. *Alcoholism: Clinical and Experimental Research, 22,* 875–882.

Mayes, A. R. (2004). Exploring the neural bases of complex memory. In L. R. Squire & D. L. Schacter (Eds.), *Neuropsychology of memory* (3rd ed., pp. 24–34). New York: Guilford.

Mayes, L., Snyder, P. J., Langlois, E., & Hunter, N. (2007). Visuospatial working memory in school-aged children exposed in utero to cocaine. *Child Neuropsychology*, *13*, 205–218.

Mazzoni, G., Cornoldi, C., & Marchitelli, G. (1990). Do memorability ratings affect study-time allocation? *Memory and Cognition*, *18*, 196–204.

McCauley, S. R., McDaniel, M. A., Pedroza, C., Chapman, S. B., & Levin, H. S. (2009). Incentive effects on event-based prospective memory performance in children and adolescents with traumatic brain injury. *Neuropsychology*, *23*, 210–209.

McClelland, J. L., McNaughton, B. L., & O'Reilly, R. C. (1995). Why there are complementary learning systems in the hippocampus and neocortex: Insights from the successes and failures of connectionist models of learning and memory. *Psychological Review*, *102*, 419–457.

McDaniel, M. A., Anderson, J. L., Derbish, M. H., & Morrisette, N. (2007). Testing the testing effect in the classroom. *European Journal of Cognitive Psychology*, *19*, 494–513.

McDaniel, M. A., & Einstein, G. O. (1989). Material-appropriate processing: A contextualist approach to reading and studying strategies. *Educational Psychology Review*, *1*, 113–145.

McDaniel, M. A., & Fisher, R. P. (1991). Tests and test feedback as learning sources. *Contemporary Educational Psychology*, *16*, 192–201.

McGaugh, J. L. (2000). Memory—a century of consolidation. *Science*, *287*, 248–251.

Mednick, S., Nakayama, K., & Stickgold, R. (2003). Sleep-dependent learning: A nap is as good as a night. *Nature Neuroscience*, *6*, 697–698.

Meeter, M., & Murre, J. M. J. (2004). Consolidation of long-term memory: Evidence and alternatives. *Psychological Bulletin*, *130*, 843–857.

Messier, C., Desrochers, A., & Gagnon, M. (1999). Effect of glucose, glucose regulation, and word imagery value on human memory. *Behavioral Neuroscience*, *113*, 431–438.

Metcalfe, J. (2000). Metamemory: Theory and data. In E. Tulving & F. I. M. Craik (Eds.), *The Oxford handbook of memory* (pp. 197–211). New York: Oxford University Press.

Metcalfe, J., Kornell, N., & Son, L. K. (2007). A cognitive-science based programme to enhance study efficacy in a high and low risk setting. *European Journal of Cognitive Psychology*, *19*, 743–768.

Metha, M. A., Owen, A. M., Sahakian, B. J., Mavaddat, N., Pickard, J. D. & Robbins, T. W. (2000). Methylphenidate enhances working memory by modulating discrete frontal and parietal lobe regions in the human brain. *The Journal of Neuroscience*, *20*(6), 1–6.

Meyers, J. E., & Meyers, K. R. (1995). *Rey Complex Figure Test and Recognition Trial*. Odessa, FL: Psychological Assessment Resources.

Middleton, J. A. (2004). Assessment and management of memory problems in children. In A. D. Baddeley, M. D. Kopelman, & B. A. Wilson (Eds.), *The essential handbook of memory disorders for clinicians* (pp. 227–254). Hoboken, NJ: John Wiley & Sons.

Miller, D. C. (2007). *Essentials of school neuropsychological assessment*. Hoboken, NJ: John Wiley & Sons.

Miller, D. C. (Ed.) (2010). *Best practices in school neuropsychology: Guidelines for effective practice, assessment, and evidence-based intervention*. Hoboken, NJ: John Wiley & Sons.

Miller, E. (1992). Psychological approaches to the management of memory impairments. *The British Journal of Psychiatry, 160*, 1–6.

Miller, G. A. (1956). The magical number seven, plus or minus two: Some limits on our capacity for processing information. *Psychological Review, 63*, 81–97.

Miller, J. A., & Blasik, J. L. (2010). Assessing and intervening with children with memory and learning disorders. In D. C. Miller (Ed.), *Best practices in school neuropsychology: Guidelines for effective practice, assessment, and evidence-based intervention* (pp. 641–672). Hoboken, NJ: John Wiley & Sons.

Miller, P. H., & Seier, W. L. (1994). Strategy utilization deficiencies in children: When, where, and why. *Advances in Child Development and Behavior, 25*, 107–156.

Miller, R. R., & Matzel, L. D. (2006). Retrieval failure versus memory loss in experimental amnesia: Definitions and processes. *Learning and Memory, 13*, 491–497.

Milner, B., Squire, L. R., & Kandel, E. R. (1998). Cognitive neuroscience and the study of memory. *Neuron, 20*, 445–468.

Moradi, A. R., Doost, H. T. N., Taghavi, M. R., Yule, W., & Dalgleish, T. (1999). Everyday memory deficits in children and adolescents with PTSD: Performance on the Rivermead Behavioural Memory Test. *Journal of Child Psychology and Psychiatry, 31*, 1051–1061.

Moscovitch, M., Nadel, L., Winocur, G., Gilboa, A., & Rosenbaum, R. S. (2006). The cognitive neuroscience of remote episodic, semantic, and spatial memory. *Current Opinion in Neurobiology, 16*, 179–190.

Mottram, L., & Donders, J. (2005). Construct validity of the California Verbal Learning Test–Children's Version (CVLT-C) after pediatric traumatic brain injury. *Psychological Assessment, 17*, 212–217.

Moulin, C. J. A., & Gathercole, S. E. (2008). Memory changes across the lifespan. In G. Cohen & M. A. Conway, (Eds.), *Memory in the real world* (3rd ed., pp. 305–326). New York: Psychology Press.

Mueller, M. M., & Palkovic, C. M. (2007). Errorless learning: Review and practical application for teaching children with pervasive developmental disorders. *Psychology in the Schools, 44,* 691–700.

Nadel, L., & Moscovitch, M. (1997). Memory consolidation, retrograde amnesia and the hippocampal complex. *Current Opinion in Neurobiology, 7,* 431–439.

Nader, K. (2003). Memory traces unbound. *Trends in Neurosciences, 26,* 65–72.

Nader, K., Schafe, G. E., & LeDoux, J. E. (2000). Fear memories require protein synthesis in the amygdala for reconsolidation after retrieval. *Nature, 406,* 722–726.

Nagel, B. J., Delis, D. C., Palmer, S. L., Reeves, C., Gajjar, A., & Mulhern, R. K. (2006). Early patterns of verbal memory impairment in children treated for medulloblastoma. *Neuropsychology, 20,* 105–112.

Nairne, J. S. (2002). Remembering over the short-term: The case against the standard model. *Annual Review of Psychology, 53,* 53–81.

Naude, H., & Pretorius, E. (2003). Investigating the effects of asthma medication on the cognitive and psychosocial functioning of primary school children with asthma. *Early Child Development and Care, 173,* 699–709.

Nelson, C. A. (1995). The ontogeny of human memory: A cognitive neuroscience perspective. *Developmental Psychology, 31,* 723–738.

Nelson, C. A., Wewerka, S., Thomas, K. M., Tribby-Walbridge, S., deRegnier, R., & Georgieff, M. (2000). Neurocognitive sequelae of infants of diabetic mothers. *Behavioral Assessment, 114,* 950–956.

Nelson, H. E., & Warrington, E. K. (1980). An investigation of memory functions in dyslexic children. *British Journal of Psychology, 71,* 487–503.

Nelson, T. O., & Dunlosky, J. (1992). How shall we explain the delayed-judgment-of-learning effect? *Psychological Science, 3,* 317–318.

Newall, A., & Simon, H. A. (1972). *Human problem solving.* Englewood Cliffs, NJ: Prentice Hall.

Niccols, A. (2007). Fetal alcohol syndrome and the developing socio-emotional brain. *Brain and Cognition, 65,* 135–142.

Nichols, S., Jones, W., Roman, M. J., Wulfeck, B., Delis, D. C., Reilly, J., et al. (2004). Mechanisms of verbal memory impairment in four neurodevelopmental disorders. *Brain and Language, 88,* 180–189.

Nolan, M. A., Redoblado, M. A., Lah, S., Sabaz, M., Lawson, J. A., Cunningham, A. M., et al. (2004). Memory function in childhood epilepsy syndromes. *Journal of Pediatric Child Health, 40,* 20–27.

Northam, E., Anderson, P. J., Jacobs, R., Hughes, M., Warne, G. L., & Werther, G. A. (2001). Neuropsychological profiles of children with T1DM 6 years after disease onset. *Diabetes Care, 24,* 1772–1787.

O'Conner, A. R., Moulin, C. J., & Cohen, G. (2008). Memory and consciousness. In G. Cohen & M. A. Conway (Eds.), *Memory in the real world* (3rd ed., pp. 327–356). New York: Psychology Press.

O'Conner, M., Sieggreen, M. A., Ahern, G., Schomer, D., & Mesulam, M. (1997). Accelerated forgetting in association with temporal lobe epilepsy and paraneoplastic encephalitis. *Brain and Cognition, 35*, 71–84.

O'Conner, M., & Verfaellie, M. (2004). The amnesic syndrome: Overview and subtypes. In A. D. Baddeley, M. D. Kopelman, & Wilson, B. A. (Eds.), *The essential handbook of memory disorders for clinicians* (pp. 15–36). Hoboken, NJ: John Wiley & Sons.

Oken, B. S., Storzbach, D. M., & Kaye, J. A. (1998). The efficacy of Ginkgo biloba on cognitive function in Alzheimer's disease. *Archives of Neurology, 55*, 1409–1415.

Olive, T. (2004). Working memory in writing: Empirical evidence from the dual-task technique. *European Psychologist, 9*, 32–42.

Olson, H. C., Feldman, J. J., Streissguth, A. P., Sampson, P. D., & Bookstein, F. L. (1998). Neuropsychological deficits in adolescents with fetal alcohol syndrome: Clinical findings. *Alcoholism: Clinical and Experimental Research, 22*, 1998–2012.

O'Neill, M. E., & Douglas, V. I. (1991). Study strategies and story recall in attention deficit disorder and reading disability. *Journal of Abnormal Child Psychology, 19*, 671–692.

Ornstein, P. A., Grammer, J. K., & Coffman, J. L. (2010). Teachers' "mnemonic style" and the development of skilled memory. In H. S. Waters & W. Schneider (Eds.), *Metacognition, strategy use, and instruction* (pp. 23–53). New York: Guilford.

Ostergaard, A. L. (1987). Episodic, semantic and procedural memory in a case of amnesia at an early age. *Neuropsychologia, 25*, 341–357.

O'Sullivan, J. T. (1997). Effort, interest, and recall: Beliefs and behaviors of preschoolers. *Journal of Experimental Child Psychology, 65*, 43–67.

O'Sullivan, J. T., & Howe, M. L. (1998). A different view of metamemory with illustrations from children's beliefs about long-term retention. *European Journal of Psychology of Education, 13*, 9–28.

O'Sullivan, J. T., & Pressley, M. (1984). Completeness of instruction and strategy transfer. *Journal of Experimental Child Psychology, 38*, 275–288.

Oyen, A., & Bebko, J. M. (1996). The effects of computer games and lesson contexts on children's mnemonic strategies. *Journal of Experimental Child Psychology, 62*, 173–189.

Paller, K. A. (2004). Cross-cortical consolidation as the core defect in amnesia. In L. R. Squire & D. L. Schacter (Eds.), *Neuropsychology of memory* (3rd ed., pp. 73–88). New York: Guilford.

Paller, K. A., & Voss, J. L. (2004). Memory reactivation and consolidation during sleep. *Learning and Memory, 11,* 664–670.

Parente, R., & Herrmann, D. (1996). Retraining memory strategies. *Topics in Language Disorders, 17,* 45–57.

Paris, S. G., Newman, R. S., & McVey, K. A. (1982). Learning the functional significance of mnemonic actions: A microgenetic study of strategy acquisition. *Journal of Experimental Child Psychology, 34,* 490–509.

Parkin, A. J., & Russo, R. (1990). Implicit and explicit memory and the automatic/effortful distinction. *European Journal of Cognitive Psychology, 2,* 71–80.

Pashler, H., Cepeda, N. J., Rohrer, D., & Wixted, J. T. (2005). When does feedback facilitate learning of words? *Journal of Experimental Psychology: Learning, Memory, and Cognition, 31,* 3–8.

Pashler, H., Rohrer, D., Cepeda, N. J., & Carpenter, S. K. (2007). Enhancing learning and retarding forgetting: Choices and consequences. *Psychonomic Bulletin, 14,* 187–193.

Pass, F., Renkl, A., & Sweller, J. (2004). Cognitive load theory: Instructional implications of the interaction between information structures and cognitive architecture. *Instructional Science, 32,* 1–8.

Piaget, J. (1968). *On the development of memory and identity.* Worcester, MA: Clark University Press.

Pickering, S. J., & Gathercole, S. E. (2004). Distinctive working memory profiles in children with special educational needs. *Educational Psychology, 24,* 393–408.

Pickering, S. J., Gathercole, S. E., Hall, M., & Lloyd, S. A. (2001). Development of memory for pattern and path: Further evidence for the fractionation of visuo-spatial memory. *Quarterly Journal of Experimental Psychology, 54A,* 397–420.

Pierce, S. H., & Lange, G. (2000). Relationships among metamemory, motivation, and memory performance in young school-age children. *British Journal of Developmental Psychology, 18,* 121–135.

Plihal, W., & Born, J. (1997). Effects of early and late nocturnal sleep on declarative and procedural memory. *Journal of Cognitive Neuroscience, 9,* 534–547.

Pliszka, S. R. (2003). *Neuroscience for the Mental Health Clinician.* New York: Guildford.

Prabhakaran, V., Narayanan, K., Zhao, Z., & Gabrieli, J. D. E. (2000). Integration of diverse information in working memory within the frontal lobe. *Nature Neuroscience, 3,* 85–90.

Pressley, M. (1982). Elaboration and memory development. *Child Development, 53,* 296–309.

Pressley, M., Borkowski, J. G., & O'Sullivan, J. T. (1984). Memory strategy instruction is made of this: Metamemory and durable strategy use. *Educational Psychologist, 19,* 94–107.

Pressley, M., & Levin, J. R. (1980). The development of mental imagery retrieval. *Child Development, 51,* 558–560.

Pressley, M., Levin, J. R., & Ghatala, E. S. (1984). Memory strategy monitoring in adults and children. *Journal of Verbal Learning and Verbal Behavior, 23,* 270–288.

Pressley, M., & Schneider, W. (1997). *Introduction to memory development during childhood and adolescence.* Mahwah, NJ: Lawrence Erlbaum.

Pretorius, E., Naude, H., & Becker, P. J. (2002). Can excess bilirubin levels cause learning difficulties? *Early Child Development and Care, 172,* 391–404.

Ranganath, C., Johnson, M. K., & D'Esposito, M. (2003). Prefrontal activity associated with working memory and episodic long-term memory. *Neuropsychologia, 41,* 378–389.

Rankin, P. M., & Hood, J. (2005). Designing clinical interventions for children with specific memory disorders. *Pediatric Rehabilitation, 8,* 283–297.

Rasmussen, C. (2005). Executive functioning and working memory in fetal alcohol spectrum disorder. *Alcoholism: Clinical and Experimental Research, 29,* 1359–1367.

Rawson, K. A., & Dunlosky, J. (2007). Improving students' self-evaluation of learning for key concepts in textbook materials. *European Journal of Cognitive Psychology, 19,* 559–579.

Rea, C. P., & Modigliani, V. (1985). The effect of expanded versus massed practice on the retention of multiplication facts and spelling lists. *Human Learning: Journal of Practical Research and Applications, 4,* 11–18.

Recht, D. R., & Lauren, L. (1988). Effect of prior knowledge on good and poor readers' memory of text. *Journal of Educational Psychology, 80,* 16–20.

Records, N. L., Tomblin, J. B., & Buckwalter, P. R. (1995). Auditory verbal learning and memory in young adults with specific language impairment. *Clinical Neuropsychologist, 9,* 187–193.

Reyna, V. F., & Brainerd, C. J. (1995). Fuzzy-trace theory: An interim synthesis. *Learning and Individual Differences, 7,* 1–75.

Reyna, V. F., & Kiernan, B. (1994). Development of gist versus verbatim memory in sentence recognition: Effects of lexical familiarity, semantic content, encoding instructions, and retention interval. *Developmental Psychology, 30,* 178–191.

Reynolds, C. R., & Bigler, E. D. (1994). *Test of Memory and Learning.* Austin, TX: PRO-ED.

Reynolds, C. R., & Voress, J. K. (2007). *Test of Memory and Learning* (2nd ed.). Austin, TX: PRO-ED.

Rhodes, S. K., Shimoda, K. C., Waid, L. R., O'Neil, P. M., Oexmann, M. J., Collop, N. A., et al. (1995). Neurocognitive deficits in morbidly obese children with obstructive sleep apnea. *Journal of Pediatrics, 127,* 741–744.

Riccio, C. A., Cash, D. L., & Cohen, M. J. (2007). Learning and memory performance of children with specific language impairment (SLI). *Applied Neuropsychology, 14,* 255–261.

Rice, M. L., Oetting, J. B., Marquis, J., Bode, J., & Pae, S. (1994). Frequency of input effects on word comprehension of children with specific language impairment. *Journal of Speech and Hearing Research, 37,* 106–122.

Richardson, G. A., Ryan, C., Willford, J., Day, N. L., & Goldschmidt, L. (2002). Prenatal alcohol and marijuana exposure: Effects on neuropsychological outcomes at 10 years. *Neurotoxicology and Teratology, 24,* 311–320.

Richardson, J. T. E. (1995). The efficacy of imagery mnemonics in memory remediation. *Neuropsychologia, 33,* 1345–1357.

Richardson, J. T. E. (1996). Evolving concepts of working memory. In J. T. E. Richardson, R. W. Engle, L. Hasher, R. H. Logie, E. R. Stoltzfus, & R. T. Zacks (Eds.), *Working memory and human cognition* (pp. 3–30). New York: Oxford University Press.

Ritchie, D., & Karge, B. D. (1996). Making information memorable: Enhanced knowledge retention and recall through the elaboration process. *Preventing School Failure, 41,* 28–33.

Roediger, H. L., Gallo, D. A., & Geraci, L. (2002). Processing approaches to cognition: The impetus from the levels of processing framework. *Memory, 10,* 319–332.

Roediger, H. L., & Karpicke, J. D. (2006a). Test-enhanced learning: Taking memory tests improves long-term retention. *Psychological Science, 17,* 249–255.

Roediger, H. L., & Karpicke, J. D. (2006b). The power of testing memory: Basic research and implications for educational practice. *Perspectives on Psychological Science, 1,* 181–210.

Rohling, M. L., Faust, M. E., Beverly, B., & Demakis, G. (2009). Effectiveness of cognitive rehabilitation following acquired brain injury: A meta-analytic re-examination of Cicerone et al.'s (2000, 2005) systematic reviews. *Neuropsychology, 23,* 20–39.

Rohrer, D., Taylor, K., Pashler, H., Wixted, J. T., & Cepeda, N. J. (2005). The effect of overlearning on long-term retention. *Applied Cognitive Psychology, 19,* 361–374.

Roid, G. H. (2003). *Stanford-Binet Intelligence Scales* (5th ed.). Itasca, IL: Riverside Publishing.

Roid, G. H., & Miller, L. J. (1998). *Leiter International Performance Scale-Revised*. Wood Dale, IL: Stoelting.

Roman, M. J., Delis, D. C., Willerman, L., Magulac, M., Demadura, T. L., de la Pena, J. L., et al. (1998). Impact of pediatric traumatic brain injury on components of verbal memory. *Journal of Clinical and Experimental Psychology, 20*, 245–258.

Rose, M. C., Cundick, B. P., & Higbee, K. L. (1983). Verbal rehearsal and visual imagery: Mnemonic aids for learning-disabled students. *Journal of Learning Disabilities, 16*, 352–354.

Rose, S. A., Feldman, J. F., & Jankowski, J. J. (2007). Developmental aspects of visual recognition memory in infancy. In L. M. Oakes & P. J. Bauer (Eds.), *Short- and long-term memory in infancy and early childhood* (pp. 153–178). Oxford, UK: Oxford University Press.

Rosen, V. M., & Engle, R. W. (1997). The role of working memory capacity in retrieval. *Journal of Experimental Psychology: General, 126*, 211–227.

Rosenbaum, R. S., Winocur, G., & Moscovitch, M. (2001). New views on old memories: Re-evaluating the role of the hippocampal complex. *Behavioral Brain Research, 127*, 183–197.

Rosenshine, B. (1995). Advances in research on instruction. *Journal of Educational Research, 88*, 262–268.

Rovet, J. F. (2002). Congenital hypothyroidism: An analysis of persisting deficits and associated factors. *Child Neuropsychology, 8*, 150–162.

Rovet, J. F., Ehrlich, R. M., Czuchta, D., & Akler, M. (1993). Psychoeducational characteristics of children and adolescents with insulin-dependent diabetes mellitus. *Journal of Learning Disabilities, 26*, 7–22.

Rudner, M., Fransson, P., Ingvar, M., Nyberg, L., & Ronnberg, J. (2007). Neural representation of binding lexical signs and words in the episodic buffer of working memory. *Neuropsychologia, 45*, 2258–2276.

Ryan, C., Vega, A., & Drash, A. (1985). Cognitive deficits in adolescents who developed diabetes early in life. *Pediatrics, 75*, 921–927.

Ryan, E. B., Ledger, G. W., & Weed, K. A. (1987). Acquisition and transfer of an integrative imagery strategy by young children. *Child Development, 58*, 443–452.

Ryan, L. M., & Warden, D. L. (2003). Post concussion syndrome. *International Review of Psychiatry, 15*, 310–316.

Sampaio, A., Sousa, N., Fernandez, M., Henriques, M., & Goncalves, O. F. (2008). Memory abilities in Williams syndrome: Dissociation or developmental delay hypothesis. *Brain and Cognition, 66*, 290–297.

Sapolsky, R. M. (1996). Why stress is bad for your brain. *Science, 273*, 749–750.

Sapolsky, R. M., Packan, D. R., & Vale, W. W. (1988). Glucocorticoid toxicity in the hippocampus: In vitro demonstration. *Brain Research, 453,* 367–371.

Savage, C. R., Deckersbach, T., Wihelm, S., Rauch, S. L., Baer, L., Reid, T., et al. (2000). Strategic processing and episodic memory impairment in obsessive compulsive disorder. *Neuropsychology, 14,* 141–151.

Savage, C. R., Keuthen, N. J., Jenike, M. A., & Brown, H. D. (1996). Recall and recognition memory in obsessive-compulsive disorder. *Journal of Neuropsychiatry and Clinical Neurosciences, 8,* 99–103.

Schacter, D. L. (1992). Understanding implicit memory: A cognitive neuroscience approach. *American Psychologist, 47,* 559–569.

Schacter, D. L. (1996). *Searching for memory: The brain, the mind, and the past.* New York: Basic Books.

Schacter, D. L. (1999). The seven sins of memory: Insights from psychology and cognitive neuroscience. *American Psychologist, 54,* 182–203.

Schacter, D. L., Rich, S. A., & Stampp, M. S. (1985). Remediation of memory disorders: Experimental evaluation of the spaced-retrieval technique. *Journal of Clinical and Experimental Neuropsychology, 7,* 79–96.

Schneider, W. (1993). Domain-specific knowledge and memory performance in children. *Educational Psychology Review, 5,* 254–257.

Schneider, W. (2000). Research on memory development: Historical trends and themes. *International Journal of Behavioral Development, 24,* 407–420.

Schneider, W. (2010). Metacognition and memory development in childhood and adolescence. In H. S. Waters & W. Schneider (Eds.), *Metacognition, strategy use, and instruction* (pp. 54–84). New York: Guilford.

Schneider, W., & Bjorklund, D. F. (1992). Expertise, aptitude, and strategic remembering. *Child Development, 63,* 461–473.

Schneider, W., & Pressley, M. (1997). *Memory development between two and twenty* (2nd ed.). Mahwah, NJ: Lawrence Erlbaum.

Schwabe, L., Bohringer, A., & Wolf, O. T. (2009). Stress disrupts context-dependent memory. *Learning and Memory, 16,* 110–113.

Scruggs, T. E., & Mastropieri, M. A. (1990). The case for mnemonic instruction: From laboratory research to classroom applications. *The Journal of Special Education, 24,* 7–32.

Scruggs, T. E., & Mastropieri, M. A. (1991). Classroom applications of mnemonic instruction: Acquisition, maintenance, and generalization. *Exceptional Children, 58,* 219–229.

Scruggs, T. E., & Mastropieri, M. A. (2000). The effectiveness of mnemonic instruction for students with learning and behavior problems: An update and research synthesis. *Journal of Behavioral Education, 10,* 163–173.

Scruggs, T. E., Mastropieri, M. A., & Sullivan, G. S. (1994). Promoting relational thinking: Elaborative interrogation for students with mild disabilities. *Exceptional Children, 60,* 450–457.

Sells, C. J., Robinson, N. M., Brown, Z., & Knopp, R. H. (1994). Long-term developmental follow-up of infants of diabetic mothers. *Journal of Pediatrics, 125,* 9–17.

Semrud-Clikeman, M., Kutz, A., & Strassner, E. (2005). Providing neuro-psychological services to learners with traumatic brain injuries. In R. C. D'Amato, E. Fletcher-Janzen, & C. R. Reynolds (Eds.), *Handbook of school neuropsychology* (pp. 425–443). Hoboken, NJ: John Wiley & Sons.

Shaughnessy, J. J. (1981). Memory monitoring accuracy and modification of rehearsal strategies. *Journal of Verbal Learning & Verbal Behavior, 20,* 216–230.

Shaywitz, S. E. (2003). *Overcoming dyslexia: A new and complete science-based program for overcoming reading problems at any level.* New York: Knopf.

Shear, P. K., Tallal, P., & Delis, D. C. (1992). Verbal learning and memory in language impaired children. *Neuropsychologia, 30,* 451–458.

Sheline, Y., Wang, P., Gado, M., Csernansky, J., & Vannier, M. (1996). Hippocampal atrophy in major depression. *Proceedings of the National Academy of Sciences USA, 93,* 3908–3913.

Sherwin, B. (1997). Estrogen effects on cognition in menopausal women. *Neurology, 48*(7), S21–S26.

Shimamura, A. P. (2004). Relational binding theory and the role of consolidation in memory retrieval. In L. R. Squire & D. L. Schacter (Eds.), *Neuropsychology of memory* (3rd ed., pp. 61–72). New York: Guilford.

Shing, Y. L., Werkle-Bergner, M., Li, S., & Lindenberger, U. (2008). Associative and strategic components of episodic memory: A life-span dissociation. *Journal of Experimental Psychology: General, 137,* 495–513.

Shuell, T. J., & Keppel, G. (1970). Learning ability and retention. *Journal of Educational Psychology, 61,* 59–65.

Shum, D., Jamieson, E., Bahr, M., & Wallace, G. (1999). Implicit and explicit memory in children with traumatic brain injury. *Journal of Clinical and Experimental Neuropsychology, 21,* 149–158.

Siegel, D. J. (1999). *The developing mind.* New York: Guilford.

Sim, A., Terryberry-Spohr, L., & Wilson, B. (2008). Prolonged recovery of memory functioning after mild traumatic brain injury in adolescent athletes. *Journal of Neurosurgery, 108,* 511–516.

Simons, J. S., & Spiers, H. J. (2003). Prefrontal and medial temporal lobe interactions in long-term memory. *Neuroscience, 4,* 637–648.

Skowronek, J. S., Leichtman, M. D., & Pillemer, D. B. (2008). Long-term episodic memory in children with attention-deficit/hyperactivity disorder. *Learning Disabilities Research and Practice, 23,* 25–35.

Smith, A. D. (2008). Memory for places: Routes, maps, and object locations. In G. Cohen & M. A. Conway (Eds.), *Memory in the real world* (3rd ed., pp. 173–206). New York: Psychology Press.

Smith, E. E., & Jonides, J. (1997). Working memory: A view from neuroimaging. *Cognitive Psychology, 33,* 5–42.

Smith, S. M. (1979). Remembering in and out of context. *Journal of Experimental Psychology: Human Learning and Memory, 5,* 460–471.

Smith, S. M., Glenberg, A., & Bjork, R. A. (1978). Environmental context and human memory. *Memory and Cognition, 6,* 342–353.

Sodian, B., Schneider, W., & Perlmutter, M. (1986). Recall, clustering, and metamemory in young children. *Journal of Experimental Child Psychology, 41,* 395–410.

Sohlberg, M. M., & Mateer, C. A. (2001). *Cognitive rehabilitation.* New York: Guilford.

Son, L. K. (2005). Metacognitive control: Children's short-term versus long-term study strategies. *Journal of General Psychology, 132,* 347–363.

Sowell, E. R., Lu, L. H., O'Hare, E. D., McCourt, S. T., Mattson, S. N., O'Connor, M. J., et al. (2007). Functional magnetic resonance imaging of verbal learning in children with heavy prenatal alcohol exposure. *Rapid Communication of Neuroscience Research, 18,* 635–639.

Spear, N. E., & Mueller, C. W. (1984). Consolidation as a function of retrieval. In H. Weingartner & E. S. Parker (Eds.), *Memory consolidation: Psychobiology of cognition* (pp. 111–148). Hillsdale, NJ: Lawrence Erlbaum.

Sprenger, M. (2005). *How to teach so students remember.* Alexandria, VA: Association for Supervision and Curriculum Development.

Squire, L. R. (1987). *Memory and brain.* New York: Oxford University Press.

Squire, L. R. (1989). On the course of forgetting in very long-term memory. *Journal of Experimental Psychology: Learning, Memory, and Cognition, 15,* 241–245.

Squire, L. R. (1992). Memory and the hippocampus: A synthesis from findings with rats, monkeys, and humans. *Psychological Review, 99,* 195–231.

Squire, L. R. (2004). Memory systems of the brain: A brief history and current perspective. *Neurobiology of Learning and Memory, 82,* 171–177.

Squire, L. R., & Alvarez, P. (1995). Retrograde amnesia and memory consolidation: A neurobiological perspective. *Current Opinions in Neurobiology, 5,* 169–177.

Squire, L. R., Cohen, N. J., & Nadel, L. (1984). The medial temporal region and memory consolidation: A new hypothesis. In H. Weingartner & E. S. Parker (Eds.), *Memory consolidation: Psychobiology of cognition* (pp. 185–210). Hillsdale, NJ: Lawrence Erlbaum.

Squire, L. R., & Zola, S. M. (1991). The medial temporal lobe system. *Science*, *253*, 1380–1386.

Squire, L. R., & Zola, S. M. (1998). Episodic memory, semantic memory, and amnesia. *Hippocampus*, *8*, 205–211.

Stickgold, R. (2005). Sleep-dependent memory consolidation. *Nature*, *437*, 1272–1278.

Stone, S. J. (1993). *The role of memory in early literacy acquisition*. (ERIC Document Reproduction Service No. ED366901).

Storm, B. C., Bjork, E. L., & Bjork, R. A. (2007). When intended remembering leads to unintended forgetting. *Quarterly Journal of Experimental Psychology*, *60*, 909–915.

Streissguth, A. P., Barr, H. M., Bookstein, F. L., Sampson, P. D., & Olson, H. C. (1999). The long-term neurocognitive consequences of prenatal alcohol exposure. *Psychological Science*, *10*, 186–190.

Stroud, K. C., & Reynolds, C. R. (2006). *School Motivation and Learning Strategies Inventory (SMALSI)*. Los Angeles: Western Psychological Services.

Sugden, D., & Newall, M. (1987). Teaching transfer strategies to children with moderate learning difficulties. *British Journal of Special Education*, *14*, 63–67.

Summers, J. A., & Craik, F. I. M. (1994). The effects of subject-performed tasks on the memory performance of verbal autistic children. *Journal of Autism and Developmental Disorders*, *24*, 773–783.

Surber, J. R., & Anderson, R. C. (1975). Delay-retention effect in natural classroom settings. *Journal of Educational Psychology*, *67*, 170–173.

Suzuki-Slakter, N. S. (1988). Elaboration and metamemory during adolescence. *Contemporary Educational Psychology*, *13*, 206–220.

Swanson, H. L. (1986). Learning disabled readers' verbal coding difficulties: A problem of storage or retrieval? *Learning Disabilities Research*, *1*, 73–82.

Swanson, H. L., Howard, C. B., & Saez, L. (2006). Do different components of working memory underlie different subgroups of reading disabilities? *Journal of Learning Disabilities*, *39*, 252–269.

Swanson, H. L., & Jerman, O. (2006). Math disabilities: A selective meta-analysis of the literature. *Review of Educational Research*, *76*, 249–274.

Swing, S., & Peterson, P. (1988). Elaborative and integrative thought processes in mathematics learning. *Journal of Educational Psychology*, *80*, 54–66.

Tailby, R., & Haslam, C. (2003). An investigation of errorless learning in memory-impaired patients: Improving the technique and clarifying theory. *Neuropsychologia*, *41*, 1230–1240.

Talley, J. L. (1993). *Children's Auditory Verbal Learning Test, Second Edition (CALVT-2)*. Odessa, FL: Psychological Assessment Resources.

Taverni, J. P., Seliger, G., & Lichtman, S. W. (1998). Donepezil mediated memory improvements in traumatic brain injury during post acute rehabilitation. *Brain Injury, 12*(1), 77–80.

Temple, C. M. (2004). Developmental amnesias and acquired amnesias of childhood. In A. D. Baddeley, M. D. Kopelman, & Wilson, B. A. (Eds.), *The essential handbook of memory disorders for clinicians* (pp. 91–112). Hoboken, NJ: John Wiley & Sons.

Temple, C. M., & Richardson, P. (2006). Developmental amnesia: Fractionation of developing memory systems. *Cognitive Neuropsychology, 23*, 762–788.

Toichi, M., & Kamio, Y. (2003). Long-term memory in high-functioning autism: Controversy on episodic memory in autism reconsidered. *Journal of Autism and Developmental Disorders, 33*, 151–161.

Torgesen, J. K. (1985). Memory processes in reading disabled children. *Journal of Learning Disabilities, 18*, 350–357.

Tremont, G., Halpert, S., Javorsky, D. J., & Stern, R. A. (2000). Differential impact of executive dysfunction on verbal list learning and story recall. *Clinical Neuropsychologist, 14*, 295–302.

Tulving, E. (1985). How many memory systems are there? *American Psychologist, 40*, 385–398.

Tulving, E. (1993). What is episodic memory? *Current Directions in Psychological Science, 2*(3), 67–70.

Tulving, E. (2002). Episodic memory: From mind to brain. *Annual Review of Psychology, 53*, 1–25.

Tulving, E., & Markowitsch, H. J. (1998). Episodic and declarative memory: Role of the hippocampus. *Hippocampus, 8*, 198–204.

Uberti, J. Z., Scruggs, T. E., & Mastropieri, M. A. (2003). Keywords make the difference! Mnemonic instruction in inclusive classrooms. *Teaching Exceptional Children, 35*(3), 56–61.

Unsworth, N., & Engle, R. W. (2007). The nature of individual differences in working memory capacity: Active maintenance in primary memory and controlled search from secondary memory. *Psychological Review, 114*, 104–132.

Vanderploeg, R. D., Crowell, T. A., & Curtiss, G. (2001). Verbal learning and memory deficits in traumatic brain injury: Encoding, consolidation, and retrieval. *Journal of Clinical and Experimental Neuropsychology, 23*, 185–195.

Van Kampen, D. A., Lovell, M. R., Pardini, J. E., Collins, M. W., & Freddie, H. F. (2006). The "value-added" of neurocognitive testing after sports-related concussion. *American Journal of Sports Medicine, 10*, 1–6.

Van Merrienboer, J. J., Kirschner, P. A., & Kester, L. (2003). Taking the load off a learner's mind: Instructional design for complex learning. *Educational Psychologist, 38*, 5–13.

Vargha-Khadem, F. (2001). Generalized versus selective cognitive impairments resulting from brain damage sustained in childhood. *Epilepsia, 42*, 37–40.

Vargha-Khadem, F., Gadian, D. G., Watkins, K. E., & Connelly, A. (1997). Differential effects of early hippocampal pathology on episodic and semantic memory. *Science, 277*, 376–380.

Vermetten, E., Vythilingam, M., Southweick, S. M., Charney, D. S., & Bremner, J. D. (2003). Long-term treatment with paroxetine increases verbal declarative memory and hippocampal volume in posttraumatic stress disorder. *Biological Psychiatry, 54*, 693–702.

Vicari, S., Finzi, A., Menghini, D., Marotta, L., & Petrosini, L. (2005). Do children with developmental dyslexia have an implicit learning deficit? *Journal of Neurology, Neurosurgery, and Psychiatry, 76*, 1392–1397.

Voelker, S. L., Carter, R. A., Sprague, D. J., Gdowski, C. L., & Lachar, D. (1989). Developmental trends in memory and metamemory in children with Attention Deficit Disorder. *Journal of Pediatric Psychology, 14*, 75–88.

Walker, M. P., & Stickgold, R. (2005). It's practice, with sleep, that makes perfect: Implications of sleep-dependent learning and plasticity for skill performance. *Clinical Sports Medicine, 24*, 301–317.

Walker, M. P., & Stickgold, R. (2006). Sleep, memory, and plasticity. *Annual Review of Psychology, 57*, 139–166.

Walker, N. (1986). Direct retrieval from elaborated memory traces. *Memory and Cognition, 14*, 321–328.

Wang, A. Y., & Richarde, R. S. (1987). Development of memory-monitoring and self-efficacy in children. *Psychological Reports, 60*, 647–658.

Ward, H., Shum, G., Wallace, G., & Boon, J. (2002). Pediatric traumatic brain injury and procedural memory. *Journal of Clinical and Experimental Neuropsychology, 24*, 458–470.

Waters, H. S., & Kunnmann, T. W. (2010). Metacognition and strategy discovery in early childhood. In H. S. Waters & W. Schneider (Eds.), *Metacognition, strategy use, and instruction* (pp. 3–22). New York: Guilford.

Watts, F. N., Morris, L., & MacLeod, A. K. (1987). Recognition memory in depression. *Journal of Abnormal Psychology, 96*, 273–275.

Webster, R. E. (1992). *Learning Efficiency Test-II.* Novato, CA: Academic Therapy Publications.

Webster, R. E., Hall, C. W., Brown, J. B., & Bolen, L. M. (1996). Memory modality differences in children with Attention Deficit Hyperactivity Disorder with and without learning disabilities. *Psychology in the Schools, 33*, 193–201.

Wechsler, D. (2002). *Wechsler Preschool and Primary Scale of Intelligence-Third Edition.* San Antonio, TX: The Psychological Corporation.

Wechsler, D. (2003). *Wechsler Intelligence Scale for Children-Fourth Edition*. San Antonio, TX: The Psychological Corporation.

Wechsler, D. (2008). *Wechsler Adult Intelligence Scale-Fourth Edition: Technical and interpretative manual*. San Antonio, TX: Pearson.

Wechsler, D. (2009). *Wechsler Memory Scale-Fourth Edition*. San Antonio, TX: Pearson.

Weingartner, H., & Parker, E. S. (1984). Memory consolidation: A cognitive perspective. In H. Weingartner & E. S. Parker (Eds.), *Memory consolidation: Psychobiology of cognition* (pp. 1–14). Hillsdale, NJ: Lawrence Erlbaum.

Wheeler, M. A. (1995). Improvement in recall over time without repeated testing: Spontaneous recovery revisited. *Journal of Experimental Psychology: Learning, Memory, and Cognition, 21*, 173–184.

Wheeler, M. A., Ewers, M., & Buonanno, J. F. (2003). Different rates of forgetting following study versus test trials. *Memory, 11*, 571–580.

Wilde, M. C., Boake, C., & Sherer, M. (1995). Do recognition-free recall discrepancies detect retrieval deficits in closed head injury? An exploratory analysis with the California Verbal Learning Test. *Journal of Clinical and Experimental Neuropsychology, 17*, 849–855.

Willford, J. A., Richardson, G. A., Leech, S. L., & Day, N. L. (2004). Verbal and visuospatial learning and memory function in children with moderate prenatal alcohol exposure. *Alcoholism: Clinical and Experimental Research, 28*, 497–507.

Williams, H. L., Conway, M. A., & Cohen, G. (2008). Autobiographical memory. In G. Cohen & M. A. Conway (Eds.), *Memory in the real world* (3rd ed., pp. 21–92). New York: Psychology Press.

Williams, J., Phillips, T., Griebel, M. L., Sharp, G. B., Lange, B., Edgar, T., et al. (2001). Patterns of memory performance in children with controlled epilepsy on the CVLT-C. *Child Neuropsychology, 7*, 15–20.

Williams, J., Sharp, G., Lange, B., & Bates, S. (1996). The effects of seizure type, level of seizure control, and antiepileptic drugs on memory and attention skills in children with epilepsy. *Developmental Neuropsychology, 12*, 241–253.

Willis, W. G. (2005). Foundations of developmental neuroanatomy. In R. C. D'Amato, E. Fletcher-Janzen, & C. R. Reynolds (Eds.), *Handbook of school neuropsychology* (pp. 41–60). Hoboken, NJ: John Wiley & Sons.

Willoughby, T., Porter, L., & Belsito, L. (1999). Use of elaboration strategies by students in grades two, four, and six. *Elementary School Journal, 99*, 221–231.

Wilson, B. A. (1987). *Rehabilitation of memory*. New York: Guilford.

Wilson, B. A. (2000). Compensating for cognitive deficits following brain injury. *Neuropsychology Review, 10*, 233–243.

Wilson, B. A. (2004). Assessment of memory disorders. In A. D. Baddeley, M. D. Kopelman, & B. A. Wilson (Eds.), *The essential handbook of memory disorders for clinicians* (pp. 159–178). Hoboken, NJ: John Wiley & Sons.

Wilson, B. A. (2009). *Memory rehabilitation: Integrating theory and practice.* New York: Guilford.

Wilson, B. A., Cockburn, J., & Baddeley, A. D. (1985). *The Rivermead Behavioural Memory Test.* Bury St. Edmonds, UK: Thames Valley Test Company.

Wilson, B. A., Cockburn, J., & Baddeley, A. D. (2003). *The Rivermead Behavioural Memory Test* (2nd ed.). Bury St. Edmonds, UK: Thames Valley Test Company.

Wilson, B. A., Greenfield, E., Clare, L., Baddeley, A. D., Cockburn, J., Watson, P., et al. (2008). *The Rivermead Behavioural Memory Test-3.* London: Pearson Assessment.

Wilson, B. A., Ivani-Chalian, R., & Aldrich, F. (1991). *The Rivermead Behavioural Memory Test for Children.* San Antonio, TX: Pearson.

Wilson, B. A., Ivani-Chalian, R., Besag, F. M., & Bryant, T. (1993). Adapting the Rivermead Behavioural Memory Test for use with children aged 5 to 10 years. *Journal of Clinical and Experimental Neuropsychology, 15,* 474–486.

Wixted, J. T. (2004). The psychology and neuroscience of forgetting. *Annual Review of Psychology, 55,* 235–269.

Wood, E., Willoughby, T., Bolger, A., Younger, J. & Kaspar, V. (1993). Effectiveness of elaboration strategies for grade school children as a function of academic achievement. *Journal of Experimental Child Psychology, 56,* 240–253.

Wood, E., Willoughby, T., Kaspar, V., & Idle, T. (1994). Enhancing adolescent's recall of factual content: The impact of provided versus self-generated elaborations. *Alberta Journal of Educational Research, 40,* 57–65.

Woodcock, R. W., McGrew, K. S., & Mather, N. (2001a). *Woodcock-Johnson III Tests of Achievement.* Itasca, IL: Riverside Publishing.

Woodcock, R. W., McGrew, K. S., & Mather, N. (2001b). *Woodcock-Johnson III Tests of Cognitive Abilities.* Itasca, IL: Riverside Publishing.

Woodcock, R. W., McGrew, K. S., Mather, N., & Schrank, F. A. (2003). *Woodcock-Johnson III Diagnostic Supplement to the Tests of Cognitive Abilities.* Itasca, IL: Riverside Publishing.

Wolters, C. A., Yu, S. L., Hagen, J. W., & Kail, R. (1996). Short-term memory and strategy use in children with insulin-dependent diabetes mellitus. *Journal of Consulting and Clinical Psychology, 64,* 1397–1405.

Work, P. H. L., & Choi, H. (2005). Developing classroom and group interventions based on a neuropsychological paradigm. In R. K. D'Amato, E. Fletcher-Janzen, & C. R. Reynolds (Eds.). *Handbook of school neuropsychology* (pp. 663–683). Hoboken, NJ: John Wiley & Sons.

Wright, I., & Limond, J. (2004). A developmental framework for memory rehabilitation in children. *Pediatric Rehabilitation, 7,* 85–96.

Wynn-Dancy, M. L., & Gillam, R. B. (1997). Accessing long-term memory: Metacognitive strategies and strategic action in adolescents. *Topics in Language Disorders, 18*(1), 32–44.

Yasik, A. E., Saigh, P. A., Oberfield, R. A., & Halamandaris, P. V. (2007). Posttraumatic stress disorder: Memory and learning performance in children and adolescents. *Biological Psychiatry, 61,* 382–388.

Yeates, K. O., & Enrile, B. G. (2005). Implicit and explicit memory in children with congenital and acquired brain disorder. *Neuropsychology, 19,* 618–628.

Zec, R. F., Zellers, D., Belman, J., Miller, J., Matthews, J., Ferneau-Belman, D., et al. (2001). Long-term consequences of severe closed head injury on episodic memory. *Journal of Clinical and Experimental Neuropsychology, 23,* 671–691.

Zencius, A. H., Wesolowski, M. D., Burke, W. H., & McQuade, P. (1991). Memory checklists: A method of teaching functional skills to brain-damaged adults. *Behavioral Residential Treatment, 6,* 1–10.

Index